Restructuring the Professional Organization

Accounting, health care and law

Edited by
David M. Brock, Michael J. Powell
and C. R. Hinings

London and New York

First published 1999 by Routledge
11 New Fetter Lane, London EC4P 4EE

Simultaneously published in the USA and Canada
by Routledge
29 West 35th Street, New York, NY 10001

Routledge is an imprint of the Taylor & Francis Group

Typeset in Baskerville by Keystroke, Jacaranda Lodge, Wolverhampton
Printed and bound in Great Britain by St Edmundsbury Press, Bury St Edmunds, Suffolk

British Library Cataloguing in Publication Data
A catalogue record for this book is available from the British Library

Library of Congress Cataloging in Publication Data
Brock, David, 1956–
     Restructuring the professional organisation : accounting,
  health care, and law / edited by David Brock, Michael Powell, and C.R. Hinings.
        p.   cm.
     Includes bibliographical references and index.
     1. Professional corporations—Management. 2. Professional
  corporations—Personnel management. 3. Professional corporations—
  Law and legislation. I. Powell, Michael (Michael J. II. Hinings,
  C. R. (Christopher Robin) III. Title.
     HD62.65.B76   1999
     658—dc21   99–12839
                    CIP

ISBN 0–415–19216–1 (hbk)
ISBN 0–415–19217–X (pbk)

Restructuring the Professional Organization

In recent years, the professional organization has undergone radical transformation. With the advent of rapidly changing markets, more sophisticated and demanding clients, deregulation and increased competition, the generalist professional partnerships have given way to larger, more corporate forms of organization, comprising increasingly autonomous specialist business units.

This volume critically examines these changes through an analysis of the archetypes which characterize accounting, health care and law practice. Key topics covered include:

- a review of the models of professional organization
- drivers of change in professions
- internal dynamics of the changes within these organizations
- new organizational forms and archetypes

With examples drawn from Australia, Canada, the UK and the USA, *Restructuring the Professional Organization* will be of interest to all students of organization studies seeking to understand the issues and problems confronting the professions as they enter the new millennium.

David Brock is Senior Lecturer in International Organization and Strategy at the University of Auckland, New Zealand. In addition to his work on professional organizations he has interests in the areas of technology-driven change; planning and strategy in universities; and planning, strategy, and human resource management in multinational subsidiaries. **Michael Powell** is Professor of Health Management also at the University of Auckland. His current research interests include changing governance structures in publicly funded healthcare organizations, organizational change and the development of integrated care structures. **C. R. (Bob) Hinings** is Thornton A. Graham Professor of Business and Director of the Centre for Professional Service Management at the University of Alberta, Canada. His work covers areas such as change in professional organizations, the emergence of organizational forms, and the recomposition of professional fields.

Contents

List of figures and tables   vii
List of contributors   viii
Preface and acknowledgements   ix

1 **The changing professional organization**   1
  MICHAEL J. POWELL, DAVID M. BROCK AND C. R. HININGS

2 **Internationalization of professional services:**
  implications for accounting firms   20
  YAIR AHARONI

3 **Global clients' demands driving change in global**
  business advisory firms   41
  TERESA ROSE AND C. R. HININGS

4 **Institutional effects on organizational governance and**
  conformity: the case of the Kaiser Permanente and the
  United States health care field   68
  CAROL A. CARONNA AND W. RICHARD SCOTT

5 **Restructuring law firms: reflexivity and emerging forms**   87
  JOHN T. GRAY

6 **The struggle to redefine boundaries in health care**
  systems   105
  JEAN-LOUIS DENIS, LISE LAMOTHE, ANN LANGLEY AND
  ANNICK VALETTE

7 **The dynamics of change in large accounting firms**   131
  C. R. HININGS, ROYSTON GREENWOOD AND DAVID COOPER

8 **Professionals organizing professionals: comparing the logic of United States and United Kingdom law practice**   154
   JOHN FLOOD

 9 **'All fur coat and no knickers': contemporary organizational change in United Kingdom hospitals**   183
   MARTIN KITCHENER

10 **Continuity and change in professional organizations: evidence from British law firms**   200
   TIMOTHY MORRIS AND ASHLY PINNINGTON

11 **The restructured professional organization: corporates, cobwebs and cowboys**   215
   DAVID M. BROCK, MICHAEL J. POWELL AND C. R. HININGS

   References   230
   Index   249

Figures and tables

Figures

6.1	Four modes of boundary redefinition in health care systems	114
6.2	The economic logic behind system integration	123
10.1	Dimensions of change and continuity in UK law firms	212
11.1	The changing professional organization	221
11.2	A typology of professional organizations	225
11.3	Location of clusters and archetypes	228

Tables

7.1	Characteristics of the P^2 and MPB archetypes	134
8.1	Numbers of clients by top echelon of lawyers	168
8.2	Total and mean numbers of work/task episodes for sample four-week period for lawyers in management committee and lawyers in alternate group	170
9.1	Structures and systems of the PB and QM hospital archetypes	184
9.2	Dominant views of the three vectors of the PB interpretive sheme	187
9.3	Continuity and change within the interpretive scheme of UK hospitals	197
10.1	Frequencies for the variables	204–205
10.2	Correlations for the selected nine variables associated with the MPB form	209
10.3	Sub-samples	210

Contributors

Yair Aharoni, The College of Management, Israel

Carol A. Caronna, Stanford University, USA

David Cooper, University of Alberta, Canada

Jean-Louis Denis, Université de Montréal, Canada

John Flood, University of Westminster, UK

John T. Gray, University of Western Sydney, Australia

Royston Greenwood, The University of Alberta, Canada

Martin Kitchener, Cardiff University, UK

Lise Lamothe, Université Laval, Canada

Ann Langley, Université du Québec à Montréal, Canada

Timothy Morris, London Business School, UK

Ashly Pinnington, University of Exeter, UK

Teresa Rose, University of Alberta, Canada

W. Richard Scott, Stanford University, USA

Annick Valette, Université Pierre Mendès-France, France

Preface and acknowledgements

The germ of this book can be traced back to a graduate organization theory class David taught in 1994. At the time he was researching aspects of autonomy, and trying to show students how contemporary organizations can offer operating autonomy yet still maintain quality of service. The example of the professional organization (*à la* Mintzberg) came to mind, the idea being that if autonomous operators were highly trained then quality control would not be an organizational problem. At the same time, Michael, also at the University of Auckland, was actively teaching and researching in the area of professional organizations. Together, David and Michael developed a symposium on the changing profess-ional organization for the 1995 Academy of Management Meetings in Vancouver that was the precursor of the book. Bob was one of the invited participants and subsequently agreed to join in developing an edited volume.

Over the next few years we met on numerous occasions: in Auckland, Dallas, Vancouver, Boston, Seattle, San Diego and back in Auckland. Dozens of white boards, countless e-mails, faxes, conference calls, and couriered manuscripts later we have produced what we planned: a volume on the changing professional organization that would be of interest to scholars and practitioners alike. More broadly, this volume addresses the contemporary complex, global, knowledge-based, service organization. It is about networks, organizational development, competition, global integration, franchising, power, and mergers; all applied to the dynamic organizations of accounting, health care, and law.

We wish to thank the contributors to this volume from across three continents who have produced original work for this volume. We are grateful for their will-ing cooperation and assistance under considerable time pressure.

There are many other people to thank: Nigel Haworth and John Deeks, Heads of the Departments of International Business and Management and Employment Relations at the University of Auckland, funded Bob's first visit to Auckland, covered additional office-related expenses, and provided the space to work on this book. Many accountants, lawyers, doctors and medical administrators gave generously of their time and ideas: Dr Dan Berkowitz, Dr Clive Brock, Richard Case, Nigel Faigan, Scott Laird, Dr William Nichols, Dr Diane Ossip and Dr David Siscovick. Stuart Hay and Stephanie Rogers at Routledge were always supportive. Leone Hill did so much with tolerance and patience to prepare the final manuscripts. Finally, we would like to recognize our partners and families who have provided encouragement and support through the arduous process of bringing the book together.

David M. Brock
Michael J. Powell
C. R. (Bob) Hinings
Auckland
December 1998

1 The changing professional organization

Michael J. Powell, David M. Brock and C. R. Hinings

- One Monday morning the CEO of a medium-sized Washington hospital discovers that the entire cardiac surgery team has resigned (to join a rival hospital). However, as an interim measure, they are quickly replaced by contract professionals.
- A large Auckland law firm considers merging with the legal arm of an accounting firm.
- A Big Five accounting firm considers selling shares in its business to raise capital for future development.

Professional organizations, such as accounting and law firms, medical practices, hospitals and universities, face increasingly turbulent and complex environments. Consequently, they are experiencing considerable change and uncertainty. Markets for professional services have been deregulated, competition is increasing both within and between professions, clients are increasingly sophisticated and demanding. Changes in technology open new opportunities for service delivery and encourage the entry of new providers. Thus, the organizational fields within which professional service firms operate have undergone radical change. Large law and accounting firms compete in increasingly competitive and international arenas. Institutional boundaries between professions, long protected by statute and tradition, have weakened as governments deregulate professional services and firms move to take advantage of new business opportunities. In response, professional organizations have changed in significant ways through internal restructuring, merger, the development of new services, and internationalization.

The above changes have come at a time when more occupations are seeking professional status (e.g. computer programmers and software designers, marketing and public relations personnel) and management both within and outside professional organizations is undergoing professionalization. Knowledge-based organizations are viewed as paradigmatic of the post-bureaucratic age (Quinn, 1993) with popular management writers pointing to the professional organization as a prototype of the effective organization of the future (e.g. Drucker, 1988; Peters, 1992). Consequently, more people are interested in the professional organization at the very time when that organizational form itself is undergoing change and has an uncertain future.

These changes are as perplexing to those who work in the professions as they are to those who study these organizations. Not long ago it was relatively simple to understand professional organizations. Mintzberg's (1979) classic delineation of the professional bureaucracy, and Greenwood, Hinings and Brown's (1990) P^2 or professional partnership model, captured the main dimensions of traditional professional organizations where the professionals (e.g. physicians or lawyers) were not only the operators but also the owners and managers. The peculiar structure of professional organizations reflected an all-pervasive 'culture of professionalism' (Bledstein, 1978) that underlay their organizational arrangements.

Less than a decade later, the same scholars suggest that the professional firm has changed in key respects (Cooper, Hinings, Greenwood and Brown, 1996). Furthermore, large professional bureaucracies such as hospitals, universities and research institutes have experienced similar challenges to their traditional organizational arrangements (Simpson and Powell, 1999; Shortell *et al.*, 1996). In the case of publicly funded professional services, governments have frequently exerted pressure for changes in governance and management that have undermined professional dominance. And increasingly competitive markets have induced professional bureaucracies to adopt more corporate and managerial modes of operation in search of increased efficiency.

Beginning from the premise that the classical models of the professional bureaucracy and the professional partnership may no longer fit the changing and more dynamic environment, we suggest that new organizational types may be emerging that need to be analysed and understood. Before extolling the professional firm as an exemplar of the new knowledge-based organization of the twenty-first century, we need to understand its emergent characteristics. This book brings together, and makes accessible to academics and practitioners alike, new scholarly work on the changing professional organization in accounting and business services, health and law. Our focus is explicitly on professional service organizations, not on the professions or professional associations as such, nor on change in the professions generally.

Accounting, health and law organizations

For reasons of parsimony and coherence, the focus of this book is on organizations in the traditional professional fields of accounting, health and law. While students of the professions have often disagreed over the definition of 'profession' and 'professionalism,' there is little disagreement that accounting, law and medicine constitute professions or clusters of professions.[1] Further, accounting firms, medical practices, hospitals, and law firms are widely recognized as professional organizations with distinctive organizational characteristics (see Montagna, 1968; Freidson, 1970; Nelson, 1988). Given that these three professions can be viewed as paradigmatic, the changes that have occurred in their organizations are likely to be indicative of what is also happening in professional organizations in other fields such as education, engineering and scientific research.

Professional organizations promise to be central information nodes in the knowledge-based economies and societies of the new millennium. Accounting and law firms provide critical forms of expertise and knowledge in the areas of performance measurement and social cohesion. With aging populations, and an increased focus on wellness rather than illness, health care organizations also become increasingly central to societal well-being.

Furthermore, the contemporary global economy is intertwined with networks of professionals and professional organizations that play important roles in its operation. From the lawyers behind large international corporate mergers, to the doctors behind pharmaceutical research and medical innovations, to the accountants who audit and value the stocks of complex multinational corporations, these professionals increasingly apply universal criteria around the world. In a reflexive manner, they play their part in the ongoing globalization of the world economy. In other words, they both experience the pressures of globalization and, at the same time, contribute to its reach.

The archetypal professional organization

Following Greenwood and Hinings (1993) we find it useful to think of professional organizations as reflecting a relatively consistent archetype or configuration. As DiMaggio and Powell (1983) suggested, it may be more instructive to consider the similarities among organizations rather than focus on the differences. Further-more, we suggest that identifying organizational archetypes is important for understanding patterns of organizational change. While individual organizations may adopt new structures and systems from time to time, sustaining change in the face of an unchanging organizational archetype is likely to be very difficult. For this reason, Greenwood and Hinings (1988) suggest that students of organizational change need to be aware that not all change efforts succeed. There are multiple change tracks. Some organizations fail to sustain their change momentum and revert to their prior state, as that is more consistent with the archetype; others get caught between the original and an emergent archetype in an apparently schizoid state. Changing the archetype itself is very difficult as it reflects deeply held beliefs and values about how organizations should be structured and operate.

Greenwood and Hinings (1993, p. 1052) define an organizational archetype as 'a set of structures and systems that reflects a single interpretive scheme'. The interpretive scheme is the key. Structures and systems do not constitute a disembodied organizational frame but rather are infused with meanings, intentions, preferences and values. They argue strongly that interpretive schemes composed of such subjective meanings underpin the objective identities of organi-zational structures and processes. Using an archetypal approach, then, involves taking a 'holistic' perspective and looking not just at organizational structure and systems but also at the beliefs, values and ideas they represent. Indeed,

Greenwood and Hinings (1993) suggest that understanding the organizational archetype, and how that may be changing, is the first step to understanding organizational change processes. This is the approach taken by a number of the contributed chapters in this volume.

We argue that professional organizations, from small professional partnerships to large professional bureaucracies, compose a broad organizational archetype with a high degree of commonality in structures, systems and, most of all, in their fundamental interpretive scheme. While there may be differences between architectural firms and law practices, the similarities are more striking than the differences (cf. Blau, 1984; Nelson, 1988). The common thread is a set of professional values, beliefs and aspirations woven into the very fabric of professional firms and organizations. Consequently, attempts to change radically their structures or systems in ways that are inconsistent or incoherent with the interpretive scheme of professionalism are likely to fail (see Chapters 6, 8 and 9 in this volume).

Archetypes and change

From this perspective, successful organizational change first requires that the interpretive scheme underpinning a particular archetype be challenged with an alternative interpretive scheme. As Greenwood and Hinings (1993) note, commitment to interpretive schemes is dynamic rather than static and unchanging. Commitment to a particular interpretive scheme within an industry or sector will be variable and subject to change. Changing levels of commitment provide a potential dynamic for change in the archetype. New interpretive schemes may be advanced that delegitimize the old, thereby leading to change.

Furthermore, structure and systems and their underlying interpretive scheme stand in a reflexive relationship with each other. Structures and systems interact with the interpretive scheme and will influence, and potentially change, the very beliefs and values that underpin them. Thus the introduction of new management structures and systems, such as new performance measurement systems into law firms, or the replacement of the traditional 'lockstep' reward system with the more individualized 'eat-what-you-kill' system, are likely to result in modification of their interpretive scheme (see Chapters 8 and 10). Such change is unlikely to succeed in the short term, however, if it cannot be presented and implemented in a way that is seen to be consistent with the overall direction of the existing interpretive scheme or with an alternative set of values that are gaining legitimacy. The sheer fact that such changes have been introduced, however, indicates that alternative preferences with respect to how performance should be evaluated and rewarded exist in these firms.

While archetypes are difficult to change as key aspects of the interpretive scheme may well be deeply institutionalized, they are not chiselled in stone. They are subject to challenge, environmental pressures, and possible delegitimation. This book raises the question of whether the traditional archetype of the professional organization has undergone substantial change such that one or more new archetypes have emerged. But first we need to recall the classical model of the professional organization.

The professional archetype

The main characteristics of the archetypal professional organization were delineated by organization theorists in the 1960s and 1970s. These theorists were, in large part, intrigued by the apparent differences between professional organizations and the dominant bureaucratic model. Writers such as Hall (1968), Montagna (1968) and Bucher and Stelling (1969) compared the structures and cultures of professional organizations with those of corporate bureaucracies and looked for distinguishing features. Of course, in delineating these distinctive features, organizational theorists inevitably contributed to the definition and further development of the professional archetype.

Hall (1968) was largely interested in exploring the different settings of professional practice and comparing the extent of professionalization and bureaucracy in those settings. In comparison, Montagna (1968) and Bucher and Stelling (1969) examined specific professional organizations: large accounting firms in Montagna's case and university teaching hospitals in Bucher and Stelling's case. Montagna (1968) found that while accounting firms were administered from within, their standards were set externally by the profession. Furthermore, professional practice was characterized by autonomy and a strong commitment to the client. Bucher and Stelling's (1969) study focused on the negotiated order of large health care organizations with dominant professional staff. They found that these organizations were characterized by fluidity and role creation as professionals sought to define their own roles within the boundaries of the organization. Consequently, hospitals experienced an ongoing process of internal differentiation or 'segmentalization' that was a function of the professional interests of particular individual professionals or groups of professionals. Such emergent structures clearly resulted in considerable conflict and competition for resources, with any consequent integration and coordination achieved through negotiated political processes. Bucher and Stelling's (1969) findings suggest that professional bureaucracies, such as hospitals, are intensely political and fluid entities. This view was endorsed by Cohen, March and Olsen's (1972) identification of one particular professional organization, the university, as a prime example of 'organized anarchy' characterized by considerable ambiguity and uncertainty.

A few years earlier, Richard Scott (1965) had described the traditional American hospital as an 'autonomous' organization where professionals enjoyed considerable autonomy and decision-making discretion. Not only did they make the micro patient care decisions but also controlled the macro level decisions about organizational policy and direction.

Freidson (1970) portrayed these autonomous health care organizations as exhibiting 'professional dominance'. That is, hospitals and other health care organizations were largely controlled by the health professionals, in particular the physicians or doctors. Hospital administrators played an important supporting role; they were there to ensure that the dominant professionals had the resources and facilities to provide the services they determined were necessary. Organizational power, however, clearly was located in the hands of the physicians. Hospitals, then, provided necessary facilities for relatively autonomous physicians whose primary loyalty was to their profession rather than to the organization. They were little more than workshops where powerful doctors performed their tasks. Freidson's (1970) study became the classic statement of the organizational dominance of powerful professionals that confirmed their 'exceptionalism' to the rationalizing tendencies of bureaucratic control.

The professional bureaucracy

Later in the same decade, Mintzberg (1979) argued that the professional organization constituted a 'professional bureaucracy', one of his five dominant organizational configurations or designs. Refining this in subsequent publications (e.g., Mintzberg, 1993), and using his own university as a case in point, he argued that the professional bureaucracy contained elements of both the professional model as delineated by other writers and bureaucratic structures. It remained, however, a distinctive configuration.

In Mintzberg's (1979) professional bureaucracy, the key component of the configuration is the operating core where the professionals provide services directly to clients. Professional bureaucracies have a small strategic apex and few middle managers or supervisors as the professional workers exercise self-management and need little supervision. Indeed, professional staff function in an autonomous manner working directly with their respective clients without much reference to each other. Nor are there generally any well developed systems of bureaucratic control, the assumption being that the professionals can be trusted to perform in the best interests of their clients and thus of the organization. The professional bureaucracy, then, cannot rely on the formalization of work processes or on bureaucratic controls to ensure high quality work. Rather, it depends on the standardization of skills, internalized values and what Ouchi (1980) called 'clan control'.

Coordination of the relatively independent professionals is achieved through the standardization of skills (conferred through professional training) which means that each professional can be relied upon to work independently and yet produce relatively similar outputs. As their tasks involve the application of knowledge and expertise to complex problems, professionals must retain considerable discretion. Furthermore, professional organizations are typically highly decentralized with different operating units loosely coupled to each other. Consequently it is very difficult for the professional bureaucracy to formulate a coherent, organization-wide strategy. In this context, strategy tends to be the accumulation of a number of individual professional projects, the initiatives of 'professional entrepreneurs'.

In part, this reflects the difficulty of agreeing on strategy in organizations of independent producers. The decision-making structure of the professional bureaucracy reflects the democratic and collegial values of the professional bureaucracy, with a high value placed on participation and consultation. In general, professionals seek collective control over the administrative decisions that affect their operations. However, as professionals need significant numbers of support staff to maximize the return on their relatively expensive time, these organizations have a well-developed structure of administrators. Administrators do not develop strategy independently of the professionals but, rather, must cajole professional leaders to support and champion their initiatives (Mintzberg, 1993).

Mintzberg's configuration reflected accurately the structural arrangements and systems of large professional organizations, whether professional firms or hospitals and universities, of a generation ago. Much has happened since he formulated his configuration to lead us to question its relevance for the new millennium.

The professional partnership

A decade later, Greenwood, Hinings and Brown (1990) developed the P^2 model – professionalism and partnership – to describe the strategic management of the professional firm. They noted that professional firms differ from other organizations in two key aspects: first, the professional partners not only own and govern the firm but also manage it, and provide the professional services; second, their primary task involves the application of expertise to complex problems which requires a significant degree of discretion. Chapter 7 by Hinings, Greenwood and Cooper develops the P^2 archetype more fully. Like Mintzberg (1979), Greenwood *et al.* (1990) found that individual professionals work independently with their clients and are largely self-contained. This has significant consequences for strategy formulation, making the strategy process quite different from that found in M- or H-form organizations. Strategic direction in P^2 organizations tends to be weak and not centrally controlled. Its successful adoption depends on consensus building among the partners, each of whom tends to operate as a separate unit within the larger firm.

From the 1960s through to 1990, then, a consistent picture has emerged of the archetypal professional organization where power rests in the hands of the professional experts, managers administer the facilities and support the professionals, decisions are made collegially, change is slow and difficult, and strategy is formulated and adopted consensually. There is little hierarchy and a relatively high degree of vertical and horizontal differentiation. Coordination and control occurs through the standardization of skills and a strong clan culture of professionalism rather than through formalized systems and close supervision.

The changing professional archetype

There is much evidence, however, that this archetypal professional organization has been undergoing significant change. Indeed, signs of change were evident even in the 1960s when the classic professional archetype was dominant. In his 1965 article, Scott suggested there were already signs of a shift from the autonomous model of professional organization to the heteronomous where professionals were subject to bureaucratic control. A decade later, Haug (1973) saw the end of professional dominance as professionals underwent a process of deprofessionalization as a consequence of the routinization of their tasks, increased consumer pressure, and technological change that gave a wider range of people access to profession expertise. Others suggested the ongoing proletarianization of the professionals whereby professionals lost their special status and were subjected to the controls of advanced capitalism in much the same way as artisans and craft workers were during the Industrial Revolution (McKinlay and Arches, 1985; Derber, 1982.). Yet other writers, such as Starr (1982) in his exhaustive study of the emergence and growth of the power of the medical profession in the US, indicated the increasing corporatization of medicine that implied physicians would be increasingly subject to financial and managerial control (see also Light, 1986). Similarly, Nelson (1988) and Spangler (1986) pointed to the increased bureaucratization and routinization of legal practice in both large firms and professional bureaucracies.

Meanwhile Chandler (1977), in his classic business history *The Visible Hand*, outlined how fundamental organizational change in large corporations occurred in the post-war decades. For example, he traced how multi-unit businesses replaced the traditional U-Form with 'a federation of autonomous offices', the rise of the managerial career (or profession), and the separation of professional managers from owners. Chandler (1977) argued that these changes were driven in part by the imperatives of managing larger and larger corporations and in part by new strategic directions. Later, we find similar tendencies in the professions. Professional organizations are now increasingly internally differentiated, with a core staff of specialized professional managers, and the traditional system of partnership governance giving way to a more corporate model. Like their corporate cousins, large professional organizations have increasingly taken on a more diversified and differentiated structure.

Support for changes in the professional archetype came from the Alberta School as well. Less than a decade after presenting the P^2 model of the professional firm, Cooper *et al.* (1996) suggest that it no longer adequately captures the dynamic changes occurring in professional firms. Based on their analysis of change in Canadian law firms, they suggest that the dominant archetype of the professional organization was shifting from P^2 to a form they term the managed professional business (MPB). This new archetype is fully presented in Chapter 7 by Hinings *et al.* and referred to by other authors in this volume. The new archetype is still emergent and retains some of the attributes of the old P^2 archetype with an overlay, or additional sedimented layer, of managerialism and business values. However, they argue it represents a clear departure from the traditional archetype of the professional organization.

Additional evidence can be adduced from changes in professional labour markets. There has been a decline in the number and proportion of professionals working in private practice and a definite trend towards salaried employment in large corporations or large professional bureaucracies (Derber, 1982; Spangler,

1986). Departures from traditional professional career paths have also become more common. Examples of these departures are:

- the employment of an increasing variety of professionals in industry-specific professional organizations, such as accountants in hospitals or lawyers in accounting firms;
- hybrid professional organizations providing 'one-stop shops' for business or professional services such as business consultancy services in accounting firms, tax and financial services in law firms, and allied health professionals working with doctors;
- professionals working in corporations or bureaucracies, such as lawyers and accountants in manufacturing and financial services firms;
- new 'professionals' working in traditional professional service organizations, such as marketing managers and public relations officers in law firms and universities.

Forces for change

What have been the main drivers of change in professional organizations? The contributed chapters in this volume point to external, environmental factors such as the deregulation of professional markets and increased competition, financial constraints and cost pressures, changes in government policy, globalization and the demands of international clients, increasingly sophisticated clients and technological change. These have all impacted on the professional organization.

Deregulation and competition

Since the late 1980s professions in many countries have seen their statutory protections for providing certain services either reduced or removed completely. This has opened the door to more intra- and inter-professional competition. In the past, for example, advertising by professionals was generally proscribed either by government statute or professional rules. Following statutory or regulatory change, advertising for professional services has now become commonplace thereby encouraging more intra-professional competition. Similarly, as statutory barriers to providing particular professional services have been removed or lessened, competing professions may enter markets that had previously been closed to them (e.g., accounting firms offering legal services; midwives providing obstetric services).

In general, the markets for professional services have also become more competitive. In some fields, such as acute hospital care, there has been a clear over-supply of beds. In the US, hospital over-capacity in an environment where cost considerations were becoming critical led to an inevitable rationalization with hospital mergers and closures in the 1990s (Shortell *et al.*, 1996). Similarly, as many Fortune 500 companies merged in the takeover mania of the 1980s, the number of large corporate clients available to accounting and law firms decreased.

More lawyers and accountants than ever before chased fewer large clients. This increasingly competitive market has encouraged rationalization and led to the adoption of more efficient structures. It also encouraged a greater focus on business development and the marketing of professional services.

Competition has become a fact of life even for publicly owned and funded health care providers in many countries, such as New Zealand and the UK. Government policy changes have attempted to create internal markets for health services that pit one healthcare provider against another in order to lower costs and encourage efficiency. In addition, these publicly owned providers have frequently been corporatized: into National Health Service 'Trusts' in the UK and 'Crown Health Enterprises' in New Zealand. The adoption of corporate governance structures was intended to shift the interpretive scheme of the hospitals from that based on public service values to a more commercial approach. Indicative of the attempted shift in interpretive scheme is the common practice of both UK and NZ senior hospital managers referring to the 'business' or the 'company' rather than to the hospital, when speaking of their organization.

Associated with the development of more competitive markets has been increased concern about costs of professional services, on the part of both private clients of accounting and law firms and private and public funders of health services. Clients frequently require professional firms to compete for contracts, to detail and justify their fees and expenses and to meet price or cost limits. Governments are using various devices, such as internal markets and capitated payment systems, to encourage increased efficiency on the part of public health care providers. In the US, where a high proportion of health services are offered in private markets, employers and health insurance funds put similar cost pressures on providers such as hospitals. The consequences have been mergers and takeovers, more explicit financial expectations, the increased use of financial incentives and more rigorous budget controls. These changes have given more power to accountants and managers in professional organizations and are most evident in new managerial systems put into place to control costs and manage resources more efficiently. Furthermore, they impact in a reflexive way on the interpretive schemes of professional organizations, raising financial and business development concerns to new importance.

Technological developments

Closely related to changes in professional markets has been technological change that in many cases has substantially altered professional work processes. For example, computer-designed and implemented audit systems have reduced significantly the complexity and labour intensity of the audit process. Consequently, the importance of the audit market for large accounting firms has declined and other products, such as business consultancy services, have risen to the fore (see Chapter 7). In health care, minimally invasive laser treatment has reduced the trauma associated with surgical interventions and the need for inpatient hospital care. It has made it possible for minor surgery to be undertaken by competing professional groups, such as family or general practitioners, in ambulatory settings. In law, contracts and other legal documents, such as wills and real estate transfers, are all on computer templates. They can often be completed by cheaper legal assistants or paralegals in the place of the fully trained but more expensive lawyers.

New technologies such as these have facilitated the routinization (or commodification) of some professional services, especially those at the low-cost end of the market. This routinization has opened the door to alternative providers and to the utilization of less specialized staff. Blood pressure, diabetes and pregnancy tests are now available over-the-counter in shopping malls and pharmacies. Nurses or pharmacists can administer them. Technological developments such as these pose major competitive and strategic threats to many professional service organizations.

Furthermore, as technological and communication advances such as the Internet enable the freer flow of information, consumers and prospective clients are more able to shop around, compare products and prices, look at varying treatment or service options and even practise self-management. Access to such information flows empowers consumers and potential clients, and enhances their sophistication with respect to the professional services they expect to receive. Together with a more competitive marketplace, this puts additional quality pressures on professional organizations. The relationship between professional and client remains unequal but is certainly less so than was previously the case.

In these and other ways, technological developments have interacted with market deregulation to advance intra- and inter-professional competition and to promote organizational change.

Globalization of services

An additional driver of change has been the increasingly international character of many professional services, particularly at the top end of the market. Multinational companies requiring consistent and uniform services around the globe have spurred the global provision of business services. In addition, professional organizations have followed clients into new markets or entered what are considered potential growth markets to provide services to new clients. Thus American law firms have opened offices in Europe and the UK; British law firms have followed suit and opened up in Europe and the US (see Chapter 8). Universities offer degree programmes around the world and compete for international students. Even health care has become an international industry. Private hospitals in Thailand advertise throughout Asia for patients who require high quality Western medicine at prices that are considerably lower than in the US or Europe. Wealthy patients travel the globe in search of advanced specialized treatment or for alternative therapies that may not be available in their own countries.

Globalization is a significant contemporary phenomenon much remarked upon with respect to business corporations, the entertainment industry, communication and the arts (Appadurai, 1996; Latouche, 1996). Its significance for professional services has been less noted but may be equally significant (see Aharoni, 1993a). Professional service organizations, whether they are accounting or law firms, universities or hospitals, are both subject to the impact of globalization and contribute to it through their own internationalization strategies. Whatever the motivations for globalization, its implications for the structure and systems of large professional firms are considerable. The chapters by Aharoni and Rose and Hinings attest to these drivers of change.

The chapters in this book discuss these changes to professional organizations and address the question of whether they portend the emergence of a new archetypal professional organization. Are the prophets of deprofessionalization and proletarianization right in pointing to the end of professional dominance? Is the 'exceptionalism' of the archetypal professional organization sustainable in the face of increased economic rationalism, deregulated professional markets and globalization? Will professional organizations succumb, as did the craft workshops of an earlier century, to the inevitable march of finance capitalism and bureaucratization? And, if there is a new archetype of the professional organization emerging, what are its characteristics?

Reflexivity in archetypal change

We have briefly considered a number of significant environmental drivers of change in professional organizations. These forces in themselves are sufficient to give rise to significant challenges to the traditional archetype of the professional organization as already delineated. While external factors, such as deregulation and globalization, undoubtedly impact on professional organizations we should not forget that organizations and the individuals within them are not merely passive recipients of deterministic forces. We need to consider the role of agency as well as that of changing environments in giving rise to organizational change which must be viewed as a reflexive process wherein the environment and organizational actors interact in such a way that change results. The environment may change, and so create pressures for organizational change; however, organizational actors have to perceive the changed environment and the need for change themselves. Furthermore, some organizations are innovative, actively seeking new products or new ways to provide services to customers, thereby contributing themselves to the changed environment.

This is as true for professional organizations as it is for other business enterprises. As Powell (1985) demonstrated with respect to the US legal profession, significant changes in the structure of a professional field may reflect the entrepreneurial actions of significant groups of professionals who are prepared to challenge existing institutional arrangements as well as the actions of governmental bodies and clients. In other words, entrepreneurial and innovative actions by professionals and their organizations interact with external changes to produce new operating environments, or to restructure organizational fields. In Chapter 4 by Caronna and Scott, we see how the organizational field of health care in the

US shifted to incorporate the health maintenance organization model of customer pre-payment and capitated remuneration systems that had been pioneered by earlier, deviant systems such as that of Kaiser Permanente. There was a change in the regulatory environment in the 1970s but the Kaiser model had already demonstrated the potential and viability of an alternative structure. The Kaiser model and similar initiatives contributed to a significant shift in thinking about the funding of health care in the US. This new structure was to become institutionalized in the 1980s as a major new form of health care provision in the competitive US market. It is important to see, then, following Giddens (1984), the reflexivity of structure and agency in changing organizational fields and in sustaining or recreating the organizational archetypes that dominate those fields.

Towards a theory of archetypal change

As we have suggested already, a complete analysis of change in the organizational fields of professionals needs to recognize both the external, environmental drivers of change and the entrepreneurial activity of professionals and professional organizations. This suggests a reflexive relationship between organizational fields and their constitutive organizations. Similarly, an adequate theory of archetypal change must include both external drivers of change as shaping the organizational field and the active role of agents in challenging existing normative constraints and pushing for new directions.

Professional service organizations are deeply embedded in institutionalized fields, with strongly held beliefs and values shaping organizational action and behaviour. Flood, in Chapter 8, emphasizes the extent to which the logic of law practice infuses the organizational arrangements of law firms. Greenwood and Hinings (1993) suggest that the push for coherence with the dominant organizational archetype will lead most organizations in a field to develop similar structures and systems based on similar interpretive schemes. The isomorphic pressure is often strong, sometimes even coercive with statutory or regulatory bodies enforcing conformity. Strongly held and institutionalized beliefs and values, such as those that constitute professionalism, make change very difficult indeed. How then does the archetype shift or change?

We need to be able to explain why and how an existing organizational archetype is disturbed or undermined such that it results in change in organizational arrangements. Institutional theory, with which the construct of archetypes is closely related (Greenwood and Hinings, 1993), naturally tends to focus on conformity to, and coherence with, institutionalized norms. Such pressure for isomorphism makes organizational change difficult. However, Oliver's work (1991, 1992) suggests the conditions under which delegitimation of particular institutions might occur thereby making possible the de-institutionalization of accepted structures, practices and processes. Similarly, we would expect a process of questioning and challenging accepted beliefs and practices to undermine the interpretive scheme that is at the foundation of the dominant organizational archetype. Change in the interpretive scheme may lead eventually to structural and systems changes. The dominant archetype, then, can no longer be taken for granted; alternative and competing archetypes surface and may gain ascendancy. We return to the emergence of competing archetypes in the final chapter.

We need to understand how this process of delegitimation of an archetype, or a set of institutional beliefs and practices, occurs. As noted earlier, Cooper *et al.* (1996) tend to see it as a consequence of external forces which change the environment in which professional organizations operate. Professional organizations must adapt and change to meet the requirements of these new conditions. Such environmental change has been a feature of the last two decades of the twentieth century. Governmental deregulation, increased competition, client demands and new technologies have all played their part.

In Chapter 7, Hinings *et al.* refer to the serious questioning in the 1990s of the usefulness and validity of the audit functions provided by large accounting firms in the face of major corporate collapses and frauds that these audits completely failed to predict. Such challenges to the value of professional services and of the special protected position and powers of professionals is reminiscent of the attacks on professional power such as Ivan Illich's *Medical Nemesis* (1975) and *Disabling Professions* (1977). Such populist critiques were supported by the revival of neo-classical economics in the 1980s that viewed professional restrictions on practice as unnecessary and self-interested restraints of trade, referring back to work by free market economists such as Milton Friedman (1962). 'Provider capture' became the byword of the reformers of the 1980s pushing for increased consumer or purchaser power and freedom (see Boston *et al.*, 1991; Hood, 1991). This was the rhetoric of governments seeking to deregulate the professions and to introduce internal markets into publicly funded service delivery systems. The message was clear: the traditional model of professional dominance, and its manifestation in organizations controlled by professionals, was subject to self-interest. In this way the professional archetype was challenged and undermined, making archetypal change easier.

Simultaneously, came the rise of general management, or managerialism, with its promise of improved efficiency and cost-effectiveness. Management had been undergoing its own professionalization with the increased popularity and prominence of the MBA degree. Highly trained managers who entered professional bureaucracies or partnerships did not simply want to support the professionals, or administer facilities. Nor were they socialized into deferring to the superior knowledge and expertise of professionals. They took a broader, macro view. They wanted to manage, to improve the coordination and pro-duction efficiency of the professional firm, and to introduce a strategic perspective. There was a significant shift in paradigm from administration to management that had significant implications for the interpretive scheme underpinning the professional archetype. This shift is reflected in changes identified in most of the contributed chapters in this volume.

So the interpretive scheme underlying the professional archetype was increasingly questioned and challenged. The challenge has not just been from external forces, however. Our theory of archetypal change must also allow for the active, agentic role of professionals and their organizations in challenging the dominant archetype and in pushing for modification or change.

We suggest that the most useful theoretical perspective to explain and even predict agentic change in archetype is derived from resource dependency theory which views organizations as acting to protect or develop or replace resource flows (Pfeffer and Salancik, 1978; Scott, 1987). Faced with resource limitations or uncertainties in one area, organizations will actively seek to develop new resource flows to compensate. Organizations in mature markets will seek to enter new markets or develop new products or services. This approach allows a focus on resource acquisition and development as a driving force in strategic organizational change. The search for new resource flows in the face of the uncertainty of traditional revenue earners is an important reason why accounting firms enter new businesses and develop new products such as management consultancy services and even legal services (see Hinings *et al.* in Chapter 7). In part, such a shift reflects a strategic intent to provide a one-stop shop for business services; in part, it is the replacement of a declining resource flow (accounting and auditing services) with another growing resource flow. Similarly, the Big Five accounting firms enter new countries, such as China, not just to follow global clients but also to develop profiles in new and growing markets (see Aharoni in Chapters 2 and 3).

There are many other examples of professional organizations pushing the boundaries of the organizational archetype in order to reduce uncertainty or develop new resource flows. Australian and New Zealand universities have aggressively moved to offer academic programmes in Asia to compensate for limited or reduced government funding. Public hospitals in the UK have responded to curbs on government funding by opening up their wards to revenue bearing private patients. Faced with heightened competition for patients, hospitals in the US have formed new alliances and networks with independent physician groups to secure their resource flows. Accounting firms have used their expertise in financial systems to leverage their entry into providing general information technology services to their clients.

The resource dependency approach allows for the active search for new opportunities and resources on the part of organizational actors as a crucial factor in organizational change. This search may lead the organizations to question traditional ways of doing business and to challenge the institutions that have long underpinned the professional archetype in order to open the door to new resource flows. In periods of environmental uncertainty and flux, organizational 'upstarts' frequently arise to challenge the status quo (Powell, 1991). The American law firm Skadden Arps (see Flood in Chapter 8) was one such upstart firm. In short order, what was once regarded as too aggressive and beyond the professional pale become accepted as legitimate practice (see Powell, 1993, for a discussion of how professional innovation becomes accepted practice). A theory of archetypal change needs to recognize this reflexive relationship between the changing environments within which professional organizations operate and the innovative and entrepreneurial activity of some of these organizations. Both environmental factors and organizational agency contribute to the delegitimation of existing archetypes and the development of new, rival, archetypes that compete with the old. The contributed chapters in this book provide an indication of the extent to which such archetypal change has occurred.

Organization of the book

The nine contributed chapters in this book present self-contained analyses of the changing characteristics of particular professional organizations. Each chapter is largely confined to one of the three professions that provide the empirical foci of the book – accounting, health and law. Aharoni's contribution (Chapter 2) is the broadest in this respect as he compares of the varying degrees of internationalization of accounting and law.

The chapters are presented in an order that reflects their primary emphasis on one of the following: the forces driving change in professional organizations, the process of change, the emergence of new or changed organizational forms respectively. This organization of the book, however, is simply indicative of the main focus of the chapters as some chapters may address more than one of these themes. This overlap in thematic coverage provides a connection among the chapters, which otherwise deal with different organizational fields in different countries.

The book draws on research in a range of countries although primarily from what might be called the Anglo-American world (Australia, Canada, the United Kingdom and the United States of America). The generalizability of the findings may therefore be questioned. However, we believe that the pressures for change that are identified are not limited to the Anglo-American countries but can be seen as global developments (see, for example, Dezalay, 1997).

Chapters 2–4 by Aharoni, Rose and Hinings, and Caronna and Scott deal broadly with the changing environment of professional practice. Chapters 2 and 3 refer particularly to the large multinational accounting firms and the growth of international or global business services firms, whereas Chapter 4 looks at the changing organizational field of health care in the US.

In Chapter 2, Yair Aharoni discusses the concept of globalization, the factors leading to it and its differing impact on accounting and law firms. He asks why accounting firms have embraced the internationalism of globalization while law firms have remained more circumspect. Rose and Hinings follow in Chapter 3 with a related analysis of the pressures for globalized business service delivery. They look at how the major accounting firms have expanded globally to service multinational clients and at how the structures of these firms have changed to meet the needs of these global clients. They suggest that the Big Five accounting firms have transformed themselves into Global Business Advisory Firms (GBAFs) which seek to provide a full range of business consultancy services, not just accounting or financial services. To service their multinational clients the 'GBAFs' have developed new client management structures and become more internally differentiated. Rose and Hinings also draw attention to the importance of individual organizational histories in shaping strategic and structural choices. Thus different firms respond to similar environmental changes in slightly different ways. However, there is little doubt as to the overall direction of change.

Caronna and Scott's Chapter 4 presents an extended case study of the one-time maverick US health care organization, Kaiser Permanente, which developed one of the first prepaid health care plans in the US. As such it was a precursor of the health maintenance organizations which diffused rapidly throughout the US after new legislation in the mid-1970s. Prior to this time, however, Kaiser Permanente was a deviant organization, ostracized and attacked by mainstream health care organizations and physicians. As the surrounding organizational field of health care changed, Kaiser Permanente moved from being an outlier to being modal, held up as an exemplar of a cost-effective system. Later in the 1980s and 1990s, the health care field changed once again in the direction of increased market competition and Kaiser again lacked congruence with its environment and needed to adapt its structures. Caronna and Scott demonstrate the importance of the organizational field in shaping organizational structures. In the early period of deviancy, professional values shaped the evolving structure of Kaiser; in the later period of increased market competition, changes were made to increase Kaiser's congruence with its environment that challenged the historic interpretive scheme underlying the traditional Kaiser model.

Chapters 5 to 8 focus primarily on internal processes of change in professional organizations. John Gray looks at the emergence of two successful new law firms in Australia and at changes in a third firm in Chapter 5. Emphasizing that the change processes in professional firms are essentially and necessarily reflexive, Gray shows how each firm's development strategy reflects its different formative intentions and the different personalities of its leaders. Interestingly, Gray suggests that increased managerial control may not represent the only future direction for law firms. Rather, he points to an emerging new type of structure that he terms the 'stars' form. Here the firm is organized around successful individual professionals and their teams, a structure and culture similar to that described by Starbuck (1992) in his analysis of the highly successful New York law firm, Wachtell Lipton Rosen and Katz.

In Chapter 6, Denis, Lamothe, Langley and Valette shift the focus to hospital restructuring in Canada where the health care system is undergoing considerable change. Emphasizing the importance of an ideological shift from provider-based to population-based health care, Denis *et al.* see boundary redefinition as a key element of health reform. They examine the pressures for 'boundary busting' inherent in the emergence of new structures (such as integrated care) and new operating units. They suggest that there are different levels of boundary redefinition in health care reform. Beginning with that involved in intra-organizational integration efforts, Denis *et al.* move to the broader horizontal or vertical interorganizational boundary redefinition required by mergers, joint ventures and integrated services, and to the boundary changes required by system-wide integration. They question the effectiveness of imposed, top–down boundary redefinition because of diluted management control in health care organizations and the strength of professional power and expertise. Rather, they suggest alternative methods of encouraging or facilitating boundary redefinition through emergent collaborative structures and by aligning structures, incentives and interactive processes.

Hinings, Greenwood and Cooper in Chapter 7 discuss the shift in large accounting firms from the P^2 archetype to a new emergent archetype, the managed professional business. They also examine the internal processes of change involved in moving from one archetype to another. Recognizing the difficulty of achieving archetypal change, Hinings *et al.* identify both the changes in interests and values necessary to precipitate change and the enabling factors necessary to make change happen. In doing so, they move the discussion of change in professional firms from the macro external environmental to inside the professional organization itself. While change in professional organizations, like that in other arenas, is usually cloaked in the rhetoric of efficiency and effectiveness, new structures and systems reflect the dominance of new interests and values. Some interests benefit from the structural and systems changes involved in moving from one archetype to another while other interests lose. In bringing interests and power relations back in, Hinings *et al.* remind us that organizational change is necessarily a political process.

The final three contributed Chapters examine the question of whether a new archetype of the professional organization has emerged. In Chapter 8, John Flood finds an interaction between the logic of differing types of law practice and organizational arrangements, which directly affects the emergence of any new archetype. Presenting case studies of two law firms, one in the US and the other in the UK, grappling with more competitive environments, Flood suggests that while there is indeed convergence between US and UK firms in some respects, in other areas differences are likely to remain significant. Arguing that law, and the localized values and traditions associated with it, infuses organizational arrangements, Flood sees limits to the transformation of the professional organization while recognizing the shift towards the managed professional business. His chapter suggests that local or national differences may continue to be important in shaping organizational structures. Consequently, the emergent archetype may differ across countries and traditions in the degree of change it represents.

Chapters 9 and 10 by Kitchener, and Morris and Pinnington respectively, continue Flood's concern with the emergence of new organizational archetypes to replace the old professional bureaucracy and P^2 forms. Kitchener looks at changes in hospitals in Wales following the radical restructuring of the UK public health system, while Morris and Pinnington survey the extent to which the structures and systems of UK law firms have changed in the direction of the managed professional business.

Identifying three major dimensions of the previously dominant professional bureaucracy interpretive scheme – its *raison d'être*, principles of organizing and evaluation criteria – Kitchener examines whether their content and meaning has changed in the restructured hospitals of the National Health Service of the 1990s. He asks whether, in the now competitive environment of the internal market, a new archetype – the quasi-market archetype – has replaced the old professional bureaucracy of the former system.

Similarly, Morris and Pinnington investigate the empirical evidence that would indicate the adoption of the managed professional business archetype, as presented earlier by Hinings *et al.*, in large UK law firms. Their chapter seeks to determine the elements of continuity and of change in professional partnerships and raises questions about transformational as opposed to sedimented change.

Using different research methods, and analysing different professional fields, the authors of Chapters 9 and 10 raise similar cautions about over-emphasizing the extent of change in hospitals and law firms in the UK. Both Kitchener and Morris and Pinnington find considerable elements of continuity in their set of professional organizations and suggest that, if a new organizational archetype is emerging, it is a composite archetype that combines the new with elements of the old. Their studies in the two powerful professions of law and medicine indicate that the interpretive scheme underlying the professional organizational archetype is quite resilient. Professionals are able to use their power to ensure that the changes that do occur are congruent with their interests and values. This is a similar point made by Denis *et al.* in Chapter 6 and indicates that it is unlikely that professional organizations will completely lose their distinctive characteristics.

In the final chapter, the editors draw together the findings and suggestions of the contributed chapters and suggest new ways of understanding the direction and extent of these fundamental changes in professional organizations. That there has been change and development is undoubted; whether this change constitutes the emergence of a new organizational archetype for professional organizations is more complex. How can we understand the new variety of professional forms that are apparent? Have professional organizations succumbed to the pressures of economic rationalization, globalization and modern finance capitalism to represent a new organizational archetype? The remainder of this volume provides some answers to these questions.

Note

1   See E. Freidson (1986), for a definition of professions.

2 Internationalization of professional services

Implications for accounting firms

Yair Aharoni

Introduction

Accountants provide an important service for business. They maintain and audit business accounts, help in tax planning, and operate as liquidators and receivers in the winding up of businesses. Since the nineteenth century the profession has flourished because of the growth in the size and complexity of business transactions (Jones, 1981), leading to an increase in investments by persons not directly involved in the business. This, in turn, has created the need for building safeguards against fraudulent use of investors' money. The need has been met by creating a system of auditing and the development of standards of both accounting and auditing by several professional associations. To date, despite much effort, these standards (and the rules for qualifying as an auditor) are far from universal. With the increased complexity of economic life the importance of auditors as custodians of the public interest has increased. Further, the more complex the tax system has become, the greater the role of accountants as tax consultants.

Accounting firms have been following the movement of manufacturing capital to overseas markets since the 1890s, when British accounting firms such as Price Waterhouse or Deloitte and Haskins Sells moved to the United States (Richards, 1981). When US multinationals expanded abroad, their auditing firms followed them. Offering an ever-widening range of auditing and tax services, they gradually increased their size and developed into professional behemoths. A series of consolidations led to the creation of the Big Eight firms (Stevens, 1981). Other mergers created the Big Six; and a further merger in 1998 made them the Big Five.

Faced with fierce competition and low prospects of growth in the marginally profitable and mature tax and audit fields, accounting firms began around the 1960s to expand their services into management consulting. Accounting firms already knew their clients and were party to their business secrets and, thus, had a head start in offering additional services. The rapid development of computers and subsequent changes in management information systems provided a further impetus for growth for these firms. Since the 1970s, the big accounting firms have climbed to the top of the list of large consulting companies, partly because information-technology consulting has grown much faster than other types of consulting.

The Big Five have become broad-based global service suppliers. The core business – that of auditing – is often the reason for the first contact with a client and has become a vehicle to secure other, more lucrative businesses. The traditional work of certified public accountants comprises between 40 and 50 per cent of total revenues. The development has not been smooth, however, with the inherent conflicts between the two critical components – auditing and consulting – leading to animosity and feuds between the two.[1] Consultants became embittered when the revenues they generated had to be used to pay costly audit litigation. Consultants are pressing for a greater share of the profits they generate and a reduction of the burden of insurance against litigation.

The fiduciary role of the auditor is the basic reason for many professional rules and standards – some of which were initiated by national voluntary organizations while others were regulated by governmental or semi-governmental institutions such as the Securities and Exchange Commission in the United States. (For the history of the profession see, for example: Jones, 1981; Richards, 1981; Winsbury, 1977; Margerion, 1980.) By the end of the 1980s, both the United States and the United Kingdom had lifted the longtime ban on soliciting or advertising for business. Since then, there have been many profound changes. 'Today', according to Gerard Hanlon (1994, p. 150), 'the emphasis is very firmly on being commercial and on performing a service for the customer rather than being public spirited on behalf of either the public or the state.'

Auditing jobs have turned into a commodity. Gone are the days when a client retained an auditor for decades, assuring accountants a steady stream of revenues. Large clients periodically invite all five firms to bid for an audit and grant it to the lowest bidder. Some observers of the industry have even proposed that firms should be forced to change their auditors periodically. Since the early 1990s, the Big Six accounting firms have also been putting together a network of law firms, creating a global system of legal services. After the merger of Price Waterhouse Coopers they became one of the largest law firms in the world, with about 1,000 legal advisors (Arthur Andersen employs 800 legal advisors).[2]

The supply of accounting services is highly concentrated – the largest five firms accounting for about 87 per cent of the world market. The Big Six, says Mark Stevens (1991, p. 17–18) 'have long been considered the only professionals capable of serving multinational corporations, a bias that translates into money, power, position and clout'.

This chapter attempts to answer three related questions: why have accounting firms become multinational, what were the key success factors, and how are the firms organized to achieve their tasks? It also explores the pressures for change in the organization. By comparing and contrasting accounting and legal services, the variables that should be taken into account in a contingency theory of multinational production are explored. The structure of the chapter is as follows. The first section briefly summarizes the major changes in the world leading to globalization. We then explore the issues related to accounting. The differences between the predictions of the theory of international production and the behaviour of accounting multinationals are analysed. Next, we highlight the organizational structure of accounting firms and explores some recent changes. Finally, some contours of a contingency theory of multinational enterprise behaviour and organization are proposed.

Globalization

One of the many indicators of the increasing globalization of the world economy is that the growth of world trade has consistently surpassed that of world output since the late 1970s. World trade grew between 1989 and 1997 at an annual rate of 5.3 per cent per annum, nearly four times faster than global output (1.4 per cent per annum) but only half the rate of growth of foreign direct investments (which zoomed over the same period by 11.5 per cent per annum). FDI outflows increased between 1985 and 1995 by 20 per cent, twice the growth rate of exports or output. The total global FDI stock almost quadrupled, from $679 billion in 1985 to $3.7 trillion in 1995. Another indicator is that sales of foreign affiliates of MNEs exceeded the value of world trade by 27 per cent (UNCTAD, 1997). In 1995, worldwide sales of foreign affiliates were $6 trillion, compared to $721 billion in 1971, claiming a steadily growing share of commerce (one-third of all manufacturing exports). Yet the human labour required for each unit of their output has diminished dramatically: from 1971 to 1991 the world's 500 largest multinational corporations have grown sevenfold in sales. Yet the worldwide employment of these global firms has remained virtually constant since the early 1970s, hovering around 26 million people.

Trade and investment have become less and less separable in the global village. MNEs access markets by both methods, and a growing percentage of world trade is composed of intrafirm transactions. It is estimated that 25 per cent of world exports are intrafirm transactions. About 60 per cent of the United States' manufacturing imports and almost half of the exports flow within the US multinational enterprises (three-quarters of commodity trade, four-fifths of the trade in technology and management services). UNCTAD estimates that if licensing, royalty and franchising payments are included, then 80 per cent of earnings for goods and services sold abroad are linked to the activities of the Unites States MNEs' attempts to achieve economies of scale and of scope (UNCTAD, 1995, p. 38). The increase in intrafirm trade is a result of attempts by multinational enterprises to link different parts of the value-added chain into a global network. Comparative advantage is now less a national phenomenon: the MNEs are able to internalize the comparative advantage within the firm, producing raw materials in one country, processing them in another and doing R&D in yet another country. One result is that it is increasingly difficult to pin down the local content in any specific economy and comparative advantage is internalized within the multinational firm.

In the global economy, capital moves from one currency to another at electron speed. The foreign exchange market had a *daily* turnover of $1.3 trillion in 1997

– compared to $190 billion in 1986 and compared to *annual* world trade of about $4 trillion. Because capital markets are instantly connected, any one national market reacts instantaneously to developments in the other markets. When Tokyo falls, all Asian stock exchanges plummet, New York declines and European markets follow. The idea that one can reduce risk by investing in different national markets may not be as applicable as once thought.

Globalization, in turn, has become possible by major advances in telecommunications and information systems. The steam engine and the telegraph shrank the dimensions of the nineteenth-century world. Today information technology is eroding borders and shrinking distances. Countries are linked with instant communications and mobile phones are a nearly universal artifact. Between 1976 and 1996, the cost of a three-minute phone call between the United States and England dropped in real terms from about 8 dollars to 36 cents and the number of transborder calls zoomed from 3.2 billion in 1985 to 20.2 billion in 1996. One transatlantic line that carried 138 calls in 1960 today transmits more than 15 million calls. CNN and other television networks allow the world to share the same images, with the same news bounced down from satellites. With the establishment of a host of web sites, any child can gain access to a wealth of information on any conceivable topic. Restrictions on the movement of knowledge and information are becoming almost impossible to enforce in the face of advances in computers and communications and decreasing costs thereof. Researchers can share information instantaneously on the Internet, and this information cannot be controlled by any government.

In a globally integrated world of change, uncertainty increases, but intellectual capital is also becoming tremendously important. According to Stewart (1997) the annual capital expenditure on information technology by US corporations now exceeds that on production technology. He estimates that the knowledge component of the output of manufacturing goods has risen from 20 per cent in the 1950s to 70 per cent in 1995.

A related trend is that of 'alliance capitalism'. With the rising costs of development, more and more firms are creating a global network for research and development, cooperating with their competitors in the world economy. Thus, according to one source, technology alliances in the fields of information, biotechnology and new materials increased from a handful in the 1970s to over 200 in the mid-1980s (Hagedoorn, 1996, pp. 173–198).

With global alliance capitalism, the walls and boundaries are being eroded not only among nations but also within firms. Walls of firms are being made more permeable by computers, alliances and outsourcing. Firms allow suppliers to access their computers to reduce the costs of inventory systems and react to the relentless and intense pressures generated by customers as well as by the capital markets.

Alliances involve the transfer of knowledge and competence between firms over time. With globalization, the issue of the proper organizational form for the relations between headquarters and subsidiaries has become important. A major issue is the degree of global integration as opposed to local responsiveness

(Pralahad and Doz, 1989). Another, is the role of headquarters in promoting innovation. Gunnar Hedlund (1986) advocated the N form, Ghoshal and Bartlett (1990) and Forsgren (1990) noted that power and authority are becoming more diffused, and different decisions emanate from parts of the corporation other than its headquarters. We shall discuss these issues after describing the globalization of services.

Globalization of services

International trade in services can be carried out in one of three possible modes of delivery. First, clients may be enticed to come to the country in which the firm is located and purchase services there. Second, an employee of the firm can be temporarily or permanently moved to the place where the customer is located. Finally, the service can be delivered across borders using telephone, fax, mail, computer networks etc. Thus, global trade in services requires international movement of factors of production. Further, the distinction between foreign investment and trade in services is not easily made. Since services are intangible and thus non-storable, they cannot be transported. They have to be produced in the place in which they are consumed, so a presence, often in the form of foreign direct investment, is needed. Indeed, the globalization of accounting – fuelled by the need of the firms to follow their clients worldwide (Aharoni, 1993b; Cypert, 1991) was achieved mainly by the creation of a multinational enterprise.

The service 'enterprise', however, is different in its governance and its rules of conduct from a manufacturing multinational. Specifically, in the production of goods, MNEs are a cluster of firms incorporated under the laws of different countries, all of which are wholly or partially owned subsidiaries of a parent firm. In contrast, the expansion of accounting MNEs as well as other professional service MNEs has been achieved by spreading and augmenting a loose collection of autonomous partnerships into a network.

Having established the network, accountants used it to diversify into more services, including mergers and acquisitions and legal services, thus increasing their size and achieving critical mass. Size has become a sign of quality and reputation and created an almost insurmountable barrier to new entrants. In fact, a pronounced trend in the 1980s was the continuing spate of mergers, acquisitions and consolidations and the attempts to create 'mega-service' firms. This trend recognized no national boundaries and was pronounced in accounting, advertising and management consulting. As already noted, accounting firms also acquired law firms. In fact, the Big Five have all entered the legal business, and lawyers have been trying to fight this trend. According to the *New York Times* (8 June 1998, p. D2) lawyers argue that accountants have duties to their clients that are in conflict with the duties of the lawyers. Indeed, on 7 February 1997, the District Court of Amsterdam upheld the Dutch bar rules banning mergers between accounting and law firms in the case that giant firms Arthur Andersen and Price Waterhouse had brought challenging the rules (Anonymous, *International Financial Law Review*, 1997). In the United Kingdom, the Law Society is anxiously eyeing interprofessional mergers since lawyers fear they will be taken over by the 'Big Six' (*Gazette*, 1997).

The transition of Eastern Europe – and later China – from a communist to a market economy that marked the 1990s created a surge in demand for accountants – not only to attest the books but to value assets undergoing massive privatization. This new demand could rarely be met by creating an affiliation with a reputable local firm – since few such firms existed. The Big Six were forced to move into these markets by sending expatriates to create firms there.[3]

The world market for business services, DRI/McGraw Hill predicted, would grow in 1996 by 3.5 per cent after inflation to $806 billion (*Business Week*, 8 January 1996, p. 107). The figures encompassed legal services, advertising, personnel supply, research and consulting, accounting, engineering, architecture and miscellaneous others. As for accounting, the world market was estimated in 1987 to be about $50–60 billion and the US market was estimated at $26.5 billion. The US market size for legal services for the same year was estimated at $75 billion, but no world market estimate was available. If the US market is used as an indicator, the market size is almost three times larger for law firms than for accounting/auditing (UNCTC, 1990, p. 144).

Yet, figures vary and definitions are not always consistent. The fee income of the Big Six in 1996 was $43.7 billion (*Economist*, 25 October 1997, p. 77), up from $33.5 billion in 1994 (*Economist*, 1 April 1995, pp. 62–3). Average profitability per partner in the Big Six has been about twice as high as in the medium sized firms (*Accountancy*, July 1997, p. 16). In fact, medium sized accounting practice has been squeezed out and firms are either huge or small. To operate globally, a firm must be very large. One result is that accounting is very concentrated with the five largest firms holding 87 per cent of the market;[4] legal services are much less concentrated. All the largest firms operate globally while many of the large legal firms are much less internationalized. Among the biggest multinational firms listed in any stock exchange, there is a clear tendency to employ large auditing firms. 'A company that seeks to entice investors to buy its bonds or shares had best provide a financial statement certified by one of the Big Six' (*Economist*, 31 January 1998, p. 20). In the UK, according to Briston (1979) the number of accounting firms with any listed companies as audit clients fell from 1,422 to 511 in the 30 years from 1948 to 1978. During the same period, the share of the eight largest firms increased from 24 per cent to 51 per cent of the UK listed companies audit. By 1991 the share was 72.3 per cent and in 1994/5 it was 78.4 per cent (Peel, 1997). Peel examines auditors' concentration ratios – across all corporate submarkets in the UK, not only the listed firms. He shows that size is a key determinant of supplier concentration.

Size has become an obsession among the largest accounting firms, with each one of the big firms looking for mergers to become number one. The reason is said to be the economies of scale achieved in computer software (Fischer, 1996), in training and in creating and disseminating information. The firms seem to think they need at least a hundred offices in the United States as well as world coverage – and are thus forced to cover high overheads. Computer systems costs have soared, too. Size also connotes reputation. Since clients cannot gauge the quality of work done objectively (and even peers cannot always evaluate the work of a consultant) – size becomes a proxy. Indeed many studies of the United States market for audit services have found evidence of a percentage audit fee premium after controlling for auditee size, audit risk and audit complexity (Palmrose, 1986). Moreover, the fee premium exists also with respect to the 'second tier'. This has been interpreted to show that the Big Six firms are able to achieve a product differentiation (Lee, 1996). They are perceived as supplying a higher quality service. Simon (1997) demonstrated that the fee premium is attributable to a subset of large auditors, not to all of them. He claims, therefore, that size *per se* does not appear to be a dominant determinant of quality. It should be noted that the relation between size and premium fee has also been studied and confirmed in Australia (Francis, 1984; Francis and Stokes, 1986), the UK (Chan *et al.*, 1993; Pong and Whittington, 1994), New Zealand (Firth, 1985), Canada (Anderson and Zeghal, 1994) and Hong Kong (Lee, 1996).

Another key factor of success is the ability to manage the human assets of the firms successfully and to balance the local needs with global requirements. Obviously, all professional service firms, irrespective of their size and the degree of their globalization, must be able to sell and deliver their services. At the same time, they must minimize the probability of the defection of top personnel. Thus, a major characteristic of a professional business firm is the need to compete simultaneously in at least two markets: the firm has to sell its services to clients and compete for contracts with the clients. Therefore, it has to focus on the needs of clients and to develop procedures and structures to serve those needs. At the same time, the firm has to compete to gain the services of the most competent professionals. It is not enough to recruit such professionals. It is essential to retain them if they are good. This means, as Maister (1982) has demonstrated, the need to grow in order to create attractive opportunities for promotion, in particular if the firm follows the rule of 'up-or-out'. In practice, these two markets are very much interconnected, since competent professionals work not only for money but also for job fulfilment and that means working on attractive contracts for large clients. In fact, one reason for the globalization of firms such as McKinsey (and auditing firms) was the ability to offer competent professionals more attractive assignments. Technology is transferred by training efforts, and firms want to assure those trained will remain. They also attempt to inculcate a similar culture and ways of operating among their many employees in different countries. Effective human resource management is extremely difficult in a global firm composed of numerous professional partnerships.

The major driver for the internationalization of the professional service firms has been the need to service their clients (Hanson, 1989). To be sure, the ease with which the internationalization has been achieved has varied. Auditing firms needed an international network to achieve the basic test of attestation of the consolidated global accounts of their clients. Law firms have been slower to move abroad. By 1980, only 24 per cent of the large-scale law firms had a presence in three or more locations (Spar, 1997, p. 10). By 1989, the 250 largest law firms in the United States established 180 overseas offices (ibid, p. 12) – less than one of the Big Six firms. Ernst and Young alone boast 660 locations in more than 130 countries. (Arthur Andersen has 363 offices in 78 countries). The reason seems to be that the major asset law firms possess is expertise in United States law – and this knowledge is perceived as not very useful to clients in overseas markets. Additionally, law firms are much smaller. Baker and McKenzie employs less than 1,900 lawyers and only the four largest law firms in the world employed more than 1,000 lawyers in 1992 (*International Financial Law Review*, September 1993). In contrast, Price Waterhouse Coopers has 135,000 employees and 8,500 partners worldwide (Vijayan and Hoffman, 1997). In the United Kingdom the twenty top legal firms earned £1.6 billion in 1993 and the Big Six earned £2.5 billion (London Economics Ltd, 1994, p. 1).

Another reason for an increased internationalization of service firms is the rising trend towards what has come to be known as the 'virtual corporation'. This firm of the future is expected to farm out almost all functions and rely on computer-based systems to create an interrelated network of suppliers, providers or vendors, each of which is an expert in some specific function, operating only in the area of its 'core competence'. All functions except the core competencies must be outsourced. The firm thus rents most of the services it needs – from data processing to telemarketing, from billing and collection to publishing or employee training. At the same time, it integrates its operations with those third-party service enterprises.

The globalization of services caused by the need to follow clients has intensified since the 1980s and some of the client firms such as ASEA Brown Boveri, did not even have a home base. The ability to provide services across national frontiers has become a key factor in the development of modern accounting practice. One result has been a competitive reaction – once one big firm moves into a certain market other firms do so too.

The information revolution redefined the parameters determining the competitive advantage of firms seeking to establish affiliates abroad (United Nations, 1993). Boddewyn, Halbrich and Perry (1986) suggested that theories of multinational enterprises and foreign direct investment are applicable to services, too. A United Nations (1993) study indeed demonstrated that business service FDI in developed countries is positively related to market size, home country business presence and openness to the host countries and negatively related to cultural distances as defined by Hofstede (1980). It is positively related (in both developed and developing countries) to global oligopolistic relations (pp. 12, 25–27, 47).

Yet, rules and predictions based on manufacturing experience may be very wrong when applied to professional services. Since the seminal work of Hymer (1976), MNEs have been assumed to work in oligopolistic industries and to have lower transaction costs. Caves (1996), summarizing many works on the theory of MNE says that 'horizontal MNEs will exist only if the plants they own and operate attain lower costs or higher revenue productivity than the same plants under separate management'. In point of fact, in services this condition is simply not necessary for a firm to become multinational. Global firms exist in industries that are far from being characterized only by global oligopolies. While some parts of the industry are global there is a myriad small domestic firms that are able to compete and to be profitable. Thus, the globalization of the accounting profession seems to be somewhat different from that predicted by theories based on the expansion of the manufacturing multinational enterprise. The same is true in accounting. The Big Six operate in dozens of countries and have sales volumes of $6 billion and more. However, there are hundreds of thousands of small firms (the medium sized firms are squeezed out). Large networks of legal firms are even smaller (Spar, 1997). The industry is not dominated by a few giant sellers, as required by the transaction cost theorem.

Organizational structure

In the professional firm the organizational structure is very different to that of a large manufacturing firm. Instead of a traditional hierarchical division of labour, one encounters more a loosely coordinated set of individual professionals. The governance structure of accounting firms is based on partnerships, with local offices as the principal place of business. Professional norms dictate that local offices are independent and central control is weak. Any change encounters difficulties in implementation, exacerbated by the authority context. A champion for change must continuously monitor the commitments of all-powerful partners (Hinings *et al.*, 1991). Very little global coordination is possible on issues such as recruiting, promoting, handling personnel problems, assigning people to projects, making sure juniors are professionally developed, getting clients etc.

Each one of the national firms directs its own affairs, decides who will be promoted to a partner position and allocates profits. Each national partnership may also decide to drop out of the network or to choose another. Indeed in 1989 two mega-mergers united Ernst & Whinney with Arthur Young, and Touche Rosse with Deloitte Haskins and Sells, thereby reducing the Big Eight to the Big Six. After the US partners approved the merger, Deloitte UK announced it would not join the new merged firm and instead linked up with Coopers and Lybrand in the United Kingdom. The Deloitte Dutch firm followed suit, backing out in favour of Cooper. An earlier offer of Deloitte Haskins and Sells to merge with Price Waterhouse was rejected by the partners of Price Waterhouse. An attempted merger of Arthur Andersen and Price Waterhouse did not materialize either.

Yet, managing partners relentlessly look for merger opportunities. In late 1997, four of the six Big Eight firms announced a proposed merger. Ernst and Young were to merge with KPMG and Price Waterhouse with Cooper Lybrand. On 13 February 1998 it was announced that the plans for the first merger had come to an end. The collapse was blamed on the cost and time of regulatory investigations and the disruption this caused to the clients. In contrast, Price Waterhouse and Coopers and Lybrand set 1 July 1998 as the official date for the merger of the two firms, having received the approval of the US department of Justice and of the European Commission.[5] Each one of the national firms was pressured to merge – following the lead of the alliance. Some firms decided to do so. Others did not. Thus the Chilean member firm of Coopers and Lybrand left and joined Arthur Andersen. Mr Wadia, Chairperson and CEO of Andersen Worldwide claimed several others would do the same.

Each partnership in the network agrees to give up some of its autonomy to achieve minimum common standards and to gain more lucrative work and increasing reputation. The formation of such networks, as well of that of strategic alliances or franchising, is still not fully incorporated into the theory of inter-national production. The network can avoid, forestall or obviate serious problems of coordination. In most cases, individual partnerships within the network have consented to some of the following (Aharoni, 1993c):

- work (and charge fees, but also pay referral fees) on cases referred by other organizations in the network;
- refer work in other countries to sister organizations in the network;
- maintain minimum standards of professional work;
- be subject to periodical reviews usually by peers to maintain quality;
- send partners or professional workers to be trained in certain methods by other parts of the organization.

Some of these networks use local names – others use a common international name. The national firms may be known by the international name or by a combined name of both the domestic firm and the international title. A third possibility is a local name where an international firm uses a local firm title even though the local firm is fully affiliated with the international one. A fourth possibility is an *association*, sometimes referred to as a *federation*. In these cases an international title is used mainly for coordination purposes. The local name is used exclusively for local practice. A fifth form is the use of *correspondents*, when the international firm does not have an affiliate. The local firm has clients other than those referred to it by the affiliated international firm but will have the right to an exclusive referral by the international firm. Sixth – and rare – is a local firm with multiple affiliations with several international firms. Finally, in a few cases the international firm operates under two or more local names (Daniels *et al.*, 1989).

The international firm's organization is intended to give all parts of the network a worldwide profile and promote the international identity to the clients. It is the preferred method among the Big Five firms, except for KPMG, which has a federated structure (see Cairns, Lafferty and Mantle, 1984). National firms enjoy a very high degree of independence in directing their affairs – Arthur Andersen is the one firm among the Big Five with a higher degree of integration, including profit sharing. The 'one firm' is a form of representative democracy of a federation of independent national firms that agree to work under a common name and follow a minimum of agreed standards. The organizational structure of such a firm has been described as based on the ideology of professionalism (Johnson, 1972; Mintzberg, 1983b) and partnership – thus P^2 (Greenwood *et al.*,

1990). A loose federation of national firms has very little tendency to centralize and transborder transactions are conducted on an *ad hoc* basis by numerous committees.

Networking and corporate culture may have been enough when Montagna (1968) wrote his analysis of professionalism, but with time the need to manage activities and integrate them has become acute. The larger size, the increased complexities of global operations and the great diversity of operations have put increasing strains on the organization. Some observers are also concerned about the significance of the proposed mergers on auditors' independence. It has been noted that the press release of all four firms announcing mergers in late 1997 ignored auditing and certainly the satisfaction an audit should provide to investors and the public (see, for example, Zeff, 1998).[6] In general, the tension between the ethos of professionalism and the management control systems has been increasing (Raelin, 1991). Since the ability to provide services across national borders has become a key factor in success, the need for integration has become essential, with a concomitant need for structural change to provide strategic direction, planning, human resources management and performance evaluation. As David McDonell, managing partner of Grant Thornton in the United Kingdom said:

> With an increasing number of businesses expanding into international markets, ability to provide services across national frontiers has become a key factor in the development of the modern accountancy practice.

To maximize the opportunities and minimize the risks of international expansion, companies need the support of advisors in different countries who are used to working closely together, and are mutually committed to the relationship.

The genuinely integrated network must be harnessed and coordinated through an organization with clearly defined strategic objectives. This central organization must ensure that all member firms share these objectives' (*European Accounting Focus*, 1994, p. 13, cited in Brown *et al.*, 1996).

Recent strains and changes

How can such huge networks be managed? The more global the firm becomes and the more standardized the solutions needed for the clients, the greater the need for integration and centralization (Aharoni, 1996). A key factor in success is becoming the ability of each location to serve clients by drawing on the accumulated knowledge and databases available to the enterprise as a whole. Insights, experience and ideas must be diffused in all parts of the organization, irrespective of their origin, hence the need for more integration and shared values and a change of the organizational structure. To provide coherence in resource commitment and enhance coordination accounting firms have introduced marketing as a staff function and moved to a system of managing partners, breaking away from the value of equity in governance. National firms are required to conform to international standards dictated by the United States headquarters, and thus, says Hanlon, the core controls the periphery. Firms have also moved to what Kobrin called 'transnational integration'. In other words, 'subunits are incomplete economic entities and their value is, in large part, derived from relationship with others' (Kobrin, 1991, p. 13). Big accounting firms are moving from the loose federation with a minimum of coordination to the establishment of new fully owned affiliates in Eastern European countries (and in China) as greenfield operations and attempts at a one firm strategy. They are also investing in 'dedicated administrative teams to pull the activities together' (Brown *et al.*, 1996, p. 72) and a council of senior partners to provide governance and guidance. Price Waterhouse incorporated a non-practising corporation – the World Firm. It has a World Board to direct and coordinate activities, to help in continuing education, in managing human resources, to create world technical standards and to monitor quality. Partners are also seconded to other national firms to help, train and advise as a part of the firm's efforts to promote the development of skills all over the world and to allow access to the collective technology, expertise and experience of the organizations. Price Waterhouse also created a European firm for regional coordination (Roberts, 1998, pp. 212–20). The parent organization finds it harder and harder to be satisfied with receiving fees for services rendered. Managing partners feel that setting standards and offering training is not enough. They attempt to provide common databases, to refer national firms to experts in other nations and increasingly – to dictate priorities in work done and coordinate activities more closely. The more the network uses a common name, the more the perceived needs of increased standardization, central planning and control. There have also been some attempts to move away from the loosely structured partnership arrangement. Changing market demands are perceived as calling for a more integrated organization. As Reynolds (1993) notes:

> Whereas international companies are legally part of the same organization in most cases accountancy partnerships are separate and distinct entities in each country. The international partnerships are agreements to co-operate, to adopt the same logo, utilize a common business approach, endorse a unitary audit manual and agreement to be checked out by the international firm. The real test for the key elements of the premier international firm is to hold together a network of up-grade national firms, which share common approaches and objectives. The rapid collapse of the Deloitte international network shows how fragile these structures can be.
>
> (p. 77)

The organizational form of partnership was originally designed for small firms and was possible because of the professional ethos. Management processes were based on a high level of consensus and partners felt they needed to be involved in *all* aspects of the business. Peer pressure on weaker performers and a relatively strong work ethics benefited management. Partners in charge of local offices were first among equals and each partner had a right of direct access to the managing partner. In Touche, for example, the managing partner was chosen by all partners for a term of three years and could be re-elected for a maximum term of nine years. Increasingly, the partnership structure is being perceived as problematic, resulting in endless committees and a lack of strategic direction. The so-called 'clan control' (Hinings *et al.*, 1991) is seen as not appropriate for a global, diversified firm with thousands of partners. Indeed, the bigger the accounting firms and the wider the range of their activities, the greater the need for coordination, planning and integration. Managing partners have become stronger, and the system of incentives has shifted to emphasize the ability to market and to earn revenues. The new generation of partners look more for profits and less for loyalty to colleagues (Bruce, 1996). Indeed, according to a survey of 137 managing partners of the Big Six public accounting firms in the United States, the major reason for the exodus of partners is their 'inadequate business development skills' (Addams *et al.*, 1997). By their mid-thirties, Wilmott and Sikka (1997, p. 839) note, 90 per cent of the Big Six accountants leave public practice and end up working for clients. Hanlon (1994) claims that these changes, as well as others in the demands of clients and desires of the state, have fuelled commercial ethos and competitive individualism. In contrast to the professional ethos of a decade or two ago, today 'the emphasis is very firmly on being commercial and on performing a service for the customer rather than being public spirited on behalf of either the public or the state'(p. 150). The traditional emphasis on collegiality and fraternity is diminishing. Partners are cajoled into cultivating business connections and bringing clients. They are promoted and retained according to their ability to raise revenues and achieve profitability. Partners are tightly controlled through cost control, personal supervision and quarterly appraisals. To some, CPAs are no more the watchdogs of the public interest, cherishing their independence and rendering an opinion beyond reproach. Instead of being professionals they are increasingly businesspersons (Dezalay, 1997). Their drive and ambition is to grow, and growth means moving away from the traditional responsibility for checking the accuracy of corporate financial statements to become a holding company of global consulting solutions in various areas of management. The conventional audit has become the least attractive of the different businesses and also the riskier – because of the huge legal settlements to which partners are personally vulnerable. Yet, 'a cataclysmic crisis in the sector may be required to induce partnerships to vote themselves out of existence' (Ferner *et al.*, 1995, p. 357).

The pressures for changes in socialization have been fuelled by events in the environment. An ever-decreasing client base, caused by a spate of mergers among clients, has intensified the competitive pressures within the accounting profession. Since the mid-1980s auditors have been allowed to advertise, and clients some-times threaten to switch auditors. Auditing has become a commodity with very little differentiation among the firms. Accountants have faced very slow growth and intense price competition. They have attempted to increase other parts of the business deemed more profitable. As a result, accounting firms are going through different stages of metamorphosis. First, they are investing heavily in information technology. To allow sharing information internally on a worldwide basis they are deploying new software, developing intranets and extending networks to support even the remotest users in international sites. Thus, Coopers and Lybrand used to operate 120 physical libraries around the US containing the organization's collective knowledge about strategic technology and business areas. Those have recently been converted to online CyberLybs on its intranet. Andersen Consulting has built a worldwide network, called Knowledge Xchange and based on Lotus Notes (Garcia, 1997). Second, the traditional tax and auditing areas are producing a smaller percentage of total revenues (see, for example, Anonymous, 1996). Indeed, audit revenue has decreased to less than 50 per cent of the total (Greenwood *et al.*, 1993). Firms are developing six core competencies: business skills, client responsiveness, personal effectiveness, social skills, thinking skills and management skills (Acher, 1998).

One obstacle to a more integrated structure is the increased tendency of some groups to file damage claims against the auditors when a firm fails (see Trapp, 1994). Auditors are perceived as guarantors of the financial system. According to the *Economist* (7.10.95) the cost of insurance against such litigation in the United States is 12 per cent of local fee income. Those litigating for damages often try to sue the whole international organization, irrespective of the country in which the claimed damage occurred. Because of the partnership structure, this heightens the vulnerability of individual partners. KPMG indeed moved to a limited liability structure. Price Waterhouse (UK), when subpoenaed by the US Senate investigating the role of accounting in the Bank of Credit and Commerce International (BCCI) scandal claimed they were separate and distinct from US practice and refused to honour the subpoenas. It said in its submission:

> Price Waterhouse firms practice, directly or through affiliated Price Waterhouse firms, in more than 90 countries throughout the world. Price Waterhouse firms are separate and independent legal entities whose activities are subject to the laws and professional obligations of the country in which they practice.
>
> (Kerry and Brown, 1993, p. 257)

In 1995 the International Federation of Accountants released a position paper calling for reducing legal liability by various legal means. The accounting firms also exploit the fears of clients of a high profile failure such as the Savings and Loans in the United States or BCCI or Baring. They promote demands for add-on services such as audit and reports of internal controls or risk assessment. In so doing they use the accounting aura of objectivity and exactness to gain more business. Accountants 'are themselves more tightly controlled than other, less responsible personnel' as they learn to be 'acceptable, trustworthy, commercially aware or whatever other term one cares to use' (Hanlon, 1994, p. 215). 'They are being exposed to greater scrutiny, market pressures and demands concerning the nature of the service delivered' (Hanlon, 1997, p. 844).

All in all, accounting firms pay less heed to the ethos of public service professionalism. They face a host of conflicting pressures from the changing environment in which they operate. Governments have moved from emphasizing the welfare state to attempts to facilitate international competitiveness. A new breed of CFOs are pressuring remorselessly for more value for their audit dollars. The combination of the transformed environment and changes in professional ethos will surely impact on the organizational structure. Thus, international work is facilitated by standardization of norms, knowledge and skills, work processes and output (Post, 1996, p. 99). The strong need for global quality assurance reduces the individual's professional autonomy and the stagnation of the auditing market has provided a trigger for greater formalization, management by objectives, budgeting systems, and new appraisal systems of performance against targets (Ferner *et al.*, 1995). The strains and tensions have intensified, and the need for a stronger centre is increasingly advocated. A dense network of international committees allowed networking, but did not solve the management problems; the conflict between the professional ethos and the commercial reality has increased. The strategy of providing integrated services was in contrast to the structure of federation of quasi-autonomous firms.

Different future paths are possible, but unclear at this stage. Thus, it is quite possible that accountants will be permitted to incorporate and the partnership will be abolished. Several of the Big Five are considering the possibility of registering a limited liability partnership and pressuring legislators to allow incorporation. What is clear is that there is no one way for internationalization. In some cases local firms remain independent but get certain services from the centre for which they are willing to give up part of their discretion. In others, there is much more need for integration. A daunting challenge in global accounting firms is not only the need to balance growth with the need for employee satisfaction and with quality services to the very demanding customers. At the same time the firm must maintain its professional ethics.

Unfortunately, much of the literature on professional service firms tends to generalize from a very small sample of firms, usually in one profession. Thus Greenwood *et al.* (1990) base their conclusions on a study of accounting firms while Løwendahl (1992) examined engineering design firms. Maister (1993, p. v), in an attempt to generalize on the basis of experience with management consultants and lawyers, emphasizes two dimensions driving the special managerial challenges of professional business firms. One is the high degree of customization, making traditional managerial principles such as routinization more difficult to apply. The second is the strong component of face-to-face communication with the client. In auditing, however, routinization is quite substantial. On the other hand, in this information society, there are many organizations employing highly qualified individuals with subjective quality assessment. What is needed, therefore, is a contingency theory, in which the variables affecting the internationalization process on one hand and the structure and processes on the other are specified.

Towards a contingency theory of globalization

Up to now this chapter has concentrated on analysing the drivers leading to the globalization of the large accounting firms and the tensions affecting their organizational structure. When other professional business services are analysed, the picture is somewhat different. In the legal profession, for example, one does not observe the same level of internationalization or concentration as among accountants. Some plausible reasons for these observed differences are suggested below. The variables proposed are a part of what might be a contingency theory of globalization.

First, auditors supply a service that is largely *standardized across countries*. Clients want the accounting firms to certify that the consolidated world financial statements confirm to the accounting standards. Thus, clients prefer a large global supplier of the service, and the service can be supplied in a standardized fashion. To be sure, accounting standards are not harmonized. In fact, the more global the business scene has become, the greater the perceived need for harmonization of accounting rules. To achieve this ambitious goal, the International Accounting Standards Committee (IASC) was established in 1973 to develop international standards of accounting. Whether or not the standards developed will be accepted is unclear at the time of writing.[7] The IASC may or may not consummate an agreement with the International Organization of Securities Commissions. If it does, international accounting standards will become the norm for securities listing (Kroll, 1997; Jones, 1998). Note that the probability that the United States will agree to abandon its generally accepted accounting principles (GAAP) is slim. However, many multinational firms conform to the US rules of generally accepted accounting principles. On the other hand, lawyers are expected to supply unique solutions to unique cases, very different because of the diversity of laws in different countries. A global service provider may not, therefore, have the same type of advantage over a local lawyer and may also face institutional barriers (Lawless, 1992).

In both accounting and legal services, professional norms call for an organization composed of partners, and the *limited liability* advantages achieved by a corporate form used by, say, management consultants, are not readily available yet to both accountants and lawyers. Accountants are forced by their clients to supply global services and therefore are willing to create networks and to overcome problems of cultural differences (Roberts, 1998).

Of course, one cannot deny the possibility that *accountants recognized the trend towards globalization earlier*. Lawyers may be late comers and in the next decade we may see them developing the same loose network to a truly unified practice worldwide.

Both accountants and lawyers need to be *qualified*. Despite mutual recognition, the professional licensing process is not global and each country has its own regulations and qualifications. Therefore, lawyers prefer the creation of a network of independent firms, each maintaining complete autonomy. One such network is the ADVOCAsia, with law firms from Australia, Hong Kong, the Philippines, Malaysia, Singapore, India and Sri Lanka (*Asian Business Review*, October 1995,

p. 54). There are also many restrictions on the practice of foreign lawyers (see Kilimnik, 1994). Lawyers also follow their far-flung corporate clients (Spar, 1997), selling the ephemeral products of information and skill. Up to now we have identified four variables:

1   The degree of standardization of the work.
2   The availability of limited liability incorporation.
3   The time by which globalization was recognized.
4   Need for certification.

Other variables are fundamental in explaining differences among professional service firms. These are:

1   Repetitive versus *ad hoc* service delivery.
2   Individual versus team-based delivery.
3   Personal versus proposal-based service sales.
4   Application of existing versus development of new solutions (Løwendahl, 1997, pp. 106–109).
5   The degree of interaction between the supplier of the service and the buyer.
6   The competence of an individual versus that of group.
7   The level of uncertainty.
8   Size of firms.
9   Regulations concerning the profession.

On the first of these variables, accounting firms enjoy a great advantage: all public firms are required by law to employ an auditor to attest to the accuracy of the financial statements. As a result, accounting firms enjoy a relatively stable demand and repetitive service, and do not have to develop a proposal each time they deliver a service. This is in sharp contrast to engineering design firms where jobs are awarded only after a complex bidding procedure. Clearly, large accounting firms servicing multinational clients face the need to audit financial statements in different countries before they attest to the accuracy of the consolidated statements. Thus one can expect large accounting firms to be compelled to become multinational. Moreover, the solution of affiliated local firms may show its limitation and the result is an increasing tension between the need to be global and the professional etiquette of a flat organization and avoidance of hierarchy. It should be noted that the more repetitive the service the easier the planning of workloads, allowing routinization of tasks and procedures, more formal organizational structure and more integration.

Accounting jobs in the large accounting firms also require the employment and cooperation of a large number of professionals over long periods of time. The different size of the projects delivered is an important explanatory variable for the existence of a diversity of firms with different strategies and a much different degree of internationalization in the same industry. As already shown, auditing includes many niches for small domestic firms. Within that industry, the Big Eight turned into the Big Six and then the Big Five because huge size is essential to service large global clients worldwide.

Accounting firms also acquire their jobs on the basis of personal knowledge and relations – not on that of proposal, as is common among engineering firms. The deep knowledge of the business gained by auditing allows a competitive edge in jumpstarting to more lucrative assignments in consulting, tax planning and even the related legal advice business. Accountants are much more dependent therefore on the marketing abilities of individual senior partners.

Auditing is a tedious repetitive service. It does not require new solutions to new problems. This fact makes it easier to plan the work, to predict the resources needed and to structure the organization. Hirsch (1989) emphasizes the importance of what he calls the S factor. Clearly the more the need for interaction and the greater the involvement of the client, the larger the uncertainty in planning workloads. Auditing is much less dependent on interaction with clients than, say legal advice or management consulting.

In auditing work, it is the reputation of the firm delivering the service that counts. In other cases, the client is interested in buying the skills of a certain individual. Thus, British Airways moved their business with Maurice Saatchi when he left Saatchi and Saatchi Plc. In contrast, while a part of the accounting work, such as tax consulting, may be based on individual trust, much of the work is based on relations with the firm – not the individual.

Further, the level of uncertainty in auditing is not very large compared to the unpredictability of winning target projects in other professional business firms. Uncertainty does exist in the ability to assess the quality of work done – and thus does have an impact on reputation. The importance of size has already been discussed.

Finally, firms must adapt to their environment: environment is of crucial importance in determining strategy and structure. More specifically, the regulatory environment may constrain internationalization and diversification. Thus, professionals need to be licensed, laws are different and so is the legal system. As another example, auditors in France are not allowed to work as consultants. All in all, professional service firms are heterogeneous and any conclusions drawn in a specific case may not be applicable in another case. The variables discussed in this section affect the ability of firms to globalize effectively.

Conclusions

For a long time, services have been regarded as non-tradable and, accordingly, confined to one location. But the major technological breakthroughs in telecommunications and computing render this notion obsolete. Service entities are finding that their survival depends on their offering services to their global clients all around the world. These firms are recognizing that adaptability and flexibility are vital characteristics of strategy (Mills *et al.*, 1983). Hence, business strategies are changing. Furthermore, professional service entities are people-centred, and managing diverse groups of persons all over the world is a real challenge. Thus, new organizational structures and relationships are being designed and implemented.

Accounting firms have moved abroad by the creation of networks of autonomous national firms. A 'one firm' culture is nurtured through training and socialization. Concurrent with growth and diversification, global accounting firms will face many challenges. The conflicts between the old professional values and the pressures to generate growth and profits will certainly intensify. The more firms try to create a superservice firm, combining auditing with legal services and consulting, the greater will be the ethical questions raised about the fairness of using auditing to secure lucrative consulting and the barriers of entry to those working only in a stand-alone profession. Moreover, the tensions between auditors and consultants will increase. Yet a stand-alone global audit firm may not be economically viable.

Most experts on strategy believe that the multipurpose conglomerate is an inefficient organization. The firm of the future, it is believed, will outsource not only some specialized functions, but also all non-core activities. Such a trend means much growth of firms specializing in benefits administration, billing, shareholders' services, telemarketing and so on. Because it uses computer networks, the ability of the core firm to control the outsourced operations is not diminished. This 'virtual corporation' will carry Adam Smith's ideal of specialization as a means of efficiency to its extreme conclusion. Nault (1997) notes that information technology made a horizontal organization possible.

The type of work done by the service firm and the professional rule of ethics determines its economic structure, its ownership structure and its human resources strategy. Professional service firms tend to be partnerships, with a high ratio of senior professionals and a high level of remuneration. In contrast, firms offering efficient execution capacity will tend to be highly leveraged corporations, with a relatively high ratio of junior professionals to partners and owners, while the billing rate per hour may be lower (Maister, 1997). In accounting the role of the 'public servant' seems to have been diminished because of the growth strategy. The culture of consensus building among professional prima donnas has changed to a more commercially dominated organization with more formalized structure and clear financial focus.

The partnership structure may be a historical vestige. It may also survive if a structural solution is harnessed to create a coordinated global system of support to the strategy of providing integrated global business services. Partnerships may become less a fragmented federation through a redefinition of the culture of the partnership and the expectations of the partners, and through networking and socialization. Pundits in management science recognize today that firms need to develop capabilities faster than their rivals. In a knowledge-based competition, the firm must 'recognize the value of new, external knowledge, assimilate it and apply it to commercial ends' (Cohen and Levinthal, 1990, p. 128). Firms may learn from other firms, for example, through strategic alliances. A multinational system may be conceptualized as a strategic alliance of its various parts. Learning organizations are not based on hierarchical structure and management formalization is low (Lane and Lubatkin, 1998).

The importance of recruiting, developing, educating and mainly maintaining the loyalty of the professionals who will be supplying the services cannot be overstated. Effective human resource management is essential to achieve better selection methods in recruiting, more efficient training, greater socialization, better career design and higher levels of loyalty. Firms attempt to inculcate a similar culture and ways of operating among their many employees in different countries. Without strong human resource management, it will be difficult if not impossible to achieve cohesion in a loosely structured global network. It will be doubly difficult to design a strategy that includes expansion into countries in which the federation cannot always rely on networks and must move to own subsidiaries. The intensifying competition among accounting firms has already forced these firms to move to more turbulent and uncertain parts of the world. This factor, and the extremely costly litigation across borders, may further reduce the efficiency of the partnership structure.

The challenge is organizational. Can strong central leadership manage a network of independent partnerships? What are the systems of human resource management, information movement, performance evaluation and planning that will allow both a response to environmental changes and uncertainties and the capability to create knowledge and disseminate it efficiently (Nohria and Ghoshal, 1997)?

There are many other problems related to organization design issues in the large accounting firms. How do these firms process information effectively? When (and how) do they use ownership, strategic alliances, cooperative ventures or networks? How will the characteristics of the professional business service firms and the key success factors faced by them affect their choices with regard to ownership and to control? Will accountants incorporate much before lawyers? Will accounting rules and standards be harmonized and globalized? These and other fascinating questions are left to future researchers. Future research may also substantiate or negate our hypotheses about variables explaining globalization.

Notes

1 At Arthur Andersen it was decided to divide the firm into two separate divisions (see, for example, Stevens, 1991, Chapter 3). Consultants are still unhappy with what they perceive as being saddled by auditors' restraints. At Andersen Worldwide, the Andersen consulting division filed an arbitration case with the international chamber of commerce in Paris, claiming irreconcilable differences and looking for independence. Arthur Andersen responded by demanding 150 per cent of the consultants' $6 billion revenues, all methodologies and technologies developed by Andersen consulting and all rights to the Andersen name.

2 Arthur Andersen has been putting together a network of law firms since the 1990s (Banks, 1997). So has Price Waterhouse (Cannon, 1997). So have Ernst & Young in the United Kingdom and Deloitte Touche Tohmatsu in France (*Accountancy*, Oct. 1997). Several large law firms also moved abroad. Until 1985, such moves were done solely at the behest of clients (Spar, 1997, p. 13). Later, firms were attracted to Europe when Europe 1992 was announced. The largest and the most well known world law office is Baker and McKenzie with 1,377 overseas lawyers out of a total of 1,897 lawyers (figures are for 1996) with a gross revenue of $594 million.

3 The trade journal *Accountancy* (1997) published many news items on Big Six firms winning the audit of large state-owned enterprises in Russia, Poland and other Eastern European countries. China allowed the Big Six accounting firms to open 27 representative offices in 6 different cities. By 1996, the Big Six were allowed to recruit 3 member

firms, 2 associate firms and a joint venture firm each (*Accountancy*, June 1997 p. 16). For
some of the administrative problems see Coopers and Lybrand in Hungary, Harvard
Business School case 9–692–112 (January 1994).

4   Before the 1989 mergers, no auditing firm controlled more than 16 per cent of the
audit market for publicly traded firms. After the merger in 1989, Ernst and Young
controlled 19 per cent – and the so-called Big Six firms between them controlled 84
per cent. By 1996, the Big Six share was 87 per cent and Price Waterhouse combined
with Coopers and Lybrand had 23 per cent of the audit pie (*Journal of Accountancy*, Jan.
98, p. 20).

5   This mega-merger was to create a firm with combined revenue of more than $13
billion, approximately 135,000 employees and 8,500 partners worldwide. It is to offer
a range of services that will include accounting, business advisory services, tax
management, human resource consulting, IT services and legal advice (Vijayan and
Hoffman, 1997).

6   Indeed, the Big Five sites on the Internet emphasize their diverse skills and unique
solutions to the clients. Price Waterhouse Coopers include audit in Assurance and
Business Advisory Service (ABAS), promising they offer 'a broad range of innovative and
cost-effective solutions'. Arthur Andersen introduces itself as 'a global, multidisciplinary
professional services organization that provides clients, large and small, all over the
world, the thing they need most to succeed: *knowledge*. Our work is to *acquire knowledge* and
to *share knowledge* – knowledge of how to improve performance in management, business
processes, operations, information technology, finance, and change navigation – so that
our clients can grow and profit. This *knowledge* comes from three sources: experience,
education, and research. In all three, Arthur Andersen excels'.

  Arthur Andersen claims it is 'a global organization with *363 offices in 78 countries*. But
for us, global is more than a worldwide presence; it's also an attitude. With a unique
organizational structure, common methods, and shared values, Arthur Andersen is
able to serve its clients, wherever they are located, as "*one firm*". Our team of over
58,000 people work together – across boundaries of competencies, functions, and
geographies – to deliver to each client a multidisciplinary, *complete solution*'.

  Arthur Andersen's practice concentrations include assurance and business advisory
services, described by the firm as 'beyond the conventional audit – that's where this
practices goes, as we work to assure the integrity and reliability of a client's information; assess the effectiveness of underlying processes; and help identify, measure,
and control a wide range of risks'. The other concentrations are business consulting;
economic and financial consulting and tax, legal and business advisory services. In the
following chapter in this book, Rose and Hinings refer to these firms as Global Business
Advisory Firms (GBAFs).

7   Kroll (1997) illustrates the advantages of increasing uniformity. Before Daimler Benz
AG could register with the New York Stock Exchange in 1993, its accountants and
auditors had to reconcile its financial statements – prepared according to German
accounting standards – to American GAAP. For all of 1993, the firm posted a net
income of DM615 million according to German standards and this turned into a loss
of DM1.8 billion under GAAP. In May 1997 the World Trade Organization (WTO)
released the guidelines for Mutual Recognition Agreements or Arrangements in the
Accountancy Sector, followed in December 1998 by the Disciplines on Domestic
Regulation in the Accountancy Sector. In general members of the WTO preferred to
be kept informed of progress by the International Federation of Accountants (IFAC)
and the International Accounting Standards Committee (ISAC), rather than take steps
to encourage the use and acceptance of international accountancy as part of a trade in
accountancy services. The IFAC proposal that 'reliance on international standards
shall be encouraged' was not included in the document. Members were not even
willing to acknowledge that international standards of accounts have been widely
incorporated (on a voluntary basis) into technical standards at the national level.

3 Global client's demands driving change in global business advisory firms

Teresa Rose and C. R. Hinings

The 'Big Five' accounting firms, now referring to themselves as Global Business Advisory Firms (GBAFs), have been practising in many countries for a number of years. But recently global servicing has become the focus of their strategies (Aharoni, 1993a), creating tremendous pressure for change in the traditional structures and cultures of the firms.

The internationalization process and the structural and cultural manifestations of that process in GBAFs are of particular interest because their reasons for expansion are different from those of other multinational enterprises (MNEs). Most MNEs have expanded to produce profitably for new customers, to take advantage of and combine a product with a factor endowment, or add value to an asset. GBAFs, on the other hand, have expanded to maintain their symbiotic relationships with clients whereby they have been contributing to globalizing while simultaneously globalizing themselves (McKee and Garner, 1996). Post (1995) states:

> The firms' dominant motive to develop international services has been to serve clients involved in a process of internationalization. The firms want to protect the relationship with their clients, and because of that they supply services in foreign countries. The client is a source of strategic, in this case, internationalizing action.
>
> (p. 9)

Changes in global markets and in the opportunities for their clients have pushed the GBAFs to increasingly 'invest in systems of global coordination and control' (Cooper *et al.*, 1994) in order to continue to serve clients.

The traditional organization of these global advisory firms lies in professional partnership: partners are simultaneously operators, managers, and owners of local or national firms (Greenwood *et al.*, 1990; Hinings *et al.*, 1991). Skills and services are widely replicated in multiple markets. These firms have moved into the global sphere by forming associations across borders between national firms (loosely coupled connections of local firms) and then by formalizing these relationships over time. Thus, their international organizational configuration is a complex network structure in which a very large number of loosely coupled connections among various partnerships (firms) support the goal of providing professional services to various types of clients' businesses (Greenwood *et al.*, 1999; Rose, 1998).

With substantive changes occurring in their clients' businesses, competitive advantage for any GBAF now arises out of the firm's ability to coordinate its semi-autonomous member firms in flexible ways. Structural flexibility is required to guarantee a high level of standardized, diversified, and quality service across all countries in which each of its numerous clients' operates. Paradoxically, this level of excellence in internal organization is more difficult in advisory firms than other MNEs because of the partnership structure and professional knowledge tasks (Greenwood *et al.*, 1990).

The purpose of this chapter is to show how the organizational structure and culture of GBAFs are changing as a result of their pursuit of large, international clients. The first section outlines a general theoretical approach to the issue of how GBAFs respond to the demands that global clients make on them. The next section deals with the pressures on GBAFs to go global and how they respond. A section that examines, in more detail, the market changes that have been taking place follows this. We then move on to show how specific client characteristics are likely to impact GBAFs. The fifth section examines the *structural* response of GBAFs to these general and specific pressures, a response involving service, functional, and geographical *differentiation*, and associated *integration*. These responses involve new roles and activities for international headquarters, regions, client management, business units and management consulting. We conclude the chapter by suggesting avenues for further research on the structural and managerial consequences of increasing international pressures, and with comments on the practical organizational concerns of professional service providers as they deal with these pressures.[1]

An approach to understanding GBAFs' global response

Since the late 1960s, a variety of writers in international business have outlined the evolution of the multinational enterprise. Vernon (1966) suggested that after developing home markets a firm expands through exports, then moves to production facilities in new markets. It sets up local subsidiaries producing at low cost locations. Stopford and Wells (1972) suggested that movement is from international divisions, to area divisions, to a worldwide product division with a global matrix structure. Recently Buckley and Casson (1998) have argued that a new research agenda on MNEs has emerged in the 1990s. They suggest:

> The new agenda emphasizes dynamic issues. It highlights the uncertainty that is generated by volatility in the international business environment. To cope with volatility, corporate strategies have to be flexible and flexibility can be achieved by several means. New dimensions of corporate strategy therefore have to be recognized.
>
> (pp. 21–22)

Similarly, Dunning (1998) suggests that many of the explanations of the 1970s and early 1980s need to be modified, as firm-specific assets have become mobile across national boundaries. Changes in the global economy lead to the growing importance of intangible assets, and particularly of intellectual capital. He argues that there is a need for companies to exploit these assets from a variety of locations.

As a result of these developments, other researchers in international management have suggested that there are considerable organizational changes taking place in MNEs (Bartlett and Ghoshal, 1989; Hedlund, 1994; Martinez and Jarillo, 1989; Nohria and Ghoshal, 1997). The evolutionary sequence here is from the multinational enterprise, and to the transnational company (to the international firm). Kogut (1985) argues that the key to global competition lies in recognizing the strategic interdependence of the various units of the MNE and leveraging that interdependence to add value to the firm globally. Increasingly, the MNE sees itself as a global entity and expects its suppliers, whether of components, finished products or services, to be able to respond in a global way.

Our thesis is that Global Business Advisory Firms have become global in order to maintain their relationships with clients who themselves have been progressing along the path from multinational to international, to transnational enterprise (Bartlett and Ghoshal, 1989; Hedlund, 1994; Nohria and Ghoshal, 1997; Stopford and Wells, 1972). The client becomes the source for the globalizing, internationalizing actions of the professional service firm. In order to continue to serve those clients who make up a large part of the fee revenues, the GBAFs have to change and 'reinvent' themselves in terms of their strategies and management practices. In particular this means developing structures and systems of global coordination and control (Cooper *et al.*, 1998).

Put simply, there are changing market demands on the GBAFs, which come directly from their clients. According to Nohria and Ghoshal (1997) and Bartlett and Ghoshal (1989) this is a transnational environment that produces simultaneous pressures for global efficiency, local responsiveness and innovative capacity. These global demands require a response from the individual firms; that is, they have to adapt in some way. The heart of our chapter is to outline what has been happening in terms of the organizational and management response to the new realities of becoming a transnational business. Strategically, they continue to be driven by the goal of serving global corporations across a wide range of services and in a wide variety of geographical settings. The changes that have come about and still continue to emerge are both structural and cultural. Our focus is on the structural responses.

Structurally, GBAF responses can be analysed through the two elements of differentiation and integration (Lawrence and Lorsch, 1967; Thompson, 1967). The changing demands of large global corporations constitute an increasingly complex environment for GBAFs, therefore, we would expect to see increased differentiation and integration to cope with that external complexity. Simply put, that external, environmental complexity is matched by increased internal, structural complexity. A number of authors have raised the issue that MNEs need to achieve 'requisite complexity'. In other words, the complexity of an organization needs to be as complex as the environment warrants (Bartlett and Ghoshal, 1989; Lawrence and Lorsch, 1967; Thompson, 1967; Nohria and Ghoshal, 1997). We are arguing that the environment of GBAFs has become, and will continue to become, more complex, leaving them facing challenges of matching appropriate levels of differentiation and, in particular, integration. What we see, empirically, is GBAFs experimenting with and implementing new integration mechanisms so that those integrative mechanisms enable them to be locally responsive, globally efficient and innovative, simultaneously.

According to Nohria and Ghoshal (1997) the most appropriate organizational form for MNEs in a complex, transnational environment is the differentiated network structure. They argue that it has the required level of requisite complexity. Such a structure has a high degree of differentiation as every subsidiary has its own resources and capabilities and as a result of this, each subsidiary is assigned different roles and responsibilities within the worldwide organization. The structure of relationships is different, depending on the nature of interdependencies between headquarters and each national subsidiary and on the nature of interdependencies among the subsidiaries. A set of shared values underpins these arrangements but they are difficult to isolate and sustain and tend to be quite emergent in nature.

Given the simultaneous pressures these firms face for global efficiency, local client responsiveness and knowledge development and transfer we expect the differentiated structure to be required in these firms. However, we also expect that the control of such a network might occur somewhat differently because with partnership governance there is not a single centre or an ultimate authority to set a strategy of relations (i.e., define the nature of interdependencies among offices) and monitor such a strategy. In the next sections we look closely at GBAFs in terms of the environments in which they operate and the specific structural responses to those environments.

The market context: the demands of global clients

Clients of GBAFs have been increasing their expectations in a number of ways (Aharoni, 1993a). First, they have higher expectations of traditional audit and accounting advice. The most lucrative clients for the firms require standardized, consistent, quality audit and accounting service across many countries. The standardization of the audit, however, has enticed many clients to take aspects of this service into their own organizations. The audit has become a commodity whose provision is lucrative only if done efficiently, and clients are increasingly driving a hard bargain for these services. Clients have also increasingly entered into litigation for audit and accounting services rendered. Essentially, clients' needs for strictly audit and accounting advice have dwindled and these services constitute smaller and smaller percentages of fee volume. The profitability from this practice area has been steadily declining (Greenwood, Rose, Hinings, Cooper and Brown, 1998b).

Coincidentally, there has been tremendous growth in the business services' market, which is encouraging GBAFs to enter new practice areas. Supporting this point, and our analysis generally throughout this chapter, we draw on partners' descriptive comments about the organization and management of the firms. These comments come out of extensive interviews conducted for a study by Rose (1998) on the evolving coordination and integration processes underlying service by these firms to their large global clients. In an interview, one partner expressed the pressure for new services in the following way:

> I think to a large extent there is movement to develop strategic relationships with professional service firms and an expectation that those professional service firms are going to be able to meet most of your needs. If not, they will be able to direct you to someone that will meet the need. While in the past, say ten years ago, there may have been a lot of relationships which were almost exclusively product focused, now their expectation is that the firm is more than a product firm. It is a professional services firm and therefore, they expect us to be able to meet their needs when it comes to process improvement, when it comes to personnel management, when it comes to information technology requirements, and management and other practice areas.

According to partners, clients want 'a firm that can deliver the same quality of product, the same product, the same service in every location'. They want 'the same level of service in all these countries'. They want 'to get full service from one firm' and they want 'seamless service'. The clients want 'high specialism' and 'a team approach instead of one individual in tax, one individual in auditing' but they also want 'a single point of contact'. Clients want 'more international expertise and more best practices from other places'. In other words, each client wants the best practices from the various local offices brought together to serve them in multiple locations.

Furthermore, and again indicated in interviews with partners (Rose, 1998), global clients expect the GBAFs to have their member firms as well integrated as they themselves are, despite differences in governance structure. Also, clients are increasingly concerned with the speed of service provided. They no longer tolerate a firm taking a number of days to figure out an answer to a simple question. Clients often want the firms to be able to provide a one-stop shop for all their professional service requirements but also expect that the partners will seek out other firms to work with (i.e., competitors or other service providers) if such an arrangement can bring knowledge to the client's situation. Recently, there have been situations where global clients have had such a complex array of service providers that they are requesting a lead firm to coordinate the services. Finally, clients expect a high degree of technological sophistication that at least matches their own, as well as a high degree of professionalism (Rose, 1998).

Market diversity

Of course, a consequence of following global clients and becoming a global firm is that the firm has to provide services in a large number of different local country contexts. The varied economic, political, professional, and cultural circumstances impact both the clients and GBAFs (Hofstede, 1980). A major difference here is emerging countries and developed countries. This is particularly pertinent because of the emergence of Asia and Eastern Europe/Russia as important new markets for business services. Resource limitations are usual in emerging countries creating problems such as obtaining and retaining professionals. There are insufficient professionals in emerging countries, especially in high demand areas such as consulting, so it is difficult for these countries to contribute to global initiatives.

Professions are also less developed in many emerging countries which means that fee rates are lower, professional standards are not always congruent with international standards, and partners have less status with global clients. Time spent on global engagements is often less lucrative than time spent on local and regional clients. The work is out of the control of local partners and therefore less desirable. This has implications for the willingness of partners in different countries to cooperate with each other and because of the historically decentralized and autonomous units of the GBAF there are few processes to deal with non-cooperating partners.

A positive side of a less well-developed audit and accounting profession is that there may be less of a foothold by auditors in the firm and fewer tensions around the development of new services. Indicated in interviews with partners in South East Asian offices, there is, relatively speaking, an acceptance of the need to develop strong management consulting divisions within the firms. Also in countries with political strategy and support of the high-technology industry (e.g., Malaysia) the development of management consulting is supported externally. The rapid growth and optimism in an emerging economy creates a readiness for new things. The limited resource situation creates a non-competitive internal environment that supports a higher level of integration across disciplines.

The important point is that there is increasing diversity, and therefore, complexity, in the marketplace of GBAFs which has to be reflected by requisite differentiation and integrative structural devices.

Client characteristics and structural responses

These changes in the marketplace, in the range and types of services demanded by MNEs and the requirement of quick, local response, are mediated through the nature of the task of a GBAF. Organization design is strongly impacted by the kind of knowledge that a task requires (Hedlund, 1994; Løwendahl, 1997; Nohria and Ghoshal, 1997). But there is an assumption in this work that task definition lies within the organization. Similarly a long line of contingency theory acknowledges the effect of task on organizational structure (Donaldson, 1985,

1996). However, neither of these research streams suggests that with certain kinds of tasks the client or customer have a critical role in task definition.[2] There is also a tendency to assume that organizational tasks are unidimensional. Within GBAFs, there is a basic division between two kinds of tasks. Audit and tax represent tasks that are to do with compliance to rules which are externally defined and which clients have to follow. Management consulting is an activity where the client comes to the firm with a problem and often with ideas about those problems, looking for advice. And within both the accounting activities and the consulting activities there are variations.

So, in GBAFs, tasks are only partly defined internally; it is central to a business *advisory* relationship that the client is involved in both defining the task and the process for carrying out that task. Not only that, the task is rarely unidimensional. This is especially true in the various kinds of consulting activities, e.g., restructuring and reengineering, strategic IT systems planning, pensions and benefits consulting. For example, Deloitte Touche in their current North American advertising emphasize working with the client on solutions (charging their unnamed competitors with 'arrogance' in their approach to clients!). This collaborative approach is also increasingly true of audit and accounting functions. KPMG have launched their Strategic Audit, promising the client a wider ranging look at the business and their involvement in solutions.

There are three particular client characteristics that are salient in defining tasks and therefore in impacting the structure of GBAFs (Rose, 1998). They are: the service and knowledge needs of the client; the reporting and operational structure of the client organization; and the history of the client and the client–firm relationship.

Clients' service and knowledge needs

Audit is basically a recurring business with a great deal of consistency. It is required by law, has specific statutory requirements, and is not threatened by economic downturn to the same extent as management consulting. The client comes to the firm and a service team is assembled. The work is fairly reactive. There is little diversity in audit and accounting expertise found across the globe, therefore, it is rather easy for a single methodology to be applied worldwide. The audit is a product that can be easily taken to the client and replicated in a number of markets. Indicated in interviews with partners and strategic documents reviewed we see that each of the GBAFs has developed a worldwide computer audit methodology and this standardized, commodified approach is used as a selling point of consistency, quality, and responsiveness. In the case of audit there is a great deal of internal control by the GBAF over the task, and its execution flows directly from the professional expertise of the accountant. Historically, the training of new accountants has been centred on the audit and accounting task.

Furthermore, the auditor–client relationship is one in which the auditor gets the client through a legal process, attempts to reduce the costs of business for the client, and attempts to reduce the client's exposure to risk.[3] The relationship is often long-term. The client is seen frequently and the firm becomes quite familiar with the inner workings of the client's organization. Client satisfaction is quite easily agreed upon. The client's perception of success is not critical to future work. Although the client's experience of the audit process is important, it is not critical in bringing the next job to the firm.

The management consulting task, on the other hand, is project-based and more cyclical than regular. Assignments are often short-term. The work is discretional and subject to economic downturn. The firm is seldom called back for the same project. It is more likely that a client's positive experience of the client–firm relationship and their favourable evaluation of the work leads to more work of a different nature. The expertise and experience is not easily replicated in every market. Management consulting work is often proactively sought, usually won in competition, and involves investment by the firm up front. There is little standardized training in management consulting (although this varies considerably by the specific consulting area), and there are few legal requirements that firms have to meet, which makes any methodological consistency difficult. While GBAFs have put effort into developing worldwide methodologies these are advisory to national partners rather than mandatory, as is the case with audit methodologies.

The management consultant–client relationship is very much a buyer–seller one in which the firm tries to convince the client that a solution (often an expensive and risky one) will increase the client's profitability and viability. The client presents the initial statement of the problem and it is the first job of the consultant to test that statement and to develop terms of reference for the assignment. There is an ongoing process of task definition, which is subject to how activities unfold over the time span of the assignment. The length of the task is highly variable but is always short compared to an ongoing audit relationship or a major insolvency. Contact with the client is also variable, dependent on the exactness with which activities can be defined and the centrality of the assignment to the client's strategy. Adding value to a client's business is key to a successful consulting assignment. Adding value requires a high degree of knowledge sharing between the clients and the consultants on an ongoing basis. It may also require the consultants to exchange information with other professional services firms (e.g., information technology) or even with competitors. The management consulting task requires the accumulation of multiple bases of knowledge and experience which come from mobility and open sharing.

So there are considerable differences between the audit and management consulting tasks and in the respective firm–client relationships associated with doing them. These differences have structural implications. One of the most obvious differences is that the skill base for audit exists similarly throughout the world, while a problem for management consulting is in attaining the critical mass of expertise capable of providing service in every location. The traditional federative form, recently held more strongly together by international headquarters and client management structures, appears sufficient for providing successful audit and accounting services worldwide. Multiple, diverse, or complex knowledge tasks (typical of management consulting) require extensive knowledge and human resource interdependencies which in turn require more corporate-like, rather than partnership-like, structures.

As a result of these issues, the structural response of GBAFs to changing client demands is complicated because it is mediated by the specific task along the audit–consulting dimension, i.e., from a regulated, externally controlled task to an unregulated, mutually controlled task. Because of this, our analysis separates the discussion between audit and management consulting.

Client structures

Another client characteristic that impacts GBAFs is their reporting structure – the extent to which decisions are centralized or decentralized, in both financial and operational matters. For example, multinational clients whose origins and headquarters lie in North America tend to have more centralized reporting and operational structures than those whose origins and headquarters are in Britain or Europe (Bartlett and Ghoshal, 1989). North American headquartered clients often require the firm to centralize and highly integrate services.

For audit and accounting the clients are the financial managers of the firms. Frequently, audit partners attribute success with clients to their ability to mirror their financial decision structures and processes. One partner describes it this way:

> We have to mirror our responsibility along the responsibility shape of the client. If a client controls everything out of head office, and works on a location by location basis then the same old story, lead partner, head office engagement partner at each location. If we have a client that works differently like in this instance, where in addition to location they break up the activities and have different heads responsible for different activities then we just have to mirror the client.

Another partner states:

> When we are doing proposals to gain new work, one of the things that a potential client looks for is how we are structured and how we will restructure ourselves to fit their needs. And it is almost a dictate [*sic*]. We could not service a group by this company unless we had reconfigured our whole service approach to drive it from somewhere else.

More specifically, the client's reporting structures are often reflected in the way the client drives fee negotiation. A client with both a centralized financial and operating structure is more likely to try to manage the total fees paid to the firm worldwide from the top. Under such conditions a lead partner within the GBAF will play a prominent and often authoritative role. (We deal with the introduction of lead partners in detail later. Suffice it to say that they are partners usually located in the city of the client's headquarters, and they have ultimate responsibility for the service received by the client.) They will dictate to each of the member firms the fee each will get for serving the client. It is also more likely that they will be involved in decisions to provide extra services in all the locations. A more usual situation is that the client has a centralized financial structure but a decentralized operational structure. In these cases it is usual for member firms to negotiate fees locally and then provide these fee estimates to the lead partner in the office which services the clients' head office. In this situation there is less involvement by the lead partner in all decisions.

Structuring for a consulting task occurs around the project requirements and involves obtaining the right expertise. However, whatever the specifics of the task, there is a strong association between client systems and the structures required to serve them, as seen in a comment made by a client service partner:

> If we are focusing on Fortune 500 companies, or we are focusing on the middle market, or focusing on entrepreneurial services, those are entirely different requirements, different fee structures, different levels of experience and expertise, etc. So much of what we do is driven by the niche that we are aiming for. I think that the firm is mainly targeting large global companies like Fortune 100 companies that are global in structure and diversified in nature which means that we will have to match that somehow. So I think that is big – if we change our strategies completely and we say that we really just want to service non-profit organizations and service entrepreneurial organizations that are trying to emerge and grow rapidly, then we would look very different than we do.

History of the client and the client–firm relationship

The third client characteristic impacting the structure and overall organization design of GBAFs is the client's history. As mentioned above, clients with their origins in North America tend to be more centralized than firms originating in Europe. As a consequence, the service provided to North American based clients tends to be more centralized – more micro-managed by the lead partner.

The historical relationship between the firm and client also impacts the extent to which the account is micro-managed. For example, the engagement tends to be less managed when the client is a long-term one. With long-term clients, there is often stability in the senior personnel that the GBAF has managing that relationship, so a greater degree of understanding and subsequent trust develops. Indeed, the client may insist on having the same people servicing it at the senior level. This is particularly true for the audit task.[4] The engagement is also more micro-managed if the client is undergoing change (e.g., geographical expansion, diversification) and thus creating many potential opportunities for the GBAF in the future. The engagement is more micro-managed depending on the historical and present risk to the firm that the client poses. In the case where the client has required the advisory firm to create external interdependencies with competitors to serve the client the engagement is also more micro-managed. Serving clients in conjunction with competitors requires additional scrutiny of the work done in the various offices in order to ensure the same guidelines for decision-making are followed. Finally, the extent to which the client has felt it wants its relationship with the firm to be highly interactive can make the engagements more micro-managed. Increasingly, partners maintain contact with clients even in the absence of current work attachments. The manner in which these relationships are maintained are likely to become an increasingly important factor affecting the ways the advisory firms integrate.

The challenge to the P² form

We suggest that these pressures on GBAFs mean that, whatever the specific structural response of individual firms, they entail a challenge to the P^2 form (Greenwood *et al.*, 1990). The P^2 form has low emphasis on strategic control, tolerant financial accountability with a short-term orientation and operates in a generally decentralized manner through a differentiated structure with few integrative devices. Cooper, Hinings, Greenwood and Brown (1996) have argued that there has been movement away from this archetype in a number of larger and more international professional service firms towards what they term a Managed Professional Business (MPB) where there is increased strategic control, greater accountability, more emphasis on the medium term, and some centralization. The MPB retains a differentiated structure but makes greater attempts at integration.

With the global pressures increasing, one particular client segment dictates that a GBAF's offices worldwide become more highly interdependent and those offices become more interdependent with competitors and other service providers when it benefits the client. These clients are diversified, have significant global reach, require multiple services that cross disciplinary boundaries, and demand efficient quality service wherever they are located. Such clients want to deal with suppliers that can efficiently provide consistent and quality services around the world. The traditional federated structure of GBAFs does not work well for meeting these demands. A form closer to the MPB is required and happening. As a result, the GBAFs are all grappling with creating a structure that capitalizes on the strong aspects of the P^2 form (local autonomy) and the integrative potential of the MPB (global efficiency). This is explicit in one partner's comment:

> Over time we may if that works and makes sense – break down the federated structure we now have for some of our more basic services – maybe it doesn't. I mean our federated structure works very well. It has served. It is our best structure. They [clients] like the fact that they are dealing with a partner in there that can do what they want and make decisions primarily. But for other types of clients [large diversified global clients], that structure doesn't work.

The need for firm balance in terms of structures that support member firm autonomy on the one hand and those that support integration among firms on the other hand is apparent in a comment made by another partner:

> Like a lot of things in life there are kind of counter balancing forces – any one
> principle taken to an extreme is a disaster. So if you want to be a totally
> centralized organization you're going to suffocate yourself. If you are totally
> decentralized you don't get any leverage anywhere and you don't get to build
> on other opportunities so you have to find a happy medium there somewhere.

One can argue that the GBAFs are exemplars of the differentiated network
structure. GBAFs are facing a transnational environment with simultaneous
pressures for global efficiency, local responsiveness, and innovative capacity
(Bartlett and Ghoshal, 1989; Nohria and Ghoshal, 1997). In the differentiated
network structure the resources and capabilities at each subsidiary are different.
Because of this, each subsidiary is assigned different roles and responsibilities
within the worldwide organization and each subsidiary's relationship with
headquarters and with other subsidiaries is governed differently. Supporting the
differentiation inherent in this network structure, is a required set of shared values
that are held by all members of the network (Nohria and Ghoshal, 1997).

However, the differentiation in GBAFs is more multi-dimensional than
Nohria and Ghoshal (1997) depict. Unlike the MNCs of Nohria and Ghoshal,
the local firms that make up the national firm have differentiated resources
and capabilities for different clients. Therefore, there must be different interdependencies created with headquarters and with other national offices for the
various clients. Sometimes this requires headquarters to be directive. Also, for
one client a national firm may have significant resources and capabilities, but
simultaneously, it may not have the resources and capabilities needed by another
client. In other words, the emerging organizational design of GBAFs can only be
understood by looking at:

1   the portfolio of client relationships existing at one time in each national firm;
2   the interdependencies among the firms that are required to provide services
    to each client; and
3   the specific structures and relationships among the structures that will ensure
    clients' needs are met.

In other words, the external network (Nohria and Ghoshal, 1997) and particularly
the portfolio of clients are critical in defining the nature of the internal differentiated network of the GBAF.

In summary, in assessing the impact of global clients' demands on the structure
of GBAFs one has to extend the explanation of global structures beyond the
differentiated network structure and delineate the specific impact of the different
dimensions of the external network in which these firms are embedded. The
structures which are most important for ensuring client service are, in part, dependent on particular characteristics of clients.

Structural responses to clients' demands

In the face of these new and changing demands, how do global business advisory firms respond? A significant set of responses revolves around new and revised structures. Notable in these structural responses is that differentiation has occurred, and continues to occur, along a number of dimensions in order for the firms to attend to the increasing complexity of their environment (Greenwood *et al.*, 1998b; Lawrence and Lorsch, 1967). The firms are differentiating horizontally by providing a broad range of services. They are offering audit, accounting, forensic and other specialist accounting services, tax services, actuarial services, corporate recovery services, personnel management services, process improvement services, and information technology services, to name a few.

The firms are also differentiating functionally by recognizing a number of experts as important for the overall practice. Experts outside audit and accounting have become so critical to the profitability of the firms that questions have been raised as to whether or not auditors and accountants are still the best equipped to be at the helm essentially driving the overall direction of the firms (Whitford, 1997). This debate has particularly revolved around the demand for consulting services by MNEs and the increasing role and profitability of consulting practices within GBAFs.

GBAFs are also differentiating geographically. The Big Ten, Big Eight, Big Six and now Big Five firms have always had strong presence in the non-communist, Western world. With the opening up of Asia and the collapse of communism they have spread their reach into these countries. KPMG, for example, operates in 127 companies through more than 750 offices. Eastern Europe, China and South East Asia are burgeoning new markets where the demand is as much for consulting activities as for audit and accounting. This geographical spread has primarily come about recently from following clients into these countries in order to respond to their business service demands (Cooper *et al.*, 1994; Cypert, 1991; Stevens, 1991).

Finally, differentiation is also occurring demographically. This has happened in two ways. First, as with so many professions the proportion of women in the GBAFs has been increasing and recently more women have been promoted to partner status. Second, with the introduction of new services, new skills are drawn on from occupational groups, which are relative novices to the world of business advisory services, e.g., specialists in SAP or PeopleSoft, and even senior practitioners tend to be much younger than senior audit and accounting partners. So the young–old distinction becomes more pronounced.

This increasing internal differentiation leads to the need for development of coordination mechanisms across member firms, functionally, geographically, and demographically (Lawrence and Lorsch, 1967; Thompson, 1967) such that a higher level of integration (unity of effort towards serving the client) can be achieved. In fact, the only way for them to meet the needs of the global market is to integrate themselves to a level previously inconceivable (Aharoni, 1993a; Greenwood *et al.*, 1998b; Rose, 1998). However, integration is particularly difficult because of their unique characteristics, context and history (Greenwood *et al.*, 1999, 1998b). Making coordination and control particularly challenging is that these firms are more widely dispersed than even the largest of MNEs. Furthermore, the partnership organization, whereby authority is widely and horizontally held, resulting in a decentralized distribution of power, makes integration difficult.

Also making integration difficult in GBAFs is that they are knowledge-intensive firms in which the expertise and experience of individuals constitute the core competence of the firm. The critical asset in these firms is reputation, which arises from the application of the professionals' knowledge to clients' problems (Aharoni, 1993a). Their critical task is for professionals to apply their expertise and experience case by case, customizing service in ways which ensure that they add value to every client's business (Aharoni, 1993a; Zeithaml *et al.*, 1990).

Concerns about knowledge capability have been central to theories of MNEs. The motive behind most MNEs has been primarily economic and strategic: to exploit knowledge to achieve economies of scale. The assumption has been that knowledge is contained in the product, the entirety of which needs to be transferred. However, the motive behind global business firms has been organizational: to serve clients' needs wherever they locate (Aharoni, 1993a; Greenwood *et al.*, 1998b; Post, 1995). The knowledge management task is thus a greater challenge in GBAFs than in other MNEs. Much of the knowledge required for service provision by an advisory firm is experiential (i.e., knowledge gained about certain clients through highly interactive processes of service), the totality of which cannot be transferred, and indeed, does not always need to be transferred. The amount of experiential knowledge transferred is not easily measurable, and further transfer cannot be mandated. What knowledge is transferred must be transformed; thus there is a major role played by the receivers of the knowledge both inside and outside the firm.

The knowledge management task is further complicated in GBAFs because the interaction with the receivers of the knowledge (i.e., clients or other professional service firms) must be monitored so that the GBAF stays sufficiently ahead of the client firm and competitors in knowledge capability in order to maximize the firm's long-term potential with each client (Løwendahl, 1997). Further complications arise from the nature of professionals themselves. Despite the criticality of knowledge creation and dissemination, and thus the importance of a supportive integrated human resource management system (Aharoni, 1995; Evans, 1992, 1993; Løwendahl, 1997; Taylor *et al.*, 1996), few professionals want managerial responsibility (Løwendahl, 1997). Most professionals value their training as service providers and their freedom through 'professional' certification to apply their knowledge, skills, and experience to client problems. Furthermore, professionals are not trained to manage so they often do not do it well (Ferner *et al.*, 1995). Also deterring professionals from management responsibilities is that the greatest financial and status rewards do not come from management activities (Aharoni, 1995). Further challenging the management of the professional workforce generally, and the management of knowledge more specifically, is the fact that many types of professionals are highly resistant to attempts at formal organization (Starbuck, 1992), which is fundamental to supporting the transferring of partners across borders that is necessary to capitalize on existing knowledge in the firms.

Despite these challenges to coordination, the general market, and specific client pressures have been sufficiently strong that GBAFs have engaged in substantive structural changes in order to better serve global clients. International head-quarters and regional structures, client management structures, business unit structures, and management consulting divisions have all emerged in response to client pressures. Each of these is an attempt to give strategic direction to the firm and to integrate the increasingly differentiated units. We discuss each in the following sections.

International headquarters and regional structures

Over recent years, every GBAF network structure has developed an international firm: this is a separate legal entity with responsibilities for global strategy (Greenwood *et al.*, 1998b). We refer to this as the international headquarters, although partners are more likely to speak of 'the international office', which is itself an indication of the difficulties of setting up such a structure. Each international headquarters comprises individuals who are appointed (or in some cases elected) to an international executive management group. The specific role and authority of the international headquarters varies somewhat by firm. But, in all GBAFs professional services are not directly provided out of the international headquarters. Some executive members maintain their own clients; many do not, another indication of the tensions over the idea of a separated management structure. The executive management group establishes the international strategy of the firm, aiming to capitalize on market opportunities and successfully serve global clients. Disciplinary developments in audit, management consulting, tax and other specialties emanate from the international headquarters. Functional work such as international marketing, international liability, technology enhance-ment, research and development, is done through international committees, groups, or task forces which are organized and facilitated by the international headquarters.

An important role of international headquarters is overseeing knowledge management. In the Big Five firms, the international headquarters is developing worldwide methodologies (e.g., automated computerized audits) that enhance standardization and the quality of the firms' services. These methodologies make sure more information and information of quality is consistently brought together to serve clients. Likewise, the international firms are devising worldwide training programmes for these methodologies and facilitating the implementation.

The international firms are also managing knowledge by identifying and tracking what knowledge exists in the firm and publishing the results in both print and electronic form. Comprehensive systems are being created that notify all members of the expertise of all individuals in the firm, the clients each individual has worked with, and the types of issues handled by each person. Technological systems that can make this information available within moments, and even bring together curricula vitae from all parts of the organization to support a competitive proposal are a priority in all firms.

The security of knowledge and information has become one of the key issues of knowledge management. The international bodies again are taking on the responsibility to devise knowledge and information management systems that alleviate clients' concerns of confidentiality. The firms are devising rules, policies, practices and procedures around knowledge accumulation, storage and dissemination, in terms of both external and internal knowledge sources. Security and confidentiality issues around knowledge have to do with the knowledge shared with customers, with other service providers, with competitors, and with people inside the firm. The firms want to sufficiently leverage knowledge but simultaneously protect and secure knowledge in the best interest of the clients and the firm.

International headquarters vary from having minimal structure (e.g., one firm has no physical presence) to having a large physical presence and operating with full-scale international profit sharing. In the cases of the firms lying within these two extremes, the costs of international headquarters are often shared. In some cases a mandatory percentage of every national firm's revenue is collected to provide revenue for the international headquarters and its projects. In these cases the proportion of member firms' fees that goes to the international headquarters has been increasing. In some GBAFs the international firm is responsible to the member firms; in others, the firms are essentially responsible to the international firm to carry out activities that work to the advantage of the worldwide firm. In all firms the responsibility and authority of the international headquarters has increased substantially over recent years.

Part of the international reach of GBAFs is the development of regional structures to implement international strategies. In each firm, the world is divided into a variety of regions, e.g., Asia, Europe, North and South America, with each having a partner responsible for bringing other partners in the region together to service global clients and to implement global strategies. The regional partner works with the chairpersons and managing partners of the firms within the region, encouraging them and assisting them in establishing and maintaining standards in their practices that are consistent with world strategies and standards. The regional partners also work with the regional firms to ensure that practices grow according to international plans; to make sure that each practice's outbound client work is referred into the international firm system; to encourage the firms in the region to develop management consulting practices; to ensure the necessary discipline, technology, and methodology training is received and utilized in all of the firms within the region; to support the resource accumulation for the development of new offices in the region; and finally, to facilitate the human resource transfers throughout the region.

Client management structures and lead partners

Given our generic proposition that global clients and their specific characteristics will have a major impact on the structures of GBAFs, one would expect quite direct responses. We see this in the strategy of each of the international firms to fully integrate service for key clients (i.e., about 20 per cent of the client base in each firm). This is done through some form of a client management structure. Client management structures exist at all levels of the organization: local, national and international. However, these structures have been primarily developed to ensure the firms can identify, market, sell, deliver and coordinate quality services to meet the demands of large multinational clients.

Essentially a client management system does two things. It develops strategies for current and future services to key global clients and it monitors the quality of those services and the satisfaction of the client with them. All individuals involved in the service to a particular client meet at least annually to discuss the strategy for serving their client. These meetings are sometimes in conjunction with the client and sometimes not. The client management structure also includes other groups that form to enhance client service. For example, all individuals serving clients in a particular industry meet annually or semi-annually to discuss the industry conditions their clients face. Individuals employing the same technology but applying it to different client cases meet to enhance their appreciation and use of the technology. So numerous groups that focus on enhancing client service are part of the client management structure of these firms.

The role of lead partner is critical to the client management structure. The lead partner is an individual in the worldwide firm responsible for ensuring that a client receives the best possible service, no matter where that client locates globally. The lead partner is expected to have the expertise required by the client (or be able to access it) and to have the big picture of the client's needs and therefore set the client service strategy. It is the lead partner's responsibility to ensure that a good flow of information about the job is provided both internally and externally. The lead partner is responsible for conflict resolution in the provision of service both among the firm's own offices and with clients, competitors or other professional service providers involved in the service. She or he is responsible for understanding the local conditions sufficiently to ensure equity in compensation to firms participating in client service. The lead partner has to ensure appropriate communication with the client. She or he maximizes the client's benefits by ensuring the transfer of ideas both internally and externally. This is a major set of tasks and a demanding job description.

Although the lead partner can be from any discipline, it is often accounting and audit partners who occupy the role. Lead partners are, usually, based at the same geographical location as the client's headquarters. To various degrees in the different firms, the lead partner is granted authority to set the strategy for client service; dictate fees to other offices; change offices to get better service; or remove, add, and transfer partners from the service team. This strong delegation of authority is new to most GBAFs and is in line with the Managed Professional Business.

While the level of authority that is inherent in the lead partner role varies from firm to firm, it is a significant amount and indeed, a change, for all of the firms. But there are constraints that remain from the P² values of partnership and professionalism. In the face of the basic autonomy of different national firms and the reluctance of partners to exercise overt authority, lead partners tend to use discretion in exercising authority. Also, as a result of the dual roles many of them play (e.g., a lead partner for one client, and the receiver of lead partner demands for a different client) there is some hesitation in exercising full authority. But there is no doubt that all GBAFs have moved strongly in the direction of having lead partners and have been increasing the authority inherent in the role.

It is on the authority and activities of the lead partner, in particular, that we see the impact of client characteristics and client–firm history. When the prestige and value of the client is significant for the office, the lead partner is more likely to be more closely involved. The availability of expertise to serve the client may also influence which professionals from which office are involved. Also, where change is imminent and new opportunities may exist for the GBAF, then there will be much more engagement by the lead partner and his or her team.

Also, the specific role and responsibilities of a lead partner are decided in light of each client's demands in terms of type of service, locations where service is requested, degree of specialization required, desire for a particular type of firm–client relationship. The amount of involvement of the lead partner in a client engagement tends to be greater when a higher level of knowledge is required. And for audit tasks, the lead partner responds by mirroring the structures of the client. For more advisory tasks, the lead partner must organize around the specifics of the project as defined by the client. In other words, the specific role of the lead partner varies in each client circumstance. If the client is highly decentralized, the task is primarily audit, and the client's operations are located where auditing expertise exists, the lead partner will play mostly an administrative role. Alternatively, if the client is highly centralized, drives a hard price target from the top, wants multiple services and demands to be informed of all work and opportunities in the locations, and sets up in places where relevant expertise does not exist, the lead partner role is much more than administrative. In this situation, the lead partner becomes involved in establishing teams of experts, ensuring the transfer of expertise, dictating work and fee rates to colleagues, and setting up joint ventures with other firms when required.

Industry business units

A further development in each of the GBAFs has been a strategic focus on substantially increasing their expertise in specific industries that are deemed to be particularly lucrative or required. Business units have been created whereby individuals from different disciplines (e.g., audit, tax, process improvement, organizational change) but specializing in a particular industry (e.g., mining, financial services, public organizations, health care, high tech) are pooled together in order to leverage knowledge and give global clients a more coherent service. The industry strategy at the local level has been extended in such a way that there are clearly defined industry groups at the regional, national and international levels as well. The primary organizational approach to this has been to routinize relationships in industry committees so that every person specializing in an industry can participate in knowledge exchange about the industry.

While all firms have developed some form of internal industry specialization there are differences in the ways in which they have done this. For example, KPMG in the USA moved to a form of organization based primarily on industry groups. This is the most 'extreme' example. Other firms have set up industry centres of excellence in different countries (e.g., Coopers & Lybrand). And all of them operate, in one form or another, with national, regional and/or international committees of industry specialists.

Unlike the international headquarters and client management structure approaches to global integration, there are some particular problems with industry specialization in emerging countries. Because there are insufficient human resources in general in these countries, and because the accounting profession is less developed, firms in these locales are not able to fully implement industry-focused strategies or engage fully in national and international industry committees. Yet, quite often, it is as global clients expand into new jurisdictions that industry specialization is needed.

Management consulting divisions

Another explicit response to the demands of global clients has been the evolution of management consulting divisions, greatly increasing internal differentiation. The GBAFs are dealing directly with the opportunity and challenge to enter increasingly into management consulting. In fact, some of the greatest structural changes in GBAFs come from their attempts to develop and offer greater and more varied management consulting services. Management consulting is quite a different kind of business than that traditionally offered by GBAFs, and it is clear that different structures and management processes are required. The implementation of consulting services has pushed the firms towards more formalized cross-border interactions. And the internal conflict that has occurred as a result of the global expansion of management consulting in accounting firms has been well publicized.

There is a range of organizational responses to expanding management consulting services on a global basis. One GBAF established a pilot project in a certain region of the world. The pilot project entailed forming an independent consulting company. This company is a corporation rather than a partnership and has a shareholder board with ten countries represented. The company comprises two structures: a legal structure and a management one. The legal structure is a holding company that does not engage in trade. The holding company acts like a headquarters and provides administrative support to its multiple subsidiaries. The management structure supports the provision of core services through a number of industry focused business units. The focus market of this structure is the multinational company operating heavily within the region and across the world. Partners from all over the world come together, concentrating on high value-adding projects.

The consulting company is financially independent. It has one standardized pricing mechanism; a cross-build-up of price by value is calculated. Only when a project takes member firms outside the region do they get into the more usual contract debates. This independent consulting company is a clear example of strategic activity that codifies, standardizes and routinizes client service, partner interactions and financial exchanges to a level never achieved in GBAFs before. Given the success of the pilot project this firm has plans to develop and implement a number of other independent consulting companies within the worldwide firm.

A parallel set of structures in this firm, also developed in response to global clients' needs for specialization, is the establishment of a number of centres of excellence. There is a centre of excellence for plant engineering and maintenance in Canada, and a centre for total quality in London. A centre of excellence for change management is based in Washington; and a centre for logistics in Chicago. These centres of excellence, like the independent management consulting company, are utilized mostly for large complex assignments involving clients who operate extensively across borders. Each centre develops a critical information base for its area of specialization. There is, however, no indication that these structures, unlike the independent consulting company, challenge the traditional partnership form, the basis of which is multiple profit centres.

In another GBAF, global consulting is again developing, first within one region of the world, with the idea that similar structures will be developed in other regions. The firm is developing what they refer to as a 'virtual organization' for their regional consulting practice. The virtual organization consists of an identifiable pool of human resources, the members of which reside in a number of countries. Unlike the previous example, there is no central administrative location. The chairperson of the virtual organization resides in one city and the managing partner in another. These two key members make all initial contacts with lead partners. They work on behalf of all global clients requiring management consulting services in the region. The virtual organization standardizes client contact for large global clients, facilitates the identification of the best practices for an assignment, and ensures appropriate movement of resources around the region. However, each country maintains its own resources and bears the cost of its own input on a job. There is no single pricing mechanism. There has been some discussion within the firm about using a standard rate based on US dollars for work done by each country.

In yet another GBAF, management consulting is being built from the ground up in one region after another. Having less developed management consulting practices at the local level, this GBAF is developing management consulting in a unified way rather than bringing together existing practices. A few years ago this firm, at the headquarters level, identified four areas in which they wanted to develop global competence and then identified the regions in the world where development would likely be most prosperous. Their focus, in other words, is on core services in key areas of the world. The outcome has also been the development of a number of centres of excellence around the world.

In this same firm, unlike the others, industry specialization has culminated in a vision for new global structures to be developed for the sole purpose of serving specific groups of global clients. The first of perhaps many of these structures are evolving in the new area of global supply chain advisory services and logistics. It is designed to bring standardization and routinization to the requirements and approaches for serving global clients with special needs. The global structure consists of individuals brought out of the national practices. It will effectively purchase these resources through a transfer pricing mechanism. Royalties are likely to go back to the original national practices. The partners in the global structure will work only on large engagements that require work to be done across many countries. They will propose, run, control, and bill a project from a central location in the world. All partners in the structure, regardless of the country in which they reside, will share the profits of the structure.

The global structure(s) codify and routinize relationships among member firms. Cross-disciplinary sharing of knowledge is somewhat routinized as the global structure brings auditors, accountants, management consultants, tax advisors and other professionals together to produce a unique set of skills. Resources (e.g., financial, HR, technology, etc.) are shared across borders, exemplifying higher routinization of the relationships among the firms than is usual for partnership form. The global structures envisioned in this firm are explicit examples of the traditional partnership form breaking down.

In yet another firm, management consulting was spun off from traditional auditing and accounting as an independent business in the late 1980s. All resources within the management consulting division are shared internationally, and a percentage (albeit small) is shared with the independent audit and accounting division. Presently plaguing this firm is conflict over which group is best equipped to provide the leadership for the worldwide firm. The accounting side has traditionally been at the helm, however, it is now the management consulting side that contributes the most revenue and holds the greatest potential for future growth (Whitford, 1997). Although clearly the most integrated firm of the Big Five, the separate disciplinary divisions and the conflicts arising between them may hinder its structural flexibility to serve large global clients with many needs.

Conclusions

In this chapter we have described the pressures imposed on GBAFs by global clients demanding more diversified, consistent, and quality service. We analysed the responses of these firms, first, by showing how they differentiate along functional, geographical, industry, service, and demographic lines, and, second, by evolving new roles and activities that allow them to attain the right level of integration across their semi-autonomous units to serve complex clients.

We examined the new integrative roles and activities in four specific structures, namely, international headquarters, client management structures, business unit structures, and management consulting divisions which are evolving in all the Big Five firms.

Interestingly, at the strategic level there are essentially no differences in the Big Five firms' responses to global pressures. All of the firms, although suggesting they are industry specialized, are actually taking on most if not all client requests, and are simultaneously seeking out new international market opportunities. All of the firms are taking explicit steps to broaden and improve their management consulting capacity. All of the firms have developed client management systems. Authority is being granted to the lead partners of client service teams such that the traditional federative form, whereby the local firms had almost complete autonomy in terms of both financial and operational decisions, is directly challenged. Furthermore, all of the Big Five are implementing technology to strategically manage both the external and internal knowledge sources more effectively. Finally, all of the Big Five firms are strengthening their international headquarters in order to ensure a higher level of internal integration.

It is important to restate that in all of the Big Five firms the overall organizational design is in response to specific characteristics of their clients. The service and knowledge needs of the clients, the organizational structure of the client, and the historic relationships between the firms and their clients essentially determine the interdependencies among units and hence determine the structures required, and the role each structure will play in the provision of service to each client.

The structural response of the Big Five clearly resembles what Nohria and Ghoshal (1997) call a differentiated network structure. However, the way subsidiary differentiation occurs (in this case, national office differentiation) in the Big Five is more complex than that depicted by the Nohria and Ghoshal analysis. In these firms structural differentiation and integration cannot be determined simply in relation to the resources and capabilities located at each national subsidiary. A single determination of the resources and capabilities of any national firm is not possible, and thus the nature of interdependency a national firm requires with headquarters or any other national firm is not unidimensional. Furthermore, the nature of interdependency is not stable over time. A local firm may have an abundance of resources and the capability to serve one client, and simultaneously have few resources or capabilities to support another client. The primary integration challenge lies in the overall firm drawing on the appropriate structures and activities that allow it to serve all of its clients efficiently and effectively at any one time. The firms are striving for enough structural flexibility to respond to each client as its needs change, and as the firm's overall portfolio of clients changes.

Our analysis in this chapter provides empirical support to the point raised only briefly by Nohria and Ghoshal (1997) that the definitive characteristics of a differentiated network structure are determined by the broader network of relations within which a differentiated network exists. Perhaps in no other organization is the broader network such a determinant of international organizational structure as in the case of the GBAFs. In this chapter we have emphasized only one aspect of a firm's external network, the clients. However, the Big Five firms are increasingly forming alliances with competitors and other service providers to meet the needs of clients which are also impacting the internal networking of the firms. One partner suggested that interrelating with other types of firms is increasingly the structural challenge they face:

> One of the real challenges we have had in coordination is joint venturing with other firms. Back when this entity [client] was formed there was effectively three types of advisors they wanted: financial/accounting, legal and technology. At one point, they asked us and we considered being the lead – say we will be advisors and we will sub-contract all the other people. They effectively wanted that. The challenge is not just within [the firm], it is within the other types of advisors. There is a set of skills there of which we have some, our human resource consulting and our pension and actuarial, the lawyers have some in their industrial relations. So sorting out between the lawyers and ourselves what we are going to do, what they are going to do, is an aspect of that engagement that is very difficult to manage.

Consequently, research that focuses explicitly on clients' roles in the structuring of these firms, from their perspective is required. Research which broadens the definition of the external network of these firms from just their client base to include the firms' relations with immediate competitors (i.e., other Big Five firms) and those networks; the firms' relations with other competitors (e.g., information technology firms, law firms) and those networks; and the firms' relations with regulative bodies are required. The very large network in which these firms are embedded needs to be realized to fully appreciate and understand their international structures and processes. GBAFs are part of, and leaders in, the restructuring of the organizational field of business advisory firms (Scott, 1995; Greenwood *et al.*, 1998a).

Notable in talking with partners in many areas of the world, and across all of the Big Five firms, is that the strategic initiatives and the structural responses (i.e., nature of differentiation and integration activities) for facilitating service to global clients may be ineffective unless the firms, in concrete ways, begin to recognize that different country contexts affect the success of any of the integrative structures. These differences mean that the same benefits of global service opportunities do not accrue to all local firms similarly. For example, local firms in developing countries are more constrained in providing global services because they are in an emerging market. Economic growth, lack of human resources, political allegiance to regionalism, and different legal requirements that add work to global assignments, all cause local firms in developing countries to reap less benefit from being involved in global client service than local firms in developed countries. When integrative structures (e.g., the international firm, global lead partners in the client management structures) do not equally benefit firms in developing and developed countries, the effectiveness of the integrative structures may be jeopardized. For example, developing countries do not have many MNE headquarters so they are often at the receiving end of colleagues' global requests. Partners in developing countries often feel 'forced' to do less lucrative work than they might find locally or regionally. Alternatively, in the rare situations when the firms in developing countries have the lead role in global service their partners do not always receive the collegial support from the larger firms that they need to serve the client. In other words, the very large local firms simply refuse to accommodate smaller local firms if the fees set for the global job are too low. Consequently, less than rational and effective means of getting the job done are sometimes employed (e.g., using firms outside the international network which creates more monitoring of work; crossing over internal territorial boundaries).

The consequences of country differences, if unattended to, may derail international initiatives meant to enhance integration and cause less efficient processes to become central to the way integration occurs. Perhaps it is when one or more of the Big Five firms recognize and deal in concrete ways with the differential advantage of global servicing for some local firms (e.g., alter transfer pricing arrangements), and the differential advantage of some of the integrative structures that we may see innovative organizational design arrangements that begin to distinguish the Big Five structurally and operationally from one another.

Where the Big Five firms presently differ, at least somewhat, is in the authority inherent in the various integrative roles and activities and in the rules and policies that support the various roles and ensure the client service process most benefits the overall international firm. Differences among the firms in this way seem to align quite distinctly with each firm's historical growth pattern (Greenwood *et al.*, 1998b). For example, if we place the Big Five firms along a continuum ranging from the firms that grew through multiple mergers to those that grew almost entirely internally, we see structural implications of these strategies. The firms that grew mostly through multiple mergers are the most decentralized in their international operations and have the most problems in accessing resources and investing in large scale international initiatives. The international headquarters is less concrete in these firms. In the firm most characterized by multiple merger growth there is not a consistent local presence or even a physical presence to the international headquarters. Also in this firm the executive body is less articulate in terms of its global strategy and is less directive. There tends to be less consistency across the firm's borders in terms of the titles held by people; in terms of the roles and activities partners do; and in terms of many of its operations. There are few rules or policies to ensure the member firms make global client service that benefits the worldwide firm their priority.

Although able to respond well locally, the firms that have grown mostly through multiple mergers struggle most with achieving global efficiency and with effectively managing knowledge. The firms at either end of the continuum (e.g., the firm whose growth has been mostly by way of multiple mergers and the firm that grew almost entirely internally) face the greatest challenges in attaining the flexibility to be simultaneously locally effective and globally efficient.

This discussion really points to the need for researchers to understand these firms' organizational histories in order to appreciate their international structuring and future structural potential. We have only spoken here of one aspect of the firms' histories when in fact organizational history is a multi-dimensional construct. Research is required to identify the various aspects of each firm's history that impacts its international structures and processes. The following research questions need to be addressed: What aspects of a firm's history matter most? What do they matter for? When exactly do they matter most? To what extent are the constraints of firm history reduced when the firms are under certain conditions (e.g., when they enter into new services or new markets; when they have extraordinary political, economic or client pressure to organize in a certain way). With adequate reflection on a firm's historical past, can the leaders of the firm essentially free the firm from some constraints of history as they expand and change?

Due to space limitations of the chapter we have not addressed the cultural changes that are required in the GBAFs to support the evolving integration roles and activities. Jones *et al.* (1997) argue that in firms such as these – where there is demand uncertainty with stable supply; where there are customized exchanges high in human asset specificity; where complex tasks must be achieved under time pressure; and where there are frequent exchanges among members of a network – social contracts and social processes, more so than legal contracts, must be the dominate aspect of governance. The requirement is a culture whereby the members of the network consider each others' needs and goals, trust one another, confide in one another and share information.

Interestingly, social contracts have been the primary processes through which the advisory firms have historically been controlled at the national level. In fact, social contracts and processes are the basis of professional ideology. However, social processes as the dominant means of control are exceedingly difficult at the international level. Heterogeneous conditions (e.g., social, cultural, political factors in various countries) make deriving and maintaining social processes difficult.

The firms are trying to establish what Jones *et al.* (1997) have recently referred to as a macro-organizational culture. They are trying to set up a common system of shared values and assumptions including industry, occupational and professional knowledge that provides explicit guidelines for behaviour and causes repeated interactions among autonomous members. They are striving for common values and assumptions about competitors, about clients, and about international service. All of the firms are striving to attain a global mentality across their membership, placing a high value on the need for better and more secure ways of sharing information. Increasingly, the commonality of values and assumptions must not only exist among the semi-autonomous members of each international firm but it appears that many similar assumptions and values must be shared among members of the industry.

In addition to building common assumptions and values across member firms, the GBAFs are engaging in other social processes that support the complex differentiated structures to which they are evolving. For example, there is restricted access to being a member of an international firm; sanctions are increasingly being imposed on national firms that do not contribute to the goals of the international firm; and there are significant discussions among the member firms about individuals' and firms' reputations in contributing to international goals. All of these social processes support a highly differentiated network structure (Jones *et al.*, 1997).

Despite these efforts it appears most likely that the social processes and subsequent shifts in culture will be insufficient in sustaining the complex networks required to serve the large clients. A number of partners during our interviews on global client service suggest that a further realignment of financial incentives is probably required to support the knowledge/information sharing kind of culture that is so critical to the success of these firms. As alluded to earlier in this chapter, partners working across borders from one another, in very different market circumstances may not always be ready to lower fees or share information because it is socially right to do so, in other words, because it is 'partnership like' and professional to do so. It is more likely that that they will, in each client scenario, evaluate the extent to which it is important to apply the social rules of partnership. In other words, they will decide whether their local contribution to the good of the international partnership, at the expense of personal or local profit will benefit them at a later date, in the case of a different client. Partners are only likely to be willing to share information at a cost to them if they feel on another occasion they will reap the financial benefits of another firm's assistance. Therefore, to assure the most efficient and effective integration for international service it is likely the firms will have to substantially alter transfer-pricing mechanisms. This will cause them to have characteristics more similar to the corporate form than to the traditional federative form. In other words, the partnership form and culture is clearly threatened by global client pressure. Research needs to address the process of partnership breakdown to understand more fully the organizational and managerial consequences of global pressures and the international structural possibilities.

We have attempted to describe and analyse some of the major structural changes occurring in global business advisory firms. These are ongoing changes, in real time, as these firms respond to evolving global markets and clients, and as their scope of operations continues to increase.[5] No current analysis can be definitive because of the speed of change for global clients and their advisors. It is this that led Buckley and Casson (1998) to argue for a new research agenda which emphasizes dynamic issues. We believe that we are dealing with such issues and that GBAFs are a particularly valuable research site because they are MNEs and a central function for them is to service other MNEs.

Notes

1   The ideas presented in this chapter derive from a program of research at the Centre for Professional Service Firm Management into the organization and management of

professional service firms in a global context. In particular, the senior author carried out an extensive study of the way GBAFs organized and managed key global accounts. This involved interviews and documentary analysis in three global business advisory firms in Canada, Malaysia and Singapore. Details of the research design, methodology and analysis can be found in Rose (1998).

2 Interestingly, both Woodward (1965) and Pugh, Hickson, Hinings and Turner (1968) suggested that there was a type of technology (jobbing) where nothing was manufactured until ordered by a customer, and then the customer had a role in the design of the product.

3 Of course, when companies collapse, auditors are often sued. Major international collapses such as BCCI, Olympia and York and the Maxwell empire, have produced large numbers of lawsuits against GBAFs

4 This issue of stability of relationship was seen as enough of an issue in auditing, because of the generally long-term nature of assignments, that the SEC in the USA directed that an audit engagement partner could not lead the assignment for more than seven years.

5 A recent trend is for GBAFs to add legal services to their portfolio of services. The way this will work through at the global level is a fascinating subject for research.

4 Institutional effects on organizational governance and conformity

The case of the Kaiser Permanente and the United States health care field

Carol A. Caronna and W. Richard Scott

Introduction

Since the end of World War II, profound changes have transformed the United States health care field[1] from a world of non-profit, free-standing hospitals and solo practitioners to a world of hospital systems, physician group practices, and managed care (see Starr, 1982; Scott, Ruef, Mendel and Caronna, 2000). In this chapter, we use case study methodology (cf. Eisenhardt, 1989b; Vaughan, 1992) to examine the relationship between these changes and the experiences of one organization embedded therein, the Kaiser Permanente Medical Care Program (KP).

We focus on the relationship between KP's professional groups, its governance structures, and the organizational field in order to advance an understanding of how institutional environments affect professional organizations. Although other researchers have taken a similar approach by examining these linkages using cross-sectional data (e.g., Cooper, Hinings, Greenwood and Brown, 1996), our work covers a fifty-year period. This historical approach allows us to examine the effects of both radical and incremental changes of the field on organizations within the field. It also allows us to examine how and if organizations adapt as their environmental context is transformed.

The case of Kaiser Permanente and the US health care field is particularly well suited for our investigation. First, KP has two major professional groups – physicians and lay administrators – with a history of varying degrees of both conflict and cooperation between them. For the most part, physicians struggled to create and maintain an autonomous professional organization (see Scott, 1965) in the face of increasing bureaucratic control. Second, KP has maintained its general structures and principles to the present day, but the health care field has changed greatly. As a result, KP's conformity to norms of medical care established by authorities in the field has varied widely. Thus KP allows us to examine a case in changing contexts and with changing relations and varying legitimacy in those contexts.

We begin with a brief review of previous studies of institutional effects on professional organizations. Then, we describe KP's history, governance structures, and relations between physicians and administrators in the context of changes in the health care field. We conclude with a discussion about the implications of our case for understanding the institutional influences on professionals in organizations and the causes and consequences of organizational non-conformity.

Institutional effects on professional organizations

A number of previous studies examine the ways in which professionals organize in relation to administrative structures. Tolbert (1988), for example, studied institutionalization processes in a sample of fifty-four law firms, focusing on the ways in which the corporate culture of the firm was perpetuated by means of selection and socialization. DiMaggio (1991) examined the process by which US art museums were institutionally constructed during the early decades of the twentieth century, concentrating primary attention on professional activities at the interorganizational (field) level. Although both studies contribute to an understanding of relations between professionals and governance, neither systematically linked specific organizations' experiences to their field.

In contrast, Hinings, Greenwood, and colleagues have produced a series of studies concerning professional staff patterns and their relation to larger institutional forces. In early research, Hinings and Greenwood (1988b) examined local government units in Britain, describing the gradual replacement of heteronomous professional staff structures (see Scott, 1965) with more centralized, corporate structures. They emphasized the role of a variety of networks and authoritative organizations (e.g., the Association of Municipal Authorities and other professional associations) in diffusing and legitimating the new governmental pattern. In later studies, they examined in detail the structures of accounting and law firms in Canada. For example, Hinings *et al.* (1991) studied an (unsuccessful) attempt to change the structure of an accounting firm from the traditional 'autonomous' professional form to a corporate model. And, Cooper and colleagues (1996) conducted two case studies of law firms in order to examine their differential acceptance of a new, manager-oriented institutional model. Although the two firms differed in the extent of their changes, in both cases, the new model did not replace the previous, professional partnership model. Rather, change reflected a more layered, dialectical pattern, suggesting the appropriateness of a 'sedimentation' metaphor.

As this latter group of studies reveals, contrary to assumptions of early work from the neo-institutional perspective (e.g., Meyer and Rowan, 1977; DiMaggio and Powell, 1983), organizations do not always adopt new archetypes disseminated through their fields or adapt to them in the same ways (see also DiMaggio, 1988). Oliver (1991) explored a variety of reasons why an organization might not conform to the demands of its institutional environment. She presents a typology of strategic responses to institutional processes that identifies conditions under which organizations may be more or less likely to conform. For example, she hypothesizes that organizations will be more likely to resist institutional pressures to conform, if conforming will bring little additional social legitimacy, if the organization has a low degree of dependence on pressuring communities, if there is a low degree of legal coercion behind institutional norms and requirements, and if the field itself is loosely coupled.

Taken together, work by Hinings, Greenwood and colleagues and Oliver suggest that both internal organizational processes and an organization's relationship to agents of governance in its institutional environment will affect the likelihood that it reacts to field-level changes and conforms to field-level models. We attempt to address all of these factors–internal processes, field-level changes, and the linkages between organization and environment–in our case study of Kaiser Permanente and the changing US health care field.

The case of Kaiser Permanente and the US health care field

In this section, we describe changes in field governance and their effects on Kaiser Permanente. We frame brief histories of the field and the organization by three institutional eras, which are marked by changes in the dominant agents governing the field. First, though, we describe the history, basic structures and goals of KP.

Historical background of Kaiser Permanente

With 9.2 million enrollees and over fifty years of experience, Kaiser Permanente is one of the nation's largest and oldest HMOs. Initially concentrated in the American west, by 1998 it had twelve divisions spread out across the US including those in Texas, Ohio and the District of Columbia. A non-profit organization, in 1996 KP's revenues totalled $13 billion, and its net income $265 million (Kertesz, 1997).

Although not the first American organization to introduce prepaid medical plans and physician group practice (Starr, 1982), KP was one of the earliest and arguably the most successful. The modern-day health plan had its roots in efforts to provide health care for Kaiser Industries workers in the 1930s. Los Angeles physician Sidney Garfield, founder of the KP Medical Care Program, began his association with Kaiser Industries in the Mojave Desert in 1933 at a Colorado River aqueduct construction site (see Smillie, 1991, and Hendricks, 1993, for descriptions of these early projects). When his on-site hospital was on the verge of bankruptcy (due to reduced payments from insurance companies and the inability of most workers to pay for their care), an insurance inspector sent by Kaiser Industries suggested a new method of financing: prepayment. With the resulting voluntary nickel-a-day payroll deduction (which all workers agreed to), Garfield's hospital was soon solvent, and later, profitable. More important than ensuring the survival of the desert hospital, prepayment changed the way Garfield's medical care was both sought and delivered. He found that workers came to the hospital earlier in the course of an illness or injury than before, and that it was in his interest to prevent such visits in the first place (Smillie, 1991; Hendricks, 1993).

When the aqueduct project was completed, Garfield replicated and improved his health plan at the Grand Coulee Dam in Washington State in 1938 and at the Kaiser shipyards in the San Francisco Bay area during World War II. The war effort brought more than 90,000 workers to Henry J. Kaiser's shipyards, many of whom stayed in the Bay area after the war's conclusion. Due to the workers' interest in remaining with the health plan, and the 'missionary' desire of Garfield and a few colleagues to continue providing a plan that 'provides so much care to the people at a cost they can so easily pay' (Foster, 1989, p. 216), the health plan was opened to the public in 1945.

Over the course of these industrial and wartime projects, Garfield and his colleagues refined the health plan so that by 1945 a set of principles was in place to guide its growth and development. Called, by various sources, the 'Kaiser formula' (Somers, 1971a) or a 'genetic code' (Cutting, 1986; Smillie, 1991), its principles have remained constant to the present day. They are: (1) prepayment; (2) physician group practice; (3) integrated medical facilities (hospitals and clinics); (4) comprehensive, preventive medical care; (5) capitation payments to physicians and hospitals;[2] and (6) voluntary enrolment with 'dual choice' whereby enrollees must be offered the choice of at least two health plans (Williams, 1971).

To fulfil these principles, the Kaiser Permanente Medical Care Program requires cooperation between the two different 'sides' of medical care – doctors and lay (non-physician) administrators. Currently, the two sides work together as members of several legally, but not functionally, distinct organizations. The lay administrators work for the non-profit Kaiser Foundation Health Plan, Inc. and Kaiser Foundation Hospitals, based in Oakland, California, which enroll members and manage facilities for all KP divisions. Twelve for-profit Permanente Medical Groups are independently owned and operated by physicians in each division. The Health Plan contracts with the Permanente Medical Groups to provide care for members and pays the medical group a capitated fee per patient. The medical group then treats the patients in facilities leased from the Health Plan. The relationship between these two sides of KP, however, has not always been so clear-cut, and the conflicts and compromises that led to the current governance arrangements are discussed below.

Although described as a 'giant mirror that reflects the struggles and uncertainties of the evolving health care system' (Kertesz, 1997, p. 61), Kaiser Permanente was not always considered representative of the health care field. As one prominent Permanente physician recalled, the organization has gone through a 'cycle of being questioned and ostracized, and criticized, to being respected, and emulated, and challenged by the competition' (Cutting, 1986, p. viii). This cycle is due to changes both in KP's governance and internal structure and to change in the field itself.

Changes in the health care field and KP governance, 1945–97

The many changes in the US health care sector since World War II include new technologies, new ways of delivering care, and new players in the health care field.

One of the most significant transformations has been in the field's governance structures: arrangements that allow one set of actors to enforce regularized control over the actions of others (Scott, Mendel and Pollack, forthcoming). Three different sets of actors have exercised field-level governance since World War II: professional providers, the federal government, and the market/corporations. Each set of actors was at the height of its power in different time periods; each change in field governance arrangements was intended to provide 'remedies' as US health care confronted new problems (Marmor, 1970).

The era of professional dominance, 1945–65

Between 1945 and 1965, health care professionals (supported by state authority) constituted the strongest and most effectively organized profession in US history and were the main agents of governance in the US health care field (Freidson, 1970; Starr, 1982; Abbott, 1988). With membership peaking at over 70 per cent of active physicians in the US during the 1940s and 1950s (American Medical Association [AMA], 1997), the American Medical Association was the professional body with the most authority. It served as an advocacy and lobbying body overseeing legislative activity controlling access to hospital privileges, patient referrals, and malpractice insurance and enforcing norms against advertising, fee splitting and corporate medicine. The majority of physicians were sole practitioners, and the AMA fought directly and powerfully against detractors and deviants as it actively constructed the health care agenda.

Few challenged the AMA's power. In this era, the federal government provided funds for support structures – medical research, hospital construction, and medical education – but did not directly pay for medical services and exercised little formal oversight in the health care field. In addition, the AMA was able to derail many attempts by federal legislators to enact national health insurance, demonstrating their power in the field (Marmor, 1970; Starr, 1982). Financing arrangements with third-party payers also had minimal effect on physicians' decision-making and their relationship with patients, since payers simply reimbursed physicians for their services. Organized medicine's centralized control of governance of the health care field lasted from the early part of the century to the mid-1960s.

In the era of professional dominance, KP deviated from the norms established by organized medicine in two ways. First, physicians practised together as a group, which meant some physicians had authority over others. Second and more important, physicians shared their authority over the programme as a whole with lay administrators. Due to the strength of professional norms and of the agents of field governance, these deviations caused KP to be a pariah organization in a hostile environment. Partly due to its rapid growth and expansion, but especially due to this hostility from the health care field, KP's physicians and administrators fought to define their roles and authority relations with one another throughout this period.

When KP was opened to the public in 1945, its internal governance structure was fairly simple. Two separate non-profit organizations enrolled members (the

Permanente Health Plan) and owned the Permanente hospitals (the Permanente Foundation) and Sidney Garfield supervised the entire programme as executive director (Smillie, 1991). He leased the hospitals from the Foundation and oversaw their day-to-day operations, was the sole proprietor of the medical group, and employed all Permanente personnel. Despite Garfield's direction of the programme, though, substantial power remained in the hands of Henry J. Kaiser.

The fact that a layman was the ultimate authority of the medical programme, and that the programme deviated from normative models of operating, caused the relationship between KP and organized medicine to run the gamut from 'active hostility to armed neutrality' (Foster, 1989, p. 223). Between 1945 and about 1960, KP was persecuted by organized medicine for a variety of alleged violations (Johnson, 1974). In 1946, the California Medical Association charged Garfield with violating the Medical Practice Act by employing an unlicensed resident and in 1948 the Alameda County Medical Association accused him of advertising to attract patients, the mass production of health care, the denial of free choice, and other types of unethical conduct (Hendricks, 1991). After Henry J. Kaiser threatened legal action against the medical society, the latter set of charges were withdrawn (Foster, 1989). Henry J. Kaiser was also attacked for having unethical 'corporate influence' over the doctors, as were the doctors, for allowing Kaiser's involvement with the plan (Hendricks, 1991). Permanente physicians were routinely denied membership in medical societies, privileges at local hospitals and board certification for specialties (Foster, 1989; Smillie, 1991; Hendricks, 1991).

These pressures prompted Permanente physicians to clarify their legal relation to Henry J. Kaiser. In 1948, eight doctors formed a partnership legally distinct from the Permanente Health Plan and Permanente Foundation (Foster, 1989; Smillie, 1991). The newly created Permanente Medical Group, a for-profit corporation, was governed by a board of directors with six permanent members and two elected members, although committee work diffused authority throughout the physician membership. That same year, Permanente Hospitals was founded as a charitable trust to run the hospitals owned by the Foundation.

Conflicts over the role and power of each part of the KP organization arose in the early 1950s. The doctors considered the Permanente Medical Group as at least equal to, if not more important than, the Health Plan and the hospitals in directing and sustaining the medical care programme. In contrast, Henry J. Kaiser and his lay administrators believed the Foundation and the Health Plan were the driving forces behind the medical care programme, and the Health Plan was the 'matrix agency' (Smillie, 1991). In 1951, Kaiser further offended the doctors by adding his name to the hospitals and asking the Permanente Medical Group to become the Kaiser Medical Group (Hendricks, 1993). Appalled at the thought of appearing to be Henry J. Kaiser's employees, the doctors refused (Smillie, 1991). Kaiser then suggested the medical group be broken into smaller, localized groups – a divide-and-conquer strategy that won him no allies among the physicians.

The doctors also resented Henry J. Kaiser's intrusion into their dealings with the AMA. At one point in 1954, Kaiser wrote a personal manifesto titled 'AMA Declares War – The Challenge is Accepted' and wanted to broadcast his challenge on television but was stopped by his top advisors (see Foster, 1989; Hendricks, 1993). Physicians felt Kaiser's very visible involvement 'deprived them of . . . professional autonomy . . . [and] the respect of their peers' (Hendricks, 1991, p. 441).

Escalating conflict was made worse by Henry J. Kaiser's increasing participation in the day-to-day operations and strategies of the KP system. His growing interest in KP began in the early 1950s, when his first wife, Bess, became ill and required round-the-clock care. Three months after Bess died in 1951, Kaiser married her live-in nurse, Alyce (Ale) Chester, and, motivated in part by Ale's health care background, began to take a much more active role in the health plan than he had previously (Smillie, 1991). This involvement was symbolized by his unilateral decision to build a 100-bed showcase, luxury hospital in Walnut Creek, California. At the time, Walnut Creek had only 5,000 health plan members. Permanente physicians argued that this hospital was unnecessary and simply too big, but Kaiser proceeded undaunted. When Kaiser suggested Ale would select the Walnut Creek medical staff, including the chief-of-staff of the hospital, the physicians felt their authority and autonomy were severely threatened and issued strong protests (Smillie, 1991).

These conflicts between Kaiser and the doctors threatened the very survival of the organization, and led to major restructuring of authority relations within KP in the mid-1950s. In 1954, trustees of Kaiser Foundation Health Plan assigned the Health Plan a president who reported to the board of trustees, and each of the three regions was assigned an overall executive director and a localized administrative structure (Smillie, 1991). It was intended that doctors and lay administrators would work together in these localized structures. However, the conflicts were not satisfactorily resolved until a summit meeting at Henry J. Kaiser's Lake Tahoe retreat in 1955.

The decisions made at Lake Tahoe were a turning point in KP's governance because, for the first time, both physicians and lay administrators were granted formal roles in system-wide decision-making. Not all provisions of what came to be known as the 'Tahoe Agreement' worked, but doctors and administrators agreed to view each other as partners, not opponents. The agreement established several decision-making teams made up of representatives from both sides. An advisory council was established with equal numbers of doctors and corporate managers and was responsible for system-wide decision-making. This arrangement, however, was short-lived due to the ineffectiveness of management by committee (Hendricks, 1993). The more successful regional management teams (in Northern California, Southern California, and Oregon) were made up of regional health plan managers, regional hospital managers and key physician administrators. A lower layer of governance was composed of area management teams of the physician-in-chief and local administrator of each hospital (Smillie, 1991).

As part of the revision of the Tahoe Agreement in 1957, the Permanente Medical Group created an executive director position (Smillie, 1991). The executive director was primarily responsible for negotiating a contract with the Kaiser Foundation Health Plan. The contract, known as the Medical Services Agreement and signed in 1958, created an exclusive relationship between the Health Plan and medical group that remained in place until the mid-1990s.

In sum, during the era of professional dominance, while the entire KP enterprise was subjected to various forms of sanctions and harassment from the wider medical establishment, struggles between their physicians and administrators reflected many of the same concerns played out in the larger field. Just as physicians in medical societies fought against the lay control of medicine, Permanente physicians struggled to develop internal governance structures that would protect their professional identities and autonomy from being subsumed under corporate control.

During this era, KP faced many threats to its existence – both internal and external. However, it managed to survive and expanded rapidly in the late 1950s and 1960s. As a highly deviant organizational form, much of its survival can be attributed to the insulation and protection it experienced in its formative years. KP was founded at remote construction sites where professional norms were less enforced, then was established in the San Francisco Bay area during World War II when a crisis mentality surrounding mobilization and the related shortage of medical services allowed different forms of medical practice to operate 'for the duration' (Hendricks, 1991). Although vigorously persecuted once the war ended, KP's founding doctors and shipyard patients had become dedicated enough to their model of medical care to continue their practice.

Probably most importantly, KP had the backing of Henry J. Kaiser. Even though he often embarrassed and frustrated the physicians, his national reputation as a champion builder of Liberty ships during World War II, access to senators and US presidents (Adams, 1997), opportunities to address the nation's health care problems (Foster, 1989), and great wealth allowed him to give much needed support and protection to KP. Thus, early isolation and the support of a charismatic figure protected KP from failure and allowed it to survive despite its nonconformity. As we will see in the following description of the era of federal involvement, KP's presence had a strong effect on the field's development in the late 1960s and 1970s.

The era of federal involvement, 1966–82

In 1965, watershed legislation passed as part of President Lyndon B. Johnson's Great Society programme instituted Medicare and Medicaid, which provided federal funding to reimburse medical care provided for the nation's elderly and poor (Marmor, 1970; Starr, 1982). Although not intended to usurp professional control, the authority of professional providers was ultimately challenged by these programmes, primarily through the increasing financial support and regulation of the field by the federal government. As it became more involved in health care financing, the government increased the number of health care related agencies and regulatory bodies and became more involved in licensing, health planning, rate setting and market building (Scott, Mendel and Pollack forthcoming). To try to control escalating medical care costs in the late 1960s and early 1970s, it introduced organizations that investigated excessive hospital stays and inefficient uses of medical resources and monitored certificate-of-need procedures (Starr, 1982). These programmes increased the federal government's governance of the field. At the same time, the power of the AMA waned as new specialty associations developed and membership in the AMA declined (Starr, 1982; Campion, 1984; Krause, 1997).

The federal government also influenced the field through its search for new models ('archetypes') of medical care organizations. As health care costs escalated, federal government and health policy experts turned to and encouraged new, more cost effective organizations. The 1973 Health Maintenance Organization (HMO) Act subsidized the development of HMOs, which involved service providers in assuming all or part of the financial risk of treatment in an attempt to control costs. In a less centralized and more loosely structured field, health care organizations experimented with horizontally integrated hospital systems and physician group practices (see AMA, 1970, for a discussion of the impact of the new physician arrangements). The federal government encouraged this search but ultimately found its authority challenged by a new set of actors.

As medical costs escalated following the passage of Medicare/Medicaid and the government and health care reformers searched for more cost-effective models of service provision, KP and other similarly cost-effective programmes began to receive widespread public attention. KP in particular was the focus of government visits and glowing press coverage. In 1967, a report of the National Advisory Committee on Health Manpower recommended the use of pre-payment mechanisms, such as those utilized by KP, over fee-for-service medicine to accomplish the 'mass delivery of medical care as a human right' (Williams, 1971, p. ii). Cost-cutting regulation in the early 1970s, such as certificate-of-need programmes, favoured KP (Smillie, 1991), and, most significantly, KP provided one of the models for the 1973 Health Maintenance Organization Act. An AMA newspaper article called KP a national showcase (Smillie, 1991), and a feature article in the *New York Times* called KP 'a good legacy of the Great Depression' (Johnson, 1974). KP was considered at the forefront of new models of organizing health care (Williams, 1971; Somers, 1971a, 1971b), and Paul Ellwood, MD, creator of the term HMO and a major proponent of these models, admitted that to ground his theories of HMOs in reality he 'had to go to Kaiser Permanente to find out how to do things' (Kaiser Permanente Medical Care Program [KPMCP], 1987, p. 17).

Once considered a pariah form, KP suddenly found itself in the spotlight of national attention as a model health care organization. To deal with this new attention, as well as the programme's growth and increasing complexity, KP augmented its governance structure with two new levels of administration: the Central Office and the Kaiser Permanente Committee. The Central Office was established informally as executive Clifford Keene, MD, arriving in 1954 at the height of the internal conflicts, began to assemble data and statistics from the various regions to create an information management system. As the administrators, medical economists and attorneys who worked with Keene gained decision-making authority, Keene's office became the *de facto* Central Office. At first, the Permanente Medical Group and the Central Office worked separately, but as the need for administrative centralization grew in light of the increasing authority of the federal government, the executive director of the medical group and the Central Office worked closely together (Smillie, 1991).

The Kaiser Permanente Committee, formed in 1967, 'constituted a maturation of the dialogue [begun in the 1950s] between physicians and nonphysicans as to the policy and governance of the programme' (Smillie, 1991, p. 221). The era of federal involvement brought many changes to the health care field, and KP was affected by these transformations in several ways. It received requests to merge with other HMOs, increase its coverage of unionized employees and provide information to others forming prepaid plans and group practices (Smillie, 1991). Because the Central Office and the medical groups conveyed different perspectives to possible merger partners and consultees, leaders of both sides of KP recognized a need to coordinate their policies. Thus the Kaiser Permanente Committee was formally created, made up of all regional medical directors (four in 1967), all regional managers (also four), and three Central Office representatives. This Committee allowed power and decision-making to be formally shared among medical directors of the medical groups, the Central Office and the regional administrators (Smillie, 1991). These changes in internal governance allowed KP to deal better with both external actors and internal authority concerns.

In addition to the KP Committee, Kaiser Permanente Advisory Services (KPAS) was founded in 1976 to provide consultative services to interested organizations (Cutting, 1986). Several retired Permanente physicians travelled the country, spreading the KP model of health care. In 1971, KP also held a symposium for public and private medical school officials to inform interested parties about their model of health care (Somers, 1971b).

Thus, in response to the increasing involvement of federal agencies in funding and regulating health care services, KP greatly strengthened its internal administrative structures. Notably, these new centralized structures relied on and formalized supportive, cooperative relations between physicians and administrators. To deal with its new found attention and praise, KP explicitly assigned the roles of ambassador and consultant to some of its members, who then actively spread KP's model of organization.

The era of managerial control and market mechanisms, 1983–present

Neither professional nor public regulatory controls, however, were able to stem the rising costs of medical care in the era of federal involvement. This failure, combined with the deregulation of many industries during the Reagan

Administration, paved the way for the expanded role of market forces in the health care sector (Starr, 1982; Scott, *et al.*, forthcoming). Marked by fragmented government regulation and declining AMA membership, in the 1980s and 1990s neither the federal government nor professional organizations possessed the centralized authority of past eras to shape the health care field outright. A new cadre of economically oriented health care policy makers and researchers argued that competitive mechanisms were the only way to control medical costs, and employers become increasingly concerned about the costs of health care corporations as the market mechanisms were constituted as the primary agents of field governance. On the provider side, more and more hospitals joined health care systems and physicians formed group practices or made similar arrangements. These corporate groups rapidly gained increasing control over the provider organizations and affiliated professionals and their administrators often had more decision-making power than physicians. On the payer side, businesses began forming purchasing alliances to increase their power in negotiations with insurance companies (Bergthold, 1990). As insurance companies had to compete for business, often by lowering rates, they began to pressure providers to reduce costs.

Several key pieces of legislation in the early 1980s encouraged competition among providers and framed the federal government's authority in terms of contracting for services, rather than its regulatory and health planning role of the 1970s. States were allowed to move Medicare patients into managed care programmes, and managed care organizations were allowed to enter into 'true risk contracts' for Medicare patients – providers could have the full risks (and rewards) of service contracting (Morrison and Luft, 1990).[3] The Prospective Payment System, part of the 1983 Social Security Amendments, set standard amounts for reimbursement for hospital services based on diagnostic categories. Thus providers had financial incentives to reduce unnecessary services, shorten the length of hospital stays, and provide medical care for less than the set rate in order to profit (Feldstein, 1986). Overall, the growing emphasis on market controls led to a heightened concern for efficiency and cost-effectiveness and to increased corporate and managerial governance of the field (see Baroody, 1981).

After being upheld as a model of health care in the 1970s, KP leaders confidently noted in the 1980s that many organizations were adopting their approaches to organizing and financing health care (KPMCP, 1987). During this decade increasing competition in the health care field caused only minor changes at KP (Kleinfield, 1983). Leaders noted that there was no general agreement as to where the 'turmoil and trends' of the health care field would lead, but KP had a clear direction and would not compromise its values. In 1988, CEO James Vohs stated in an interview that he expected KP to continue to be competitive and grow in the 1990s (Traska, 1988).

KP's age and experience in the field gave it an initial edge over other medical organizations (Levine, 1996). However, it soon began to experience the pressure of competition when less restrictive HMO models (e.g., individual practice associations, network forms) grew more rapidly than group/staff models (for research on changing proportions HMO types, see Christianson *et al.*, 1991). In 1994, for the first time KP experienced no membership growth while at the same time the HMO industry grew 12 per cent and other group/staff models grew 5 per cent (KPMCP, 1994a; Anders, 1994).

KP reacted to increasing competition by cutting costs through eliminating layers of bureaucracy, removing 770 middle management positions in Northern California alone (KPMCP, 1994a; Appleby, 1997). It also devised new system-wide performance measures to better communicate the quality of its services to current and potential members and their employers (KPMCP, 1994b). In 1993, KP's Northern California region was one of the first health plans in the nation to release a Quality Report Card, which was developed by the Permanente Medical Group in collaboration with Andersen Consulting and used more than 100 performance measures (KPMCP, 1994b). KP also was part of a new initiative made up of cooperative group health plans, large employers, and the National Committee for Quality Assurance that created the Health Plan Employer Data and Information Set (HEDIS). HEDIS measures indicate performance levels of different health plans in an attempt to help employers better understand how their health benefit dollars are spent.

KP began using HEDIS measures in 1994 as a way to communicate their performance to both internal and external actors. Previously, KP did not measure performance systematically, with regions collecting data in different ways. But faced with the constraints of the era of managed care, KP CEO David Lawrence noted that:

> purchasers and members will not wait for us to make slow, step-by-step progress in [the critical areas of reducing costs and improving members' care experience]. If we don't make improvements rapidly and exceed their expectations, they will take their health care needs to our competitors. Key to making necessary improvements is knowing how we measure up now.
>
> (KPMCP, 1994b, p. 1)

Regions also established directors of performance improvement, measurement and quality assurance.

However, these efforts were not enough for KP to remain competitive. By the mid-1990s, KP had to adjust further its strategies and health plans to become congruent with the more flexible HMO models in order to compete successfully. Conforming to the managerial imperative, KP hired new executives from outside the health care industry (Kertesz, 1997) and used management consultants (Smoller, 1996). It experimented with point-of-service plans, which allowed members to see non-Permanente physicians at a higher co-payment rate, in the late 1980s and made these plans available to all plan members in 1994 (Kramon, 1989; Winslow, 1994). Faced with an oversupply of hospital beds in many of its regions, KP moved to close some of its facilities and build alliances with other community hospitals to treat its patients (Wasserman, 1996; Appleby, 1997; Kertesz, 1997). Philosophically, these decisions were very hard for the organization, as they violated its long-standing principles (Anders, 1994; Appleby, 1997).

In the midst of increasing competition, changes to its structures included incorporating new actors into KP's governance system and restructuring existing authority relations. In 1996, KP formed contracts with employee (e.g., nurses) unions that allowed union oversight of KP business plans that affected unionized workers (Kertesz, 1997). That same year, the twelve Permanente medical groups formed a national body, the Permanente Federation. The Federation created a common governance structure for the twelve groups in order to simplify relations with the national office of the Kaiser Foundation Health Plan (Kertesz, 1997). The Permanente Federation includes the Permanente Company, which is responsible for business development and geographical expansion. The Permanente Company's board of directors consists of both Permanente Federation and medical group executives, but only one representative from the Health Plan.

KP's governance structure was also affected by a series of mergers and new affiliations. To boost its membership KP acquired, in 1996, several small HMOs in New York state and the District of Columbia. It also merged with the Group Health Cooperative of Puget Sound in Seattle, Washington (Kertesz, 1997), an HMO founded in 1947 (Luft, 1987), and in 1998 formed a strategic alliance with AvMed Health Plan in Florida, a 400,000 member organization. Each of these mergers affected KP's governance. For instance, in the case of AvMed, KP executives now serve on AvMed's board of directors, and AvMed executives serve on KP's local boards in Georgia and North Carolina.

Internally, KP took several measures to streamline its business operations. In January, 1997, it merged its Northern and Southern California Kaiser Health Plan and Hospitals regions to consolidate operations and reduce administrative overhead (Appleby, 1997). It also divided its regions into small customer service areas in an attempt to direct patients to resources in the most cost-effective way (Appleby, 1997).

In all, these various changes in the 1990s gave external actors more authority over KP. Merger partners and unions gained formal authority through their integration into KP governance. Purchasers of health plans, such as employers, gained indirect informal authority as a side-effect of increasing competition; KP had to increase efforts to demonstrate its quality and performance in order to attract customers. Thus its leaders had to consider purchasers' potential reactions and interests when making decisions. This growing number and diversity of actors with governance authority was accompanied by a renewed distancing between administrators and physicians.

Summary of field and KP governance changes

In sum, during the second half of the twentieth century, profound changes in the US health care field resulted in new ways of organizing and new governance structures. Previously in undisputed control, professional organizations lost their dominance as first the federal government and then the markets became stronger forces governing the field. However, a backlash against potential decreases in quality has left the health care field in search of new remedies.

As KP reacted to these field-level changes in governance, its own governance structures became much more formalized and complex than when Sidney Garfield essentially ran the entire programme by himself. In the 1950s, conflicts between physicians and lay administrators led to the formation of legally separate organizations and the creation of various management teams made up of members of both sides; in the 1960s and 1970s, transformations of the health care field prompted centralization; and in the 1990s, increasing competition encouraged mergers and affiliations. Over the course of this history, relations between physicians and administrators ranged from antagonistic and strained to supportive and cooperative.

Effects of field governance on Kaiser Permanente

In this section, we attempt to make sense of how transformations of the field influenced these internal organizational changes as well as what the case of KP reveals for the study of conforming and non-conforming organizations.

Field influences on internal governance

Agents of field-level governance can have strong effects on the structures and behaviour of organizations embedded in the field. These agents may be state agencies, which exercise coercive power and regulative authority, professional and trade associations, which exercise normative authority, or large-scale corporate structures, which exercise the powers of 'private governments' (see Scott, 1995). Equally important are those field-level actors, whether public or private, that are capable of creating and disseminating models, templates, or archetypes of organizing (see Greenwood and Hinings, 1993; Suchman, 1995).

Analyses of the power of regulative agencies are provided by Tolbert and Zucker (1983), who examined the ways in which selected states required municipalities to adopt civil service reforms; and by Baron *et al.* (1986) in their study of the role of US wartime agencies (such as the War Production Board and the War Management Commission) as they mandated and in other ways promulgated general models for bureaucratizing employment practices. DiMaggio (1991) describes the role of the Carnegie Corporation and the American Association of Museums as vehicles for defining and promoting a particular model of art museum in the US context. And Orru *et al.* (1991; 1997) discuss the broader institutional and cultural factors that led to the adoption of different models of business organizations in South Korea, Taiwan and Japan.

In the case of US health care, the three main field agents of governance differed in the modes and mechanisms they employed to exert control. Organized medicine exercised normative authority, advocating professional autonomy and unconstrained care. The federal government tried to stem the rising costs of health care at first by employing regulative authority and later by endorsing new, non-traditional models of service financing and provision. And market governance employed exchange mechanisms to introduce concerns for efficiency and even profit into the health care field by stimulating competition. Each of these agents of governance and the changes they brought to the health care field had strong effects on internal governance structures and professional relations at KP.

At the time when professional associations were the main agents of governance in the health care field, KP was highly incongruent with normative ways of financing and providing medical care. Internally, KP physicians and administrators were engaged in their most complex, antagonistic governance negotiations. Although some of this complexity was due to the newness of the organization and its early growth, the antagonism was a reflection of the strength of the AMA and other medical societies in determining the norms of the field. In the era of professional dominance, the AMA fought against doctors who deviated from their normative model of the solo practitioner reimbursed on a fee-for-service basis. All Permanente physicians were trained in this profession, and thus knew they were rejecting their profession's norms by working as employees of Sidney Garfield in a prepaid group practice. Consequently, they broke rank with professional associations, but they did not reject the AMA's resistance to the involvement of lay administrators in governing health care. Permanente physicians knew the AMA perceived that Henry J. Kaiser was their boss and assumed they worked for a lay administrator. Consequently, they actively tried to distance themselves from him and his staff. They formed their own medical group, sought at least an equal share of authority over the programme and insisted on formal governance relations. Although denied the control of the health care field held by other members of their profession, Permanente physicians fought for control in their more limited sphere of influence. The conflicts between doctors and administrators, particularly in the 1950s, mirrored the conflict between KP and the health care field.

In the 1960s and 1970s, the federal government's increasing authority in the health care field created both a more centralized and a more positive context for KP. No longer considered a deviant, KP's congruence with the field increased as the field changed around it. New regulations favoured organizations with prepaid health plans, physician group practices and, most importantly, evidence of cost control. Thus KP and like organizations needed to make fewer changes than traditional organizations to comply with these regulations, but they suffered the same administrative burdens. The development of the Central Office and the Kaiser Permanente Committee were, in part, driven by the centralization of funding and regulation under federal authority and the need to consolidate knowledge about new programmes.

These changes in governance were also influenced by the attention focused on KP as an exemplar of one of the new models of medical care. The Kaiser administrators and Permanente physicians realized they needed to coordinate their messages about the programme in order to present a consistent front to the media and organizations seeking advice. This coordination did not reflect the tensions of earlier times, but rather both sides of the organization came together in a new spirit of cooperation. Part of this cooperation was due to the solidification of acceptable, roughly equal authority relations between doctors and administrators. Arguably, it was also due to the lack of significant field-level wars between administrators and physicians in this era, and the positive attention from the government and media that mostly celebrated KP and its unique governance structure. Embedded in a more positive professional climate and showcased in the national spotlight, cooperative relations between agents of KP governance seemed axiomatic.

Field-level validation of KP continued in the early 1980s, as legislation that encouraged managed care reinforced KP's ways of practising medicine. However, increasing costs and competition led to new pressures on all service providers from insurance companies, employers and patients. As KP's congruence with the field decreased, its vulnerability to these pressures increased, leading to change its governance structures and professional relations. Part of this change involved integrating merger partners and other external actors into KP governance. Another adaptation involved the increasing attention accorded to consumer interests. More efforts were expended in devising methods of demonstrating health care quality and techniques of marketing KP services to consumers, which gave administrators formal ways to evaluate the performance of physicians and other medical staff.

An even more significant change involved a greater separation between the Health Plan and Permanente physicians. By allowing Health Plan members to see non-Permanente physicians, albeit at a higher co-payment rate, Kaiser administrators made the first major break of their exclusive relationship with the Permanente medical groups. Although we do not have enough evidence to assume causality, it is notable that the Permanente medical groups have recently formed their own, national-level federation and their own business planning arm, the Permanente Company. It is also notable that the Permanente company is mainly concerned with geographic expansion, yet only has one Kaiser Foundation representative on its board of directors. As KP faces increasing competition, its major players have renegotiated their authority relations once again.

In sum, when organized medicine had strong, centralized authority over the health care field, Permanente physicians worked actively to differentiate themselves from the medical programme's lay administrators. When the federal government singled out KP as a model medical organization, it formed centralized committees, which relied on cooperation between physicians and administrators, to deal with the resulting attention from the media and advice-seekers and increasing regulation of the field. When corporations and the market became the new agents of field authority, KP took a variety of measures that changed its governance structures in order to stay competitive. It merged with other health care organizations, opened its plan to non-Permanente physicians, and saw a decrease of Kaiser and Permanente joint decision-making. Thus, field-level transformations had a variety of effects on KP over time, even though KP maintained its principles and basic model of care. At times, agents of field governance fostered internal conflict, then cooperation; persecuted, then celebrated KP; and buffered KP from, then exposed it to competition. Notably, this variety of effects had more to do with transformations of field-level governance than any adaptation on KP's part.

Lessons from a non-conforming organization

KP's lack of major adaptation in the era of professional dominance is particularly interesting. Considering the amount of persecution it suffered from organized medicine, why did KP maintain its highly deviant form? According to Oliver (1991), an organization that will not benefit from increased legitimacy, does not depend on pressuring communities, cannot be legally coerced, and exists in a loosely coupled environment, will resist institutional pressure to conform. These conditions, however, are the exact opposite of KP's experience in the 1940s and 1950s. Conformity would have solved KP's legitimacy problems, eased relations with medical associations that controlled hospital access and board certification, and reduced the amount of legal coercion to which it was subject. At the same time, conformity would have caused KP to abandon its principles and, most likely, disband. KP simply could not conform, not because of a loosely coupled institutional context (in fact, the context was very tightly coupled in that era) or an independence from pressuring communities, but because it was so different from its context, any adaptations would render it radically transformed or result in its demise.

KP's nonconformity may be the exception to Oliver's rules, but it suggests an expansion of the conditions under which some organizations do not conform to their institutional contexts. It also suggests how new models develop in organizational fields. Previous work by Leblebici and colleagues (1991) described the endogenous development of new, innovative models of organizing in the US radio broadcasting industry. During the period 1920 to 1965, this industry's innovations were introduced by 'marginal participants in the market [and were] later adopted by leading members [of the field] driven to do so by intense competition' (Scott, 1995, p. 70).

The case of KP and the US health care field suggests different factors leading to the legitimacy and diffusion of models of organizing. Unlike the innovative radio stations, which were often located in rural communities and participated in peripheral segments of the market, KP was not marginal to the health care field at the time its model gained popularity. Although KP deviated from field-level norms, it did so with the strong support of Henry J. Kaiser, a large membership base, and a growing national presence. Also, KP was not simply a passive organization with no influence on the diffusion of its innovations; it actively disseminated its model through the KP Committee and KPAS. And in the 1960s and 1970s, its model of organizing was adopted by other field participants because of its cost-effectiveness and congruence with new regulations, not its competitive value. Innovation, then, can be developed by deviant but visible and influential organizations; these organizations can take an active role in the diffusion of their innovations.

In sum, KP's influence in the late 1960s required at least two conditions: (1) changes in the field created new needs that traditional models of organizing could not meet; and (2) KP's model could meet these needs. Thus the transformation of the field was both cause and consequence of the diffusion of the KP model.

Conclusion

The case of Kaiser Permanente and the US health care field offers two main contributions to an understanding of the complex relations between institutional environments and organizations. First, the case illustrates the process by which some organizations indirectly adapt to field-level norms – in contrast to more typical forms of adaptation – when their deviant models of organizing become legitimized and diffused throughout the field. Second, the case suggests revisions of Oliver's (1991) typology of non-conformity: some organizations resist making changes that would appease field-level actors, not because of various weaknesses of field governance (as Oliver argues), but because of their radical ideological commitments to non-normative models. In both respects, examining the experiences of non-conforming and illegitimate organizations, especially ones that survive for many years, offers important directions for broadening institutional theory.

Our simplified version of the US health care field's development and Kaiser Permanente's history, however, leaves many questions for future research. At the organization level, we need better understanding of how and why deviant models of organizing become legitimate. The case of Kaiser Permanente indicates that addressing a new field-level need can increase an organization's legitimacy, but it is likely that there are other, perhaps more important, factors. Also, given that field participants influence the creation, modification and reproduction of fields (Giddens, 1979, 1984), how do deviant organizations affect field norms, and what role do they play in the legitimation of their own models?

At the field level, it is important to consider how the degree of field structuration or coupling (e.g., DiMaggio and Powell, 1983; Greenwood and Hinings, 1996) affects the creation of new models and legitimation of existing models. Are deviant models more likely to gain legitimacy in tightly or loosely structured fields? More specifically, how do differences in the amount of agreement among field participants on norms, models of organizing, and who has legitimate authority, as well as the amount of interaction between participants, affect legitimation processes? And is there variance in this process across different types of fields and professions?

Based on our own historical examination of Kaiser Permanente and the US health care field, we believe that the complexities and dynamics of the relationship between organizations and their institutional environment are more apparent and better understood in longitudinal than cross-sectional designs. Thus we encourage students of organizations to examine organizations and their institutional environments historically and longitudinally – in explorations of the questions we raise, or in related attempts to advance the institutional perspective.

Notes

1 We use the term 'field' to refer to an organizational field – a community of organization with a common meaning system, made up of organizations that produce similar services or products, key suppliers, consumers and regulatory agencies (DiMaggio and Powell, 1983). Following this definition, the health care field is made up of service providers (e.g. hospitals, physicians), purchasers (e.g., government, employers, individuals), intermediaries (e.g., health insurance organizations) and governance units (e.g., professional associations, public agencies and corporate systems) (Scott, Ruef, Mendel and Caronna, 2000).

2 Capitation payments are set amounts given to service providers, determined on a per-patient, per-annum basis. Typically, these payments are in lieu of fee-for-service reimbursement.

3 Specifically, the Omnibus Budget Reconciliation Act in 1981 allowed states to move Medicare patients into managed care programmes, and the Tax Equity and Fiscal Responsibility Act in 1982 allowed managed care organizations to have 'true risk contracts' for Medicare patients (Morrison and Luft, 1990).

5 Restructuring law firms
Reflexivity and emerging forms

John T. Gray

Why do law firms restrucure?

The business services sector plays a vital role in facilitating the growth of other sectors in the developed economies (Castells, 1996). Business services typically comprise law, accountancy, computer firms and management consultancies. Different professions directly compete in some market services but not in others (Australian Bureau of Statistics [ABS], 1997). For example, accountancy and law compete directly for taxation advice and corporate governance services but not for auditing. Many law firms have restructured recently in the face of increasing competition from other professions and para-professions, particularly in parts of the market that are lucrative and growing, such as corporate commercial transactions.[1] At the same time, they have moved from traditional professional monopoly market niches, because of deregulation of some aspects of their licence to practice. In Australia, this has led to a decrease in staples such as conveyancing[2] and an increase in corporate commercial legal services. There is, of course, a tendency in market behaviour that accessible sectors of high return will attract competitors, increasing innovation and furthering growth (Schumpeter, 1934; Porter, 1985). As market distortions such as statutory barriers to entry are removed, the tendency becomes more pronounced. Gray *et al.* (1998) in an attempt to analyse law firms' strategy in changing markets, reviewed a decade of literature and surveyed lawyers to discover which issues received most attention in the Australian legal industry. Increased competition, changed customers' demands, globalization, and information technology were the chief contextual reasons why partners of law firms believed they needed to restructure their firms.

Customer demands have changed as corporate organizations have become more focused in their activities. Law firms no longer enjoy tight, loyal customer relations, due to their clients' managerial practices used in reducing to core businesses and in contracting out other functions. Tenders are regularly called, panels of providers formed and performance regularly reviewed. Corporations now frequently employ in-house counsel, whose chief role is to manage business services provided to the corporation. Law firms that once relied upon long-term relationships and a record of service to customers now find new customer demands requiring them to adjust their practices.[3] Whilst globalization is an indefinite concept its practices affect law firms. For example, business services increasingly become subject to corporate management through globally convergent ways. That is to say, networks are established and important practices replicated internationally. So a multinational firm's relatively standardized business practices affect its choice of business service provider. All of this is speeded by technology that permits rapid exchange of information (Karpin, 1995; Castells, 1996). Thus global ways can be transmitted rapidly, customers can survey their lawyers' performance on-line, and these processes and accelerate business services.

What is restructuring?

A commonly found metaphor for organization is a building (Bolman and Deal, 1997, pp. 37–40). Metaphors of building make the notion of restructuring seemingly transparent. Blueprints are drawn up, a framework is erected and construction proceeds in accordance with design. When the building/organization is complete then it is commissioned and people work within it. Apart from maintenance, the structure remains until a major refurbishment occurs, and part of the building process is repeated. Within this tradition, we continually build organizations and we may rebuild, or restructure them, also.

A less common metaphor is that an organization is a whirlpool, a structure in flux, a vortex of identifiable patterns formed through ever changing molecules of energy. It was Barnard (1948, p. 14) who suggested that such a metaphor was 'a realistic thing to one who gets into it, and it seems real enough to anyone who watches it. When you use the name nearly everyone knows what you mean, and there is no other name commonly covering the same thing'. This is suggestive of serendipity, permeation and uncertainty. It reminds us that although individual molecules of water are constantly replaced they pattern the flows of the whirlpool. It reminds us that the molecules are not equally influential in the patterning. It leads us to consider where, and if, boundaries could be drawn of the whirlpool/ organization. It reminds us that individual elements, 'inside and outside' the whirlpool, constitute and are constituent of the whirlpool. It makes us think of what we might do to restructure a whirlpool. Within this perspective, a variety of unequal forces are mingling constantly and continuously organizing.

When law firms restructure what happens? Is the organizational hierarchy changed and systems produced to settle people into behaviour that is appropriate in the new structure? Is restructuring a continual building of organization or is it a continuous process of organizing? This distinction lies at the juncture of the argument as to whether partners and staff in law firms are cultural dopes (Garfinkel, 1967) who act within predetermined structures or powerful agents who do as they wish. If organizations are continually rebuilt into structures that dominate then those within them are cultural dopes. If organizing is a continuous process then those who comprise the organization are free agents. These are extreme representations, neither of which is satisfactory. The world is no more composed of free agents than it is of determining structures. Surely there must be some sense of reflexivity between these agents and these structures?

Reflexivity

Indeed, reflexivity is particularly observable in law firms, for partners are individually influential but, most frequently, less influential than the partnership that they form. Giddens (1976, 1984) attended to this problem of the 'dualism of structure and agency' and argued that it, and therefore organization, should be reconstituted in terms of a duality, 'in which power and structure are interpenetrated' (Clegg, 1989, p. 138). He argues that to concentrate upon the reproduction of the forms, including organizations, which constrain human behaviour, is too deterministic a position. On the other hand, he asserts that 'voluntaristic social theories, such as ethnomethodology or phenomenology, concentrate upon human agency as knowledgeable, creative and constitutive of reality' (Giddens, 1984, p. 4) and therefore produce claims for individual agency which are unrealistic. A more satisfactory explanation is, he offers, that actors are constitutive of structure as well as constituted within it and that there is *a duality of structure and agency*. Repeated actions pattern behaviours but are constrained by others' actions and combined memories of patterns.

By organizing, lawyers constitute their firms and society. When law firms restructure, those influential within them[4] act concertedly to pattern behaviours. They, their staff, customers, competitors and fellow lawyers are involved in a reflexive system of organizing. They are neither cultural dopes nor free agents. Whatever they do affects structure. Structure constrains whatever they do. Restructuring is a continuous process of organizing but the remembered patterns of structure inter-permeate the process and constrain it.

Ranson, Hinings, and Greenwood (1980) used structuration to explain what it is we do when we organize. Later, Greenwood and Hinings (1988) introduced the concept of archetypes to the study of organizations and their restructuring. They joined with others and specifically applied archetypes to empirical studies of professional firms in accountancy and law (Hinings *et al.*, 1991; Cooper, Hinings, Greenwood and Brown, 1996). By incorporating structuration and archetypes we develop theory that helps us understand not only what it is we do when we restructure but also more particularly how law firms restructure.

Three cases of Australian law firms, that I introduce now and develop in a later section, will demonstrate approaches taken to restructuring that are both complex and reflexively related. Turner and Hardy[5] are two talented lawyers who left a medium sized corporate practice to set up their own firm in the mid-1980s. Turner, the firm's joint founder and managing partner reflected:

> We didn't want to do Mums and Dads' law. We wanted to make a difference. You can't make a difference in a large firm, but at least you don't do Mums and Dads' law. So we looked around and realized that you have

to focus. You've got to offer something special, otherwise the big guys will eat you.

Turner and Hardy, due to the professional interests of founders and their strategic industry analysis chose to focus on the communications industry. The firm has been extremely successful, has grown rapidly and now also offers general corporate commercial services and sophisticated information technology legal services. It is now a medium to large firm. It doesn't do Mums and Dads' law.

Conner Bertrand was founded by partners who also left two of Australia's largest firms and established a firm for the pleasure and practices of its partners. It would not be burdened by centralized strategy making, formalism and revenue dispersion. The partners had several large and one huge client that followed them into the new firm. Each of its partners is extremely talented but its name partners are renowned lawyers and rainmakers[6] of the first order. They are stars: talented, sought after, creative, difficult, essential, expensive, crafty. They focused on corporate commercial law. They settled finely on top tier, difficult, corporate commercial law thus differentiating the firm and maintaining capacity for high margin pricing (though a small firm they price at large firm rates). Their move was more recent than Turner and Hardy, functionally focused rather than industry focused, but equally as successful.

The third firm is Fahey Dickson. It grew over some fifteen years through a conscious strategy of merging from the small, long established Fahey, sited in one city, to a very large national firm with international alliances. It has three hundred partners. Fahey had twelve. Sturrock, one of the firm's leading corporate rain-makers, and its managing partner during most of the large mergers recalls:

> We didn't start the urge to merge but it was like, 'Get big or get out.' Some of us had to decide would we form our own firm, join a large firm or grow this one. The Big Three, as it was then, just had all the corporate business. It's interesting, exciting, lucrative business. It's my practice. We started with some smaller firms we knew in Sydney, and, well you know the rest.

In the next section I will trace how these firms restructured. I will concentrate on fairly recent events as I do this, fully recognizing the importance of historical context, and that restructuring is a process not an event.

How do law firms restructure?

The first thing to say is that law firms are restructured by a continuous reflexive system of organizing. Those in law firms are continuously involved in a process of organizing that is affected by influential agents in their society and their organizing affects society. As with the metaphor of the whirlpool, all forces mingle, and at given times some are more influential than others. Nonetheless, for purposes of exposition, we can trace the elements that are chiefly implicated in the organizing system. The first of these are contextual constraints (Ranson *et al.*,

1980). We can consider these as including, significantly, those factors listed in the opening section of this chapter: increased competition, changed customers' demands, globalization and information technology. In tracing the chief elements implicated in organizing, we should stress that law firms are embedded in their own complex (Granovetter, 1985) and are constrained by patterns and agents within it. The activities of the lawyer will be limited by statute and by professional practice requirements of a certificating body, socialized by many things, including the college of law attended. Moreover, these very activities affect the systemization of the law including how law firms are structured. Compliance with conservative methods will reinforce those ways. Introduction of successful innovation may produce changes in legislation, practice rules or syllabus. All of us are trapped within this web and are weavers of it, though some have more influence than others. Those who follow societally accepted design rules reinforce those rules and their associated disciplinary practices (Foucault, 1977). Law firms are constrained by the environment within which they operate. The economy, law, and norms all help shape this environment. But they are also subjected to factors inside the firm that they have rather more control over, such as strategy, size, technology, and resources deployed, all of which also affect and constitute their environments. They are structured in ways that reflect these mixes and the prevailing practices of the industry.

Australian statutes, and the rules of their professional association, currently require lawyers, to practise law only within businesses legally incorporated as sole traders or partnerships.[7] Thus, if lawyers were to establish limited liability corporations in which law was practised they should do so against an overall currently accepted design rule, or constraint. They may be disciplined to return to the original design rule or this new behaviour might, in time, be acceptable and become the new design rule. Whichever way they move they affect the design rules.

Law firms restructure by attending to these contextual constraints and interpreting what can be done about them. Increasing competition in law from accountants has seen the Sydney branch of Andersens International expand its legal staff from eight in 1996 to eighty in 1997. Law firms have adopted strategies designed, in part, to address this competition. In an unusual move, Gadens Lawyers have established a separate business, Gadens Accountants, to directly confront the competition, learn from it and use some of its methods. However, as Flood avers (in Chapter 8 of this book) most law firms attempt to differentiate themselves from accountants. This is a difficult and precise strategy if it is to be successful. On one hand, law firms copy aspects of accountants' customer service, project teams and people management, whilst on the other, they emphasize relationship marketing, individual brilliance and collegiality. By enacting a strategy, constrained by context, partners organize their firms.

Turner and Hardy strategically organized to fit the context that its founders noted. It focused on an industry that was likely to grow as Australia moved from a monopoly supplier of telecommunications to a duopoly and, at least in policy, now moves to free competition. Deregulation opened opportunities for lawyers who 'could do communications law and move quickly. The big guys did communications as part of their general corporate commercial practice' noted a partner at Turner and Hardy. The global context of this industry deterred accountants from moving into it as they did not have sufficient legal resources or specialist network and, of course, the confluence of communications and information technology enabled, as well as caused, huge growth. Thus the partners structured their business in ways that used most of the significant contextual factors to their advantage. Turner and Hardy rapidly discovered that customers' demands in this industry required the law firm to interlock its customers both with sophisticated computing networks and sophisticated organizational systems. From its inception Turner and Hardy was tightly centralized and managed inside the firm despite its external reliance on networks. Initially this was personalized in its managing partner but as it grew from a small firm to its current medium large status its hierarchy was organized around partners' practices and functional specialties.

Conner Bertrand was formed ten years after Turner and Hardy. Economic conditions were similar, in as much as Australia was rapidly booming from a recession. However, they were dissimilar in as much as information technology had changed organizing practices. Corporations had been hollowed. Networks and strategic alliances enabled professionals to work at excellent levels outside the infrastructure of very large firms. The interests of partners coincided with a niche in the market that did not attract other professions. Conner Bertrand's managing partner calls this, 'One hundred per cent law. If they want eighty per cent law then they can use accountancy lawyers. We don't do flow work. We do difficult, get it right or get dead law.' Technology permitted it to operate at very low leverage rates. The reputation and networks of its partners attracted huge clients and gave access to a superior referral network of suppliers. Indeed, it was the demands of one of these clients that helped decide the firm's formation. This client used two of Australia's largest firms for its taxation and corporate matters. Conner Bertrand includes partners from both of those firms and is better fitted to add value to that client. The firm's huge reputation for excellent law but small size had made it a popular referral when larger law firms faced conflicts. 'We do the work for their client. We do it excellently and that reflects well on the referring law firm. What is more to the point, we are not interested in poaching their clients and they know it' (Bertrand). The firm has remained small, because it suits its strategy and its partners' interests. It has an emergent strategy that comfortably fits interests and context.

Fahey Dickson faces all the significant contextual constraints that we have named, but strategically they have resolved these into a drive to differentiate the firm from competitors. Their New South Wales managing partner argues that, 'all the Big Six face these pressures but the critical issue is the commodification of services. We all do excellent law so the client sees us as easily replaced. Accountants can make that worse; though, they haven't so far got the legal clout to compete at our level'. Fahey Dickson uses its national network to cement corporate relationship marketing. 'If a Queensland partner has one of the banks then he has to be introducing other services and other states to that bank. That doesn't just happen. It needs agreed strategy and marketing. It needs discipline and lawyers hate discipline. It needs partners who think about the partnership and are supported when they do. That support at Fahey's comes in the form of excellent systems and managers.' Fahey Dickson has used its considerable resources to analyse the market, agree national strategy at partnership level and delegate its management team to organize within strategy. It emphasizes building relations with current customers, particularly its corporate counsels. It identified core customers and has offered them service standards beyond normal industry performance. It organizes its legal groups in projects that reflect its client's practices and it backs these up with personal quality assurance from senior partners. It monitors international global law matters through its alliances and consultancy. It withdrew from alliances in Asia several months before that region's economic meltdown and has discussed merger with a fellow member of the Big Six – as a defensive strategy against UK or US firms.

Each of the firms faces, at the micro-level, different contextual circumstances, whereas in the macro-context their constraints are similar. Contexts are phenomena that attract the interest of actors and are then interpreted by these actors. What one actor sees as a problem, another may see as an opportunity and yet another may not note at all. Turner and Hardy adopted an obvious strategy by focusing on the communications industry that has subsequently boomed. Well, it was obvious in hindsight!

Contextual constraints affect how law firms are structured. All lawyers are socialized into expecting that the normal form of legal business is collegiate partnership. This is seen as accommodating values of professionalism, independence and community service. There are, however, pressing economic environmental pressures that suggest that senior equity partners introduce more managerialist features into the firm. Corrs, Chambers, Westgarth is a large law firm represented in several Australian states. It is embarking upon a strategy of integrating these state firms into a national practice. It has employed a non-lawyer as its chief executive officer and is re-arranging its affairs so that meetings of partners approximate those of boards of directors with the CEO to implement decisions. One sees this type of managerialist governance in several medium firms, and most of the largest firms. Whilst managerialism is extant in Australian legal firms, it is not universally welcome. Some lawyers see strategy, marketing plans and the appointment of non-legal functional managers as inevitable responses to changes in the environment, as commercial realism. Others see such practices as diminishing the nature of professional practice, as bureaucratization. When reminded that managerialism was increasingly prevalent in corporate law firms, one of Bertrand's partners responded, 'That's dreadful. Don't you think that's dreadful? I don't want law to be a bureaucracy, I prefer a college. Law is still a lifestyle thing.'

Turner and Hardy started with a similar view of collegiality but, as it grew, it installed more systems and became managerial. Fahey Dickson, in its attempt to differentiate, emphasizes collegiality that involves the client. 'We do lockstep.

Equal partnerships impose real management discipline and differentiated payment schemes cause clever accounting. The more outwardly managerial we become the more we look like our competitors.' Law firms are constituent and constitute their context. They affect and are affected by it. Influential partners interpret context and influence others to organize in ways that are possible given context.

Ranson *et al.* (1980) argue that such different patterns of judgement result from the lawyer's interpretive scheme and that consequent patterns of behaviour, such as language, rituals, use of artifacts, comprise provinces of meaning. To continue with our argument of inter-permeability, a lawyer will be socialized by his or her institutional world, which is seen as the rational means of action, and will interpret events from this developed *schema*. Additionally, the lawyer's behaviour will help to construct the social reality. Ranson *et al.* (1980, p. 6) give the example of a professional who has an underlying interpretive scheme that acknowledges the manner in which one should respond to clients, colleagues or others. This is normally not articulated, but some elements of this professional mantle, such as autonomy, public service, and ethics may be explicitly stated in certain instances. The argument suggests that we have interpretive schemes that we learn through environmental socialization. These schemes enable us to understand our world. Indeed they channel our understanding of our world. Others share interpretive schemes like ours. Thus we operate similarly and reinforce our understanding. These interpretive schemes are not normally explicit but can be. Groups such as lawyers, whose socialization or contextual constraints are intense, will have strongly entrenched interpretive schemes. Lawyers behave and speak in a consistent manner whilst in court or respond in a broadly consistent manner to cases which could be seen as in 'conflict of interests'. Lawyers express the belief that the form of business within which they operate is part of the mantle of professionalism. But, then again, these artifacts of ritual, of language, may be differentially used. Here then we need to look at populations, at groups, which share meanings. We need also to recall that context will affect provinces of meaning and be affected by them and thus populations will construct their provinces of meaning within contextual constraints.

We cannot assume that the partners and staff of law firms will be unanimous in their values. Homogeneity, if it is seen, may be a mirage. The individuals, who make up the group, or the population, will each have variations around some imaginary mean of acceptance of the values of the population. There will be some just barely accepting of the population's values so as to remain members, and indeed their fissiparous behaviour may eventually cause new design rules, which will change future patterns. There will be others perfectly conservative of pre-existing values and some wavering around the mean of this imagined values bell curve. But values of a population are not inert characteristics like height or eye colour (that seem immutable on a short timescale). They are affected by the more powerful in the population who can control necessary nodal points and promulgate their translation of values. So the founders of firms, such as Turner Hardy, or Conner Bertrand have more say in the values of the firm than a new recruit (Trice and Beyer, 1994). They have more say also than the national managing partner of Fahey Dickson for their influence is direct. Bertrand told me that, 'Conner just stands at his door and bellows', if he wants to cause an effect. Fahey Dickson's national managing partner operates through state managing partners, practice heads, committees and strategy. Any bellowing is corporately polite and politically fraught.

Gray *et al.* (1998) argued that interpretation of professionalism was a critical issue in provinces of meaning and organizing law firms. Partners, such as those at Conner Bertrand, who looked upon law firms 'as partnerships of colleagues akin to seventeenth century corporations' emphasize independence, tolerance, autonomy and disdain systemic controls. Because of Conner Bertrand's context its partners can exercise those values. Turner and Hardy, on the other hand, have no concerns about introducing managerialist features. Performance, accountability, customer responsiveness, these need management systems, strategy and control. Fahey Dickson has been decidedly more managerialist than it now is. It is trying to ameliorate these tendencies so that it can differentiate itself to clients and lawyer recruits from its competitors. Provinces of meaning are inextricably linked to context: interpreted by influential coalitions of partners. And of course interest affects one's motivation to seek positions of influence. Positions of influence will contest with each other to create dependencies of power (Ranson *et al.*, 1980) in populations and thereby achieve domination of the province of meaning. When we undertake certain roles and attach more or less power to one role or the other we are structuring an organization and we do so inter-dependently of contextual constraints and provinces of meaning. So when Corrs decides to appoint a non-legal chief executive officer it is their influential coalition that interprets contextual constraints such as increased competition and does what is possible given the firm's provinces of meaning.

Each of our case firms has equity partners and salary partners. At Turner Hardy strategy is authorized by meetings of equity partners but is formulated and enacted through the managing partner, Turner. Information concerning the firm is promulgated in separate editions to the two classes of partners. Partner admission is by proposed candidacy to the partnership. As the managing partner assesses all staff annually he can provide sensitive advice to the firm. Financial reviews, billing history and work in progress are monitored by the managing partner. The control system is centralized for a firm of this size. This reflects the history of the firm, its rapid growth, its information technology, and the immense capacity of its managing partner.

Conner Bertrand partners meet regularly on an informal basis but rarely on a formal basis. When I last visited the firm, it had not held a formal meeting of partners since it admitted its last partner, several months previously. However, as the managing partner told me, 'We are always in each others' offices or around the table. Conner and Bertrand are the strategists and I just adjust their excesses. By the time matters are decided we have all had a say but C&B normally prevail.' Partners have considerable leeway, rules are few and often ignored where they do exist, but all partners are very experienced, appreciate the collegiality of the firm, and pattern their behaviour in ways that support it.

Each of the actors in an organization has interests and may act to support those interests. Thus is power seen to be accomplished – in terms of the realization and frustration of interests. Ranson *et al.* (1980) acknowledge these features of agency and interest but, in doing so, their exposition relies heavily on resources dependency theory to explicate dependencies of power. By contrast, Clegg's theory of 'circuits of power' (1989) presents a model of social systems that includes these notions of agency and interests but is extended by discussion of facilitative power and dispositional power. He argues that these three types of power are implicated in complex circuits in which vital control points are contested. It is the outcome of these contests through which dependencies of power form. Clegg's theory is consistent with the concept of dependencies of power expressed by Ranson *et al.* (1980) while extending it beyond resources dependency. Applying it to the cases considered here casts further illumination in areas that resource dependency does not illuminate.

Patterns of power in the three firms are remarkable exactly because they are unremarked by those within the firm. At Turner and Hardy the managing partner is centrally implicated in strategic decisions. At Conner Bertrand the name partners are centrally implicated. At Fahey Dickson the core is shifting and those who wish to be influential need to attend to a wide electorate. The patterns in each firm are followed tacitly by staff and partners. These patterns reinforce dependencies of power and will only be restructured through some balancing of contextual constraints, and provinces of meaning. So to restructure, law firms must organize each of these elements in a way that is efficient so that it maintains competitive advantage and legitimate so that it is consistent with expectations in its professional field.

We can add another consideration to how law firms structure, the notion of archetypes. Lawyers have dense networks of relationships that reinforce accepted ways of patterning including the way they organize their firms. They know what is appropriate when they organize. It is consistent with, and legitimated by the professional template of how a law firm should be organized. Greenwood and Hinings (1988) explain this as 'particular interpretive schemes coupled with associated structural arrangements constitut(ing) a design archetype'. Archetypes are types whose construct 'becomes a function of the isolation of clusters of ideas, values and beliefs coupled with associated patterns of organizational design' (Greenwood and Hinings, 1988, p. 295). They agree that organizations have a limited number of configurations, structures and strategies and that:

> configurations are composed of tightly interdependent and mutually supportive elements such that the importance of each element can best be understood by making reference to the whole configuration.
>
> (Miller and and Friesen, 1984, p. 1, cited in Greenwood and Hinings, 1988, p. 294)

As we have discussed, these elements can be viewed as contextual constraints, provinces of meaning and dependencies of power. Fahey Dickson approaches a

Managed Professional Business archetype. So does Turner and Hardy. This is consistent with research that indicates MPB is the emergent archetype (Hinings *et al.*, 1991; Cooper *et al.*, 1996). However, Conner Bertrand operates as a Professional Partnership (Cooper *et al.*, 1996) and is determinedly non-managerial. There is sufficient differentiation within the legal profession for both of these archetypes to be extant, though one would expect one to be more popular (Gray *et al.*, 1998; Cooper *et al.*, 1996). Paradoxically, we can consider archetypes as both constraints and catalysts to restructuring law firms. Institutional forces (DiMaggio and Powell, 1983) constrain law firms to organize similarly for the purpose of legitimacy. However, innovations in organizing practices will introduce new archetypes that compete for ascendancy in their social niche. So it seems that in many instances where P^2 was the preferred dominant archetype, MPB now is in evidence (Cooper *et al.*, 1996).

It is more than a search for legitimacy that does this. Innovation typically involves a search for efficiency. Firms attempt to find coherence in the way they organize. Ranson *et al.* (1980) provide an explanation for the processes that occur when those in firms seek coherence, which is the equilibrium state. Other writers have suggested that coherence among several elements will establish a stabilized organization. Notably, Mintzberg (1979) and, Miller and Friesen (1984) have argued that the basis of organizational coherence is the relationship between structure, strategy and environment. In this model, strategic decision-makers shape the structure of the organization to retain competitive advantage and bring about fit, with changed or changing circumstances.[8] Greenwood and Hinings (1988) note some of these arguments of Mintzberg (1979) and, Miller and Friesen (1984) but argue that these should be tempered by Ranson *et al.*'s (1980) establishment of coherence as emergent from the relationships between provinces of meaning, contextual constraints and dependencies of power. Their argument is that each of the inter-connected elements will tend to equilibrium so that the firm's strategy can proceed. This equilibrium may be contested and unbalanced, hence dynamics in organizations, but the most frequently observed state will be equilibrium. In suggesting that 'coherence comes from the consistent relationship between an interpretive scheme and an organization's structures and systems' Greenwood and Hinings (1993, p. 1058) succinctly elaborate their argument:

> There are two convincing theoretical reasons for anticipating that organizations will develop structures and systems consistent with a single interpretive scheme. Miller and Friesen (1984) provided one such explanation with their concept of 'momentum,' describing organizations as evolving towards archetypal coherence because for any firm it is better to be one thing consistently than to be a combination of ill fitting parts. In effect, they acknowledged the economic benefits that flow from coherence. A rather different explanation recognizes organizations as composed of groups whose positions of relative advantage and disadvantage are shaped by the organization's design . . . Structures and systems allocate scarce and valued

resources and indirectly legitimate and perpetuate distributive inequalities by the consistency of the cues and messages transmitted. An organization's 'dominant coalition' will seek to remove discordant structures because of the risk of challenge of the status quo.

If we examine organizations in an institutional field we notice that they are organized similarly (DiMaggio and Powell, 1983). If structuring causes organizing then there must be a design preference that is learned institutionally. This design preference, design type, emanates from a shared cognition, an interpretive scheme. Therefore Greenwood and Hinings conclude that:

> A design archetype is thus a set of ideas, beliefs and values that shape prevailing conceptions of what an organization should be doing and how it should be judged, *combined* [sic] with structures and processes that serve to implement and reinforce those ideas.
>
> (1988, p. 300)

We are now in a theoretical position from which we can answer, 'How do law firms restructure?' They[9] restructure, or structure for that matter, by reflexively assembling the elements of contextual constraints, provinces of meaning and dependencies of power into organizing modes[10] that tend to coherence. Organizing modes are legitimate if they correspond to templates found in the profession.[11]

An example of restructuring

Law firms are constituent and constitutive of their society. They are organized in modes that are reflexive of provinces of meaning, dependencies of power and contextual constraints. Their institutional field contributes structuring templates as an important part of their external contextual constraints. These templates are formed reflexively as those within the firms have differential power to affect coercive, normative and mimetic forces. Their market environment contributes imperatives that constrain the firm to stability or change. Within the firm contingent factors constrain those who are influential in the way that the firm may be organized. Dependencies of power are established and maintained by influential coalitions or agents by contests in circuits of power. These interpret contextual constraints and provinces of meaning as they persuade their electorate to act in a concerted fashion.

Those in the electorate are variably committed to the agenda and this commitment is variably contested. Provinces of meaning are significant in these contests. Lawyers are knowledge workers. Their practice is learned from professional templates ameliorated by the values espoused by the dominant coalition within the firm. Provinces of meaning are ideational constructs with variable understanding, interpretation and commitment formed by those in the firm. Each of these elements inter-permeates all others. Actors are practically or discursively conscious of these elements and their ensemble.

We can note that some firms' organizing modes are coherent whilst others are incoherent. Coherent organizing modes are sought by influential coalitions as they promote efficiency and legitimacy. In all of this, actors interpret the elements and organize as they are capable, within their mutual constraints. Gray *et al.*, (1998) established that firms could be analysed within this scheme and their organizing modes interpreted against ideal types. They observed that the Sydney law firms in their sample adopted organizing modes that approached the archetypes described by Cooper *et al.* (1996). Seven firms organized in accordance with the managerialist archetype of Managed Professional Business. Seven firms organized in accordance with the traditionalist archetype of Professional Partnership. The remaining firm had been organized managerially but appeared to be returning to traditionalist organizing. However, at the time of the research it could not be judged as more managerialist or more traditionalist.

The tendency of these firms to adopt either managerialist or traditionalist organizing modes shows the utility of the archetypes P^2 and MPB which have been discussed in many other parts of this book (beginning with Chapter 1). Both Turner & Hardy and Fahey Dickson would fit near the MPB ideal type. Moreover, both have moved historically from P^2 towards MPB. However, Conner Bertrand is a very successful firm that sits rather uneasily on a scale that admits of two archetypes only. As I said earlier, its partners are stars: talented, sought-after, creative, difficult, essential, expensive, and crafty. These are words that one applies to stars and Conner Bertrand's name partners. I believe that stars may represent an emergent form of organizing and perhaps another archetype.

When Starbuck (1993) described Wachtell and Lipton he spoke of exceptional talent. Indeed, he argues cogently that if we are to make a difference when we do organizational analysis we should eschew the analysis of average cases and concentrate upon the exceptional. After all, he says, if we wish to study high jumping in order to improve elite performance it makes little sense to observe a wide range of talent (Starbuck, 1993). Well I suspect that the time for stars is now.

First, in Australia and the UK contextual circumstances are ripe for such ventures. When Conner Bertrand was formed three of its founders left a large firm that had suffered a very large embezzlement by one of its partners. Huge amounts of partners' time, talent and earnings were used to remedy the matters. The distraction that this caused highlighted liability issues and the subsidization that rainmaker partners make to others in their firms. At the same time a client was seeking tighter linkages than were possible with the law firms from which the partners came. By forming Conner Bertrand, partners were able to add value to this client's business in a way that they could not in their previous firms and more tightly control their own business. They focused on corporate commercial law, which is booming in Sydney. They focused finely on top tier, difficult, corporate commercial law thus differentiating themselves and maintaining capacity for high margin pricing.

These circumstances may have some unique features but we can see that variations of them are available now and will proliferate in the future. Liability issues will not lessen. Rainmakers will not cease chafing that they subsidize others.

Clients will continue to seek tighter linkages. Technology and globalization will lessen the importance of size to a law firm or its client. Lawyers will leave firms and take clients with them. The contextual constraints that saw Conner Bertrand emerge will permit others to do the same. They will be tightly focused by industry or specialty and will exploit circumstances.

We have seen these firms in the past but often they have been transitory. Partners leave a firm that has an organizing mode near either extreme MPB or P^2 and form a star that flares brightly but shortly merges with another firm. Circumstances in large law firms are now such that I predict the form will not be as transitory. Some will flare and merge. Most will flare and stay. For this to happen it requires three vital organizing forces. First, the organizing mode its partners select must be coherent. However, selection is not made by it, selection emerges through partners' actions. In this it is vital that the affairs of the firm can be managed. Now, in Conner Bertrand this was done by its unobtrusive managing partner. His role was not that of a powerful managing partner more the role of a producer of a theatre. Without his stars, who were also co-directors, he had no theatre. Without their producer the stars could not behave as freely and creatively as they wished. The producer's role at Conner Bertrand was to attend closely to the actions and moods of the stars, to translate their strategy into action, to smooth conflicts between partners and staff, to keep the show on the road. In this instance I must say that the person involved showed admirable managerial and political aptitude and, though he may deny it, the firm could not have survived in its star form without him. Thus, one of the contextual issues for stars to solve is the production function. I do not think it matters whether the producer is a strong willed manager (as is the case in at least one other star firm I know), or a servant leader (Fairtlough, 1994) as in the case of Conner Bertrand. The important feature is that the role of the producer is consistent with the values expressed by the partners.

At Conner Bertrand the partners had worked with each other, some quite closely, in other firms. They espoused values of collegiality, professional excellence and professional enjoyment[12] in the formation of the new firm. These espousals were backed with enactments (Schein, 1985) as the firm negotiated its first matters,[13] grew, took on extra staff and partners. If collegiality implies democratic decision-making then Conner Bertrand is not collegial. However, if collegiality implies an elite taking advice, debating, listening, deciding and negotiating support before implementation then Conner Bertrand is collegial. Its strategy making seems emergent, and indeed its partners would deny any elaborate strategy making process, but the firm is tightly focused and strategic. The very trick of this is that the partners involve others. Though no one is under the illusion that the name partners are not the most powerful and will not prevail, debate does occur and interests are protected. One could trace each of the circuits of power (Clegg, 1989, p. 214) in Conner Bertrand and note their interdependence and completeness. When I knew the firm it was organized so that its power, values and context cohered. Organizing is a continuous process and the partners, stars, producer, partners, staff, work together to keep their professional world patterned.

Conclusion and paradox

We can draw five major conclusions and one major paradox from the material in this chapter. First, to restructure law firms the concept of reflexivity needs to be in the forefront of our theorizing and practice. Professional service firms are dissimilar to industrial organizations with their typical vertical coordination. Their organizing practices are more similar to network enterprises that are described by the intersections of semi-autonomous systems (Castells, 1996, pp. 150–200) in which interests, values and contexts are shared. By reflecting momentarily on the traditional way of organizing law firms, the professional partnership, we realize that law firms have always organized internally like networks. Lawyers have only recently accepted the managed professional business with its strategic integration and control as a legitimate organizing ideal. The partners at Conner Bertrand run their firm as if it were the intersection of semi-autonomous systems. Most of these systems are within the firm. Indeed the systems are the partners and their practices. Some of these systems are outside the firm. When the firm was founded it had no litigation capacity and relied exclusively on a network of barristers.[14] It has subsequently appointed litigation partners and staff but still relies heavily on network to overcome its diseconomy of size. Conner Bertrand is a spectacularly successful example of a small firm that fits the star ideal. It more vigorously adopts network enterprise than the other firms mentioned, yet they all use networking. Its success in this organizing mode reflexively affects the legitimacy of network enterprise and I predict will influence others to copy. If we take the notion of reflexivity seriously we must recognize that our own theorizing affects organizing choices. By limiting our organizing ideals we reduce industry complexity. This theoretical reduction will lead, if we are sufficiently influential, to limits on actual organizing.

Second, law firms are organized by their dominant coalition in ways that are possible given the prevailing provinces of meaning and convincing interpretations of contextual constraints. Power and values are relatively overt in law firms, so debates, campaigns and symbols are employed to convince electorates that the coalition has identified critical issues in the environment and proposes strategies that are consistent with values within the firm and the profession. Fahey Dickson demonstrates the need for electoral support for strategy by its systems and size. Turner & Hardy and Conner Bertrand, have been successful because their founding partners retain power consistent with the values and context of their firms. Our understanding of law firms is limited if we reduce our theorizing to structures of law firms.

Third, coherence of contextual constraints, dependencies of power, and provinces of meaning is sought for purposes of efficiency and legitimacy. Turner & Hardy were able to coherently organize their law firm in ways that were unusual with contemporary practices but sufficiently usual to be legitimate. Law firms in Australia did not specialize in this industry. They did not connect so tightly with their clients. Turner & Hardy organized swiftly because of size and vitality and grew quickly because of market and talent. Partners are constrained in their organizing choices. They are not free agents. They are constrained by a societal structure, in which the mores of their profession are paramount for legitimacy and the realities of the market are paramount for efficiency. Turner & Hardy have been able to balance legitimacy and efficiency and their success has reflexively affected their profession and their market.

Fourth coherence of organizing mode is problematic given reflexivity, the conservative nature of the profession and its changing context. As Morris and Pinnington (1998b) have discovered in the UK, lawyers are slow to change their organizing practices and emphasize preference for past ways. Hinings *et al.* (1991) and Cooper *et al.* (1996) observed that firms oscillate between organizing modes but that a preferred archetype is observable within a profession. So law firms are constrained in their organizing choices by their profession's preferences. Nevertheless, firms do succeed and analysts report their success. Success and publicity encourage diffusion of these ways and their legitimation.

Fifth, preferred professional organizing choices or archetypes have been limited in discussion to either Professional Partnership or Managed Professional Business (Greenwood and Hinings, 1993; Hinings *et al.*, 1991; Cooper *et al.*, 1996). These are useful in typologizing law firms on a continuum but they may limit strategic thinking to either one type or the other. It seems likely that there are several other types. This has always been theoretically possible but my observations concerning stars suggest that it is empirically likely.

Sixth, and paradoxically, the partnership form provides opportunities for lawyers to restructure their firms in ways that are sufficiently managerialist to satisfy customer demands and counter competition but sufficiently professionalist to satisfy colleagues' demands and counter competition. Each of the firms I mentioned has been able to organize its affairs within the constraint of partnership. Each has been creative and strategic in their actions. They have reflexively organized consistent with the law industry within which they are embedded. If those who manage law firms concentrate upon reflexivity, coherent organizing modes and archetypes they will be able to employ the advantages of network enterprise that partnerships infer and overcome the disadvantages of conservatism that partnerships confer. An uncritical reading of the literature on professional organizations could lead one to the view that there is no alternative but that firms will become more managerialist in face of the challenges that I have outlined, that they will approach the Managed Professional Business, rather than the Professional Practice. Matters are much more complex than that. The cases mentioned in this chapter and my recent research (Gray, 1999; Gray *et al.*, 1998) convince me that firms organize reflexively and that any convergence towards an archetype will be ameliorated by interesting exceptions. Some of these may be so liberating, (as stars are) that they will affect other fields.

In conclusion, I can say that the observations I made in the Australian law firms help me build a theory that emphasizes reflexivity, coherent organizing modes and archetypes but the theory permitted me to understand what law firms do when they restructure. Law firms face similar challenges to other business service professions yet have responded differently. Normatively, they have been more conservative than accountants. Mimetically, they have been less entrepreneurial. Statutorily, they have been sheltered by higher barriers to entry. Nonetheless, the three cases that I have used demonstrate that some law firms are adept at restructuring to face challenges. Within a conservative profession one can find particularly innovative practices. The trouble is there are too few of them. It is problematic that an industry that faces such challenges is slow to change, whilst some of its (well known) number, rapidly adapt. Practitioners in the industry and academic analysts have a project to trace the diffusion of innovative organizing practices and track them longitudinally. The project will need to address the institutionalization of organizing practices and their transmission. It appears that the professional field of law is in the process of recomposition and that we shall observe some interesting organizing choices during that recomposition. I have suggested that stars will contribute a new popular archetype and believe that reflexive analysis will reveal others.

Notes

1 This makes up about 32 per cent of law firms' current business (ABS 1997, p. 10).
2 Conveyancing refers to the transfer of real title from one person or entity to another.
3 This is clearly demonstrated in Flood's discussion of solicitors briefing barristers in a later chapter within this volume. To paraphrase him, the barrister is the boss, the solicitor is second in charge, and the customer makes the third and pays.
4 These are typically equity partners, managing partners, chairpersons. This group occasionally includes chief executive officers or general managers. Which of these may form the dominant coalition is a moot point in any case.
5 I have developed the cases from actual firms but have altered names and some details for this chapter.
6 Rainmakers are lawyers who bring large amounts of business to a firm and generate business for other partners.
7 For jurisdictions where incorporation is permitted the conflict between a sense of professionalism and managerialism may not be as overt. Nevertheless, in Chapter 10, Morris and Pinnington report that this phenomenon is observable in the UK and Cooper *et al.* (1996) report the same for Canadian experience.
8 We can understand that any strategic decisions will emanate from the interplay of the three elements of contextual constraints, provinces of meaning and dependencies of power and are embedded within society (Granovetter, 1985).
9 Of course law firms are not 'they'. It is the influential, within the scheme that I have outlined, who structure law firms.
10 I prefer this to organization or organizations as it consciously refers to a process, a 'going on' by which a mode of rationality is patterned. Because of institutional legitimacy, economic efficiency, or domination, organizing modes tend to coherence.
11 It is plain from Greenwood and Hinings' empirical research (Cooper *et al.*, 1996; Hinings *et al.*, 1991) that professions do transmit institutional templates of legitimate organizing.
12 At this firm and many others I have been told by partners how important it is that their firm should be fun to work in. At first I thought this disingenuous but I have come to realize that it is a sincere expression. Top lawyers believe that long hours and arduous professional work does not preclude enjoyment. Indeed if they do not enjoy what they do, why do it?

13 One major matter dominated its first years. Subsequently it has shown that its excellence attracts matters from large firms with conflicts of interest, which refer respected clients to Conner Bertrand. It does not tender, nor panel and it has always had a surfeit of work.

14 NSW continues with a separate bar. Solicitors can plead cases. Barristers specialize in litigation. Barristers by statute must practise as sole traders

6 The struggle to redefine boundaries in health care systems

Jean-Louis Denis, Lise Lamothe, Ann Langley and Annick Valette

'It is imperative that the system ensure coordination and cease the current mode of functioning in which a range of discontinuous and incomplete services are offered in cafeteria fashion'. *(Rochon Commission report, 1988, p. 412)*

'Professional bureaucracies are not integrated entities. They are collections of individuals who join to draw on the common resources and support services but otherwise want to be left alone.' *(Mintzberg, 1979, p. 372)*

'Each operating unit involved in the continuum of care – prevention, primary care, acute care, rehabilitative care, and maintenance care – should have "the system" embedded within it.' *(Shortell et al., 1996, p. 27)*

'Integrated delivery is a forced idea. It doesn't happen naturally.' *(Michael Abel, CEO of Brown and Toland Medical Group, San Francisco, quoted in Haugh, 1998)*

The quotations above illustrate one of the central challenges of change in health care systems in the 1990s. Those on the left are examples of calls for breaking down boundaries to achieve greater integration and coordination in the organization and delivery of health services. Those on the right reflect the barriers to integration and collaboration in a world traditionally made up of autonomous professionals and health care providers structured as 'professional bureaucracies'.

In fact, integration as a boundary redefinition process appears to be a key underlying theme in the emerging discourse on health system change at multiple levels. At the system level, discourses about population health and health promotion suggests a need to traverse sectoral boundaries in developing health policy (Hayes and Dunn, 1998). At the inter-organizational level, 'managerial' discourses about the need to improve efficiency and develop critical mass to justify advanced technology exert pressure for boundary shifting moves such as horizontal mergers, outsourcing and networks of shared services. In addition, discourse about the need for a community orientation, client-focus and continuity of care are leading to demands for vertically linked services and integrated systems of various kinds (Shortell *et al.*, 1996). Finally, at the intra-organizational level, ideas about patient-focused care and continuous quality improvement are leading to a push for cross-functional teams and programme management, both of which require previously autonomous units to collaborate more intensely. Even within operating units, the trend towards client-focused care is generating calls for closer inter-professional collaboration.

In other words, boundary-busting is endemic in the current wave of health care system change. Organizations whose structures were apparently founded on the principles of 'pigeon-holing' and professional autonomy (Mintzberg, 1979) are being required to dismantle the pigeon-holes and to either renegotiate their frontiers (as in mergers, for example), or more fundamentally, to recognize and deal with their mutual interdependence on an ongoing basis.

In this chapter, we draw on a variety of empirical experiences within the Canadian health care system (especially Quebec) to examine the dilemmas associated with integration and boundary redefinition at different levels. The empirical base includes studies of emergent clinical operating units (Lamothe, 1996) and of various attempts to achieve intra-organizational change (Lozeau, 1997; Denis, 1988). It also includes ongoing studies of teaching hospital mergers (Denis, Lamothe and Langley, 1998) and of collaboration between hospitals and community clinics (Bégin and Labelle, 1989). Other relevant work deals with the impact of regional planning (Denis *et al.*, 1996) and with the role of regional agencies in the regulation of the health care system (Denis and Valette, 1997, 1998; Denis, Langley and Contandriopoulos, 1998). Most of these studies involve in-depth qualitative process analysis. In this chapter, we draw on this base to look at the stimuli for change and to examine the reactions that these initiatives engender. We analyse the reasons behind successes and failures and attempt to draw theoretical and practical conclusions about more or less propitious ways of meeting the challenge of creating health care systems capable of adapting to evolving needs.

Two key elements form the backdrop for this analysis. First, we note how changing ideologies of health care manifest themselves in the Canadian health care system and are stimulating efforts towards greater integration. Second, we examine the nature of collaboration in professional bureaucratic forms of organization and note how this may affect attempts to achieve integration. Our conclusions in this area build on negotiated order theory (Strauss *et al.*, 1963, 1964) and are illustrated by a recent in-depth study of operations in a large teaching hospital (Lamothe, 1996). A central argument of this chapter is that an understanding of the natural patterns of collaboration in professional organizations is essential to comprehending the fate of boundary-crossing initiatives at different levels. This argument is elaborated in subsequent sections.

Changing archetypes and the Canadian health care system

Chapters 4 (by Caronna and Scott) and 9 (Kitchener) in this volume describe the appearance of competing institutional archetypes for the organization of health care in the US and UK. In Canada, these trends are reflected in an ideological shift away from a 'provider-driven' system and towards what we call a 'population-driven' health care system. The old 'provider-driven' philosophy emphasized professional and organizational autonomy, the treatment of illness, the dominance of institutional care, and centralized government regulation.[1] Increasingly, governments have been very critical of this previously dominant philosophy. For example, a Quebec government health commission report called it a '*system held prisoner by the various interest groups that move through it*' (Rochon *et al.*, 1988, p. 407) at the expense of the population to be served. The emerging 'population-driven' archetype is characterized by a concern with population health and health care needs and by an emphasis on community-based services, integrated system design, local management and democratic citizen control. The structural solutions proposed in the Quebec report include the introduction of programme-based (rather than institution-based) funding, more emphasis on community services, as well as increased powers to regional bodies to ensure greater coordination and accountability.

In fact, proposals for changes in organizational design across Canada are consistent with the underlying changes in interpretive schemes. There is wide agreement among policy elites that health services should no longer be organized as a loosely coupled set of autonomous providers but should become an integrated system capable of providing continuous care across organizational and professional boundaries and accountable to the populations served. This often involves merging separate organizations, creating regional health authorities to manage the system and instituting some kind of programme-based funding. In parallel with these shifting ideas about health care organization at system and inter-organizational levels, the discourse about internal organizational design has also emphasized the need for integration and continuity. One manifestation of this is the 'TQM/CQI' movement that emphasizes the use of multidisciplinary and multifunctional teams to develop improved patient-care processes (Berwick *et al.*, 1990; Health Canada, 1993). Another has been the introduction of new ways of structuring hospitals that can better integrate physicians into a unified proactive management structure, countering traditional dual hierarchies in which physicians were seen as independent entrepreneurs with few organizational responsibilities and administrators were seen as passive providers of resources for the development of professional practice (Ackroyd *et al.*, 1989).

In summary, the new ideology of health care delivery is associated with structural changes that demand greater collaboration and integration across organizational boundaries at all levels. While other countries and jurisdictions have experienced similar philosophical changes, their solutions have often been somewhat more radical, involving deeper system-wide changes such as the development of internal markets and competition (e.g., Enthoven and Kronick, 1989; Saltman and von Otter, 1987; Jérôme-Forget White *et al.*, 1995). As we shall see, a key feature of health care reform in Canada is the extent to which its attempts at redesign have tended to rely on bureaucratic processes and the realignment of hierarchical structures of roles and responsibilities. This chapter will reveal the strengths and limitations of these mechanisms for achieving behavioural change in professional organizations.

A final key observation must be made before proceeding. This is that despite the influence of the new population-driven philosophy on reform proposals, the two archetypes form competing sources of legitimacy that coexist within the changing system. In fact, the 'provider-driven' archetype is not only the representation of an ideology but also the representation of an existing power structure in which large provider organizations such as major teaching hospitals and their highly specialized medical elites have a commanding role. In a country where the public health care system is seen as a question of national identity (Rachlis and Kushner, 1994), where access to care is a key political issue and where individuals still often rely on hospital emergency rooms to obtain primary care, this structure of influence is not easily ignored. In the emerging community care sector, where values fit best with the 'population-driven' archetype, power resources are weaker: budgets are much smaller, administrators are less well-paid, doctors and professionals are less prestigious and board members and community organizers are often less well-connected. In other words, the power structure that could be questioned by moves towards a population-driven system is intimately implicated in the decisions that will lead to its reform: change is partly *endogenously* generated. As we shall see in our discussion of boundary-breaking initiatives, this endogenous process of system evolution tends to generate compromise solutions that overlay elements of a new archetype onto structures of the old (Cooper *et al.*, 1996). The solutions chosen are thus often captured by some of the same dynamics that caused the problems they were intended to solve.

Emergent structures of collaboration in professional organizations

The previous section summarized some of the ideological pressures that are leading to calls for integration and boundary crossing within and between health care organizations. But what does this mean in practice? In order to comprehend the impact of these calls for change, we argue that it is first necessary to understand how professional organizations traditionally function. More specifically, it is crucial to understand the nature of professional collaboration at the operational level because it is here that fundamental boundaries are defined and it is here that most concrete boundary-crossing initiatives must penetrate and take root if they are to be successful. In this section, we draw attention to some of the main features of work organization and coordination in a complex professional bureaucracy where a variety of professional groups must collaborate to produce a range of outputs. We reach beyond Mintzberg's (1979) characterization of this organizational form as a federation of autonomous experts by drawing on negotiated order theory and a recent study of operations in a large teaching hospital (Lamothe, 1996) to generate a more nuanced picture of professional collaboration. Three features of collaboration within health care organizations seem particularly important to understanding the fate of boundary redefinition initiatives: *emergent operating units, differentiated professional influence* and *diluted managerial control*.

Emergent operating units

Mintzberg (1979) notes that the operating core is the key part of a professional organization because it is here that critical decisions about the content of work are made by professionals uniquely qualified to determine appropriate courses of action for a given client. The formal organizational chart thus often has little to say about what goes on at this level. Divisions by medical department and by professional group provide identification for their members (Champagne *et al.*, 1998) and indicate the broad framework within which they operate but do not specify how work will be carried out. Although Mintzberg (1979) insisted on the individual nature of professional practice, in reality, various specialists and professional groups need to collaborate in some way to get the work done. Lamothe (1996) examined how distinctive forms of coordination among professionals (negotiated orders) emerged organically around different categories of patients within the hospital she studied. This produces a variety of semi-autonomous 'operating units' that do not have formal existence in the organization chart, but which form the *de facto* elementary structures of the organization. Collaboration within these units tends to take different forms depending on the uncertainty of the task and the technology used.

For example, when patients can be clearly categorized by medical problem and associated with a standard treatment (e.g., as in ocular surgery), standardized and routinized work processes develop using a relatively limited number of coordination mechanisms. Medical control over technologies favours medical control over the operating unit and the collaborative structure adopts a hierarchical model. At the opposite extreme, when patients' problems become extremely complex requiring a multiplicity of treatments and technologies controlled by different professionals, a new form of categorization by patient type may develop (as in geriatrics). In Lamothe's (1996) study, this new approach favoured the emergence of an ideology in which the global treatment was seen as the integration of individual treatments and in which the multidisciplinary team was seen as the main technology. Here, the doctors' knowledge ensured that they became the *de facto* team-leaders, but mutual adjustment among professionals became a key coordination mechanism.

The two extremes described rely on different mixes of coordination mechanisms but both seem to be relatively functional in terms of the efficiency and effectiveness of patient care given the differences in context. When patient categorization was less clear, Lamothe (1996) found more open systems of coordination in which interactions among specialists and professionals took the form of segmented interventions communicated through chart inscriptions. While this approach appeared adequate in some conditions, under extreme uncertainty about which specialty categorization should dominate this form of coordination could be quite problematic.

The main point of this discussion, however, is to draw attention to the existence of emergent 'negotiated' organizational boundaries in professional organizations that coexist with formal structural boundaries. Professionals constantly and naturally coordinate across these boundaries to do their work. However, the specific form that this coordination will take develops and stabilizes organically through informal ongoing interactions. While uncertainty and technology are crucial factors affecting the form of coordination, different individual groups of professionals may stabilize their interactions in somewhat different ways (e.g., Barley, 1986). Tacit rules and mutual trust developed over time help to hold operating units together (Lamothe, 1996). Any outside intervention that aims to alter boundaries must thus deal with these emergent social units and forms of collaboration. It must also deal with the intrinsic power relationships and incentives that structure emergent collaboration and produce these local and varied negotiated orders. This brings us to the second key element underlying professional collaboration.

Differential professional influence

Negotiated order theory (Strauss *et al.*, 1964) as well as Crozier and Friedberg's (1978) theory of activity systems draws attention to the strategies individuals and groups use to position themselves favourably within the organization by maximizing their control over sources of uncertainty. These strategies and the resources behind them determine the forms of negotiated equilibrium that will emerge among professional groups as they interact. A group has particularly effective strategies when it succeeds in gaining control over tasks which are the principal source of unpredictability in the production process (Crozier and Friedberg, 1978). In hospitals, and to a lesser extent in other areas of the health care system, physicians have traditionally been the dominant group. Through interaction, an equilibrium state emerges, as other groups must cooperate in order to survive. Cooperation is essential to the preservation of the basis on which present and future privileges stand (Crozier, 1964). This sets the basic web on which reciprocity relations among the various professional groups are knitted. This active involvement corresponds to role creation activities described by Bucher and Stelling (1969) and to Abbott's (1988) description of professional domain redefinition in which certain professional groups are hierarchically subordinated to others.

Because of their central role in defining treatment needs, physicians in hospitals have thus traditionally had a dominant influence on the shape of structures for collaboration within the emergent operating units described above. In general, it is through a system of implicit rules, by which it controls developments, that this group keeps other professionals in various forms of subordinate relationships (Lamothe, 1996). This group's power is also reflected in greater access to the administrative structure and relative independence from managerial control (e.g., in Canada, physicians are not on organizational payrolls). Since boundary-crossing initiatives usually involve changing the structure of collaboration among professionals, the role of dominant professionals cannot be ignored. Moreover, since their political strategies, like those of others, are strongly influenced by individual and group interests, the economic and professional incentives that guide their behaviour are crucial to understanding how such initiatives will be received and how emergent boundaries are likely to organically evolve. Finally, note that self-interested negotiations surrounding professional practices involve patients whose own sources of influence are often limited. Strategies for protecting professional autonomy can generate emergent patterns of collaboration that are not necessarily ideal for the patients served. The perception that this occurs has been one of the driving forces behind calls for change.

Diluted management control

The web on which reciprocity relations are knitted among professionals extends to the upper level of professional organizations. However, only groups with control over the critical zones of the organization will tend to be strongly represented here (Thompson, 1967). For example, governance structures in hospitals have traditionally incorporated a formal and informal division of leadership roles among three poles of internal influence: a board of directors representing the community, the chief executive and management team, and the medical staff (Denis, Langley and Cazale, 1996). This structure dilutes the power of management and creates a need for collaboration and emergent negotiation not only in the operating core but right to the top of the organization.

In hospitals, doctors' success in keeping a dominant position over other professions gives them the status to impose themselves as privileged negotiators with the administrative group. They play an important role in the selection and distribution of resources essential to their specialized practices and their negotiations on these matters have a major impact on the orientations taken by the hospital. Also, the role played by the medical hierarchical structure on the implementation of administrative decisions has a direct impact on the nature and the volume of production activities. The administrative group exercises an integrative role largely related to its responsibility over budgetary controls, and a support role through its control over logistics. The interplay of contradictory forces at the top contributes to the stabilization of the system. On one side, the medical group fights to preserve the unpredictable characteristics, impossible to rationalize, of the activities they control. On the other side, through greater rationalization, the administrative group attempts to improve the efficiency of operations and is constantly tempted to '*push planning further than what would be rationally wise*' (Crozier, 1964).

Through these processes, the clinical operating core has often had considerable immunity from managerial influence partly because of information asymmetry (Girin, 1995), partly because of institutionalized power-sharing and partly because of the dominant professional group's skill in protecting the core from attempts at standardization and rationalization that would hamper its capacity to adapt organically. Indeed, many (Mintzberg, 1979; Cohen and March, 1986) have noted that the managerial levers for control in professional bureaucracies tend to be largely indirect involving limited control over structures and incentives and often leading to a form of custodial management that preserves rather than threatens professional practices (Ackroyd *et al.*, 1989). This diminishes the likelihood that managerial intervention will be capable of altering emergent boundaries. Perhaps for this reason, many of the pressures for boundary change noted earlier have been promoted by new organizations outside the traditional provider elite (e.g., consultants, regional boards and authorities in Canada). However, as we shall see later in our more detailed discussion of system integration, this can pose other problems.

Overall, this analysis of three aspects of emergent collaboration in professional organizations paints a more complex portrait of the context in which changing ideologies of health care delivery must take root. It reveals certain fundamental dynamics, which will affect attempts to traverse boundaries at all levels. First, professional work often requires horizontal coordination and formal organiza-tional and structural boundaries do not appear to constitute insurmountable barriers to the development of emergent collaborative modes of functioning when individual professionals see this collaboration as necessary to achieving their goals. Conversely, the existence of a formal structural grouping will not necessarily define lines of collaboration: in other words, operating units tend to be emergent and are based on repeated interactions in the course of work. Second, some professionals have greater influence than others on the emergence of informal collaborative arrangements and such arrangements cannot be expected to appear unless compatible with the goals and strategies of key individuals and groups. Any attempt to change collaborative relationships within and across organizational boundaries to improve patient care is more likely to work if appropriate incentives are there to support them. Finally, severe limitations of managerial power to force change in collaborative patterns are evident. These limitations are based on information asymmetry (in a large organization, there may be substantial ignorance at top levels of the many varied ways in which operating work is carried out), a corresponding inability to dictate professional behaviour, and the dilution of available levers for action by the need to negotiate their use with the professionals affected by them. To summarize, we argue that both intra-organizational and inter-organizational boundary-crossing initiatives aimed at improving integration must take into account emergent patterns of professional collaboration because these are both critical for success and elusive from control through administrative fiat or structural reorganization.

In the next section, we draw on empirical evidence and on the theoretical elements introduced above to analyse how the forces for boundary redefinition generated by changing ideologies of health care delivery interact in practice with the natural patterns of collaborative behaviour described above. As we shall see, some attempts at integration seem to be decoupled from patterns of emergent collaboration, generating conflict and even possible destruction of functional behaviours. At the other extreme are initiatives that generate considerable peripheral activity but fail to influence the nature of professional practice significantly because they reproduce or reinforce traditional power structures and modes of collaboration in the way they are implemented. The potential for positive change appears to lie somewhere between these two extremes. Our analysis is carried out at four different potential levels of integration. This section is followed by a discussion in which we draw some preliminary conclusions concerning means of achieving the objectives of improved service coordination, while taking into account the natural dynamics of professional collaborative processes.

The dynamics of boundary redefinition in practice

Figure 6.1 illustrates four types and locations of boundary redefinition within the health care system. It shows how this field is penetrated by multiple forces for change that affect both clinical practices and the overall structuring of the system. To develop an understanding of the dynamics of the formation and transformation of organizational boundaries, we evaluate these boundary redefinition trends along four analytic dimensions. The first dimension, called *the nature of boundaries*, concerns the principles by which professional activities are segmented and illustrates the challenges faced at each level of analysis. The second dimension, labelled *the drivers of change*, refers to the specific economic, technological, ideological and political pressures driving boundary change at that level. The third dimension, labelled *mechanisms for change*, identifies various instruments and management tools that have been proposed for achieving the objectives of integration. These mechanisms can be roughly ordered from 'harder' mechanisms involving changes in formal *structures* and/or *incentives* to 'softer' approaches based on organized horizontal *interaction*. Finally the *risks* dimension summarizes our assessment of the problems associated with a particular form of boundary change and the potential for different variants of it to produce (or not) an effective reconfiguration of practices.

Each of these dimensions is considered for four levels of boundary redefinition: *intraorganizational*, *horizontal*, *vertical* and *systemic*. The last three refer to different forms of interorganizational boundary-crossing. *Horizontal boundary redefinition* concerns relationships between organizations offering similar types of health care services. *Vertical boundary redefinition* implies the development of linkages between organizations offering services at different levels of care (e.g., acute care and primary care). *Systemic boundary redefinition* refers to attempts to reconfigure entire systems of organizations by traversing management boundaries, reducing provider autonomy and potentially forcing other forms of horizontal and vertical integration. At the limit, this may imply a new conception of the system as responsible not just for delivering health care but as accountable for the health of the community (in conformity with the emerging 'population-driven' archetype). Below, we elaborate on this analysis and draw on examples from empirical studies to examine how certain specific boundary redefinition initiatives have fared when confronted with the dynamics of professional organization described in the previous section.

Form of integration	Intra-organizational integration	Inter-organizational integration		
		Horizontal integration	Vertical integration	Systemic integration
Nature of critical boundaries	• Internal structural boundaries • Emergent operating unit boundaries (core)	• External structural boundaries • Emergent operating unit boundaries (core)	• External structural boundaries • Ideological boundaries • Emergent operating unit boundaries (interface)	• Senior management boundaries • Possible questioning of all other forms of boundaries • Intersectoral boundaries
Drivers • Economic	• Budget constraints, rationalization	• Economies of scale	• Emphasis on cheaper care alternatives	• Reduction of waste and duplication
• Technological	• Increased professional specialization	• Decline in hospital care, critical mass	• Technologies for ambulatory care, information technology	• Information technologies, move to ambulatory care
• Ideological	• TQM/CQI, empowerment, evidence-based medicine, etc	• Synergy, centres of excellence	• Population health, community care	• Population health, community care
• Political	• Interests of administration, nurses in promoting roles	• Survival for threatened organizations	• Interests of primary care providers in promoting roles	• Interests of managers, bureaucrats in control
Mechanisms 'Harder' ↕ 'Softer'	• Programme structures, patient-focused care • Multidisciplinary teams, problem-solving teams, etc.	• Horizontal mergers • Joint ventures • Shared services • Joint committees	• Vertical integration (common governance) • Contracting, shared services • Joint problem solving	• Centralized governance • Internal markets • Programme funding • Planning committees
Risks	• Standardization without regard for varying needs • Disinterest of dominant professional group • Programme definition that fits poorly with emergent needs	• Destruction of tacit knowledge and social capital in operating core and organization • Bureaucratization • Costs of complexity	• Dissociation between formal relationships and autonomous arrangements • Distrust and avoidance • Costs of complexity	• Costs of complexity • Growing bureaucracy • Reduced competition • Demoralization of unit management and professionals

Figure 6.1 Four modes of boundary redefinition in health care systems

Intra-organizational boundary redefinition

The nature of critical boundaries

As described earlier, intra-organizational boundaries in health care organizations are of two types: structural boundaries that reflect the formal groupings of the organizational chart and emergent boundaries that reflect *de facto* operating units providing care to specific categories of patients (Lamothe, 1996). These emergent units coordinate activities in different ways depending on task uncertainty, technology and local patterns of negotiation among professionals. However, because they are affected by differential power relationships, these local nego-tiated orders can be more or less well adjusted to the needs of patients (or clients) and may be more or less efficient. This leads to interest in finding better ways to coordinate practice, intruding on professional autonomy and often involving an attempt to redefine both structural and emergent boundaries (see Figure 6.1).

Drivers of change

There are several specific drivers of changes at this level. For example, economic constraints pressure decision-makers to seek ways of standardizing and rational-izing medical practice based on the belief that efficiency gains are possible (see, for example, Lomas and Contandriopoulos, 1994). In addition, increasing professional specialization has led to a need for more effort in integrating different contributions to care for patients with complex health problems. At a more ideological level, quality management strategies (borrowed initially from the private sector) such as 'total quality management' (TQM), 'continuous quality improvement' (CQI) and 'patient-focused care' promote the integrated organiza-tion of health care delivery around improved services to the patient (Lozeau, 1997; Berwick *et al.*, 1990). These normative discourses essentially question the adequacy of a form of work organization based on the autonomous and emergent dynamics we described above. Finally at the political level, certain groups may see in the new discourses a way to enhance their influence in the negotiated order. For example, nurses' efforts to establish their independent professional role can lead to a shifting of boundaries that previously favoured doctors (see, for example, Pollitt's (1993b) analysis of quality management models in the National Health Service). These strategic games between professions have also been accompanied by more determined efforts by managers to intervene in the organization of professional practice. The work of Quinn *et al.* (1996), Leonard-Barton (1996) and Blackler (1995) on the management of intellectual capital provide clear illustrations of this.

Mechanisms

Several mechanisms for boundary redefinition at this level have been proposed, varying from 'hard' structural changes to 'softer' forms of integration. On the 'hard' side, programme structures involve changing from a formal organization based on departmental divisions to one based on activities (Leatt *et al.*, 1994). The success of such initiatives will depend greatly on the capacity of these programmes to create new interfaces between autonomous professional logics without destroying emergent operating units that incorporate extensive mutual learning over long periods of time, and whose accumulated tacit knowledge and social capital contribute positively to the effectiveness of patient care. A 'softer' form of boundary-crossing is represented by the development of multidisciplinary teams (frequently associated with the TQM/CQI movement). In theory, this approach has the potential to alter considerably professional practice (D'Amour, 1997) by forcing the coordination of operating work by mutual adjustment. At another level, teams may be mobilized for the development of uniform protocols and 'critical pathways' intended to specify optimal patterns of medical intervention based on the best available scientific evidence (Sackett, Richardson, Rosenberg and Haynes, 1997) but in fact acting as a conduit for the standardization of work processes. In summary, a variety of mechanisms are being put forward, all of which imply greater integration across boundaries in professional practice and many of which introduce limits on professional autonomy.

Confronting experience: illustrative examples

How have such initiatives fared in practice? In the Canadian context, two examples from empirical research illustrate some of the issues involved in achieving change. The three key elements of the emergent structure for professional collaboration identified in the previous section are clearly implicated in the observed dynamics.

The first example concerns the implementation of quality management and process review in several Montreal hospitals (Lamothe, 1996; Lozeau, 1997). The mechanisms observed were mostly 'soft' in nature, building on informal *interaction* rather than formal *structures* or changed *incentives*. These initiatives had some limited success in support areas. However, despite considerable management rhetoric, they had no impact whatever on emergent clinical operating units where their potential should have been highest (Carman *et al.*, 1996; Weiner *et al.*, 1997). In fact, these efforts failed to penetrate the natural structure of emergent collaboration among professionals, mainly because the dominant professional group (physicians) was uninterested, uninvolved and often only tentatively solicited. Managers and other professionals tended to assume (probably with good reason) that physicians would not participate (Lozeau, 1997) and avoided confrontation on the issue, ensuring the reproduction of established negotiated orders and the continued immunity of operating units from managerial influence. This pattern has been noted by others (Berwick *et al.*, 1990) and illustrates one of the ways in which professional dominance tends to perpetuate itself. In these cases, there was an obvious decoupling between the institutional discourse that led to the adoption of the quality management approaches and the way in which they were implemented, ensuring preservation of the status quo (Meyer and Rowan, 1977).

Some research has in fact found that implementation of quality management approaches in clinical areas is more likely if there is active physician championship (Weiner *et al.*, 1997; Carman *et al.*, 1996). Others have argued that physicians need to be able to see the benefits to them before they will get involved, and that the managed care environment of the US may provide the needed stimulus (Chesanow, 1997). Finally, Boerstler *et al.* (1996) suggest that success in this area occurs where hospitals have a previous tradition of clinical or outcome research. All this tends towards the conclusion that deeper change is possible if the dominant professional group leads it and can be persuaded to want it, and if the new pattern of activity and interaction required is not too unfamiliar. We see here explicitly how 'successful' change in the professional organization tends to be partly conservative and endogenous, implicating old patterns of influence in the creation of the new, and building on existing emergent forms of collaboration.

A similar pattern can be seen in our second example. This involved a change in *incentives* (compensation scheme for doctors) aimed at encouraging greater multi-disciplinary collaboration among doctors and nurses in nursing homes (Denis, 1988). The empirical study showed that changes in collaborative behaviour were indeed facilitated by the change in incentives, but only where both physicians and nurses showed interest in promoting such collaboration. The goals of physicians were clearly predominant in determining outcomes, again demonstrating the perpetuation of dominance relations and the endogenous nature of these processes.

Summarizing the risks

Overall, the effectiveness of intra-organizational interventions aimed at boundary redefinition remains uncertain. As can be seen, professionals, especially doctors in hospitals, have a great ability to resist pressures for change that do not fit their goals. Reformers (managers, political decision-makers and experts) may propose and sometimes impose transformation projects that are incompatible with the logic of professional production and that fail to take into account the varying needs of different emergent units. Clearly, the issue at this level is to develop the capacity to design new interfaces (e.g., between doctors and organizations, clinician accountability for resource use) without undermining informal coordination mechanisms that are fundamental to the capacity to apply expertise effectively (Quinn *et al.*, 1996).

Horizontal boundary redefinition

The nature of critical boundaries

This type of boundary redefinition involves inter-organizational collaboration between organizations with similar missions (e.g., between two or more acute care institutions or between two or more primary care organizations). At first sight, this is an initiative that mainly involves the opening of formal *structural* boundaries between organizations. However, drawing on our previous discussion, it also appears critical to consider the impact of horizontal integration on the pattern of collaboration in emergent operating units. This is because operating units offering similar services in different organizations may have developed quite idiosyncratic negotiated orders that may have to be questioned and renegotiated to achieve the results expected from integration.

Drivers of change

The forces driving horizontal integration among health care organizations include efficiency gains, better use of technologies and the creation of centres of excellence (Markham and Lomas, 1995). Horizontal integration is also expected to reduce destructive competition between health care organizations within a given market and should allow the emergence of new forms of synergy and cooperation. At the more political level, several hospital managers and boards have latched onto horizontal integration and merger as a means to ensure survival in a world where the importance of institutional care (especially in the acute-care sector) is declining. At the same time, inter-organizational relationships often create tensions between the desire for autonomy and the need for cooperation (Pfeffer and Salancik, 1978; Benson, 1975). In practice, conflict over which partner will dominate often underlies negotiations to collaborate.

Mechanisms

A wide range of means have been proposed to increase horizontal integration and collaboration among health care organizations (see Figure 6.1). Shared service agreements, co-financing of technology, strategic alliances for the development of new services and fully fledged mergers are some of these. Each has different repercussions for the organizations involved. For example, shared service agreements and strategic alliances appear more reversible and less demanding than mergers. They also probably have much less significant effects on professional practice. The example given below from our empirical work examines the boundary redefinition issues raised by mergers, one of the 'harder' forms of horizontal integration.

Confronting experience: an illustrative example

Our ongoing study of the processes associated with two mergers of three teaching hospitals suggests that this is an extremely demanding and complex operation for managers, professionals and other organization members (Denis, Lamothe and Langley, 1998). Teaching hospital mergers involve a multiplicity of forms of restructuring at different levels of the organization. First, they require integrating diverse organizational cultures that favour different conceptions of the role of management and of the nature of relations between the medical staff and the administration. These cultural parameters describe divisions of roles that have evolved gradually over time and that are judged to be acceptable and functional for that specific organization. In fact, these patterns directly reflect the emergent negotiated orders at the top of the organization that we described in our section on emergent structures. They are combined with divergent perceptions of the organization's role within the community and the health care system as a whole. The different organizational cultures conflict during the merger, with each attempting to maintain its legitimacy despite commitment to a major merger project. The job of management is particularly complex in this situation, as they must renegotiate a new legitimate role among these opposing forces.

At the clinical level, the combination of teaching hospitals represents a major upheaval, attacking the foundations of emergent operating units (Denis, Lamorke and Langley, 1998). In our study the mergers fundamentally challenged the existing organization of medical practice and the way in which physicians and nurses saw their roles. Few physicians saw any interest in transforming practice habits that had developed organically over time and that represented a legitimate strategy for meeting their revenue objectives. For nurses, the transfer of services to another site represented a significant modification of their working environment in terms of the practice norms that they had learned to master. These dynamics combined with a certain conservatism among professionals and managers wishing to preserve their organization strengths rendered boundary-crossing change extremely difficult. As a mode of horizontal integration, the mergers encountered enormous barriers. Thus, beyond the obvious demolition of structural boundaries, we see that the merger project threatened the established negotiated order within each organization. In this process, the negotiation of a new clinical order appeared essential but was extremely difficult. These observations are confirmed by reports of difficulties experienced with other attempts to implement horizontal mergers in Canada. For example, in a study of mergers of rural hospitals Demers and Bégin (1990) noted the power of the medical elite to combat merger proposals that seemed to threaten its interests.

Summarizing the risks

The difficulty and uncertainty surrounding such processes indicate that the benefits of horizontal integration are less obvious than suggested in the literature at least in the short term (e.g., see the critical analyses by Markham and Lomas, 1995; Robinson, 1997). In addition, our observations indicate that the success of a merger depends on the informal dynamics of restructuring the clinical operating core over which management actually has relatively limited control. This also suggests that there is a need to find better means of rendering the frontiers of professional practice more dynamic. Experience with these mergers illustrates forcefully the problem of creating interfaces between autonomous operating units with their own internal logic and consistency. It also dramatically reveals the enormous complexity involved in reconstructing a multiplicity of different professional operating units simultaneously and of grasping the logic of the whole. The costs of this type of operation both financially, and in terms of the time required to relearn new modes of functioning, are often greatly underestimated, as are the difficulties of managing and operating a professional organization on several sites. Obviously, softer and more limited modes of horizontal boundary redefinition may be less costly, while also offering fewer potential benefits. For example, rationalization of purely administrative services, while still difficult, is easier to achieve than integration of professional services because their modes of functioning are more susceptible to rational planning and more easily imposed by managerial fiat.

Vertical boundary redefinition

The nature of critical boundaries

Vertical integration is a form of inter-organizational collaboration that involves the coordination of work between organizations occupying different positions along the continuum of care (e.g., between acute care and primary care organizations). Linkages are thus created between organizations that previously functioned with minimal coordination. Our earlier analysis of intra-organizational and horizontal integration indicated the importance of considering both structural boundaries *and* emergent operating unit boundaries. These two types of boundaries are also affected by vertical integration. However, in addition, *ideological* boundaries may also come into play in a major way (see Figure 6.1). For example, when acute and community care organizations must collaborate, their practice philosophies are often completely different, reflecting the divide between 'provider-driven' and 'population-driven' archetypes. The 'provider-driven' philosophy is more closely associated with acute care and the 'population-driven' archetype better fits the ideology associated with primary care. As we shall see, the differing philosophies generate considerable tension concerning modes of collaboration even when there is agreement that linkages are needed.

Drivers of change

Economic considerations are pushing the provision of care to the most cost-effective level, which is often community rather than expensive acute care. New technologies are contributing to the equation by allowing this transfer. This requires developing smoother linkages between levels of care. As indicated earlier, strong normative discourses associated with the 'population-driven' archetype also signal to providers the importance of finding new ways of offering services. These have often been adopted by payers looking to save money and by certain public and private providers who see in these initiatives a way to enhance the value and status of their contributions.

Mechanisms

'Harder' forms of vertical integration involve eliminating structural boundaries and placing linked organizations under the same management. Other forms make interdependence explicit by introducing market mechanisms for contracting (a central element of the 'New Public Management' described by Ferlie *et al.*, 1996). Vertical linkages may also involve 'softer' modes of collaboration such as agreed referral protocols, guidelines and joint problem solving. These different approaches have in fact given rise to debates in the literature between those favouring formal structural integration (Shortell, 1997) and those favouring virtual integration via various forms of contracting and alliances (Robinson, 1997). These debates also reveal themselves in the jockeying for position between acute care providers attempting to consolidate their role by absorbing primary care providers (in fully fledged vertical integration), and the smaller and less prestigious primary care organizations fighting to retain their autonomy and increase their power in the system (preferring a form of virtual integration that gives them a potentially important role as purchasers of care). As noted earlier, these battles lines are drawn across an ideological divide that reflects to some extent the two competing archetypes or philosophies of care. This brings us to some observations from recent and ongoing studies of attempts to develop such vertical linkages in Quebec.

Confronting experience: illustrative examples

Our empirical examples in this section concern observations of a variety of attempts to promote better coordination across the continuum of services but especially between acute-care hospitals and community clinics (e.g., Daoust, 1998). These changes were initiated following reductions in the budgets for institutional care and the transfer of funds to the community clinics, which would become responsible for post-operative care and the organization of home care for vulnerable populations in the community. In most situations observed, a 'soft' interactive approach involving the maintenance of organizational autonomy and the development of joint agreements and protocols was favoured. Compared with the dramatic effect of the horizontal mergers described in the previous section such 'soft' vertical linkages might be expected to have a relatively modest impact on emergent operating units and power structures since hierarchical reporting relationships and the central core of operations remain largely intact. The changes proposed seem essentially to be at the level of the development of new interfaces based on the principle of complementarity. In practice, however, the situation is more complex. For example, community clinics whose traditional ideology and emphasis has been on preventive and long term care have reluctantly found themselves obliged to develop new patterns of behaviour for dealing with acute post-operative patients. The consequent ideological tensions created within the clinics are accentuated by the transfer of nurses and other personnel from the acute-care hospitals.

Perhaps the most striking observation, however, is how difficult it has been to involve dominant professionals (physicians) in making the new collaborations work. In one case, while nurses and managers from hospitals and community clinics worked intensively together to develop a new inter-organizational referral system, doctors simply undermined their efforts by ignoring the planning meetings and taking no part in the development of protocols whose effectiveness depended on their collaboration (Daoust, 1998). Their dominant role in the negotiated order, the inability of managers to direct their behaviour, and the lack of obvious incentives produced a truncated process that was unlikely to deliver the expected patterns of collaboration. Meanwhile, the physicians invented parallel ways of providing ambulatory care services in hospitals or private clinics under their own control. In other words they responded to pressures for change by developing their own emergent modes of operation that protected their interest but that were decoupled from management intentions.

It should be noted that this phenomenon has not occurred everywhere. Moreover, it is not obvious that such physician initiatives are necessarily dysfunctional from the patient's perspective. However, it again illustrates the powerful role of the emergent processes of negotiation described earlier in determining the fate of boundary redefinition initiatives. Note also that while 'harder' versions of vertical integration might introduce new levels of management that could intervene more strongly in forcing collaboration among certain levels of employees, the evidence from our observations of intra-organizational collaboration suggest that aspects of professional production dominated by physicians would be just as likely to escape direct control (see also Bégin and Labelle, 1989).

Summarizing the risks

Ideological boundaries add to the complexity of inter-organizational linkages in vertical integration, potentially contributing to distrust and avoidance of real collaboration. This is possible because dominant professionals cannot be made to participate in activities that do not seem essential to them. Even when the need for integration is perceived, certain groups may prefer to duplicate activities under their own control rather than submit to processes and ideologies that others would impose on them. However, the solution of collective problems such as the coordination of care for the frail and elderly ideally requires the invention of new care strategies and the commitment of key actors to a common project. Relational capital between actors belonging to different organizations, and complex tacit knowledge developed among these communities and their patients are important assets in such efforts. But a long process of adjustment and learning can only create these.

Systemic boundary redefinition

The nature of critical boundaries

System integration involves the introduction of some form of coordination device that integrates all organizations within a given geographical area or system of care. The aim is to reorganize activities across all forms of structural boundaries, both horizontal and vertical, in order to create fluid ('seamless') networks of services (see Figures 6.1 and 6.2). System integration encounters the difficulties noted earlier of dealing with both emergent professional boundaries and ideological frontiers associated with different levels of care. In this sense it resembles vertical integration (a more bilateral phenomenon). However, because of the introduction of common governance and the integration of multiple organizations, it adds an additional level of complexity, crossing traditional management boundaries and ensuring that individual organizations lose some autonomy. In addition, system integration may ultimately open the door to intersectoral boundary crossing as regional or local health agencies collaborate with other kinds of public and private organizations having a potential impact on health (e.g., education, municipal services, etc.).

Drivers of change

Despite the multiplicity and complexity of the boundaries to be penetrated, there is considerable interest in this type of boundary reconstruction at present (e.g., organized delivery systems as proposed by Shortell *et al.* (1996), regional governance and integrated systems in Canada, town–hospital networks in France). System integration is seen as both a way to improve continuity of services

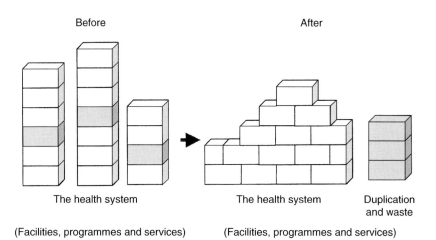

Figure 6.2 The economic logic behind system integration
Source: Image adapted from Edmonton Capital Health Authority's 1994 business plan

in a context where evolving technology allows increased emphasis on ambulatory and home care, and a means to achieve substantial economies by avoiding unnecessary duplication and competition between providers. A particularly striking rendering of the economic logic behind system integration, inspired by a diagram in the Edmonton Capital Health Authority's (1994) first 'business plan,' appears in Figure 6.2. This trend is also influenced by the reformist discourse of the emerging archetype described earlier which emphasizes the need for the creation of a population-driven system accountable to the community. Finally, at the political level, this form of integration is favoured by health care planners and policy analysts promoting a more 'rational' approach to the organization of health care resources.

Mechanisms

The mechanisms for system integration vary. The most radical form involves the creation of a single governing board responsible for planning, funding, coordination and operation of all services in a territorial area or for a given clientèle. Less radical approaches could include the development of a coordinating body that leaves individual organizations more autonomous but which forces active negotiations of their respective domains (Denis, 1997). Other interventions may involve programme planning and funding that organize services across multiple boundaries.

Confronting experience: illustrative examples

This form of integration has the effect of reducing the autonomy of individual organizations and, correspondingly, it often increases the distance between the operating core and the actors who are effectively involved in managing or coordinating it. In our studies, we have seen that this can have both positive and negative effects (Denis, 1997; Denis, Langley and Contandriopoulos 1998; Denis and Valette, 1998). On the positive side, more distant structures may sometimes have wider leverage over direct and indirect mechanisms for managerial action capable of producing dynamic and potentially positive change (e.g., control over resource allocation, structures and incentives). The action of such coordinating agencies may also be less restrained by the entrenched patterns of professional power described earlier in the chapter. For example, the new regional authorities in Quebec and across Canada have been the source of numerous innovations and attempts to render health care systems more responsive (including vertical and horizontal boundary crossing).

However, distance from operations can render the action of system governance bodies insensitive to varying local realities, and also raise questions of legitimacy. The locus of power may be divorced from the locus of knowledge required to use it intelligently. There is a danger that system integration may crush the flexible, emergent and organic nature of professional collaboration under a wall of standardizing bureaucracy that is both demotivating and ill-adjusted to the varied patterns of coordination required for different client populations (Lamothe, 1996). (The right-hand image of Figure 6.2 is not encouraging in this respect!) The challenge of this form of integration is thus to find ways of intervening that limit the perverse effects of a poorly adjusted system while supporting its ability to dynamically and organically adapt to changing needs.

One positive example comes from a study of regional planning for mental health services in Quebec (Denis *et al.*, 1996). The regional body organized a major planning effort with local sub-regions with the objective of developing a programme structure for the provision of mental health services. The analysis of this experience shows that the pertinent unit for the planning of mental health services is the sub-region where both a significant social network and the knowledge of local needs exist. In this case, the boundaries between actors and organizations had already been penetrated and mechanisms for coordination at this level already existed. However, the system-level initiative was able to build on this embryonic collaboration, enhancing the learning across ideological frontiers, and provide support for positive developments. The existence of ideological dissension between producers working at different levels of the health care system in areas such as mental health (Denis, Langley and Contandriopoulos, 1998) and HIV/AIDS (Champagne *et al.*, 1995) reinforces the need for a long mutual learning process. Such a process may develop following a decision to proceed to system integration. On the other hand, this will be difficult to impose by fiat: a new negotiated order has to be developed and stabilized organically through mutual adjustment. The role of the system level of coordination is mainly to offer incentives, resources and space that can influence the pattern of negotiation and encourage the development and/or reinforcement of such collaboration.

Summarizing the risks

In summary, the dangers of this form of integration lie in the costs of complexity and bureaucratization associated with increasing distance from operations. While this distance may provide greater potential for introducing frame-breaking change, it can also lead to insensitive and misguided attempts to impose standardized approaches, leading to demoralization on the part of unit management and professionals. In addition, there is a disturbing aspect to the idea that all health care providers within a given area might be perfectly coordinated and controlled from the centre. While services may possibly be better aligned and more continuous, the monolithic nature of the system may offer limited recourse to the consumer. For this reason, in many areas of Canada, attempts have been made to introduce mechanisms for democratic deliberation and accountability into plans for systemic integration.

Discussion

We began this chapter with two sets of quotations illustrating the tension between the pressures for integration inherent in current discourse on health care reform and the nature of operating work in professional organizations. We have attempted to deepen the analysis of this fundamental conflict and to examine its practical consequences. We first drew on recent research and on 'negotiated order' theory to develop a more complex portrait of the nature of health care organizations as arenas for professional action. We then examined how the forces for change interact in practice with these professional arenas at different levels of analysis using a variety of empirical studies of the Canadian health care system. In our concluding comments, we first draw together these observations to identify some common challenges and then examine the potential contribution of three modes of intervention to achieving productive change.

The challenges of boundary redefinition

To an outside observer, the health care system appears to be traversed mainly by *structural* boundaries, which define the frontiers of different organizations and departments. These structural frontiers have often been fiercely attacked by political authorities and policy makers because they are seen as counter-productive in terms of services to the population (e.g., Rochon *et al.*, 1988). However, the emphasis on the need to change structural boundaries misses the importance of other barriers to integration that may at the same time be more significant in terms of their potential effects on patient care, and also more resistant to change.

Specifically, we noted that professional organizations are characterized by *emergent operating units*, *differential professional influence* and *diluted managerial control*. Emergent operating units represent the collective constructions that have taken form over time among local professional communities in order to deal with uncertainties and to solve problems of cooperation in an acceptable fashion (Friedberg, 1993). The good news about these units is that their existence implies that professionals have no difficulty working together across structural boundaries when their interests and their task needs require them to do so. The bad news is that whether they are functional or not for the clients served, or cost effective, these emergent units structure the habitual behaviours of professionals and are particularly resistant to change through managerial fiat. This is because the professionals that negotiate their frontiers over time retain a high degree of autonomy and because they become strongly attached to modes of operation that both define their identity and accommodate their interests. *Differential professional influence* and *diluted managerial control* ensure that integration initiatives that involve altering the patterns of professional practice (as proposed in the initial quotations) cannot succeed unless dominant professionals see the benefits of change and are willing and able to invest in developing a new (*emergent*) *modus vivendi*. In addition, as we have seen, *ideological* barriers, reflecting the philosophies of the 'provider-driven' and 'population-driven' archetypes can add to the complexities of achieving certain types of inter-organizational linkages by decreasing the likelihood that professionals will recognize the advantages of new forms of collaboration.

Overall, our empirical analysis suggests that poorly calibrated attempts at boundary change can encounter two extremes of potentially dysfunctional consequences. In the more common of the two scenarios, intra- or inter-organizational collaborative efforts essentially reproduce existing negotiated orders because dominant professionals see no reason to change their behaviours. In an alternative but perhaps more damaging scenario, imposed structural changes (e.g., as in mergers) can result in the destruction of valuable tacit knowledge and social capital embedded within emergent units that may be difficult and time-consuming to recreate. Both of these two extremes are associated with each of two fundamentally different types of coordinating mechanisms that have tended to dominate in Canadian reforms ('soft' interactive mechanisms and 'hard' structural mechanisms respectively). In the next section, we will argue that a third type of mechanism (alignment of incentives) needs to be used more extensively in conjunction with the others to achieve deeper and potentially more productive change.

Promoting adaptive change by aligning structures, incentives and interactions

The role of structure

Health care managers and policy decision-makers often rely on structural solutions to promote changes in the organization of health care and to establish new forms of linkages among categories of professionals and between professionals and their organizations. Some of these changes involve creating integrated structures with broad scope (e.g., mergers, integrated systems) that will have more power to force changes at lower levels. This has been the typical pattern in Canada. To operationalize their integration mandate, these entities may then try to impose new structures at a more micro-level. However, as we have seen, when such changes fail to take into account the shape, diversity and emergent dynamics of clinical operating units, they can be ineffective or possibly even disastrous. Yet, there is a real need both to enhance service integration and to re-establish boundaries at a human level that make sense in terms of the operating work of professionals. How can this be done?

One approach is to acknowledge formally small-scale emergent operating units that have so far remained informal, but that implicitly recognize the need for horizontal collaboration. Such 'programme' units are needed to become the new foundations of constantly growing structural entities as they allow professionals to find coherence in the production of specific care activities. Different categories are currently being used to define such programme units: types of patients (mental health), population groups (elderly), and specialized services (neurosurgery).

Although conflicts between proponents of each of these are ongoing, the pluralistic nature of health care services will most probably call for a mix of them. Systems that were once composed of mission-specific organizations may well have to become systems composed of programme-specific services adopting a variety of different modes of functioning.

With the population health approach, the local community is being introduced as another basis for unit definition. Although this may bring health care services down to a manageable scale, especially in rural areas, the superimposition of client programmes may be needed to meet efficiency imperatives. Overall, the point is that micro-structures must be designed to recognize the varying logics of varying professional activities. However, to produce evolution in these logics, structural forms need help from other mechanisms.

The role of incentives

A key mechanism for change, so far little used in the case of Canadian reforms, involves changing the structure of *incentives* driving professional and organizational action. The central role pooled remuneration schemes could play in changing the dynamics of collaboration in teaching hospital mergers are one example. The potential for capitation systems (involving fixed payments per client enrolled) to ensure that professionals are made both clinically and financially responsible for services is another. To achieve productive change via incentives, the rules of the game must be made clear and professionals must be able to see the benefits accruing to them in terms of the development of their clinical practice. In the context of this chapter, note that incentive manipulation is a mechanism that tends to produce less standardized solutions than structural transformations because it leaves considerable autonomy in the hands of professionals who then elaborate strategies to achieve certain results. Obviously, no reward scheme can produce a given behaviour with certainty (Giacomini *et al.*, 1996). As one of our intra-organizational level examples showed, incentives can send ambiguous signals subject to interpretation. But they can induce behavioural changes if professionals are involved in collective processes of deliberation around their meaning and objectives. This brings us to the third mechanism for promoting changes in forms of collaboration.

The role of interactions

This approach involves providing occasions for provider and professional groups to interact among themselves in order to invent collective solutions. For example, in concrete terms, this can involve the use of working groups, joint committees, and planning task forces. Although such forms of participation may be seen as somewhat utopian, they can lead to learning and to change in the systems of ideas that guide professional action (see the analysis of the potential for public deliberation developed by Bohman [1996], the work of Denis and Valette [1997], on the role of representations in the transformation of health services in regions of

France, and Oakes *et al.* [1998], critical appreciation of the role of business planning as a pedagogical tool in the Alberta museum system). Again, this is a mechanism that allows variety and sensitivity in the development of solutions. However, its impact can be greatly increased when it is combined with the second approach (the development of compatible incentives). Some of the examples we described earlier showed how unreinforced interactive exercises could reproduce traditional modes of negotiation, leaving emergent patterns of collaboration barely disturbed.

The last two mechanisms aim at promoting changes in professional systems without undermining their fundamental autonomy and identity. According to knowledge-based organization theorists (e.g., Blackler, 1995), the way professionals structure their activities and use their expertise are constitutive of their identity in a given organizational setting. Destabilization of identity without complementary mechanisms for stabilizing operational units may represent a major loss of expertise and knowledge capital. Major structural reforms are at risk of creating a decoupling between the logic of knowledge and the logic of professional management. In this regard, incentives and interactions (preferably in combination) may represent appropriate mechanisms to reconcile needs for change and new learning with the preservation of knowledge capabilities.

This perspective is consistent with the literature on the governance of collective action (Ouchi, 1980; Eisenhardt, 1989a; Friedberg, 1993). *Structural* reform is based on the principle of hierarchy where changes in formal boundaries are supposed to induce changes in the distribution of influence, the locus of control and in the behaviour of agents. The various structural reforms we examined do not always pay much attention to the uncertainties inherent in such processes. Changes in formal structure do not necessarily create more certainty. They simply provide a new arena to develop professional strategies. In considering the limits of structural changes, many authors have proposed market-like reforms for health care systems. These propositions are often based on recognition of the need to reinforce or renew the structure of *incentives*. Proposals based on public competition or on the implementation of internal markets aim to change the role of professionals in the governance of health care organizations and system by coupling financial and clinical responsibilities. Despite potential problems regarding professional autonomy, these reforms have the advantage of co-opting professional expertise and experience in the management of care. Finally, increasing occasions for *interactions* among professionals implies a clan type of governance logic. This involves the development of local norms based on mutual adjustment among professionals searching for adaptive solutions to improve care.

In conclusion, although several writers on the transformation of health care systems examine the question of professional regulation, few have examined how various boundary-shifting reforms affect the definitions and logics of professional practice. In our view, to achieve desirable reform, new incentive systems need to be designed to promote change while retaining the support of professionals. No reform can attain its objectives if professionals do not participate in the renewal of their implicit rules of operation. In addition, given the uncertainties about appropriate interventions, and also concerning the way in which various actors will respond to incentives, it seems desirable to invest in approaches that mobilize professional participation. Pilot projects and collaboration with professional communities interested in achieving change seem to offer a useful avenue. These would provide guidance on the use of different forms of incentives and on how different initiatives for change are interpreted.

However, there are no simple answers in fields where internal and external complexity are increasingly combined (Løwendahl and Revang, 1998). While exogenous forces have served to shake health care systems out of a long period of relative calm, change that appears dramatic on the surface is often at bottom inherently conservative because of the endogenous nature of critical decisions (see also Cooper *et al.*, 1996; Montgomery and Oliver, 1996). This manifests itself as much in the 'hot' conflict and demoralization of professionals faced with upheaval of their professional routines during the teaching hospital mergers as in the 'cold' indifference to managerial change efforts during TQM programmes and inter-organizational collaboration attempts. Between the two extremes, we see more constructive adaptation, usually when change builds on latent potential and when professionals want it or can be brought to believe in it. The great challenge is to find ways to promote and maintain such adaptiveness while recognizing that any change (including changes in incentives) will implicate the old in the definition of the new.

Notes

1 In Canada, health care is publicly funded and administered. It has always been a provincial responsibility, although partially regulated by the federal Canada Health Act (1984) that establishes five guiding principles (universality, comprehensiveness, portability, accessibility and public administration), supported by financial transfers covering a portion of the costs. The Act allows the federal government to penalize provinces that do not comply with these principles. However, the force of this measure is waning as federal contributions have been declining (from 50 per cent of public expenditure in the 1970s to 30 per cent in 1994) (National Forum on Health, 1997).

7 The dynamics of change in large accounting firms

C. R. Hinings, Royston Greenwood and David Cooper

In our previous work (Greenwood *et al.*, 1990) we suggested that professional partnerships, in general, have had, historically and traditionally, a particular approach to organization and strategic management – the P^2 form.

> Our thesis is that professional partnerships constitute an organizational type by virtue of their distinct strategic management practices. The configuration of controls used by their centers differs from previously identified patterns such as Williamson's M- and H-forms of organization.
>
> (Greenwood, *et al.*, 1990, p. 748)

However, many professional service firms, especially the larger ones, are undergoing change with an emerging alternative organizational form, which is much more oriented towards 'standard' corporate practices. We have called this form the Managed Professional Business (Cooper *et al.*, 1996). Other writers have attested to the importance of change in these organizations although not necessarily emphasizing the same elements (Stevens, 1981; Nelson, 1988; Galanter and Palay, 1991). There seems to be a growing consensus that major changes are taking place in professional service firms. But, Hinings *et al.* (1991) and Greenwood and Hinings (1996) have argued that when an individual firm attempts to introduce a managerial innovation, there are a number of problematic elements and the dynamics of the change process have to be examined.

The aim of this chapter is to examine some of these processes of change. Prima facie, we would expect it to be difficult for a firm organized as a professional partnership to change, primarily because of the way those two features, the professional, and the partnership, interact on the authority system. As Hinings *et al.* (1991) have stated, the professional organization emphasizes collegiality, peer evaluation, autonomy, informality, and flexibility of structure. Collegial, group based policy decision-making is juxtaposed with individualized, autonomous day-to-day activities. As a result dealing with long-term, strategic change is difficult because of the lack of an organizationally prescribed, hierarchical system of decision-making which can be mobilized when necessary.

While it is possible to talk generically about professional service firms, the actual pressures for change, and the processes of responding to those pressures, will vary by sector and market, e.g., small accounting firm/large accounting firm; small law firm/large law firm. Therefore, this chapter concentrates on large accounting firms. The first section examines the elements of the traditional archetype, the P^2 as the organizational context and starting point against which the pressures for change have to be understood and evaluated. The second section details the pressures for change on large accounting firms and the emergence of a new organizational field of professional business services. The third section outlines the emerging alternative archetype, the Managed Professional Business and what changing to such an organizational design type means. The fourth section suggests how the process of change unfolds in those firms. The fifth section comes to conclusions about further research.

The traditional archetype: P^2

'Traditional' in some ways is a difficult word. We use it in two senses. The first is factual, meaning that historically many, if not all, accounting firms have been organized like this. The second draws on the concept of legitimacy, suggesting that this form is seen as the proper and appropriate way of organizing, even when some firms have been organized in a different way. This second meaning gives strong credence to the idea that changing to a new archetype by a large number of organizations requires that the new form has been legitimized within the industry sector or organizational field. It is the idea of legitimacy, rooted in beliefs, values, ideologies and their interpretative component that leads to the idea of archetypes.

We are not dealing with the theoretical justification for an archetype approach here; this has been done in our previous work (Hinings and Greenwood, 1988a; Greenwood and Hinings, 1988; Greenwood et al., 1990; Greenwood and Hinings, 1993). An organizational archetype is a configuration of structures and systems, which have a common orientation. This common orientation is provided by an underlying interpretive scheme. And such an archetype is legitimated within the organizational field of which it is a part (Scott, 1995).

Historically, the accounting industry has been dominated by the P^2 form (Greenwood et al., 1990). It is labelled 'P^2' because of the twin components of partnership and professionalism. This form has an interpretive scheme and configuration which is relevant to a complex organization of geographically dispersed professionals working within the legal framework of a partnership. As Hinings et al. (1991, p. 376) put it:

> A professional service firm has a primary resource and work force of a group of trained professionals who have agreed to work under the same organizational umbrella. An important characteristic of such firms is that these professionals agree to share ownership as a group of partners.

Table 7.1 gives details of the P^2 form (and also the Managed Professional Business (MPB), which will be discussed later). In the P^2 form, the common, institutionally legitimated orientation or *interpretive scheme* centres on two elements, *governance* and *task*. Governance encompasses three beliefs: the fusion of ownership and control which is embedded in the notion of partnership; representative democracy as the basis of both strategic and operational decision-making; and the non-separation of professional and managerial tasks, with the result that managerial tasks revolve among the owners (partners). In terms of how tasks are to be performed, there are four beliefs: that professional knowledge is primary and central; that control and evaluation is exercised by peers; that work responsibility is indivisible; that strong links with clients and understanding their problems, is central to task performance.

The archetype approach denies the neutrality of organizational systems and structure and argues that those design elements are ways of capturing and operationalizing the underlying interpretive schemes. For the P^2 archetype the professional/partnership interpretive scheme means that, in terms of *systems*, there will be weak *strategic control*, enshrined in little analytical emphasis and consensus decision-making. With regard to *market and financial control* systems, there is tolerant accountability over achieving targets, even when those targets are specific, and targets are always short term, with a year being the longest period envisioned. Finally, for *operating control*, the P^2 archetype operates through decentralized processes with little central involvement, with the exception of control of standards and quality which is the primary focus of involvement.

Structurally, one of the special characteristics of organizations dominated by professionals is that they build their own roles rather than fit into preset ones. This produces spontaneous internal differentiation based on work interests. Informality in work groups tends to be the norm and work groups are put together on the basis of the ability of the members to work together and with clients. As a result, there is a low level of *specialization* and the criteria for such specialization is a mixture of professional divisions and personal interest. The professional nature of the primary tasks means that much is left to the individual professional group.

Integration and coordination is left to the professionals with only low-level support staff. There are few tiers (Maister, 1982) and little use of cross-functional teams at either the management or operational levels. There are also generally few formal rules, with the exception of professional standards. The latter are regularly inspected through review procedures. Integration is primarily achieved through one-on-one meetings between partners and other professionals and through the generic meetings of the partnership group.

Pressures for change

In the final quarter of the twentieth century the environment within which accounting firms provide their services has not stood still; far from it. Indeed, our argument is that the changes that have occurred have been relatively rapid and dramatic, producing strong pressures for organizational change. We look, briefly,

Table 7.1 Characteristics of the P^2 and MPB archtypes

	P^2 archetype	MPB archetype
Interpretive scheme	*Governance* Fusion of ownership and control A form of representative democracy Revolving managerial tasks among the owners Local office as the centre of commitment *Primary task* Professional knowledge Peer control Work responsibility as indivisible Strong links with clients Widely distributed authority Minimum hierarchy	*Effectiveness / efficiency* Management Client service Competition Marketing and growth strategies Rationalization Productivity
Systems	*Strategic control* Rationality – low analytical emphasis Interaction – consensus decision-making *Marketing–financial control* Specificity of targets – precise financial targets Tolerance of accountability – high Time orientation – short term *Operating control* Range of involvement – low Primary focus of involvement – professional standards and quality of service Decentralization–centralization – decentralized	*Strategic control* Rationality – moderate analytical emphasis Interaction – more directive decision-making *Marketing–financial control* Specificity of targets – precise financial and market targets Tolerance of accountability – low Time orientation – short term and long term *Operating control* Range of involvement – medium Primary focus of involvement – professional standards, quality of service, planning, marketing and compensation Decentralization–centralization more centralization –
Structure	*Differentiation* Level of specialization – low Criteria of specialization – professional divisions and personal interest *Integration* Use of integrative devices – low Use of rules and procedures – generally low, but emphasis on standards and quality	*Differentiation* Level of specialization – medium Criteria of specialization – professional divisions and functional difference *Integration* Use of integrative devices – medium, development of hierarchy and cross-functional teams Use of rules and procedures – still emphasis on standards and quality but more rules generally

Source: Adapted from Cooper *et al.*, 1996.

at two aspects of that environment, the markets for the services which accounting firms provide, and the institutional context within which they operate. Markets have been restructured in a relatively short period of time and patterns of demand for the various services provided have altered significantly. We examine three aspects of these firms' markets: increased competition for accounting services; growth in the demand for other business services; and globalization. With regard to the institutional context we examine the nature of the regulatory framework within which accounting firms operate. We deal with two aspects: the attack on the legitimacy of the accounting profession and firms; and the role of the professional associations.

Market dynamics

Competition for accounting services

Many writers, academics and journalists, have pointed to the increasingly competitive nature of markets for accounting services. Central has been the commodification of the audit. Until the 1980s, auditing and associated accounting services were the centrepiece of activity, producing anything up to 70 per cent of fee volume. Since then, audit fee volumes have been decreasing and profitability declining; in some firms audit is now down to less than 50 per cent of fee volume. It is also no longer possible for accounting firms to differentiate themselves in terms of the audits they do. Clients are more disposed to threaten to switch auditors even if, in practice, they rarely do (Greenwood, Cooper, Hinings and Brown, 1993).

As Wooton, Tonge and Wolk (1990) point out, the growing maturity of the audit industry internationally, together with the removal of strictures against advertising, has made competition between accounting firms more vigorous. This is echoed by Russell Palmer, formerly CEO of Touche Ross International, when he noted:

> The maturation of the professional . . . can be seen in fierce price competition that, not long ago, would have been considered undignified. The fighting is almost hand-to-hand between firms that, trying to secure footholds in companies, offer to conduct audits at the lowest possible cost.
>
> (1990, p. 85)

As audit becomes more of a commodity the relationship between the client and the accounting firm becomes more commercialized. In our own research an important and long-standing client asked its auditors to produce a short statement stating why they should be reappointed as auditors and what value their audit added compared with any other auditing firm. As recently as the late 1980s the audit was accepted by clients as a necessity and therefore required little or no questioning. Now the accounting firm has to produce justifications to the client.

Another market change that reduces the demand for traditional accounting services has been the mergers and acquisitions activity of the 1980s and 1990s. For the audit core it means that there are less large clients again producing more competition and lower profit margins. But mergers are a two-edged sword, as they have increased the market for other services such as valuations, insolvency and consulting.

Growth in the demand for other business services

The demand for extensions and additions to traditional audit and accounting services has been going on for quite some time, but really picked up speed in the 1980s and 1990s (*Business Week*, 1988; *The Economist*, 1988; *Fortune*, 1998). Clients have looked for more general business advice on strategy, restructuring, and various new ideas about organizing such as TQM, reengineering, EVA and help with introducing management information systems such as SAP and Peoplesoft. This has resulted in a rapid growth in demand for management consultancy services and associated work in information technology. Similarly, clients are requiring more accounting work, which is of a business advice nature such as corporate restructuring, insolvency, valuation and tax advice. Also, litigation support and forensic accounting services have emerged together with the recent development of environmental accounting (Lawrence, 1993). These market developments produce a great deal of special work that is very profitable and highly competitive. In addition, the major accounting firms are in the process of becoming law firms, adding law practices to their already wide range of services. In the merger between Price Waterhouse and Coopers and Lybrand, and also in the proposed and failed merger of KPMG and Ernst and Young, the announcement did not mention traditional accounting services, but emphasized synergies in consulting and industry specialization. All of this has culminated in these firms dropping their description as accounting firms and speaking of themselves as 'business advisory firms' and 'professional service firms'.

Globalization

There is also the development of 'globalization' (Aharoni, 1993a). For a long time the Big Five accounting firms, and their predecessors, have prided themselves on their international coverage and their ability to provide the same quality of audit service to a client anywhere in the world. Increasingly, the largest manufacturing and service firms have moved from being multinationals to being truly international as they begin to lose a close connection with a specific country (Nohria and Ghoshal, 1997). These international large clients demand a wide range of services deliverable anywhere in the world. They require more systematic links with the professional service firms that serve them. When Thorne Ernst and Whinney (TEW) was created in Canada in the mid-1980s, they stated:

International strength is increasingly important. . . . To serve its clients effectively, wherever their operations are located, any major CA firm must be able to draw upon a strong network of associated professionals around the globe.

(TEW, 1986, p. 1)

Accounting firms are repeatedly stressing the growing internationalization of business and the necessity of accounting firms to follow suit. Being large is associated with tight and extensive international coverage. The largest accounting firms see their market dominance as built on their international reach and strong linkages with multinational organizations. And much of their recent growth, and the impulse for mergers has come from a stated strategy of providing 'one-stop shopping' and 'seamless' service to their multinational clients who are the major users of their services. As their business is dependent on what is happening in other organizations, accounting firms have been affected by what has been happening to their clients. This has included the impact of the mergers and takeover activity of the 1980s and the internationalization of an increasing number of clients.

Institutional dynamics

Accounting firms operate within regulated environments, where institutional entry is defined and controlled by professional gatekeepers (the accounting professions), the state (government departments concerned with occupations and professions) and other bodies (such as market regulators). These institutional gatekeepers could either block some of the effects of the market dynamics or help in the restructuring of the sector. To examine this we need to look at the legitimacy of the profession and its activities, and the role of professional associations.

The attack on the legitimacy of the accounting profession and firms

The role and purpose of audit have come under scrutiny in the last decade. As *The Economist* (1992, p. 19) put it, 'an audit of auditors would be scathing. They have missed impending company collapses and become too close to company managers'. The same refrain is heard in the USA and Canada (*Report on Business Magazine*, 1998). The response of the accounting profession and the Big Five firms is defensive, citing an expectations gap. Part of the decreasing legitimacy of what auditors do is fuelled by speculation that auditing may have become a 'loss-leader' in order to pull in special services for the other parts of the firm. There has been an increase in litigation against accounting firms that has become so severe in the USA that the Big Six produced a joint statement in 1992 which began by saying 'The tort liability system in the United States is out of control' (Statement of Position, 1992, p. 1). The role and probity of the accounting profession is under scrutiny. This scrutiny has been reinforced in the USA and Britain by the actions of government appointed regulatory watchdogs. In the USA the SEC has been examining the role of accountants, especially with regard to audits. In Britain the Thatcher government became involved in a general examination of professional bodies as part of attempts to break their monopolies.

The role of the professional associations

The various chartered accountants' institutes regulate individuals, not firms. Their concern is with ensuring that accountants are properly educated and trained and that they act with probity in the public interest. But with the increasing task complexity of accounting firms, issues are raised about education and training. In the Western world, the various bodies have recognized the changing nature of the accountants' world in a number of ways. One is by diversifying themselves, moving away from a concentration on audit and accounting and recognizing the wide range of activities that accountants are now involved in. In Canada, for example, the CICA introduced the notion of 'Interest Groups' covering, inter alia, business advisory services, information technology, environmental management (Gaston, 1992). This is the accounting profession reaching beyond the core disciplines of accounting, auditing and tax. It is recognition of the changing nature of the accounting firm, particularly the larger ones, and legitimating those changes. These actions also legitimize and encourage the move of accountants into related fields and attempt to maintain the certi-fication control of that body.

Another response has been for the professional associations to formally examine their role and purpose, coming up with strategic visions and mission statements, which, again, emphasize their generic role as business advisors rather than their specific role as accountants. Allied to this is the continuing search for mergers between the various accounting professions to present a stronger, united front.

The recomposition of the organizational field and the pressure for a new archetype

So, there are a number of changes taking place in the institutional context of accounting firms among them being increasing scrutiny of the role and probity of the profession; an increasing diversification of services; and an emphasis on the firm as more general business advisors. In these market and institutional dynamics we begin to see a recomposition of the organizational field of accounting. DiMaggio (1991, p. 267) suggests that the question of where organizational fields come from has received inadequate attention in institutional theory. We are suggesting that the external unfolding of new market conditions and the similar unfolding of institutional changes are all part of sectoral restructuring and that, in a heavily institutionalized environment, there has to be a process of deinstitutionalization and reinstitutionalization around new organizational forms.

Powell (1991, pp. 199–200) suggests that institutional change comes from a number of sources, including the recomposition of organizational fields. What we see happening for large accounting firms is the recomposition of the organizational field. As Powell (1991, p. 200) puts it:

> When the structure of fields changes in such a profound fashion, established organizations scurry to protect their interests and to reestablish rules and practices that favour the status quo. But boundary changes also bring upstarts to the fore and create the possibility for a redefinition of rules and assumptions that favour newcomers or challengers at the expense of incumbents.

Professional service firms in accounting are reviewing their fields as they seek to re-establish their growth trajectories and feel compelled to broaden the range of services offered. In doing so, the emergence of new specializations and the escalating importance (from a revenue generating standpoint) of others (especially management consultancy) is leading to the reconsideration of licensing arrangements, training and career patterns, and the creation of a business services organizational field. A number of the major accounting firms are defining themselves publicly as 'business advisors'. In 1988, one of the (then) Big Eight had a mission statement which stated:

> To be known by Key Decision-makers as the Leading Provider of Distinctive, Creative Business Advisory Services of Superior Quality delivered by Teams of Skilled Individuals adding Significant Value to the Performance of Our Clients.

The emphasis here is on business advice; there is no mention of accounting. What we see is the development of capabilities in new services, all of which derive initially from accounting, but increasingly move further away from that core definition of the firm. Redefinition has been and is occurring in the individual members of the Big Six (recently become the Big Five).

Essentially, accounting firms have been diversifying at an increasing pace. Diversification is of two kinds. One is the move into allied accounting fields, e.g., forensic accounting, corporate restructuring. The other is the move into allied non-accounting fields, in particular management consulting. These fields involve hiring non-accountants and this is part of redefining the institutional field. Accounting firms have moved from a sole concern with audit, accounting and tax, to adding insolvency and corporate restructuring practices, management consulting, forensic accounting, personal financial planning, and environmental accounting. Lawrence (1993) shows how firms move into forensic and environmental accounting and then develop institutionalization strategies to legitimate their professional role. Accounting firms are struggling to cope with the rapid growth of a demand for management consultancy services at a time when demand for their traditional staple, accounting and audit services is growing slowly (*Business Week*, 1988; *The Economist*, 1988; *Fortune*, 1998).

The institutional context contains the historically legitimated practices and strategic recipes which inform the sector, generally, and individual organizations, specifically. Amongst other things, these recipes and practices contain prescriptions and proscriptions about acceptable organizational structures, systems and ways of managing (Hinings and Greenwood, 1988b). It is the interaction between the market and institutional contexts which encourages or discourages the emergence of new archetypes and defines what those archetypes are. We now have to address the question of how these market and institutional dynamics have led to pressures to alter existing, professionally based, organizational practices.

The managed professional business

Accounting firms, then, have been subject to increasing competition, locally, nationally, and internationally and the institutional context has been one that encouraged a positive response to those market pressures. What are their strategic responses and how do these translate into organizational terms? Strategically, growth has always been central to the strategy of large accounting firms. While the language of 'market share' is not always formally used, it is a key element.

An important and obvious change resulting from the search for growth has been the emergence of larger and larger firms since the 1970s. In that time accounting firms have moved from the Big Ten, to the Big Eight, to the Big Six and, most recently, the Big Five. This has produced firms which are very large multinationals employing over 100,000 people and billing billions of dollars. They are highly geographically dispersed within any one country and throughout the world. KPMG, for example, has 750 offices in 127 different countries. This kind of scale immediately poses the question of their effect on the internal organization and operation of the P^2 form. Much existing organization theory would argue that the impact of increasing scale is to produce more specialization, standardization, formalization and decentralization, all of which may be inimical to common sense conceptions of the professional partnership. The 'second tier' of firms (e.g, Grant Thornton, BDO) have followed a similar, but more muted growth path.

As part of this growth, non-accountant professionals have been added to the firms. Most are in 'line' positions, such as tax lawyers, management consultants, IT professionals, while others are staff, including marketers and human resource managers. The addition of other professional services and staff challenges the P^2 form. So, the internal unfolding of the accounting task in itself produces pressures that emphasize management as an issue, especially strategic management, and except in the most hegemonic industry sector, there will always be alternative organizational forms (Kondra and Hinings, 1998).

What is the emerging alternative to the P^2 form in large accounting firms? We have called it the Managed Professional Business (Cooper *et al.*, 1996). Each word is important; it is still professional in the sense that its core work is carried out by professionals. But there is an increasing emphasis on the fact that it is a business and that it has to be systematically managed. Table 7.1 outlines the elements of the MPB.

What kind of *interpretive* scheme underpins this archetype? The developing underlying common orientation is to see the accounting firm as a business. Of course, professional service firms have always been businesses in the sense that they are economic units who sell services to clients and make profits from those services. But the partners and other professionals have usually defined themselves as being in a special kind of business. This new orientation tends to be exemplified by statements like 'we are a business like any other business', i.e., *it de-emphasizes difference* from other economic entities.

There are a number of other words and phrases which are part of this alternative interpretive scheme. They are 'productivity', 'client service', 'competition', 'marketing and growth strategies', 'cross-selling' and 'rational-ization'. Of course, all of these are commonplace nouns and adjectives in, e.g., a retail store, a consumer products manufacturer or a printer. But they are quite unusual in the P^2 form. They represent the importation of the language and style of business. To have a strategy and to use marketing would still be regarded as unnecessary and even as 'unprofessional' by some accountants. In this new interpretive scheme there is much less concern with governance or professionalism *per se*. Governance through partnership may even be seen as something that gets in the way of efficiency. Recently KPMG in the USA has floated the idea of turning their management consulting practice into a public company (and have hired an investment bank to look at the possibility). In the MPB, professionalism is taken for granted. The keys are efficiency and effectiveness and an important way of achieving this is through rationalization of structures.

The *systems* to support the MPB introduce a strong, top–down, analytical strategic capability.

Strategic control becomes much more important. Systems are designed to increase rationality. There are attempts to look beyond one year of operation and data begins to be assembled to help guide decision-making. It is not the formal use of analysis and scanning that one would find in many corporations, but strategic planning processes are put in place within national units and attempts are also made to produce international strategies. Decision-making becomes somewhat more directive. The Managed Professional Business introduces, rationalizes and bureaucratizes the process of strategic planning. This is not a wholesale adoption of corporate practices; it is the introduction of management systems to help guide professional activity.

Market-financial control becomes more central to the operation of the firm. Not only do specific targets remain for financial purposes, but market targets are introduced. The focus on client service means that mechanisms for monitoring client relationships are introduced, including client satisfaction surveys. At the level of the international firm, client management systems are set up to ensure that a major client is served the same way in Bangkok, Sydney or Vancouver. The degree of tolerance for missing targets reduces and there are real attempts to adopt a more long-term time horizon, although without compromising the short term.

Operating control also changes in the MPB archetype. The range of corporate involvement increases as planning, marketing and human resource functions are seen as more vital to the operation of the firm. There is still an important and primary focus on quality standards. But increasing attention is paid to the compensation of partners. In this archetype, there is more emphasis on inequality in compensation, tied to performance. In fact, compensation issues often come to the fore. One of the problems that professional service firms have to deal with is that partner contributions to profit vary (Morris, 1992a). In the P^2 archetype there may well be seniority based lockstep profit allocations. In the Managed Professional Business where the partnership is more concerned with present and future economic return than past and present professional contribution, performance related compensation systems are introduced.

Along with this goes a move to more centralization. Firms will now appoint a chief operating officer, one of whose tasks is to scrutinize in detail the performance of offices and individual partners and take action where necessary. Centralization is also seen in the new client management systems where a lead partner is appointed with strong responsibility for directing partners in other offices, setting fee levels and hours to be worked.

Structurally, differentiation increases in two ways. There is more professional specialization, a result of strategic and marketing emphases and the idea of differentiated markets. And the emphasis on effectiveness and efficiency leads to the beginnings of functional specialization as marketing and human resource specialists are introduced to the firm. However, this is done in a particular way. While these non-accounting specialists enter the firm, they are still under professional control. Almost without exception there will be an accountant designated as the 'personnel partner' or the 'marketing partner' to serve as a channel of communication to other partners. There is less ability to build personal roles and more bureaucratic definition of them, i.e., less spontaneous internal differentiation.

Structural *integration* is increased in a number of ways. Hierarchy becomes more important with the development of 'partners-in-charge' or practice heads of what are, in effect, departments. These PICs have responsibility for the business plans of their units (e.g., audit, tax, insolvency, financial advisory services, small business, information technology, management consulting) and for the evaluation of other partners and all staff. More teams develop to deal with 'cross-selling' between specialist areas. Coordination and control is a more bureaucratized process. As a result, more rules and procedures are introduced.

To some extent this description of the MPB may seem like an incremental step from the P^2 archetype. This is not the case and it highlights the rationale for the concept of archetype and the emphasis on the underpinning nature of interpretive schemes. For example, the initial introduction of marketing into a professional service firm is not 'just' adding a function; it has to be undergirded with a new way of conceptualizing the relationship of the firm to its clients and environment generally. Similarly, introducing a partner in charge of other partners is a crucial break with the value of equity in governance and it has to be led by a change in interpretive scheme. Hinings *et al.* (1991) show how the introduction of what could seem like quite minor managerial changes from a corporate perspective failed in an accounting firm because they were seen as radical in the way they challenged existing interpretations of governance and professionalism. So the MPB archetype represents a real break with past practice.

The dynamics of change

The fact that an alternative archetype has emerged and has achieved a degree of legitimacy, both among large accounting firms and within the profession generally, does not mean that it will be adopted either uniformly or easily. The dynamics of the change process involved in moving from the P^2 archetype to the Managed Professional Business are potentially complex. At the basis of this process is the configuration of values, interests, power and capability (Hinings and Greenwood, 1988a; Greenwood and Hinings, 1996). And these configurations arise from the internal differentiation of these accounting firms into a multiplicity of different groups. There is something of a paradox here. The very processes of growth through diversification that have produced greater internal complexity and the drive for the new MPB form, through that very complexity can make the adoption of the new form more difficult.

It is internal differentiation that lies at the heart of the political nature of organizations. Much of the work on differentiation and conflict in organizations (Lawrence and Lorsch, 1967; Nystrom, 1986) shows how technical boundaries between departments and sections are reinforced and buttressed by cognitive boundaries. These different organizational groups are likely to have alternative ways of viewing the purposes of the organization, the ways in which it might be appropriately organized and how actions might be evaluated. In accounting firms, historically, this has been seen in the tensions between accountants and management consultants but the potential for more tension increases because of internal complexity. One aspect that has been introduced recently has been the introduction of support specialists such as marketers and human resources personnel who define themselves as professionals. The diversity that comes from extending the range of services of professional firms and the introduction of other professionals increases the potential for political activity.

Of course, a political model of organizational change not only starts from groups with different beliefs and interests, it also incorporates power (Clegg, 1989). Organizationally defined groups vary in their ability to influence organizational change; they have differential power. Some groups and individuals are listened to more keenly than others. Some have more or less potential for enabling or resisting change. The relations of power and domination which enable some organizational members to constitute and recreate organizational structures according to their preferences thus becomes a critical point of focus (Pettigrew, 1985; Ranson *et al.*, 1980; Walsh *et al.*, 1981). The operation of values, interests and power can only be conceptualized and understood in relation to these differentiated groups.

Clearly, our approach suggests that the changes in market and institutional context are dynamics that push for changes in organization and management within accounting firms. But what is it that will precipitate change inside these firms? For change to even be on the agenda two things have to be in place. One is that there has to be a certain level of dissatisfaction with existing approaches to management by some group or groups. The other is that there has to be some articulation of an alternative approach to management by some group or groups. These are *interests* and *values* and we call them *precipitating dynamics* because they start and give direction to an organizational response to contextual pressures.

Precipitating dynamics

Interests

One of the dynamic elements in reacting to contextual pressures is the satisfactions and dissatisfactions of groups and individuals with the existing distribution of resources (in a broad sense), and their motivation to enhance or sustain their shares of scarce and valued resources. The notion of interests refers both to the distribution of scarce resources and to the orientation and motivation of members to maintain and enhance their sectional claims. Within the organizational literature the notion of interests has appeared only sporadically, but the structure of an organization represents a differentiation of functional tasks from which there flows a distribution of scarce resources. The process of functional specialization distinguishes one set of organizational incumbents from another by differentially affording them scarce wealth, status and authority; built into the organization is a structure of advantage and disadvantage (Pettigrew, 1973; Benson, 1977; Walsh *et al.*, 1981). Interests are concerned with the aims of functionally discrete groups to secure a sufficient and fair share of organizational resources and are expressed through a motivation to enhance or defend a particular distribution of those resources.

This image of an organization as an aggregation of groups locked in battle for scarce resources can be overstated. There are always circumstances that limit, or hold in check, the nature of the struggle. But organizations are composed of groups with their own perceived interests, which motivate them to struggle for a favourable pattern of resource allocations. And the intensity of the struggle and the pressure for change in existing allocative mechanisms will be a function of the amount of dissatisfaction with the share of resources going to particular groups. The number of dissatisfied groups and the intensity of their dissatisfaction can be a critical dynamic of change.

In accounting firms the introduction of new services leads to increased conflict over resources. Greater internal differentiation produces increased conflict between groups (Langhorn and Hinings, 1987). It happens in two ways. The first is that the introduction of a new service represents an investment decision and resources have to be allocated to support it in the early stages. This has occurred with decisions to introduce services such as forensic and environmental accounting, executive search, and in the drive to open up offices in countries such as Russia, China and other Eastern European and South East Asian countries (Cooper *et al.*, 1998). The first of these, introducing new services, is also related to the decline in profitability of some established services, e.g., audit, and that of others increasing, e.g., insolvency, management consulting. As a result there are attempts to reallocate resources of accommodation and staff, and the prestige that goes along with this. In accounting firms that have individualistic 'eat-what-you-kill' values underlying their compensation systems, interest dissatisfaction will be high when the system fails to respond to new patterns of revenue and profit generation.

Recently, two major 'fault lines' have developed in accounting firms as interests diverge between groups. The first, and most publicized, is that between accounting groups and management consulting groups. At the moment, in Andersen Worldwide, there is a dispute between the consultants and accountants which is before the courts and threatens to split the firm completely. The consultants feel that their contribution to the firm is not properly recognized in the way in which resources of compensation, authority, and status are distributed in the firm. There are similar disputes in most firms, but it is particularly strong in Andersen because of the very large differences in work between the consultants and accountants. Andersen attempted to cope with these tensions in 1988 by dividing the organization into two business units, Arthur Andersen and Andersen Consulting.

The other division is between young and old. Under the P^2 model, older partners, e.g., over 55, who had contributed in the past, but were no longer making a substantial financial contribution were allowed to 'retire' gracefully by involving themselves in the activities of professional associations and generally running down their work life. This fits with the values of collegiality and partnership. But with the pressures of the late 1980s and 1990s to produce, younger partners have shown themselves to be unwilling to support their older colleagues, given that they are pressured more and more to develop new clients, cross-sell, and be ready to work with major clients anywhere in the world at a moment's notice. So, the Big Five have 'downsized' older partners; revamped compensation systems; examined pension systems. There is a constant tension around the issue of producing over a lifetime and within this partnership itself may become less desirable.

One further tension over interests which is not yet as well developed as the others, but with the introduction of the MPB is likely to get stronger, is between line professionals and staff professionals. The P^2 does not have the line–staff distinction; the MPB does. There are two particular functions that are developed, one being marketing and the other human resource management. As large accounting firms become more strategically and managerially focused in delivering a wide range of integrated services, so marketing moves from an activity which is the responsibility of every partner, to one which is driven from a central unit selling the firm as an entity (Greenwood, Hinings, Brown and Cooper, 1997). Also, as these firms have grown they have needed HR managers to deal with the large numbers of support staff and, latterly, to introduce and coordinate managerial education and training. Both marketing and HR staff identify themselves as professionals, as experts in their own particular areas, but often find that they are not given what they see as their 'due' in expertise. And, both groups are committed to introducing the MPB.

Values

Values are the commitments of groups and individuals in an organization to particular interpretive schemes, i.e., that of the P^2 or the MPB. There are four patterns of commitment that could be found in accounting firms:

1   widespread commitment to the P^2 interpretive scheme (status quo);
2   widespread commitment to the MPB interpretive scheme (reformative);
3   low commitment to either the P^2 or the MPB (indifference);
4   substantial commitment by different groups to both the P^2 and MPB (competition).

It is important to emphasize that *it is groups and individuals* who have commitments. This keeps in the forefront the political nature of change and stability. Our research suggests that many accounting firms are moving into situations of competitive commitment (Greenwood, Hinings and Cooper, 1999). On the one hand there are the proponents of status quo interpretive schemes, emphasizing the validity and necessity of professionalism and partnership with its value components of individuality, autonomy, participation in decision-making, and local domains. On the other hand there is the alternative interpretive scheme of a more corporate approach incorporating values of collectivity, executive action, bureaucratic rules, national and international arenas of activity. Since the 1980s there has been increasing questioning both externally and internally of the management and operation of these firms, producing alternative values for interpreting the nature of the organizational context and the meaning of professionalism and partnership.

Because internal diversity has been increasing, various kinds of coalitions arise. The MPB is likely to be embraced by the newcomers to the system, such as those in management consultancy, corporate valuations, mergers and acquisitions in accounting firms. It is also being voiced by those with responsibility for the overall management of a firm, and sometimes by younger partners. It is particularly those in support and managerial positions and with national and international responsibilities who interpret the organizational context as requiring more strategic direction, marketing expertise, and central direction. It is more likely to be the auditors and tax accountants who will be committed to the P^2 form of organizing.

The existence of competitive commitments challenges and destabilizes organizational arrangements. Such a challenge may result in a reorientation if the challenging interpretive scheme becomes dominant. However, the change initiated may be aborted or unresolved if the supporters of the prevailing interpretive scheme successfully resist change. While the Big Five accounting firms are at somewhat different stages, all of them exhibit competitive commitments but with the challenging interpretive scheme becoming dominant. We see this in the appointments made since the mid-1990s to senior positions locally, nationally, and internationally. It is at the local, operational partner level that most commitment to the P^2 archetype is found. The partner fallout from the mega-mergers of 1989 and the 'layoffs' of the early 1990s have reduced the numbers of those vocally committed to the old archetype.

Any major change in an organization illustrates the interconnection between values and interests and an important research question is to unravel this connection. Changes towards a more managerial and corporate form of organization in accounting firms are usually formulated in value, strategic, and efficiency terms, e.g., achieving service excellence, becoming number one, relating better to clients and so on. Underlying these phrases are economic goals of 'market share', increased partner income, greater profitability of services. The initial consequences of these in terms of organizational change are to alter the distribution of resources between organizational groups. As the process of reallocation takes place, e.g., from audit to management consulting, so the balance of satisfaction and dissatisfaction will alter. Dissatisfaction with resource distribution in an accounting firm will itself be expressed in value and efficiency/effectiveness terms. A particularly difficult reallocation to deal with is that from principal professional roles to managerial and service support roles, something that we regard as increasingly under discussion in accounting firms.

Enabling dynamics

The particular configuration of interests and values in an accounting firm, along with the contextual pressures, will precipitate change, giving it a direction. Dissatisfaction over the existing distribution of resources means that those dissatisfied organizational members look for alternative ways of organizing. With commitments leaning towards the Managed Professional Business, a potential direction is given to that change.

In short, our argument so far is that different groups within accounting firms are likely to have different interests to enhance or defend and espouse different values for change or stability. With an increase in the number of distinct groups within these firms, the room for the interplay of different values and interests is increased. But in any such interplay some groups' values dominate and their interests predominate, whereas those of others are sub-dominant or repressed (Alford, 1975). Organizational arrangements are constituted in accordance with members' values and interests; but the act of organizational design is the privilege of *some*, not all, organizational actors. To understand why this happens requires us to examine how certain groups are enabled by their position in an organization to effect change. Some voices are heard, others are ignored.

So, what is it that enables some views to win out, to be enabled, to actually start change in a particular direction? As a starting point we argue that there are two generic dynamics to the process of being heard and prevailing in the political struggle: power and capability.

Power

Power is a capacity to determine outcomes and structures are used to obtain and utilize power (Hickson *et al.*, 1971; Pfeffer, 1981). Existing powerful groups are frequently tied to prevailing values and resource distributions because these are the basis of their power. In accounting firms audit groups still retain a central role both because of their regulatory underpinning and the way all accounting training is centred on this function. As Starbuck, Greve and Hedberg (1978), Tushman and Romanelli (1985) and Miller (1990) show, powerful actors remain committed to prevailing values and interests in the face of internal and external pressures to change, because doing so serves their interests.

The suggestion is that those in power at any given time are usually committed to the status quo. This may be because, for example, audit partners act to maintain their own values and interests which are well served by the existing arrangements. A somewhat different interpretation is that such powerful partners are captured by prevailing modes of thought and are unable to visualize a different way of operating. Whichever interpretation is more plausible in a particular situation, they both touch directly on the importance of power and the ability to control decision premises as a key dynamic or suppressor of change.

Our use of power as a dynamic of change rests upon a distinction between the extent to which power in an organization is relatively dispersed between a multiplicity of groups, rather than focused and concentrated within a narrowly drawn coalition or elite. This is the distinction between a *concentrated* power structure and a dispersed one. With concentrated power there is restricted access to key decision processes and information sources; power is in the hands of an elite. A *dispersed* power structure has more open access to decisions and information; a variety of organizational groups have access to power.

Hinings *et al.* (1991) and Blau (1984) have shown in professional accounting firms and architectural practices that the partnership form of ownership makes strategic change difficult because of the individualized, autonomous nature of power. But, increasingly in the Big Five accounting firms this dispersed power structure has been changed in a more concentrated direction. The change, however, has been towards concentration in the hands of auditors. Increasingly this is under attack towards a new form of dispersion, between different groups. Some of the publicized accounts have centred on battles between audit and consultancy, especially in Arthur Andersen.

The power structure is especially important where there is a competitive commitment to alternative interpretive schemes. The interpretive scheme reflected in the organization will be consistent with the ideas and beliefs of the elite where there is a concentrated power structure, e.g., the audit group. In such an organization the power structure acts as an instrument of the elite facilitating the status quo despite opposition. We might also anticipate that a concentrated power structure would enable the elite at least to begin the process of reorientation. A dispersed power structure, however, would not lend itself to an imposed choice. Major change would be unlikely to occur unless there was a widespread commitment to an alternative interpretive scheme (i.e. the reformative commitment).

The important point is that there is not a simple relationship between the two power structures and likelihood or ease of change. It is not the case that a concentrated power structure facilitates change whereas a dispersed power structure is obstructive. A concentrated power structure can facilitate imposed change or obstruct change; which it will be is dependent upon the commitment of the elite to particular interpretive schemes. In one of the biggest accounting firms in Canada there was a '*coup d'état*' in which a group of four stood together for election on a platform of taking the firm into an MPB mode. They won and then, through a concentrated power structure began the process of implementing a new structure and systems that were geared to giving direction to the firm and to collecting information about ongoing performance.

This was a firm which previously had a dispersed power structure, which was able to obstruct change but not facilitate it when commitments became more competitive. It required a shift to a concentrated structure for change to occur. Had there been a reformative commitment already, then a dispersed power structure would have done the job of changing the organization. In short, the role of power is intimately related to the pattern of commitment within the accounting firm.

Capability

Change in an accounting firm is enabled, not just through power, but also by the capabilities and competencies of actors. It is the operation of power that renders a decision on whose interests and values will prevail. However, the further implementation of the requisite values, structures and systems (the new archetype) requires the necessary skills and experience to effect the desired changes. Enabling change involves both behavioural skills and experience, such as leadership and knowledge of change processes, and technical skills and experience, such as knowledge and experience of the new way of organizing, in this case, the Managed Professional Business. In order to introduce new management forms accounting firms require:

1 sufficient skills for the generation of commitment and excitement over the prospect of change; and
2 have an understanding of what it wishes to do (i.e. the nature of the changes to be obtained).

Currently, in accounting firms, there has been increasing concern with the rhetoric of management, and specifically, the Managed Professional Business.

Their strategic recipe is to introduce strategic planning, formal marketing, centralized control in a management committees and specialized, high level, administrative support. Moving an accounting firm from the P^2 to an MPB requires the mobilization of expertise on the technical details of the new archetype and on the processes of change. Child and Smith (1987), in their analysis of transformation at Cadbury's, examine 'the market for the transfer of design concepts and technical knowledge required to effect the transformation of a firm's products, processes or organizational mode' (p. 19). Hinings *et al.* (1991) showed how managerial innovations in an accounting office of a Big Six firm failed because of the lack of technical *expertise* in doing what the new form required, together with the difficulties that one set of accountants had in explaining to other sets how the new organization would work and be better. The issue is understanding how one does strategic planning, human resource management and marketing in a large accounting firm. At the moment this tends to be an arena for experimentation.

In addition, the managerial changes that accounting firms are introducing challenge values about partnership and professionalism that established groups have. Most of the new ideas about organizing emphasize specialization for everyone and a stable departmentalization within the firm. This constitutes a radical challenge to the P^2 form and emphasizes the importance of capability in transformational leadership.

Since the 1980s, strategic, transformational leadership has acquired an important place in analysing change (Tichy and Ulrich, 1984; Pettigrew, 1985; Tushman and Romanelli, 1985; Schein, 1986). Howard (1991) has written in a similar vein for professional service firms. There is a particular emphasis on senior executives as institutionally defined leaders; on leadership as a matter of defining overall values, strategy, and mobilizing commitment to symbols; and of leadership as crucial in major organizational change because it involves restating values, directions and organizational forms. Institutional leaders play a key role in developing, maintaining and altering the interpretive scheme of an organization. As Tichy and Ulrich (1984, pp. 240–241) put it, quite starkly, the transformational leader is 'one who commits people to action, who converts followers into leaders, and who may convert leaders into moral agents'.

Some of the structural and system changes entailed in the interpretive schemes of the MPB are technically difficult to do. Setting up international teams to manage major clients is not easy, especially when there is little teamworking experience. Bringing together partners from Canada, the USA, the UK, Spain, South Africa, the Philippines and Brazil to manage the Coca-Cola relationship creates high levels of diversity in a situation where past practice has been to work independently. Similarly, installing an information system that turns up material on the work that has been done on a particular client regardless of which specialty has carried it out is difficult and requires a lot of investment in hardware and software.

So, the adoption of the MPB requires an accounting firm to have an elite who are committed to that archetype, who have the power to at least begin the process of change, who have themselves, or have access to, technical and behavioural capability in the new archetype and change management, and who can work with enough discontent in the firm to harness it to change. Each of the Big Five start at a different point in the historical process and with a different mix of these factors; all of them have been making moves which are meant to enable change to the MPB archetype. A particular problem for accountants is going beyond seeing their own capability as central to management; the issue for them is recognizing something called 'management' which goes beyond the financial.

Taken together, the existence of particular and specific knowledge and skills and the nature of leadership form what we would call the capability of an organization to achieve change. They enable change to take place or reinforce the status quo.

Summary and conclusions

There is clear evidence that accounting firms are undergoing change at local, national and international levels. To understand what change actually takes place we have to examine the dynamic processes within a firm, which direct and enable that change. These dynamics are based on the pressures from the market and institutional context, the way in which interests and values precipitate and give a direction to change, and the extent to which the distribution of power and the existence of technical and social capability enable that change.

Firm context is conceptualized by partners (and other groups) as a *pressure* for, or initiator of, change. While we would argue that the firms themselves are important actors in creating that context, nonetheless, markets are seen as changing and becoming more threatening. Similarly, the role of these professions is being questioned. However, to understand any response, the pattern of value commitments to existing or alternative interpretive schemes, and the distribution of material interests are conceptualized as *precipitators* of the direction of change. It is from these that we can know whether there are pushes for alternative ways of organizing or not. Power and capability act as *enablers* of the change process: dependencies of power and domination allow the resolution of conflicts between organizational groups over value preferences and sectional interests, and organizational capability enables appropriate competencies to be brought to bear.

Two important general points underlie this approach. One is the importance of conceptualizing values, interests, power and capability as the properties of groups, and our suggestion that much of the change that has occurred incrementally in professional service firms has increased the diversity and visibility of groups. The other is that change (or inertia) can only be understood through the *joint action* of the five basic dynamics. It is not a matter of modelling their individual contribution to change, but of showing how they combine in different ways to allow or block change.

Context does not operate independently upon organizational forms but is interpreted through filters or meanings and aspirations (Ford and Baucus, 1987). The distribution of power is not disconnected, either from that context or from interpretive schemes or organizational arrangements. In particular, where there is a competitive pattern of value commitments the role of power will determine which interpretive scheme is utilized to order structural arrangements. Furthermore, the extent to which a destabilized organization progresses along a path of change or becomes stuck between beginning and end points will be a function of organizational capacity. The particular direction followed, in other words, will depend upon the manner in which changes occur in one or more of the dynamics and the triggered response in the others.

This chapter has argued that the market and institutional pressures in the world of the Big Five accounting firms have led, since the 1980s, to the emergence of an alternative archetype, the Managed Professional Business, to the historical archetype, the P^2 form. Indeed, the P^2 form is being destabilized and greater legitimacy is being given to the MPB. It is clear from our research that all of the Big Five are to a greater or lesser degree moving towards this new archetype. But it is a difficult (and painful) process. We have attempted to outline some of those dynamic processes at work. For the new archetype to succeed, the reorienting organization requires powerful actors committed to new ideas and the organizational capability to implement them.

A few cautionary remarks are in order. Accounting is made up of six giant multinationals, which are located in most countries in the world and tend to be very geographically spread within those countries. Being a multinational is also producing pressures for the development of a Managed Professional Business. Being geographically spread makes centralized control difficult. As is always the case with pressures for change, and responses to those pressures, there are always contradictions and unintended consequences of the action taken. An important research task is to examine these. To do it requires something of a refocusing of much of our thinking about change; it requires conceptualizing it as, first, a very uneven process (no neat stages), and second, as an inherently political and conflictual process.

A second remark is that we are clearly writing about large organizations relative to their sector. There are small accounting firms specializing either in particular service, e.g., forensic accounting, mergers and acquisitions, small business, or in particular localities. It is the large firms which are under pressure to restructure to the new archetype. Of course, these firms are dominant in the industry in terms of fee volume, relations with large corporations and training of future accountants. An interesting area of research would be the so-called 'second tier' accounting firms.

One further cautionary remark is that the analysis we are putting forward is most appropriate to English-speaking countries where there is a considerable degree of similarity of accounting practices. In non-English speaking countries the picture may well change. For example, there are countries where accounting firms are not allowed to be involved in management consultancy because of a perceived conflict of interest. What becomes interesting here, as the Big Five accounting firms strive to become more integrated as international firms, is how they cope with these differences of code and culture.

While the Managed Professional Business may not look like a 'new' organization from the viewpoint of an organization theorist, from the vantage point of a partner in an accounting firm it is very different. And it is the interpretive scheme component, in particular, that defines that difference. As a number of partners have said to us, in the new organizational world partnership doesn't mean anything anymore. Partners are merely highly paid employees. Nothing could be a more indicative statement about the possible demise of the P^2 form and the emergence of the MPB.

8 Professionals organizing professionals

Comparing the logic of United States and United Kingdom law practice

John Flood

Introduction

> Once you've got a major client, the rest follow like sheep. You can be a lousy lawyer, but if they like you, they'll come. It's the herd instinct. Look, if I'm general counsel of a large corporation, no one can criticize me if I retain Kirkland and Ellis. It doesn't have anything to do with how good they are, just how big they are. So you take a risk when you hire someone smaller.
>
> (Tischmann, Senior Attorney)

This partner was rationalizing his success in obtaining clients, keeping them and using them as a means of acquiring the mantle of senior partner as soon as the current senior partner retired. While this is a common feature of corporate law practice in the United States, it has not been the driving force behind United Kingdom law firms. But I will argue that English large law firms are now becoming captive to the same forces as American firms. For example, to balance the quotation above, an English planning lawyer was described thus:

> 'All my friends are my clients,' [Cooper] claims. 'I don't have a private life.' That is the only possible explanation for the fact that he personally billed £1.75m last year.... That means that Cooper's department ... billing £2.4m, was responsible for more than ten per cent of ... Gouldens' gross fees last year ... Cooper claims that he probably works 4,500 and 5,000 billable hours a year – which boils down to between 12 and 13 hours *every single* day of the year – and an average of nearly £400 an hour if based on a strict hourly basis. 'Work it out,' he challenges, 'I start at 7a.m. and start charging, charging, charging.'
>
> (Dillon, 1992, p. 25)

The stereotypical American law firm organization followed the principles laid down by Cravath early in the twentieth century (Swaine, 1946; Nelson, 1988; Galanter and Palay, 1991). Those who aspire to partnership in the firm must undergo a tournament with each other to establish who will win the prize of election to membership. Associates embark on a range of cases over a seven or eight year period at which time they are evaluated. If they succeed, they become partners; if they fail, they must leave the firm. Within this partnership model inhered the values of collegiality and the sharing of profits and losses. Indeed, it went further as liability was unlimited, as befitted a professional. The prime capital a lawyer possesses is human, which consists of skills, experience, reputation and relationships with clients (Galanter and Palay, 1991, pp. 89–90). When lawyers have surplus capital, the firm hires more associates to absorb the surplus, thus intensifying the tournament.

English law firms have not typically followed the Cravath pattern. Histories of the City law firms (e.g., Slinn, 1984; Dennett, 1989; St George, 1995) show a more benign form of collegial dictatorship which operated by restricting the size of the partnership and relying on unqualified clerks for some areas of work. However, cultural patterns of organization in English firms have altered and in many ways become similar to the American model.[1] But the transformation has not been complete, nor is it likely to be so. There is a range of institutional factors that militate against the assimilation of the two legal professions. Among these are differences in legal education, formal distinctions between different units of the legal profession (e.g., barristers and solicitors), regulation of unauthorized practice e.g., the practice of law is more tightly regulated in the US (cf. Rhode, 1981) and relationship of the profession to the state (Abbott, 1988; Johnson, 1993; Baldwin, 1998). And finally their developments have not been isochronal with each other (Flood, 1989).

If we historicize organizational practice among lawyers, we cannot omit the roles of professionalism and professionalization. Ideas surrounding the concepts of collegiality, development of expertise, incorporation, unlimited liability, multi-disciplinary practice, ethical standards are either deeply embedded in or sometimes antithetical to professionalism (cf. Greenwood *et al.*, 1990). These are continuing tensions that professional service firms tackle, or, in other terms, 'organizational change represents not so much a shift from one archetype to another, but a layering of one archetype on another' (Cooper *et al.*, 1996, p. 624).

In this chapter I examine the relationship of work and organization in American and British law firms, which I argue is reflexive (see Flood, 1996). For the purposes of this analysis professionalism is treated as an epiphenomenon while the assertion of power and authority in law firms is treated as a dependent variable which can be explained by the network of client relations in the firm and the ways work is distributed. This goes beyond a view dependent solely on the internal workings of the firm. Of course the wider, ever-changing environment is crucial to how law firms function.[2] Corporate law firms are products of histories, ideologies, cognitive scripts and reclaimed narratives that persist through time (cf. Powell and DiMaggio, 1991; Greenwood and Hinings, 1996). But here I look more towards work than external effects, such as the state. I use two main sources of data, namely, an ethnographic study of corporate lawyers in Chicago (Flood, 1987) and interview studies of City lawyers in London, especially in relation to the market for advocacy services (Flood, 1996; Flood *et al.*, 1996). The first case study focuses on the work of lawyers in general; the second concentrates on one sphere of activity, namely, litigation and advocacy. These two studies are quite different, both in method and scope, and are obviously not comparable *pari passu*, but they serve to illustrate differences across the US–UK divide in intra-law firm organization and the role of lawyers *vis-à-vis* clients. From these perspectives they are informative and complementary. In both studies I have taken a small slice of lawyers' work and relationships and investigated these in depth and used them to make a more general point about the manner in which lawyers present or articulate their organizations and attempt to represent distinctiveness. In both, the client is the point of convergence. In the first case study the client is seen as a means to power in the firm. In the second the client is instrumental in the redistribution of work between two sectors of the profession and the way that bears on a solicitor's place in the firm.

Large law firms are intrinsically risk prone enterprises, always in competition with other professional service providers – e.g., accounting firms, investment banks, consultants – for clients, both domestically and internationally. Risk is also present in the structure of law firms, since partnership connotes sets of constrained choices that are based not on office but on perceptions by others that some partners will necessarily have more symbolic capital available to them which confers privilege and status. This idea of risk permeates through the organization and, as Beck writes, 'coping with risk can include a *reorganization of power and authority* (1992, p. 24). For example, the major change in the firms' relationships with clients over the past twenty years has been the shift from long-term, embedded, comprehensive relationships to shorter-term transactional interaction (Nelson, 1988). Rather than use a single law firm for all legal matters, clients shop around for expertise drawing on different firms for various skills. How the selecting is done is open to question. In some cases the selection is not strictly objective insofar as it is based on the single criterion of being the right firm for the job. There is an element of spreading the work among 'favourite' law firms to keep them happy.[3] Joe Flom said, perhaps disingenuously, of his firm, Skadden Arps:

> We are building a series of boutiques, or specialists, in individual areas with enough overall strength in terms of quantity so that we can put 30 or 40 people to work on an emergency basis without destroying the continuing business of the firm. . . . If you are lucky and get the people working together on a transactional basis, it works quite well. When I say transactional basis, and I think this is the essence of where corporate practice is going, people are coming in for specific transactions. They are not looking for somebody who is in the same clubs that they are in. They are looking for somebody who will do a particular job, and do it well.
>
> (Federal Bar Council, 1984, pp. 95–6)

Therefore the ability to sustain client links over the long term is essential for partners who wish to claim authority within their firms, that is, partners have to work continually to maintain their domination over other lawyers (Bourdieu, 1990, p. 129).

Professional service firms are not simply constellations of diverse interests that mingle for the sake of profit. On the contrary, it is their histories, always evolving, that create their interest. Although the behaviours of the lawyers in the firm may be patterned in some respects, that is not to argue that their actions are determined by any specific modalities. Bourdieu puts it this way, 'The conditionings associated with a particular class of conditions of existence produce *habitus*,[4] systems of durable, transposable dispositions . . . as principles which generate and organize practices' (1990, p. 53). The possibilities and potential for change in law firms, amongst others, are both repressed and reproduced by *habitus*. The obverse of this picture is that professional service firms are also client-driven organizations. One of the most famous examples is the law firm, Freshfields, which has enjoyed a long-term relationship, about three hundred years, with its chief client, the Bank of England (Slinn, 1984). When comparing medical practice to legal practice Heinz and Laumann (1982) demonstrated that the choice of legal specialty in the corporate hemisphere was provoked by client pressure and need rather than intellectual interest, as in the case of medicine. Most corporate law firms depend on repeat business based on retainers. Without clients who pay these fees lawyers cannot practise, unless they are in government or are members of corporate legal departments. Clients, then, are the lifeblood of the law firm. But unlike blood, which reproduces itself in the marrow and replenishes itself on oxygen, clients do not always possess those propensities for self-reproduction. Law firms, especially corporate ones, must therefore receive continuous transfusions of clients in order to exist and to thrive. This requires firms to compete vigorously both to find clients and then to keep them (cf. Abel, 1989; Sander and Williams, 1989). Getting clients is not a talent equally distributed among professionals. Little has been written on the topic: Bourn's study (1986), for example, focuses on how businesses find lawyers. Mostly, client-getting is part of the arcane nature of practice.

The lawyer–client relationship entails a structural coupling of cultures so that trust is possible between the two. This coupling comes about in part through the process of attracting and retaining clients. It is replete with contingency. Both clients and lawyers are mobile. Clients can change lawyers and lawyers can move to different firms. With the decline in the durability of partnership during the 1980s, mobility has increased dramatically (see Eisler, 1991; Caplan, 1993). Both sides play with calculations of risk and develop trajectories of trust through the building of the lawyer–client relationship. There is an enormous impact on the culture of the firm and as relationships develop, the power relations within the firm alter and shift to reflect the new dimensions of economic intensity. Committee assignments change, partners' shares rise and fall, associates find their patrons have immense patronage or none at all. To extend a metaphor of uncertainty I term this aspect 'managing the cultural organization of uncertainty'.

To understand 'markets for legal services', I adopt White's interpretation (1981). Rather than assuming that markets are arenas theoretically populated by producers and consumers (although of course to an extent they are), White asks questions not normally broached by economists. The key one is: 'Why, when even the largest of firms wants to offer a product new to it to the public, does it usually do so by acquiring the persona of a firm belonging to an existing market?' (White, 1981, pp. 517–18). The burgeoning market for advocacy services in the UK case study illustrates this. In some respects solicitor advocates want to be like barristers, while in others they claim a difference which says, in effect, besides being advocates we are *also* solicitors. White's (1981, p. 518) sociological view of markets sees them as 'self-reproducing social structures among specific cliques of firms . . . who evolve roles from observations of each other's behaviour . . . I insist that what a firm does in a market is to watch the competition in terms of observables'. Advocacy lends itself to 'observables' superbly.

Markets for expert knowledge tend to be small and sustained through relatively stable memberships. These memberships are socially structured and depend on developing trust and order (Granovetter, 1985; Baker, 1990). Reputation plays a significant role, as Leifer indicates: 'A small and identifiable group of producers, attached to brands, develop stable and distinct reputations among consumers and hold onto stable market (volume) shares. The reputations are not arbitrarily distributed across producers, but are often tied to market share' (Leifer, 1985, p. 443). Markets here are sets of roles adopted by the players in attempts to maximize their welfare. We also need to understand the effect of status as perceived by producers and consumers. Since reputations are unevenly distributed, perceived differences in quality frequently result in high-status producers receiving more customers than low-status producers. Moreover, the business flows to them with minimal or no costs of advertising (Podolny, 1993). Such a market is difficult to enter and price will not be the crucial determinant in selecting a professional.[5] The connections between status and quality are at best fuzzy; they depend on incomplete signals about status from producers, buyers and interested third parties. There are also time lags in the signalling process. The embeddedness of social relations within markets can help to facilitate the distribution of signals, but consumers are usually risk-averse and will require proof of levels of quality (Podolny, 1993, p. 838). In the case of advocacy, while it is an observable activity, a consumer can incur high transaction costs when retaining new advocates.

The US case study

The ethnography here is of a Chicago law firm, which I call Tischmann Weinstock and Levine (Flood, 1987). The firm's name is a pseudonym and I have changed a few details in my description of the firm to make it harder to identify, but these changes do not affect the analysis. I will first present a brief picture of the social structure and work of the firm and then explain how the research was done.[6]

The firm is composed of about ninety lawyers who practise in tax, real estate, business, estate planning and litigation. Tischmann considers itself a general practice firm. Within the largest practice areas are litigation, real estate, and corporate, all of comparable size. The lawyers are evenly divided in number between partners and associates. Tischmann has a policy of maintaining an approximate one-to-one partner-to-associate ratio, an inducement it uses to counteract the lure of the megafirms to potential associates (cf. Galanter and Palay, 1991).[7] The firm's clients range from large multimillion-dollar companies to wealthy individuals with large estate-planning and corporate needs. The majority of the corporate clients were controlled by five of the partners. By controlling the major clients, these five partners were thus able to exercise considerable authority in the firm. Tischmann is more fortunate than some insofar as it is an established firm that has built up expertise in certain areas for which it has earned a strong reputation. Its client book, which lists all clients and the jobs being done for them is substantial: over 220 pages long. In the markets of the 1980s and 1990s, however, a strong reputation is ultimately ephemeral, which Tischmann has recognized.

History of clients at Tischmann

Tischmann had an advantage, which to some could also be a disadvantage, of being a minority Jewish firm in its early days of the 1920s and 1930s. Jewish lawyers and other professionals were barred from the mainstream, white Anglo-Saxon Protestant firms, so they formed their own firms that served Jewish clients. For some years, in effect, there existed an alternative parallel Jewish economy. Exclusion by others brought cohesion within the group. In these early days, Tischmann was composed mainly of German Jews. They established their client lists through personal networks based on such institutions as the Standard Club in downtown Chicago. Gradually, as the influx of Jews from Eastern Europe strengthened, they joined the firm and added their networks of clients to the others. Clients requested such services as incorporating companies, putting together real estate deals, and planning estates, but there was little litigation. Some of its early clients became multinational companies and outgrew the firm. Thus, Tischmann was primarily a facilitative law firm: its members counselled, negotiated, and advised rather than litigated conflicts.

One feature of the early period lingered through to the 1970s. Individual lawyers thought of clients as their personal property, not those of the firm. Although the firm existed, the constituent lawyers did not always think of it as an entity to be continued with clients being served by generation after generation of lawyers. For example, it was common for no prior arrangements for another lawyer from the firm to be assigned in the event of a death or retirement. Firm consciousness, then, is a fairly recent phenomenon. The clients, too, viewed their relations with lawyers in much the same fashion: their affairs were handled by an individual lawyer and not by the firm. Once it was established that, although lawyers had 'rights' in a client by virtue of having brought that client into the firm, the firm 'owned' the client. Of course, there was no way this rule could be enforced against clients; they were free to view the situation any way they wanted. The consciousness of Tischmann as an entity was established when the firm decided not to alter its name according to the composition of the partners who ran the firm. The name would no longer reflect congeries of personnel, but instead would symbolically identify the firm as an enduring entity. This feature of nomenclature raises the issue of 'branding' as an index of quality, which I will return to below.

During the 1980s the trend towards the concept of the firm being the key representative of the client received a setback. For example, through aggressive marketing, Finley Kumble attempted to dominate the legal market by acquiring law firms and raiding others for their best 'rainmakers' (Flood, 1994). Stevens (1987, p. 42) quoted the managing partner, Steve Kumble, as articulating the philosophy that:

> Lawyers bring in clients and law firms service them. I don't care what anyone says about a firm's history or traditions or any such nonsense. Except for a few clients who are still deep in the stone age, you don't get hired that way. Clients go with the lawyer they know, the lawyer they've worked with, the lawyer who delivers for them regardless of his firm's place in the pecking order. Sure you have to be able to service that client once he's on board, but it's the individual who gets him there. . . . Those who fail to see this, and thank heaven there are many of them, overrate the power of the firm and underrate the power of the lawyers that make it work.

Interestingly, this is in direct contrast to others' views. For example, Peter Brown (Federal Bar Council, 1984, p. 90) expressed his sentiments thus:

> The large law firm has now become an American institution in itself. Lawyers in big firms are no longer accountable to individual clients. Rather, they are accountable to their law firm. Law firms are the entity, not the individual. The objective of the large law firm is simply to make money and to grow bigger in order to make more money. To a large extent, the client has been left out in the cold.

Getting clients

The simplest method of obtaining clients is to inherit them. It is painless and requires little original effort. What it does require is a patronage relationship so that a senior lawyer can devolve his 'empire' to a protégé. The senior partner in Tischmann had one of the biggest clients in the firm, a large corporation (and its head), which he had served for many years. As he began contemplating his retirement, he started to give more and more responsibility to a younger, though fairly senior, partner who had done a considerable amount of work for this client. The junior partner had worked alongside the senior partner for many years but had never been considered a co-equal. Some of the lawyers in the firm were worried that the client, who was known to regard the senior partner in an avuncular light and looked to him for advice on all sorts of business and personal matters, might not transfer his esteem, and therefore business, to the new partner.

Because this partner was younger and had not engaged in the same extensive counselling relationship with the client as had the senior partner, the relationship lacked intimacy. Others thought the relationship would alter and become more formal, technical, and arm's length. Most considered it likely (or hoped) that the client would stay with the firm.

Sometimes problems exist where younger lawyers should be inheriting clients and the older lawyers refrain from passing along responsibility. This leads to the younger lawyers defecting from the firm. Two senior partners at Tischmann had such reputations. Their philosophy was that junior and middle range partners should serve the senior partners' clients rather than be concerned with clients of their own. This attitude frustrated the junior partners. They could see no future for themselves except as the 'minders and grinders' (Nelson, 1988) of these partners and their clients. Any clients they tried to bring into the firm were labelled 'inferior' by the senior partners, who believed their clients were the *crème de la crème*. The only solution for the junior partners was to leave and move to firms that would encourage their drive and ambition.

The usual method for getting clients takes place outside the firm. It entails joining clubs, being involved in business ventures, giving seminars to chambers of commerce, having a well-connected family, and more; but most of all it entails being lucky. One partner, who had some of the most valuable clients in the firm, made his first connection with a big client in the elevator of his apartment building. The story had acquired the status of legend, but demonstrated the element of serendipity in business where personal relations are of paramount importance. A neighbour of his was complaining one day that he could not find a lawyer to handle a corporate problem his commercial real estate company was having difficulty with. The partner offered himself, and that became the start of a constant supply of work from the company, which continued even when the neighbour moved to another part of the country. As the partner's reputation in this field of work grew, so did his range of clients. In the space of a few years he became one of the most powerful members of the firm, with his clients generating several million dollars' worth of business a year.

Another partner, whose cousin was extremely successful in starting his own companies, received the legal business the companies generated. As the cousin prospered, so did the lawyer. One side effect of having a cousin well known in the securities business was that other securities people knew of him and were willing to give their legal work to the lawyer. While attending a securities conference one day, the lawyer enlisted two new clients because they knew his cousin and needed a mid-West lawyer. This lawyer also thought carefully about what kind of conference or seminar he would attend: 'It's no good going to a seminar that is full of lawyers. I'm not going to get any business out of them. I need a place that's full of securities people and accountants; they're the ones who can bring me real business.' He would also sign himself up for conferences but not attend. 'I don't need them, but when people look through the lists of participants they'll see my name and that of the firm. And with luck, if they need a securities lawyer, they'll call me.'

Giving seminars can be an important way of legitimately publicizing and marketing the firm. One labour lawyer who was trying to develop a satellite practice in one of the Chicago suburbs was a frequent speaker at chamber of commerce seminars. When the lawyers were asked to present a paper at such a seminar, they would put together a package about the firm. It would list the lawyers and their fields, and try to emphasize the distinctiveness of the firm. But with a general practice firm, proving distinctiveness is often hard to achieve.

The brochure presented an interesting insight into how the firm perceived itself:

> Founded in 1905, Tischmann still maintains its original philosophy that its lawyers are both attorneys and counselors. We offer expert advice on legal questions and advice is given with an eye to the broader context in which the legal questions arise. By identifying both legal and non-legal considerations, we can recommend action which is not only legally sound, but which will produce the best overall results for our clients.
>
> In the firm's view, the ever-increasing complexity of doing business in today's regulatory climate increases the importance of the role of the lawyer as attorney and counselor. The practice of law can no longer be a 'reaction' to problems as they arise. If possible, the lawyer should counsel and advise the client in hope of anticipating the many problems the client may face in the future. We feel that by careful and innovative lawyering, we have met and will continue to meet the challenges of today's law practice.
>
> The firm has a reputation for creative lawyering in which our lawyers find ways to accomplish the results the client seeks. While our lawyers have a broad range of experience, each has also developed special expertise in a specific substantive area of the law. As a result, each Tischmann client should expect to be in 'one to one' contact with his or her personal lawyer who knows and understands the client's business. At the same time, each client knows that each lawyer is able to call upon the knowledge and experience of other lawyers in our office to provide the best planning and solutions to specific legal problems.

Firm brochures fundamentally say the same thing, which makes one difficult to distinguish from the other. One can derive an idea that legal work (and by extension, professional services' work) is fundamentally fungible. Once a 'legal device' has been created, e.g., the 'poison pill', it cannot be patented and is open to copying by others (Powell, 1993).[8] The work is essentially reputational, hence the similarity of these brochures.

Brochures themselves rarely, if ever, produce a client, but personal contacts with the audience, say personnel directors from local businesses, do succeed in bringing in clients. The particular partner involved in developing the suburban practice found that many businesses needed counselling on how to negotiate with labour unions that wished to become established. The suburbs are traditionally places where businesses go when they leave the inner city, often to avoid unions' power. The chambers of commerce, then, were ideal avenues for him to use to tap into this market. He also produced a newsletter for the firm, which told the attorneys how the suburban practice was faring. Most of its six or so pages were given over to the fruits of client development and seminars given by the lawyers, e.g., 'The seminars are definitely gaining exposure for Tischmann's suburban office and the number of suburban clients is steadily increasing.' There then followed a list of lawyers and clients brought into the fold. The seminar reports were glowing: 'Bill Smith's [a Tischmann partner] November 1 seminar on 'Interest-Free and Other Below-Market Loans' attracted a standing room only crowd for this office. Attendees were representatives from Merrill Lynch, Touche Ross, Porte Brown, Tempo Graphics, Royal Fuel, Detterbeck and Company, and Peacock Engineering.'

For the Tischmann lawyers a popular method for getting clients was through being on the opposing side of a case. A partner with several large corporate clients said he acquired them all this way. He had been involved in large real estate partnership transactions and had handled them sufficiently well that the people on the other sides had sought him out for future deals. Attracting a client by this manner meant that a client had 'proof positive' of a lawyer's ability.

The most frequent form of client-getting is via networks. Bourn (1986, p. 59) found that 75 per cent of her sample of businesses located attorneys through networks of friends and colleagues. Typically, such a request is: 'I need a lawyer who can handle a securities issue for me. Do you know anyone?' According to Bourn, the next largest category is that of personal knowledge (29 per cent) where the potential client actually knows a lawyer. The lawyers at Tischmann were plugged into many networks, not just chambers of commerce, but also charitable foundations, especially Jewish ones, schools, political activities, both Democrat and Republican, and bar associations. Besides formal membership in bar associations through joining sections and becoming officers in them, bar associations can sometimes produce unexpected effects.

In 1984, the American Bar Association held its annual meeting in Chicago, in part to inaugurate its new downtown bar centre. This occasion provided an opportunity for many Chicago law firms to act as unofficial hosts to out-of-town lawyers. Tischmann was among them. The majority of the firms were holding their receptions in hotels and restaurants. Tischmann, or rather its management committee, decided to hold a reception during the meeting, but something out of the ordinary, something distinctive. The firm planned its reception to be in the top storey of a department store. The same summer that the American Bar Center was opening, a new, very fashionable and expensive, luxury department store, Neiman Marcus, opened on Michigan Avenue, one of the main downtown shopping centres, near to the bar centre. Tischmann reserved the top floor restaurant and part of the food hall.

In order to make the reception a success, the Tischmann management committee hired a consultant. His task was to help the lawyers use the reception as a vehicle for promoting the firm and increasing business – to plan it as a military campaign. The first step was acquiring the lists of those attending the ABA meeting, and then combing them for people the lawyers knew. Those that were considered good 'business prospects' were invited by the lawyers that knew them. In addition, a request was sent to every lawyer in the firm asking for a list of 'notables' who should receive invitations. Ultimately, more than a thousand invitations, with *handwritten* envelopes, were sent. Brigades of secretaries, messengers and paralegals were dragooned into writing the envelopes. The consultant had told them that handwritten envelopes would inspire a warmer response among those invited.

As the date for the reception approached, the consultant was brought into a breakfast meeting at the firm, which every lawyer was commanded to attend. The memorandum from the partner in charge of the party to all attorneys and summer associates was headed, 'Re: Survival Techniques at Parties':

'Peter Smith, Director of Marketing and Director of Midwest Law Firms Group at XXX Accounting Company will be hosting a one hour meeting on Wednesday morning of this week at 8:30 a.m. in the 32nd Floor Conference Room at which he will be sharing some ideas which he has in regard to creating the appropriate image at cocktail parties. Attendance by all is expected. We would like to be finished by 9:30 a.m., therefore, please be there promptly at 8:30 a.m.'

Over sweet rolls and coffee, the senior partner spoke about the importance of the occasion as a means of publicizing the firm and raising its business profile. Many of the lawyers attending were disconcerted about the event; it was expensive, the rental cost was nearly $10,000 for the evening, and it seemed a most artificial way of generating business. The consultant lectured about how the party should be conducted. His main emphasis was on how to change the conversation from social talk to business talk, and then finding the appropriate moment to hand over a business card. He warned that no opportunity should be missed to switch a conversation from social to business; otherwise the talk would be 'wasted.' About 230 of those invited agreed to come, but the partner in charge told the lawyers to write to those who could not attend, offering future assistance if ever needed. A few days before the reception, the event received some publicity from a local newspaper as one of the events to attend during the ABA meetings.

After the reception, considerable follow-up work was done. The partner in charge distributed another memorandum on the 'ABA Party:'

> Attached hereto are the following:
>
> 1 List of guests who attended the party;
> 2 List of guests who indicated that they would be in attendance but who did not come to the party;
> 3 Copy of three signatures from our guest books which we are unable to read – if anyone recognizes any of these please let my secretary know; and
> 4 Your guest list as submitted to the ABA Party Committee for placement on the computer.
>
> I find it difficult to prepare letters for others and, therefore, in lieu of my suggesting a form of letter, I would rather suggest that the following points

could be covered in the letter and that the style of the same should be yours rather than mine:

1 Thank them for attending;
2 Possibly mention something either legal or otherwise relative to what you may have discussed at the party;
3 Possibly some reference to their work on an ABA committee; and/or
4 A possible line such as 'looking forward to working with you in the future.'

When, finally, the paperwork was removed to the file room, it occupied six expandable folders: the total cost of the reception was $18,000. In effect, the party was a public relations exercise that left the firm with no real way of establishing how much business had been generated.

Keeping clients

The dream of most lawyers is to find clients who will keep them for the remainder of their careers. Shearman and Sterling's representation of Citicorp, a client that generates millions of dollars in fees every year, is paradigmatic. The trick is to capture a client, especially a corporate client, when it is small, and then to grow with it. One partner at Tischmann who had a publicly held company for a client said he originally obtained the client because. 'The guy who runs it and I knew each other from years ago and grew up together.' He felt he had nurtured the client through its formative years into its present state. Consequently, he was very protective of, and defensive about, the client. When the client became involved in litigation, the lawyer called in a litigation partner to assist him. He was, however, concerned about clearly establishing the line of authority from the outset: every decision had to go through him; the litigation partner would have no direct contact with the client. Moreover, the differences in approach between corporate attorneys and litigators disturbed him. At one stage the litigator argued that they should seek an award of counsel's fees from the court. The corporate partner was adamantly opposed because he did not want the client to think that fees would be taken care of by some external agency. 'I like to be concise with clients,' he said, meaning clients should be aware of whom, and how much, they will pay. He went on to say that if the litigator wanted to work with him on this case he should share the same frame of reference: 'We better be on the same beam.'

This kind of extreme paternalism is common among the senior lawyers. At least three were enmeshed in such relationships with their clients, and their success was thought to depend on paternalism, which raised fears about what would happen to the clients' relationship with the firm when these lawyers retired. This was brought to a head in one extreme case when a senior lawyer died nine months after joining the firm as part of a merger. There were grave fears over whether the newly merged Tischmann, as a unit, had developed sufficiently strong links with this lawyer's clients to fill the void caused by his death. But even paternalism has its limits. One senior partner had no problem being aggressive and forceful with clients who were contemporaries with or younger than him. With older clients, however, he averred that 'I am deferential; I let them tell me what to do; I won't argue with them.'

Keeping clients content is sometimes wearing for the lawyer, but it is part of the game of being a lawyer and therefore must be accepted. Very wealthy clients seem to be the most capricious. Two partners, one senior, the other in the middle range, visited a client in the suburbs to discuss a new theory they had developed for his case against the trustees of a large charitable foundation. The client made them drink about four scotches before they could really discuss matters; moreover, they were worried whether he would accept their ideas. At first, he liked the idea; later he equivocated. The senior partner tried to reinforce his idea by saying, 'It's no worse than Kirkland would do for you.' The same client once called the partner at 10 p.m. to hear the partner's final speech in a case. They talked until 3 o'clock in the morning. The next day when the jury brought in a verdict in favour of the client, the client leaned over to the lawyer and said, 'Well, at least you got that f***ing right!'

Another wealthy client was involved in extensive litigation during the course of which he had discarded several lawyers. When a Tischmann partner received the case, he thought it a 'mixed blessing', never knowing if the client would depart. During the discovery phase of the litigation, the opposing party requested some personal papers from the client. These papers included explicit, often critical comments about his lawyers, past and present. The issue was so sensitive, that the papers were given to a paralegal, who was then locked in a room and instructed to 'white out' all remarks about the partner. The remarks about the current lawyer–client relationship were excluded from discovery on the grounds of lawyer–client confidentiality. Even the partner himself was forbidden to see the unexpurgated papers.

To keep clients, lawyers must both follow their demands and, on occasion, anticipate them. One large client felt it would be a good idea for Tischmann to open a branch at its mid-West headquarters in the suburbs. Tischmann complied. (The venture was unsuccessful, however, since it failed to generate substantial amounts of new business.) Another client, in cooperation with a partner, had been pressing for a branch office in another state, but the firm was wary about committing resources to the proposed plan because of the failure of the suburban venture.

Anticipating clients' demands can best be illustrated by the following example. A partner who inherited, from a senior lawyer, a small but rapidly growing company as a client visited the company for its annual general meeting. While the lawyer was talking to the president of the company, the president told him that the company was implementing a change in its corporate structure. The actual legal work was, however, being done by another law firm. The partner was shocked and asked why the work had not been given to him. The president said he believed Tischmann had no expertise in this kind of work and so he had looked elsewhere. Because the type of structural corporate change being sought was relatively new, the partner had not anticipated that his client would need this kind of work. No amount of persuasion on his part could make the president redirect the work to Tischmann. The firm still 'possessed' the company as a client, but it had failed to obtain a substantial and profitable piece of business from it.

The archetypal means of retaining clients is to cross-sell services to them. Thus, if a client came to the firm with a single task in mind, such as a real estate transaction, the firm would attempt to entice the client into using the firm's tax, ERISA, or litigation departments as well, and, if possible, put the client on a retainer so there was a constant stream of money coming into the firm. But cross-selling is a delicate matter. If a client, for example, is referred to a lawyer because of some special expertise, the lawyer may not be able to cross-sell the client. A partner who was a specialist in an arcane area of tax law had many clients referred to him for that particular matter alone. It was understood by those who referred the work, although never openly articulated, that he would never attempt to poach the clients or he would face the sanction of no further referrals. Even if, therefore, referred clients asked about other services in Tischmann, he had to refuse them for fear of upsetting the lawyer who had referred them.[9] But if a client came without a referral, then it was understood that open season had been declared.

Another form of cross-selling sometimes occurs between lawyer and client. A partner who worked for an investment bank was expected to refer Tischmann's clients to the bank, thus establishing a symbiotic relationship. This type of symbiosis was taken a step further when a big client of the firm asked the partnership to form a limited partnership with it to enter a real estate deal: Tischmann had little choice but to comply or face dwindling interest from the client.

'*Making rain*'

Lawyers who bring in substantial numbers of clients are called 'rainmakers'. One central consequence of being a rainmaker is to be bestowed with power and wealth. That is, rainmakers control the firm and receive the largest draws of the partners.[10] They win seats on the management committees of firms and thus obtain positions with the authority to help create and influence policy and the future direction of the firm. At Tischmann there were seven lawyers on the management committee, all of who were substantial client finders and minders. They also constituted the highest remunerated group in the firm.

Most American law firms use the 'eat what you kill' method of remuneration. Rewards are directly based on the business generated by a lawyer (Gilson and Mnookin, 1985). Firms make no allowances for equality or equity. Each partner must maximize his or her own rewards. In the UK system a 'lockstep' arrangement is the norm (see Morris and Pinnington, Chapter 10, this volume). Here incoming cohorts of partners constitute a class that is given the same level of rewards. Each year the level is raised until the class reaches a plateau near retirement when the levels are reduced. The rationale of the system is that the firm retains a corporate identity and refutes the cult of the individual. Improved rewards come through increasing the firm's business at large.

In this section I will show how although a lawyer may control a large number of clients, that degree of control does not of itself indicate whether a lawyer will be considered either a rainmaker or a member of the firm's elite. In Table 8.1, I have rank ordered the lawyers in Tischmann by the numbers of clients attributed to them. These figures are derived from the 1986 Tischmann client book. The attribution is made on the basis that a lawyer is considered in control of a client, i.e., belongs to the lawyer, when that lawyer is designated, in the client book, as the billing partner. Only in a few cases have some lawyers not actively generated their entire clientele. Instead, they have been granted clients by another lawyer for some reason. For example, when one large corporate client split into two entities, the original billing partner continued with one while the other part was assigned to another partner. In all other cases the lawyers generated their own business and therefore possess their own clientele. These clients are broken down into two categories, individual and corporate (following Heinz and Laumann, 1982),

Table 8.1 Numbers of clients by top echelon of lawyers

Lawyer and status	Number of clients		% of total clients	
	Individual	*Corporate*	*Individual*	*Corporate*
1-sp	153	143	9.6	15.2
2-sp	137	68	8.6	7.2
3-sp	140	37	8.8	3.9
4-sp	82	50	5.1	5.3
5-sp	44	43	2.8	4.8
6-sp	44	43	2.8	4.8
7-sp	49	39		
8-sp	54	22		
9-sp	64	22		
10-jp	57	23		
11-sp	49	18		
12-sp	47	18		
13-mp	41	26		
14-mp	26	46		
15-sp	39	29		
16-mp	38	28		
17-mp	28	26		
18-jp	19	26		
19-mp	18	20		
20-mp	93	13		

Source: Adapted from Flood, 1987.

Notes: The lawyer number includes the status of the lawyer in the firm as follows: *sp* = senior partner, *mp* = middle-range partner, *jp* = junior partner.
  The next rank is 'senior associate' (*sa*) – the highest ranked *sa* was 29 (with 5 individual and 24 corporate clients).
1 the next 12 lawyers (ranked 21 to 32) include 2 *sp*, 5 *mp*, 3 *jp*, and 2 *sa*, and have an average of 25 individual and 11 corporate clients.
2 the remaining lawyers have no significant numbers of clients, but the firm totals according to the Tischmann client book are 1,594 (individual) and 939 (corporate).

which reflect the types of clients Tischmann handles. The lawyers, too, are separated into the status groups of senior partner, middle partner, junior partner, senior associate, middle associate and junior associate. As might be expected, senior partners control the majority of the clients.

These numbers, very crudely, indicate who are and who are not the rainmakers in Tischmann. The low numbers signify one of two things: that either the lawyers are relatively new associates who would not be expected to have any clients yet, or lawyers who have been unsuccessful at finding clients. The following lawyers have the most clients (i.e., they have large numbers of both individual and corporate clients).

In the case of three, most of the clients are individuals (79 per cent). What the numbers fail to indicate is who has the most active clients. Although a lawyer may have a large roster of clients, they may only bring in small amounts of work. To be a successful rainmaker, a lawyer must have clients who are sources of regular, continuous work. Thus, a lawyer could have only one or two clients, but these could be enormously profitable, if they were large institutions. So, while simple numbers help to paint a picture of who is likely to be successful within the firm, they do not tell us who is a consistent rainmaker. The profile of the rainmaker can be obtained through somewhat different means, however. As I mentioned above, there is certain congruence between the most successful rainmakers and the members of the management committee.

In Table 8.1, the actual members of the management committee are lawyers 1, 2, 3, 4, 5, 9 and 15. The mean number of their clients, both individual and corporate, is 150. The list excludes some who one might expect from the aggregate numbers of clients would be included, e.g., 6, 7, 8, 10, 12, 14 and 20. However, their mean number of clients is only 77.5, approximately half the number of the management committee, which is insufficient for inclusion on the committee.

Admittedly, a management committee this large would be unwieldy, but there have to be good reasons for excluding such potential members. On the whole, individual clients do not carry as much weight as corporate ones. Many of the clients of lawyers 7, 8 and 22, are estate planning clients. That is, much of their legal work is done on a once-only basis. The client supplies the relevant data and the lawyer draws up the appropriate plan; and unless the client's situation changes radically or there is an abrupt exogenous change, as with the 1986 Tax Reform Act, the plan is not altered. Hence, these lawyers' clients are not, in part, 'continuous feed' or 'repeat player' clients. Other reasons for exclusion from the management committee are self-selection through, e.g., old age (as in the case of lawyer 7 who was in his eighties), poor health, and semi-retirement (as in the case of lawyer 12).

To attempt to locate a rational basis for identifying successful rainmakers, I analysed the time records of all the attorneys in Table 8.1 for two sample two-week periods in March and October. These records provided information on, amongst other things, which lawyers did what tasks for what clients and for which lawyers as billing partners (i.e., to whom the client belonged) and for how long.

A task here is defined as an episode of work carried out on behalf of a client, e.g., a telephone call, or drafting a letter.[11] Taking the two groups of lawyers with the highest numbers of clients in the firm, namely, the members of the management committee and the group of alternates, we can compute the group means of numbers of tasks per the management and alternates groups per the clients for each group. Table 8.2 illustrates the derivation of these means by showing the total numbers of episodes of work for the sample four-week period for each lawyer in the two groups.

Table 8.2 leads to certain conclusions about which lawyers, in terms of possessing business-producing clients or the lack thereof, would or would not be counted as major rainmakers in the firm. The management committee group is far ahead of the alternates group with a mean number of episodes of work per group of clients of 901 compared to the alternates' mean number of 225.6. Lawyers 20 and 22 are not recognizable as legitimate candidates because their levels of tasks are so low (33 in each case), despite the relatively high number of clients on their rosters, 93 individual, 13 corporate and 44 individual, 2 corporate, respectively. Conversely, lawyers 4 and 5 have extremely large numbers of tasks to their credit, 1,385 and 2,205 respectively: they also happen to be the two most powerful lawyers in the firm.

Those between the two poles who are on the management committee, except for one member, share a minimum of 400 tasks for the period. The exception is lawyer 3, who has only 327 tasks with a preponderance of individual over corporate clients. His position is politically charged since he belonged to the firm Tischmann merged with and the two firms had to be represented on the committee. Lawyer 7 would have been the natural choice (with 346 total tasks), but he removed himself on the grounds of age and lawyer 3 was the next in line. This also helps to explain why lawyer 8 is no longer a member. He stepped down when the merger took place to allow the other firm to put its representatives on the committee, although he could validly have claimed a seat.

Table 8.2 Total and mean numbers of work/task episodes for sample four-week period for lawyers in management committee and lawyers in alternate group

Management group		Alternate group	
Lawyer	Total work episodes for each lawyer	Lawyer	Total work episodes for each lawyer
5	2,205	8	430
4	1,385	7	346
9	754	6	338
2	633	10	328
1	588	14	157
15	415	12	140
3	*327*	28	*33*
Totals	6,307		1,805
Means	901		225.6

Source: Adapted from Flood, 1987.

Putting aside this anomaly, 400 tasks in a four week sample period would appear to be the threshold for membership on the committee. Clearly, then, lawyers 6, 10 and 14 are not candidates. Another distinguishing feature is that, again except for one lawyer, the members of the management committee have at least one corporate client for which there are more than a hundred tasks in the sample four-week period. Lawyers 4 and 5 demonstrate their pre-eminence in this area by having very high numbers of tasks per client. Lawyer 4 has two clients, *Alpha* and *Beta*, with 274 and 198 tasks per sample four-week period respectively. Lawyer 5, who is by far the most successful and powerful lawyer in the firm, has four clients who generate enormous amounts of work: *Gamma* with 848, *Delta* with 347, *Epsilon* with 256, and *Zeta* with 251 tasks in the sample four-week period. Lawyer 2 has at best 77 tasks for a single client, but this is counterbalanced by his having 633 total tasks, the fourth highest total. Lawyer 6 comes close with one corporate client generating 95 tasks, but his total is low at 338 tasks in the sample period.

Perhaps one anomaly is lawyer 1, who had the highest numbers of clients, both individual and corporate, of any lawyer in the firm, namely, 153 (individual) and 143 (corporate); but his number of tasks is only the fifth largest in the firm. His situation (along with lawyer 20, who out of 93 individual and 13 corporate clients had only 33 tasks) illustrates the problem inherent in relying on numbers of clients as an indicator of business activity.

The statistics also show how reliant the lawyers are on a relatively small number of clients, despite having large numbers on their roster. For example, with the exceptions of lawyers 1 and 3, the ten biggest clients per lawyer in Table 8.2 account for at least 60 per cent of each lawyer's business, in most cases higher. These lawyers, then, probably typical of most, have fairly concentrated practices: a few clients provide sufficient work for a successful practice. The two exceptions, lawyers 1 and 3, have rather more diffuse practices with 57.9 per cent and 58.4 per cent, respectively. These lower percentages are probably a reflection of the exceptionally large range of clients each possesses, especially individual clients.

The foregoing represents a sketch of the successful rainmaker: a lawyer who has corporate clients that generate continually high levels of tasks which keep other lawyers within the firm in work. A lawyer who merely has a large number of clients on the books is not necessarily successful if most of those clients are moribund: a static picture can therefore lie. Instead, it is obligatory to examine the amount (flow) of work transacted through a lawyer. Lawyers having few clients who demand large amounts of legal work on a regular basis are easily more successful and possess more symbolic capital (social and economic) than those who have many clients that require work only from time to time. The high rates of capital acquisition enable the successful lawyers to dominate the management of the firm and plot its direction. However, they are reluctant to become involved in the day-to-day aspects of management, preferring instead to allocate that work to middle range partners.[12]

The UK case study

The British legal profession has undergone significant change in the last decade or so. Solicitors have been granted rights of audience in the higher courts; legal aid is coordinated under franchising arrangements; multinational practices are common; and the government has interposed more regulation in the form of bodies such as the Lord Chancellor's Advisory Committee on Legal Education and Conduct (ACLEC) (cf. Johnson, 1993).[13] And, more importantly, for corporate lawyers the City of London was effectively deregulated and reregulated by the 'Big Bang' of the 1980s. London truly became one of the troika of global cities servicing global capital (Sassen, 1991). City solicitors have long been aware of the foundation of their role. In 1977, in evidence to the Royal Commission on Legal Services (the Benson Commission), and in 1989, in reply to the British government's Green Paper on the work and organization of the legal profession, the City of London Solicitors' Company and City of London Law Society put forward the argument that English law was a product marketed by English lawyers throughout the world. For example, in the 1989 reply, the City of London Law Society (1989, p. 5) said:

> The advantages of English law as a 'product' enable solicitors to contribute to this country's balance of payments some £250,000,000 per annum in invisible exports and constitute an important part of the attraction of the City of London as a world financial and insurance centre.

Rather like the big American corporate law firms, English corporate law firms really began to expand in numbers and size in the 1970s. The main fuel was provided later by the Big Bang and then augmented by firm mergers. It is important to stress, however, how small the typical City firm was in the post-World War II period. Slinn (1984, p. 159) notes of Freshfields, 'In 1946 there were seven partners, fewer than at least two of the other leading City firms, Linklaters & Paines and Slaughter and May, each of whom had twelve partners'. And following lifting of the restriction on partner numbers, Slaughter and May had 24 partners in 1968 (Dennett, 1989, p. 236). As partnership became a normal expectation for assistant solicitors, the partnership track has extended from around five years to eight to ten. The length of the track depends, on part, on the structure of the partnership – whether it is two-tiered with salaried and equity partners or solely equity partners. The former lengthens the process (Flood, 1996, p. 177). A change which is emerging in the 1990s is the lack of desire on the part of some assistants to achieve partnership. They view the prize as too costly in terms of the other aspects of their lives. Instead, they elect for a form of permanent senior assistantship (cf. Flam, 1993; Morris and Pinnington, Chapter 10, this volume).[14] This suggests the 'Cravathization' of UK firms is not complete. Moreover, most City firms use lockstep reward systems. The rationale for the approach is that it breeds collegiality and cooperativeness rather than competition between lawyers (cf. Gilson and Mnookin, 1985). One possible consequence is that UK lawyers feel less pressure to generate billable hours compared to American lawyers and are therefore not in a race with such sharply measured outcomes.[15]

Getting and caring for clients

The key element in attaining partnership is clearly business-getting, which is continually reviewed through the partner's career. This has been epitomized by a tribute to Sir George Allen, a founding partner of Allen & Overy, on his retirement in 1952, which said, 'He completely identified himself with his client . . . always gave himself wholeheartedly to the client's interests' (Allen & Overy, n.d. p. 2).

The British legal profession has traditionally hived off advocacy as a separate activity. Whereas solicitors start litigation, it has been the custom for barristers to present the case in court. In 1992 that division was breached by the government, which allowed solicitors to become eligible to act as advocates in the higher courts (Flood *et al.*, 1996). Although the take-up of these rights has been slow, the consequences for the organization of law firms is profound.[16] Among those, for example, who have been perplexed over hiring two sets of lawyers to conduct a case are American clients who are used to dealing with a single firm that both prepares and presents litigation.[17] This section uses the illustration of the division of labour between solicitors and barristers to explore how organizations, in relation to clients, are perceived by the actors.

A corporate solicitor explained the manner in which referrals had been handled and are viewed now:

> A client who knows you inside out. You know the client inside out. You know all of the facts. You could recite this case backwards. You have gone through all of the settlement negotiations and they break down and then the client says, 'Right sue them.' With our existing system I then say, 'I will now introduce you to Mr So and So or Ms So and So who is a barrister. He or she will prepare the pleadings for the case and I will instruct them to do this. Then when we go to court he or she will stand up and will argue your case.' Explaining that to someone from overseas is like explaining to a Martian our legal system . . .
>
> You all know who the boss is. Boss one is the client. You know who the second boss is, it is the instructing solicitor. The roles in the past, for perfectly understandable reasons, have been that the roles have become completely reversed and it has become boss one is the barrister, boss two is the solicitor and boss three or maybe not the boss at all is the client.

There are cost implications to taking advocacy in to the solicitor's firm. A junior partner reflected on how barristers in commercial chambers appear to earn much more than senior partners in a City law firm, while charging less.

> On an hour by hour basis barristers work out cheaper to use, except perhaps for the very, very senior QCs. Barristers may end up earning a lot more

money but that is because they do not have to pay the same rents, they do not have to pay for the same office rates, they do not have to keep the same thing like this going. This all cuts into the cost, but it also means that for every hour of time that we give to a client in the law firm we have got to charge more for that in order to make a profit than the barrister who is sitting down at the bar . . . So that is a major disincentive to try and say to clients we will do all of your cases.

In many ways the division of labour between solicitors and advocates has to be decided fairly early in a case so that the best team of experts can gathered, as a partner related:

If you've got a large case, or a large problem for a client that may become litigious, you will start to put together a team of people to help the client at an early stage and that team may well comprise a senior barrister, a junior barrister, whom you would consult at the very outset to introduce them to the problem because it is something that you would want them to work on with you as the problem progresses. We would not on any case of substance run everything ourselves right to the last minute and then suddenly get in a barrister.

These views were not universally endorsed, however, by other lawyers. One senior partner said:

I certainly do not see any merit in saying to my clients you have got to double-man this case just so there is a future for the bar. My clients are not impressed with that idea.

The need to attend to the client's needs, to keep the client informed, and to maintain with the client a two-way communication link, was emphasized generally. The close contact with a client was seen as a big difference between what solicitors and barristers do. An assistant solicitor said,

The barrister rarely has to worry about clients – big advantage. They do have to worry about PR. They do have to make sure that the client is happy, but primarily they do not have to worry about that. They can just do their specific job in their specific way and give it back to the solicitor, and it is the solicitor's job to pass it out. So client liaison is so much a solicitor's job.

The head of the litigation department in the same firm felt not only that the roles of the advocate and the solicitor, especially if a partner, are different, but they may even be antithetical.

I suspect that all of the requirements of an advocate are antithetic to the ethos of a partner in a City law firm, certainly as we are currently structured.

A partner in a City law firm is meant to be a 'client-getter' and a 'client-pleaser' and, much less important, but nonetheless important, available to his partners. As I have said, I don't think that any of that is something that an advocate can readily do consistently with the requirements of his role as an advocate. It may be that I have been putting it at a very practical level; I get my leg mercilessly pulled by clients and partners if I'm not available every hour of the day at the end of the telephone at my desk. It's bad enough going out for meetings, it gets much worse if you go to a trial for a few weeks.

The problem of reconciling the requirements of being a City partner raised by the firm's clients and fellow partners and colleagues, with the need to become unavailable so as to prepare a case, and later present the case perhaps for days on end, were felt by the other firms. A junior partner argued, 'We are not geared to providing the time to people required to prepare for cases and we have not had the experience that junior counsel have had day in and day out in the tribunals where they practise.'

It is indicative that, while the problem of combining the role of client-pleaser with advocate, the presenter of a case in court is perceived in similar terms in all firms. There are important differences in perceptions of how the problem can be resolved. What is seen as an antithesis or an incompatibility between the two roles in one firm, is perceived as a mere management problem for another.[18] The senior partner in one of the latter firms explained:

> The burden of preparation is quite high and that means the solicitor advocate has to then be able to manage his practice so as to keep all of his other clients happy and that's something which I don't think any of us have yet really had to focus on. One of my partners was in a four week hearing, and another one is set for October which could run six to eight weeks. He wonders, 'How am I going to handle the rest of my clients?' That's a management issue.

The role of City firm solicitors as the sole contact point for clients is undoubtedly creating problems for firms that wish to expand their advocacy services. It is also seen as a major difference between barristers and solicitors. Most interviewees, for example, felt that direct professional access between clients and barristers had made little difference to their professional practices, because barristers had limited skills, or desire, to deal with clients directly. The clash of cultures between solicitors and barristers was also expressed in other terms, relating to differences between the two branches of the legal profession. One identified difference was that of the barrister as a loner and the solicitor as the team worker. A head of litigation pointed out:

> Barristers are not very 'house trained'. We have many years ago now taken a couple in-house and it was a disaster on their side. They sort of operated as if they were still sole practitioners taking up pretty much any client that they wanted, to do whatever they wanted and it just does not really work.

The loner mentality was seen to be totally incompatible with the work of a City firm, and especially the role expected of partners by their clients. As the head of litigation in another firm argued, 'Access to partners is very important for our clients because of, normally, their profile and the type of cases they bring to us, so it is important that they feel that partners are dedicating time to their case.' The head of litigation in one firm felt there was a big contradiction between lawyers as negotiators and as advocates.

> Another reason for keeping the role of an advocate separate from that of the manager of the team and from the solicitor, if you like, is that when you come to settlement discussions most advocates, and that means at the moment barristers, will tell you that they would rather not get involved in settlement discussions for the very good reason that if you are an advocate you want to see things slightly black and white. Your case is white and his case black. To be a successful negotiator, settler, you have got to see the shades of grey in the situation.

Career structures

For many established solicitors the changes in the advocacy rules are of marginal effect on their own careers. The main impact of the change is received by the junior members of the law firms. This distinction places an age-related tension on firm development. The head of litigation in one firm was facing this problem.

> We have to meet the expectation of junior lawyers, most of whom are now joining the litigation department with the expectation that not only in their working lifetime but within the short to medium term they will be conducting cases, perhaps not monsters but at any rate cases, and they are expecting us to provide not only with the training but also with the experience. We must live with the challenges that arise for us everyday. Challenging is this: First, how do we get our people to have sufficient advocacy experience that they can compete effectively with the bar? . . . The second question is: how do we structure ourselves internally to provide that service?

The same senior partner explained how the older members of the firm, like himself, were not likely to benefit directly from increased advocacy exposure.

> By the stage of my career that I have reached I can actually bring something to the party that the clients expect me to bring which is a certain amount, I suppose, of experience, you know, 'Well, I have done this before.' I don't think that the client would find it terribly attractive to substitute that for, 'Well, I am now going to do the advocacy, I know that I have never done it before, but I will have a go at that as well.' The other reason for it is I suspect that it will take something like ten years or so before you will see solicitors standing up and handling complex cases before the high court.

Some lawyers believed that developing an advocacy capacity was a means of achieving a competitive edge, which centred only on inter-firm struggle.

> Certainly no one wants to get left behind. That's exactly where the emphasis is coming from at the moment. It isn't coming from the client. It isn't coming from the attitude at the bar. It's coming from fierce competition between City firms to be able to say, 'We can add something different. We are a 'one-stop shop', if clients buy that.'

It is clear that a range of pressures are being felt by City law firms, both from within as junior lawyers wish to expand their portfolios of skills and symbolic resources, and from without as clients press to see a more rational system that is synchronized with others outside the UK. However beleaguered solicitors may feel, their concerns are being amplified with the forces to globalization of legal services which are themselves being influenced by the moves of the large accounting firms to establish and legitimate multidisciplinary practices (MDPs), in some cases by taking over law firms (cf. Brill, 1985).

Discussion

Comparing the two case studies in particular, and US and UK legal professions in general, we can see that the UK legal profession is subject to pressures of change far greater than in the US. Plausible reasons for American stability can be found in the substantial domestic market enjoyed by American lawyers and the influential role of the Securities and Exchange Commission in international capital markets work. Further causes are located in the role of the American attorney in putting deals together: attorneys are depicted as quarterbacks coordinating the strategy of deals in alliance with bankers and others (Fitzpatrick, 1989). British lawyers have always assumed the role of underlabourer in deal-making, the lead role going to the merchant and investment banks. These reasons have enabled American lawyers to concentrate on work without being troubled to the *same extent* by external competition.

Change in the law firm

Both case studies, then, illustrate the role of *habitus* in declaring the conditions of their respective fields. 'Durable dispositions' are displayed in the work of getting and keeping clients and in the attempts to come to terms with the creation of new markets and a new division of labour. The forces for and against change become apparent as these lawyers struggle with their modes of working. The processes of institutional change may be quickly imposed from without, but the response internally can be slow (or fast) depending on where in the institution the change is occurring and where it meets resistance. One of the points I put forward at the beginning of this chapter was the reflexive nature of legal work and organization.[19] Law firms are infused with law, because they are legal arrangements and composed of lawyers, and they also stand apart from law, because they demand an association based on voluntaries (which has its material rewards).[20] This varies between countries: the US has a far more individuated system based on meritocratic rewards, and the UK has a more collectivized system, which rewards groups through lockstep. Thus the goals of the collective are competing with the desires of the individual, although it would be reasonable to say they are not incompatible.

The American example shows that power and authority lie in the individual's command of clients and the resources that can be committed to them. Rain-making is highly applauded. In Britain it is possible to command many clients, but still be subject to the will of the collectivity. The firm is perceived as an entity that endures and outlives the individuals. Yet, in part, these are idealized and romanticized conceptions of law firm organization. Actors are capable of selecting action because of irrational reasons, e.g., because they perceive others might be following a particular course of action and therefore they must be publicly seen to do alike (Han, 1994). This can occur even if the consequences are deleterious to the actor.[21]

> Institutional factors often lead organizations to conform to societal norms even when formal enforcement mechanisms are highly flawed. Frequently cited institutional influences include historical legacies, cultural mores, cognitive scripts and structural linkages to the professions and to the state. Each, in its own way, displaces single-minded profit maximization with a heightened sensitivity to the organizational embeddedness within a larger social environment . . . [That is,] organizations adopt many practices and structures, not for efficiency reasons, but because the cultural environment constructs adoption as the proper, legitimate, or natural thing to do.
>
> (Suchman and Edelman, 1996, p. 919)

Therefore, although there are stark differences between the two types, there are similarities insofar as neither can step away entirely from the 'normal' model of a law firm. If they were to do so, even if it were in the individuals' self-interest, the perceptions of the public and others would be shocked. It is unlikely that a wholesale reconfiguration of the law firm partnership could take place as long as the present norms and ethics of law practice exist. Forms of incorporation and limited liability that have been explored by law firms have been genteel, to say the least. The law firm as an organization requires the patina of professionalism in order to justify itself as organization and to its lawyer-members. It may be seething with dissension and difference (Martin and Meyerson [1988] quoted in Schultz, 1995): the classification of partners as junior and senior creates subcultures that can be oppositional to each other. Yet the public face of the organization will strongly attempt to portray itself as smooth and unriven.

Knowledge markets

In the UK case study I showed the perceptions of a change in the market for legal services. The sediment was truly stirred by expansion of advocacy services. Similar effects are being observed among welfare lawyers, as the government changes the funding structure of legal aid (cf. Sommerlad, 1995). Perhaps the bigger game is being played in the corporate sphere at the global level. If two jurisdictions, New York and England, have come to dominate world markets in law, the organizations that deliver those services will have to compete. The deregulation of the British financial markets in the 1980s and the creation of the single European market in 1992 were signals for US law firms to enter the British market by setting up firms in London and elsewhere. The Courts and Services Act 1990 enabled the establishment of multinational law practices in the UK, which allowed foreign firms to associate with, merge with British law firms or employ British lawyers (Flood, 1996). The first wave of big American firms to move into London offered, by English standards, large salaries (Flanagan, 1998). The lure was powerful and British lawyers were joining American firms. One of the effects was to import American firm organizational modes to London. A few firms began to shift their remuneration systems from lockstep to 'eat what you kill'. And as the struggle over which lawyers could deliver the most expertise in capital markets work, English firms began to set up offices in New York and elsewhere in the US. At first, both US and UK firms played safe by offering services based on their own jurisdictional skills. Over time, however, they each began to offer expertise in both types of law (Swann, 1998).[22] The transfer market between UK and US law firms is now a regular occurrence. Lawyers move but the firm retains its identity. For City firms 'branding' as an index of quality assurance is critical.

Both in the US and UK law firms are retelling their histories as part of an intellectual enterprise that endows them with legitimacy. In addition to individual lawyers increasing their symbolic capital, the firm is also creating capital. We see this in part through the fixity of naming that law firms have adopted; no longer do names change with the partners – the image of the brand is central to the identity of the organization. Simple regulation, inscribed in codes of conduct and elsewhere, has become inadequate to capture the complexities of global corporate life. The malpractice insurance schemes run by the professional bodies are largely for the benefit of a public suffering incompetent service delivered by small firms and solo practitioners. Large firms potentially face negligence claims amounting to millions of pounds and dollars; thus they take out extra cover beyond the professional bodies' thresholds. How esteem, status and prestige are conserved and raised becomes an important issue for corporate law firms. For the top echelon of firms in the US and the UK, their names are brands, which clients know are unlikely to be adulterated by commingling with accounting firms, for example, become guarantees of 'excellence'. The result of staying with the brand is that the organization cannot so radically alter its structure as to become unrecognizable. While it may move from a more traditional partnership mode to a more managerial style, it does not and cannot affect the integrity of the original structure. Mergers and lateral hiring of staff have undoubtedly increased in frequency, but success, internally and externally, is still measured by the strength of organic growth (Lee, 1997, p. 21). As this suggests, the normative structures of professions render them peculiarly resistant to concerns of economy or efficiency.

Multi-disciplinary practice is seen by some commentators as inevitable (Scott, 1998; *The Lawyer*, 1998a).[23] Law firms below the top rank have actively discussed forming alliances with Big Five accounting firms, while stopping short of full merger (Lindsay, 1998a). The dangers to institutional integrity and legitimation in such alliances have been submerged of late. Arthur Andersen has been able to form alliances with Spain's and Scotland's largest firms without demur (Lindsay, 1998b). But Andersen's attempt at establishing an alliance with a City law firm, Wilde Sapte, courted disaster (Flood, 1998). The entire courtship was conducted in the public gaze and when Andersen's spurned Wilde Sapte, the law firm began to atrophy. The failure was partially due to two key rainmakers leaving Wilde Sapte for another firm – after they had voted for the alliance. A large, 250-year-old City law firm was snubbed. The extent of the damage to the reputation of Wilde Sapte is yet incalculable, but the intensity of the reaction to the failure has introduced caution among other potential suitors. The rupture with the law firm's established culture was significant and abrupt. This suggests that interfering with the image inscribed on an established law firm is a high-risk venture. The brand could be devalued beyond recall.[24]

To conclude, if law firms are gradually adopting new configurations in their organizational schemas, from, say, P^2 to MPB, the reason may be that others are doing so and therefore the herd instinct comes into play – even if there is no rational reason for the change. Control of an organization does not necessarily indicate how change should be managed. Even departmental structures are fragile: some firms prefer to cross-cut them with joint-expertise groups so that collectivities of lawyers are brought together for specific purposes, e.g., crisis management. Adaptation to new markets introduces uncertainty and random factors that are not immediately amenable to rational planning, e.g., should intra-firm advocates be insulated from clients and other lawyers? If they were, how would that conflict with client control and the maintenance of authority in the firm? Cooper *et al.* (1996) are right when they argue the case for the sedimentation approach to law firm organization. While firms may oscillate over the spectrum of P^2 to MPB, most, however, are combinations of the archetypes. What is clearer is that international competition and the threat of multidisciplinary practices from the accounting firms are forcing English corporate law firms to revisit their traditions, billing becomes more aggressive, lockstep begins to pall. Incentives to remain with a firm for the long term fade and career mobility becomes the norm. These sorts of conditions will conspire to cause the P^2 archetype to weaken and instead favour the MPB.

Notes

1 Those below partner level, in both systems, have always been treated as employees with minimal standing in the firm (see Spangler, 1986).

2 For example, the Lord Chancellor's Department (1998) has issued a White Paper that proposes to grant complete rights of audience to solicitors from their initial qualification. This would place them in direct competition with barristers.

3 Personal communication from City solicitor, August 1998.

4 *Habitus* is the system of dispositions (i.e., 'virtualities, potentialities, eventualities') of actors in a particular field that is continuously subjected to everyday experiences and is therefore an integral part of social action (Bourdieu and Wacquant, 1992, pp. 133–135).

5 For example, the market for auditing services among large corporations is dominated by the Big Five accounting firms which possess the numbers of auditors and cost structure that enable them to undertake, say, the auditing of Ford (see Han, 1994).

6 I examined the firm's web site in July 1998 and found Tischmann contained many of the same attorneys as ten years before. The composition of the management committee hadn't changed significantly in the intervening years. Perhaps one notable element was that the retirement of senior lawyers appears to have more of a voluntary flavour than in the UK where it is usually mandatory at between 60 and, more rarely, 65 years of age. I noticed on the web site that one lawyer in Tischmann who in the 1970s was in his own 70s, was still presented to be in active practice.

7 Using the ranking system of law schools devised by Heinz and Laumann (1982), I found that 50 per cent of the firm's lawyers graduated from elite law schools (Harvard, Yale, Chicago, Michigan), about one-quarter from prestige law schools (Northwestern, Duke), and about 10 per cent each from regional schools (Illinois, Iowa, Notre Dame, Wisconsin) and from local schools (Chicago–Kent, Loyola, De Paul). The range of the billing rates, at the time of the research, was from $70 to $225 with a median of $115.

8 The lifespan of ideas may be very short. A leading New York bankruptcy lawyer remarked that his briefs and other documents would appear on the Internet shortly after they were filed. He even had his own arguments quoted back at him, without attribution. Personal communication, December 1996.

9 Sometimes cross-referrals *within* a firm are also conducted with great caution and the consideration of keeping the client within one's firm grip. For example, a partner may never pass work to another 'aggressive' partner within the same firm. Personal communication from City solicitor, August 1998.

10 From the figures, I was able to see at Tischmann, the top attorneys in the firm received over four times the amount awarded to the junior partners.

11 An analysis of the manner in which work was recorded showed that on average 55 per cent of a Tischmann lawyer's time was spent in talk on the phone, at meetings, in conferences, etc. For senior partners 95 per cent of their time was billed as talk; for middle-range partners, 65 per cent; for junior partners, 50 per cent; for associates, less than 15 per cent (Flood, 1987).

12 There was one item about which the management committee was firm, namely, the recording of time sheets and billing. Any lawyer who was tardy in submitting time sheets didn't receive his or her salary cheque for that month until the sheet was completed.

13 The Lord Chancellor's Department (1998) has proposed that ACLEC should be abolished.

14 Personal communication from City solicitor, July 1998.

15 The average annual billable hours target for UK lawyers is around 1,400 hours. In the US it can be anywhere between 2,000 to 2,500 hours per year (Alcock, 1998).

16 The Lord Chancellor's Department (1998) estimates that out of approximately 60,000 solicitors in England and Wales only 600 have become solicitor-advocates.

17 The importance of these perceptions can be demonstrated by the example of the Commercial Court in London, which is staffed by a small cadre of elite judges. A full 80 per cent of its caseload involves one overseas party, and 50 per cent of the caseload involves both parties being foreign. Therefore it is a forum of choice for many non-UK corporate litigants. See the International Centre for Commercial Law web site at http://www.icclaw.com.

18 Tischmann, like most US law firms, had no problems with this division of labour. Whoever the client belonged to was the client 'carer-pleaser', but many litigation cases were referred from the corporate and property departments so the litigator would be responsible for the case but not the client.

19 Reflexivity is also a major theme in John Gray's chapter (5) in this volume.

20 I am not denying that partnership is underdeveloped jurisprudentially; quite the contrary, but partnership requires a high degree of consensus. Some law partnerships still require unanimous votes for organizational change. The City firm of Denton Hall refused to merge with two other City firms because a single partner objected (Hoult, 1998, p. 15).

21 For example, in the rush to open overseas offices, law firms didn't always analyse the need for one, and so many were closed after a short but expensive time (Flood, 1996).

22 Work does not always follow expected patterns. For example, the US firms have been strong in privatization work in Eastern Europe, an economic process pioneered in the UK; and UK firms have been at the forefront of utilities regulatory work in the US, which has a longer tradition of this type of regulation than the UK.

23 In the US there are restrictive rules on who can deliver legal services and how audit services can be combined with legal services. These rules inhibit the formation of MDPs in the US (Cannon, 1997).

24 Both the American Bar Association and the Conseil National des Barreaux in France have initiated inquiries into MDPs because they fear the legal profession will fragment with their implementation (*The Lawyer*, 1998b; Tyler, 1998). The Paris Bar has gone further requiring MDPs to 'reveal to their local Bar the legal and financial structure between the lawyers and the other professions involved' (Tyler, 1998, p. 16).

Acknowledgements

I am grateful to the editors David Brock, Bob Hinings and Michael Powell, for their encouragement and helpful comments. Andy Boon and Eleni Skordaki helped with the development of the ideas and critically read drafts, for which I thank them.

9 'All fur coat and no knickers'

Contemporary organizational
change in United Kingdom
hospitals

Martin Kitchener

Introduction

Until the early 1990s, Mintzberg's (1979; 1983a) notion of the 'professional bureaucracy' provided an adequate basis from which to understand the nature of many professional organizations. In particular, the attention drawn to the influence of professional autonomy and decentralized decision-making helped to explain prevailing configurations of structure and power in United Kingdom hospitals. The aim of this chapter is to consider the extent to which these characteristics have survived recent socio-economic and political shifts (see Greenwood and Lachman, 1996, pp. 563–72).

In the UK, contemporary studies of change in public sector professional organizations have tended to concentrate upon the structural implications of the introduction of so-called 'new public management' (Hood, 1991; Pollitt, 1995; Ferlie *et al.*, 1996). This term is used to refer to the uneven introduction by state agencies of a collection of loosely linked, and sometimes inconsistent, doctrines. These include fiscal restraint, a preference for market forms over bureaucratic structures, and the adoption of private sector management techniques. Early research into the impact of the new public management (NPM) has reported the fragmentation of organizational forms, attempts to enhance the managerial control of professional work and the replacement of hierarchical control with contractual relations (Hoggett, 1996; Clarke and Newman, 1997).

This chapter combines concepts from institutional theory with empirical data to analyse contemporary developments in one field of public sector professional organizations, British National Health Service (NHS) hospitals. In 1991, the UK government sought to transform the institutional framework of this sector through the introduction of a quasi-market (LeGrand and Bartlett, 1993, pp. 1–12). The key element of this NPM reform saw the division of public health care organizations into provider and commissioning or purchaser units. For the first time, provider units such as hospitals were required to compete for contracts to provide health care services to the new commissioning bodies (p. 12). At the organizational level of analysis, this reform led to the first significant alterations to the configuration of UK hospitals since the creation of the NHS in 1948

Table 9.1 Structures and systems of the PB and QM hospital archetypes

	The PB hospital archetype	*The QM hospital archetype*
Structures	Distinct professional collegiate and administrative hierarchies.	Clinical directorates, market-customer based. Hybrid professional-manager roles.
Systems	Poorly developed management information systems. Asset base managed externally.	Enhanced management information systems. Asset base managed internally.

(Kitchener and Whipp, 1997; Kitchener, 1998). These changes are summarized in Table 9.1 where they are represented in terms of movement from a professional bureaucracy (PB) hospital archetype towards a quasi-market (QM) archetype.

As Table 9.1 shows, the PB hospital archetype was characterized by the distinct professional and administrative hierarchies described by Mintzberg (1979; 1983a). By contrast, the QM archetype represents an alternative form of hospital organization based upon clinical directorates or medical cost centres. Within this new structural form, senior hospital managers have greater independence from regional health agencies and an emphasis has been placed upon the development of hospital management information systems. The aim is to produce the cost and quality information that hospitals need to compete within the quasi-market. Managers are also expected to manage and maintain their asset base fully recognizing their capital costs.

Beyond these alterations to formal hospital structures and systems, the reformers who introduced the quasi-market hoped to alter prevailing attitudes and beliefs regarding the appropriate organization of hospital activity (Department of Health [DoH], 1989). Had these changes occurred, the QM archetype would have been expected to achieve legitimacy and stability (Zucker, 1987). By contrast, a failure to secure the legitimacy of the prescribed change in attitudes and values would indicate a lack of coherence within the archetype and, possibly, its fragility.

Following Hinings and Greenwood (1988a), this chapter considers the extent to which the intended changes occurred in prevailing views of what UK hospitals should do, how they should do it, and how they should be judged. The aim is to assess the coherence and stability of the recently introduced QM archetype of professional organization. Analysis of these issues is contained within the six main sections of this chapter.

The first section introduces the concepts that are used in the chapter. In the second, the research design and methods that were adopted for the study of change in UK hospitals are described. The third section presents an analysis of dominant beliefs and values about the PB archetype. Section four describes the ways in which these prevailing attitudes became challenged by the state through the NPM reform agenda. In section five, the characteristics of the QM hospital archetype are outlined. Section six draws on study data to compare the intended and prevailing attitudes concerning the QM archetype. It is suggested that a failure to gain professionals' support for the intended attitude changes has led to the co-existence of new structures and systems with a hybrid interpretive scheme that maintains established values and attitudes.

Archetypes, tracks and sedimentation

Greenwood and Hinings (1988, p. 294) propose that the study of continuity and change within organizations can 'usefully begin' by the specification of 'archetypes' and the 'tracks' that organizations take in moving from one archetype to another. Drawing on the work of Miller and Friesen (1984), they contend that archetypes emerge within 'fields' of interrelated organizations. This occurs because the constituent organizations seek to demonstrate their legitimacy to resource providers by adopting institutionally accepted configurations (Meyer and Rowan, 1977; DiMaggio and Powell, 1983). Greenwood and Hinings' (1988) view of archetypes stresses not only the similarity of internal structural forms and systems but also the importance of a common orientation, or underlying interpretive scheme, that offers ideological coherence to the configuration (Ranson *et al.*, 1980).

The notion of tracks of change is used to help trace an organization's movement between and within archetypes. A distinction is made among tracks of inertia or little change, tracks that run out of steam (unresolved excursions), and tracks that produce a new archetype (transformations). Greenwood and Hinings (1993, p. 1057) predict that internal stakeholders' perceptions of the legitimacy of the interpretive scheme will influence the stability of an archetype and, hence, the tracks of change that are followed.

Miller and Friesen (1984) and Oliver (1991, p. 146) suggest that, because vested interests and their power bases become intertwined with a particular archetype, change tends to proceed along tracks within rather than between archetypes. DiMaggio and Powell (1983, p. 148) argue that it is 'isomorphic' pressures – such as coercion from resource providers, mimicry, and the influence of professional groups – that encourage adherence to established archetypes. Ackroyd *et al.* (1989) agree that managerial action in professional organizations is often limited to 'custody' over existing archetypes. This arises, they suggest, from the emphasis that professional-managers place upon maintaining stable working conditions for their professional colleagues.

The more recent empirical work of Cooper *et al.* (1996) implicitly draws on these insights to acknowledge that previous applications of the tracks perspective have tended to concentrate upon transformations and so overlook examples of unresolved excursions. By contrast, they draw on the example of Canadian law firms to explore the emergence of an organizational archetype that comprises 'sedimented' structures and ideologies. This geological metaphor is used to represent change not so much as a shift from one archetype to another, but as a layering of one archetype on another. The sedimentation concept points particularly to the persistence of values, ideas and practices under conditions where formal structures and processes seem to change.

Drawing upon these concepts, and following Hinings and Greenwood (1988a, p. 295), this chapter presents the first systematic analysis of previously intended and emergent beliefs about three principal 'vectors' of UK hospital activity:

> (1) the appropriate *domain* of operations i.e. the broad nature of an organization's *raison d'être*; (2) beliefs and values about appropriate *principles* of organizing; and (3) appropriate *criteria* that should be used for evaluating organizational performance.
>
> (Emphases in original)

The research methods and design used to investigate these issues are described next.

Research design and methods

This chapter draws on data collected during two early investigations into the impact of the quasi-market in UK hospitals. These projects required the use of comparative-intensive case studies to generate a foundation of understanding in the area and to reveal existing and emerging interpretive schema, structures and systems (Kitchener, 1994, p. 209). The first study was sponsored by the Economic and Social Research Council (ESRC) and investigated organizational change in NHS hospitals between 1991 and 1993 (McNulty *et al.*, 1994). The second study more directly considered the emergence of the QM archetype through comparative-intensive case studies at three groups of Welsh hospitals between 1991 and 1995. A plurality of perspectives was derived from interviewing a wide range of stakeholders including health care commissioners, hospital managers, doctors and nurses. Over a hundred interviews were conducted. These were supplemented by periods of observation and the examination of archival material. This inclusive approach ensured that the hospital archetypes emerged as reflectors of meanings which acknowledge the negotiated order in hospitals and the possibility of local variations (Cooper *et al.*, 1996, p. 629).

In the absence of detailed and reliable primary data that describe the configuration of hospitals before the mid-1980s (Pollitt *et al.*, 1991, p. 64), the PB hospital archetype was constructed largely on the basis of the experience of respondents and from secondary data. The consistency of data that emerged from these sources suggests that the PB archetype may reliably describe the general form of many UK hospitals before the early 1990s. The QM hospital archetype is derived largely from primary data collected during the two studies.

The PB hospital interpretive scheme

Following negotiations between the state and the medical professions, most UK hospitals joined the NHS at its inception in 1948. The majority then developed similar configurations of structures and systems. These common features are described in detail elsewhere (Kitchener, 1998) and summarized in Table 9.1 as the PB hospital archetype.

The key structural characteristics of the PB archetype include the location of UK hospitals within the wider NHS hierarchy and the distinction, within hospitals, between administrative hierarchies and collegial professional structures. The systems dimension of the PB archetype concerns the range and sequence of activities involved in hospital management. Traditionally, there was limited investment in this area because the ideology of the archetype stressed the requirement to allow hospital doctors to manage themselves (Mintzberg, 1979). Many senior managers were committed to this view and so information systems remained 'too feeble to provide . . . evidence of the need to change' (Miller and Friesen, 1984, p. 94). Even after the introduction of general managers following the Griffiths reforms of 1983, the defining features of management systems remained those identified by the Department of Health and Social Security (1983) and previous inquiries: poor financial accounting mechanisms, and a lack of standardized cost and performance data.

The rest of this section analyses the dominant beliefs and values about the three principal vectors of activity that underpinned the PB hospital archetype. These features are summarized in Table 9.2 and considered, in turn, below.

Raison d'être

From 1948, there was widespread agreement that the *raison d'être* of UK hospitals was to provide the organizational bases from which medical practitioners could deliver given treatments, free at the point of delivery, in a stable and collaborative environment. There was also an expectation that stability would be assured through annual funding increases from central government. In general, this occurred, and the emphasis that was placed upon stability fostered strong professional networks that involved the transfer of ideas, information and even some resources between hospitals (Harrison and Pollitt, 1994, p. 36).

Principles of organizing

The characteristic principle of organizing within the PB hospital archetype was the distinction between the medical and administrative domains of activity.

Table 9.2 Dominant views of the three vectors of the PB interpretive scheme

	PB interpretive scheme
Raison d'être	Collaboratively organized and stable hospital care.
Principles of organizing	Loose-coupling. Strategic and operational professional autonomy. Distinct administrative and professional domains. Pigeon-holing.
Evaluation criteria	Service quality as determined and monitored by professionals

Administrators, working within a domain that embodied an ethos of hierarchy, control and procedures, accepted that they were not expected to intervene in clinical areas (Freidson, 1994). By contrast, the medical domain was based upon notions of autonomy, self-discipline and adherence to professional standards. These ideological differences led to poor communication and an enduring demarcation between the two 'loosely-coupled' domains (Weick, 1976).

Within the medical domain, the objective of hospital doctors to secure autonomy and protect occupational closure was never entirely free from external challenge by the competing claims of, for example, nurses and the professions allied to medicine (Abbott, 1988; Ackroyd, 1996). The cause of hospital doctors was advanced, however, through a series of *ad hoc* accommodations and concessions between the state, hospital administrators and the medical profession (Larson, 1977, p. 179; Phelps-Brown, 1983). When they joined the NHS in 1948, for example, hospital doctors surrendered their economic autonomy, or right to determine their remuneration. In return, the state allowed them to maintain high levels of operational autonomy, or the right to set standards and control medical performance. This operational autonomy allowed doctors to make decisions that were only loosely constrained by guidelines issued by the state and professional bodies (a process described as 'pigeon-holing' by Mintzberg, 1983a). The power that this process gave to doctors lends weight to Harrison and Pollitt's (1994, p. 35) view that 'contrary to the usual assumptions of textbook management, managers were not the most influential actors in the organization; doctors were'.

Evaluation criteria

The autonomy of hospital doctors was reinforced through the reliance that was placed upon peer review as the primary means of defining and assuring service quality. As a result, the pre-eminent logic governing service provision in the PB hospital archetype was quality, as determined and monitored by professional providers.

The attitudes and values that supported these vectors of the PB hospital interpretive scheme did not simply prove to be a barrier to transformation. Their wide acceptance and cohesion provided a clear position against which successive cases for reform were negotiated by the state, hospital managers and health care professionals (Brunsson and Olsen, 1993, p. 3). Even the Griffiths reforms of 1983 which stressed cost-effectiveness and managerial efficiency were 'limited in comparison with the continued influence of medical autonomy and financial limitations' (Pollitt *et al.*, 1991, p. 61). As a consequence, resistance and inertia from managers and professionals combined to ensure that when change initiatives challenged vectors of the PB interpretive scheme, they were 'thwarted, sidetracked or aborted' (Kitchener and Whipp, 1997, p. 52).

Challenges to the PB interpretive scheme

During the 1980s, the PB archetype continued to provide the world's most comprehensive and least expensive hospital services (Davidson, 1987). Despite this fact, high-technology medicine and an ageing population combined to place substantial organizational and financial strains on the NHS. In addition, the attitudes and values that supported the PB interpretive scheme came under sustained attack from the neo-liberal ideology of the successive Conservative administrations from 1979 (Pollitt, 1993a). The critique rested on the conception of professional bureaucracies representing professionals' interests over those of tax-payers and consumers. Enthoven (1985) claimed, for example, that medical dominance suppressed consumer information and restricted the development of health care. In response, the political reformers advocated a new set of attitudes and beliefs based upon the ability of markets to achieve superior performance and reduce clinical autonomy.

By the late 1980s, some of the medical professionals who had been incorporated within the management of hospitals following the Griffiths Report (DHSS, 1983) combined with the government to press for change. Whilst their agendas may have differed, a growing consensus began to appear for the fundamental reform of the PB hospital archetype. This view was summarized by an orthopedic surgeon from one large acute hospital in Wales:

> Everyone in the health service thought there had to be a big change . . . the nurses wanted more pay, the government wanted to spend less and limit our [doctors'] power . . . and we wanted to stop them doing this and get them to spend more money . . . something had to give.[1]
>
> (Personal interview, 1993)

In the face of this momentum for change, the political reformers were presented with a number of options. These included overt rationing, increased expenditure, and the expansion of private health care (King's Fund Institute, 1988, p. 24). After rejecting these options, and after ignoring the failure of a market simulation exercise, the government took Enthoven's (1985) advice and split the NHS into purchaser and provider units. Kitchener (1998) reports that individual UK hospitals responded by pursuing a variety of tracks of change. These differences of experience are explained, in part, by variations in the extent to which management teams in hospitals sought to build influence and momentum for change through symbolic management tactics.

Despite the different tracks of change followed by individual hospitals, by the mid-1990s a new hospital archetype had emerged (Kitchener, 1998). The structural and systems characteristics of this QM hospital archetype are represented and contrasted with the PB archetype in Table 9.1. The main features of the new configuration are summarized below.

The QM hospital archetype

In terms of change at the level of the UK hospital sector, while providers were expected to compete for contracts with purchasers, the UK health market differed greatly from the economists' notion of perfect competition (LeGrand and Bartlett, 1993, pp. 1–12). In particular, providers were not expected to maximize their profits. Nor were they necessarily privately owned. Whilst hospitals were re-labelled as 'trusts' to signify their increased independence from direct state control, they remained subject to considerable influence from government agencies (Ranade, 1995, p. 136).

For these reasons, the proposed archetype represented a 'quasi-market' form that differed significantly from the purer market models that exist in US health care (Montgomery and Oliver, 1996). The UK quasi-market archetype did, however, embody an increased orientation towards a market for heathcare services that contained pressures for competition among provider organizations.

Internal structures and systems

In terms of the internal structural characteristics of the QM archetype, 70 per cent of hospitals adopted the clinical directorates model of organization (Rea, 1995, p. 232). This form is based upon medical cost centres, or clinical directorates, that are responsible to hospital boards of directors. Although this model was never a formal government policy, it became legitimized through a variety of normative, coercive and mimetic isomorphic processes. Hospital managers were, for example, encouraged by professional bodies such as the National Association of Health Authorities and Trusts (NAHAT) and the Institute of Health Service Management (IHSM) to adopt the model. In addition, commissioning officials 'steered' hospital managers to adopt clinical directorates through policy directives that were issued through memoranda and briefings for senior managers.

The immediate priority of the quasi-market was to control escalating costs and erode what was seen as the dominance of profligate professionals (Dent, 1996, p. 879). As a consequence, the main shift in the systems dimension of hospital configurations was the increased emphasis that was placed on the development of management information systems to support the contracting process between purchasers and providers.

The intended interpretive scheme

In line with the main aims of NPM, the policy reformers hoped that the new institutional framework would encourage 'management ideas [to] provide the dominant intellectual framework within which the health service thinks about itself and its role in society' (Davidson, 1987, p. 23). This attempt to replace the dominance of professional 'ideas' with management 'ideas' involved promoting the belief that 'simply injecting more and more money is not, by itself, the answer' (DoH, 1989, pp. 2–3). In place of the stability offered by annual increases in state funding, hospitals were to become market oriented in the following way:

> The hospital Trusts will earn revenue from the services they provide. They will therefore have an incentive to attract patients, so they will make sure that the service they offer . . . respond[s] to what people want locally.
>
> (DoH, 1989, p. 24)

A key aim of this initiative was to encourage UK hospital doctors to resemble American-style 'corporate clinicians' by tying medical staff and administrators closer together through competition with other hospitals (Schulz and Detmer, 1977, p. 8). As part of this government project to have professional expertise 'on tap' rather than 'on top' (Pollitt, 1993a), the reformers sought to introduce managerial performance indicators and make the audit of patient care the joint responsibility of hospital doctors and managers. The legislation that introduced the quasi-market stressed, for example, the 'need':

> To develop and publish indicators of hospital performance which cover the quality as well as the efficiency of the services provided. . . . Every consultant should participate in a form of medical audit agreed between management and the professional locally.
>
> (DoH, 1989, pp. 36–40)

The logic of conducting audits whereby patient care processes are benchmarked according to performance criteria and subjected to managerial review is clear, given the importance that costs should play in a market. The next section assesses the extent to which attempts to alter prevailing conceptions of hospital activity have occurred.

The emergence of a hybrid interpretive scheme

Raison d'être

While strategy in the PB archetype concentrated on the plans of the individual professional (Mintzberg, 1979, p. 364), within the quasi-market hospital managers began to develop embryonic business plans. These adopted a more aggregate connotation of strategy referring to, for example, increasing the market share of hospitals. During the early 1990s, reflecting this development, phrases such as 'competition' and 'marketing' began to emerge within the QM archetype.

Sometimes using the new language, clinicians began to report that managers had encouraged them to work towards the new hospital business plans by increasing their opportunistic behaviour. This most commonly included them marketing their services to purchasers and becoming involved in various income generation schemes. Throughout the UK, politicians and their officials sought to legitimize the new language and commercial activity in the press, and through the requirement that hospital managers attend what were termed 'cultural change' seminars. A senior consultant at one of the case hospitals gave his view of these pressures:

The message is clear from the Government and its various bodies that they think that . . . competition will provide the most effective coordination of health resources and enable close clinical involvement in planning and development at all levels of management.

(Personal interview, 1992)

The combined influence of these prescribed and recommended practices frayed, to some extent, the consensus surrounding elements of the PB hospital interpretive scheme such as stability and cooperation. In their place, an alternative imperative, competition between hospitals, began to emerge. This notion failed, however, to secure widespread legitimacy amongst professionals. Their resistance and inertia can, in part, be traced to the professional ideology which stresses deference to the needs of the patients rather than to the paying customer (Keat, 1991, p. 223). Doctors seemed particularly uneasy with the perception that, within a market, managers could override their operational autonomy by prioritizing the treatment of those patients who generate income. A senior consultant explained a perception that he felt was dominant amongst his colleagues:

The new market has a second-hand car salesman image . . . and antagonizes a lot of us medical professionals. . . . Market thinking is foreign thinking to hospital doctors. People don't like to think of competition. It is a bad term to use. . . . It conjures up the wrong mission for us who believe we are here to treat the patients in need, not those who bring in the cash.

(Personal interview, 1994)

This anxiety was combined, in some cases, with the unease that clinicians expressed at the possibility of a shift of power away from hospital doctors towards health commissioners. In the summer of 1992, a consultant geriatrician felt that:

Some psychopathic, aggressive purchasers will now ignore our advice and refer on the basis of cost rather than patients' interests.

(Personal interview, 1992)

Interview data collected between 1992 and 1995 further suggested that doctors 'detested' the emergence of what one termed the 'shabby commercialism' of the market (personal interview, 1995). Many expressed concern with, for example, the amount of money that was rumoured to have been spent upon the production of glossy promotional brochures, income generation schemes and the hiring of management consultants. A nurse spoke for a number of her colleagues when she said that she felt that these developments were a waste of time and 'all fur coat and no knickers' (personal interview, 1994).

Other professionals agreed with a senior clinician's description of the quasi-market as an 'unpopular broad agenda for rationalization, creeping privatization and movement towards the North American corporate model' (personal interview, 1995). As part of this view, many clinicians feared management attempts to prevent them from holding clinical sessions in hospitals other than the one in which they were based. Hospital managers seemed increasingly eager to abolish what one termed 'this scope for divided loyalties' (personal interview, 1994). Many doctors continued, however, to view this practice as an important part of their right to determine effective care practices. As one doctor explained, they also felt that its erosion might fragment the professional networks that enhance patient care:

> When I joined hospital management, if I was short of equipment I knew I could ring one of my colleagues to borrow even a £20,000 piece of equipment. That doesn't happen any more I'm afraid. Some people still do you favours on a personal level and everybody pulls their fingers out in emergencies, but I don't know what will happen when my generation retires.
>
> (Personal interview, 1993)

Hospital managers were left in no doubt about professional concerns regarding what they felt to be challenges to their operational autonomy. This point was made when a director of a trust reported a conversation with a consultant. Whilst the doctor was perceived, by the director, to be 'generally in favour of some of the changes':

> The consultant told me that even when he became a [clinical] director, he would still dig his heels in and would not budge on professional issues. He made that clear. Last month, a manager told him that he was 'over' on one contract and should transfer a bed from one ward to another so that another contract could be satisfied. He told the manager to 'stuff it' in a nice way and tried to explain that this would not be acceptable to any professional.
>
> (Personal interview, 1995)

Against this background of resistance to the intended shifts in dominant views concerning the *raison d'être* of hospitals, the next section considers prevailing views regarding the appropriate organization of hospitals.

Principles of organizing

Proponents of the quasi-market hoped that the introduction of the clinical directorate structures would raise the level of integration between the medical and managerial domains and so encourage hospitals to reduce their reliance upon the founding principles of pigeon-holing and professional autonomy. Under the new structures, the managers of clinical directorates, usually consultant grade doctors, became responsible for clinical budgets and a premium was placed upon their commercial management skills.

Data collected between 1992 and 1995 suggest that many professionals felt that the major impact of the clinical directorate structure had been the intensification of time and budget pressures. One clinical director articulated the view held by many of her colleagues that the new role involved 'lots more paperwork, more meetings, more stress and less clinical involvement' (personal interview, 1994). Two consultants admitted to having cancelled clinical sessions in order to 'keep up with the paperwork' (personal interview, 1995). Whilst some professionals welcomed the greater responsibility attached to their new roles, others felt that they had been coerced into acceptance through, for example, the requirement for them to demonstrate managerial activity to achieve their 'merit pay' awards. There is, however, little evidence to suggest that the increased blurring of the boundaries between the medical and administrative domains resulted in enhanced managerial control of professional work. This view was supported strongly by the majority of the clinicians including the clinical director of obstetrics and gynaecology at one case hospital:

> Most of us accept now that we must get involved with the administration of the Trust. Even though it takes a lot of time, I don't really mind looking after the budget for the department or having to go to all these board meetings. . . . In a way we are helping them [managers] to do their job . . . but there is no way they should ever be allowed to mess around with medical decisions about they way we do our jobs, no way. The day that happens, I'm off to the States where I can earn some real money.
>
> (Personal interview, 1994)

This evidence suggests that professional staff accepted, to some extent, the clinical directorate structure. In some cases, senior clinicians appreciated the opportunity to take the new medical-manager hybrid posts. It was clear, however, that professional staff would continue to resist managerial attempts to restrict their autonomy within the new structure.

Evaluation criteria

Since the 1991 reforms, the government has succeeded in generating the information to publish league tables that represent aggregated hospital performance data. Unlike the case in the US, however, monitoring the performance of individual clinicians remains within the medical domain. In the case of hospitals, this process continued to occur under the dominance of particular consultants who questioned the legitimacy and purpose of collecting the required data through the proposed managerial audits. One consultant put their concerns to the researcher in this way:

> Who are these people judging and monitoring us? What are their qualifications? What are their achievements? What are their standards and values? The increased monitoring affects our self-esteem and confidence. It creates an environment of mistrust. . . . There are an awful lot of good, hard working professional people in this hospital that are being prevented from

doing a good job because of unreasonable demands being placed on them in terms of form-filling.

(Personal interview, 1994)

Whilst audit committees were established in some of the case hospitals in the early 1990s, doctors participated on a voluntary basis, selecting the subjects they wanted to examine rather than being directed by managers. Concern with technical aspects of medical care dominated, with little interest shown in resource use as an issue. Later, the medical audit Working Paper that followed the introduction of the quasi-market conceded the principle that: 'the quality of medical work can only be reviewed by a doctor's peers' (quoted in Harrison and Pollitt, 1994, p. 130).

Doctors had, therefore, been successful in resisting the increased managerial control of their work, which would have occurred had clinical audit become the primary method of quality assurance. The result has been that peer review is still widely perceived to be the primary means of quality control. It is conducted by doctors, and on a voluntary basis. This position remains far removed from a managerial process of quality assurance that the reformers hoped would allow externally driven performance analysis to diminish medical power and so reduce costs.

Discussion

This chapter has described two alternative archetypes that are extant in the field of UK hospitals. First, primary and secondary data were combined to show that, following the birth of the NHS in 1948, most UK hospitals developed similar structures and systems that were underpinned by a common interpretive scheme. These similarities were represented as the PB hospital archetype which shares many characteristics with Mintzberg's (1979; 1983a) notion of the professional bureaucracy. The structures and systems of the archetype were characterized by distinct medical and administrative domains. The defining feature of the PB interpretive scheme was the consensus that supported professional autonomy, stability and the peer review of practice as the primary means of quality assurance.

Other studies have demonstrated that these characteristics of the PB hospital interpretive scheme were not limited to the field of UK hospitals (Ranson *et al.*, 1980). Elements such as the widespread support of the distinction between clinical and administrative domains were also revealed in the Denis, Langley and Cazale (1996) study of Canadian hospitals. Similar features also emerge from Metcalfe and Richards' (1990) study of the UK civil service, and Greenwood and Hinings' (1988) research into UK local government agencies. Each of these works identify parallel combinations of widely held values and attitudes that reduced the opportunities for significant change within fields of interrelated professional organizations.

The second part of this chapter provided an analysis of the conditions under which the prevailing PB archetype was challenged. As Oliver (1992) would predict, a combination of the NPM doctrines, changing government regulations and internal performance crises provided sufficient momentum to 'de-institutionalize' elements of the PB archetype.

The fact that, after some forty years of stability, this occurred for the first time lends support to the 'punctuated equilibrium' thesis of change (Romanelli and Tushman, 1993, p. 1156). Under this view, organizational life is characterized by 'long periods of the maintenance of a given configuration, punctuated by brief periods of multifaceted and concerted transition' (Miller and Friesen, 1984, p. 23). This chapter has shown that the predominant condition within the field of UK hospitals has been the negotiated and incremental change of the PB hospital archetype (Kitchener, 1998). Only since the introduction of the quasi-market in 1991 have coercive, normative and mimetic forces (DiMaggio and Powell, 1983) combined to produce a new set of hospital structures and systems to challenge the dominant archetype. These were represented as the QM hospital archetype.

The findings presented here indicate that it was the intention of the reformers to alter prevailing attitudes towards the key vectors of hospital activity (DoH, 1989). In particular, the introduction of the quasi-market represented an attempt to dislodge dominant conceptions of what UK hospitals should do, how they should do it and how they should be judged. In some ways, the aims of this initiative were similar to those described in Greenwood and Hinings' (1988) study of UK local government agencies and Cooper *et al.*'s (1996) study of Canadian law firms. These authors report institutional pressures to shift similar professional bureaucracy archetypes towards 'corporate bureaucracy' or 'managed professional bureaucracy' archetypes. Each of the emergent configurations share characteristics with the intended QM hospital archetype. In particular, all emphasize the managerial appraisal of professional work and the importance of professional organizations becoming 'more business like' (Cooper *et al.*, 1996, p. 643).

Table 9.3 compares the prevailing attitudes under the PB hospital archetype with those intended by the reforms, and those that have emerged since 1991. To emphasize that the emergent hospital interpretive scheme shares prescribed elements with some that have endured from the PB archetype, it is labelled the 'hybrid' interpretive scheme. As Table 9.3 shows, the intended shifts in dominant attitudes occurred regarding only one of the key vectors of activity. Professionals have come to accept, albeit under some coercion, the new clinical directorate structure of hospital organization. It is ironic that this shift was not originally intended by the reformers. Beyond the acceptance of the new principles of organizing hospitals, the intended alterations to prevailing beliefs regarding the *raison d'être* and criteria for evaluating services were not viewed as legitimate by key stakeholders. The great majority of professionals interviewed in this and other studies (e.g., Goldacre *et al.*, 1998) viewed the intended beliefs and attitudes unfavourably.

As this chapter has shown, the increased use of commercial language within hospitals suggested early success in the reformers' aims to encourage notions of competition and the managerial accountability of doctors to individual hospitals

Table 9.3 Continuity and change within the interpretive scheme of UK hospitals

	PB interpretive scheme	*Intended QM interpretive scheme*	*Hybrid interpretive scheme*
Raison d'être	Collaboratively organized and stable hospital care	Competitive health care provision. Market orientation	Increased opportunistic behaviour. Reduced collaboration. Emphasis on stability
Principles of organizing	Loose-coupling. Strategic and operational professional autonomy. Distinct administrative and professional domains. Pigeon-holing	Reduced operational and strategic autonomy of professionals. Enhanced managerial control of professional work	Maintenance of professional autonomy and pigeon-holing. Clinical directorates. Professional-manager hybrid roles
Evaluation criteria	Service quality as determined and monitored by professionals	Emphasis on managerial definitions and monitoring of service quality	Service quality as determined and monitored by professionals

rather than to their professional bodies. Whilst hospital managers are now less willing to allow clinicians to provide services to competing hospitals, little evidence emerged to suggest that the primary loyalty of UK hospital doctors has shifted from their peers and professional associations to general managers or to their hospitals. The notion of the 'corporate clinician' (Schulz and Detmer, 1977, p. 8) has yet to take hold in the UK.

In addition, the maintenance of peer review as the primary means of quality assurance suggests that UK doctors have so far proved successful in protecting themselves against managerial attempts to scrutinize and control their work (cf. Haug, 1973, p. 195; Reed, 1996, p. 577). The fact that some hospital doctors have accepted medical-manager roles within a more integrated formal structure should not, therefore, be conflated with either a loss of their professional autonomy or a replacement of key elements of the PB interpretive scheme.

These findings infer that prevailing conceptions of what UK hospitals should do, how they should do it, and how they should be judged did not become 'normatively fragmented' (Oliver, 1992) to the same extent as reported within Greenwood and Hinings' (1988) study of UK local government agencies. This situation highlights the continued power of medical professionals in shaping the outcomes of state policy. It also raises significant questions regarding the extent to which it is possible for managers or policy makers to secure shifts within the interpretive scheme of UK hospitals.

This chapter also reports the uneven and inconsistent adoption of change in professional organizations, a finding also noted by other researchers in this area. Such uneven change adoption is the consequence of the tension that emerges when, on the one hand legitimacy is sought through the adoption of prescribed configurations, while at the same time, the required attitude changes are viewed as incompatible with dominant professional belief systems. This chapter would seem to lend some empirical support to Oliver's (1991) prediction that, in these cases, tactics of buffering may emerge to disguise non-conformity with institutional pressures. In the case reported in this chapter, the widespread adoption of the clinical directorates model of internal organization masks the fact that key elements of the prescribed QM interpretive scheme were not accepted by the still-powerful professional groups. In particular, professionals resisted the threats to their operational autonomy that were perceived to emanate from increased managerial control of their work and consumerist notions allied to market orientation.

This pattern seems to be consistent across a number of fields of professional organizations. Montgomery and Oliver (1996) report that many US health care organizations adopted prescribed formal structures in response to HIV policies. The level of adoption varied, however, in response to practical considerations such as the determination of professional groups to uphold their autonomy. In a similar vein, Slack and Hinings' (1994, p. 821) study of change in Canadian sports agencies showed that whilst there has been a 'general shift' towards bureaucratic forms, key decision-making processes have 'not changed substantially'. Drawing from private sector examples, Hinings, Brown and Greenwood (1991) and Cooper *et al.* (1996) describe parallel processes, which involve the development of new structures that do not fully displace the prevailing interpretive scheme.

Cooper *et al.* (1996, p. 643) suggest that, because these findings show that 'organizations are structures in process', the language of sedimentation 'may be preferable to that of transformation' to describe change in professional organizations. Indeed, the examples of law and accountancy firms, local government agencies, and the UK hospitals reported here indicate that the responses of professional organizations to discontinuous change often accommodate existing together with new forms of organizing. In the case of UK hospitals, new structures co-exist with a hybrid interpretive scheme in which established attitudes and values persist.

Conclusion

This chapter has shown that, despite the intentions of political reformers, the introduction of a quasi-market has not led to the transformation of UK hospitals. Instead, the concept of sedimentation more accurately represents the process by which the 'coat' of hospital structures has changed whilst the 'knickers' of prevailing power relations, attitudes and values remain largely intact. This outcome suggests that Mintzberg's (1979, 1983b) notion of the 'professional bureaucracy' may continue to provide an appropriate basis from which to understand the nature of professional organizations in this field.

Note

1 All personal interview references and quotes are taken from a study of organizational change in UK hospitals that was completed in 1996. The research design and methods of this study are described in the second section of this chapter.

10 Continuity and change in professional organizations

Evidence from British law firms

Timothy Morris and Ashly Pinnington

Introduction

Change in partnerships of professionals has become an important aspect in the work seeking to understand how occupations claiming the privileged status of a profession are evolving. A key theme is the growing importance of 'business-like' behaviour and values. This refers to heightened competition for clients and income at the expense of more 'gentlemanly' (*sic*) conduct, concern for short-term fee maximization instead of the provision of dispassionate advice to a stable set of clients, and the replacement of a generalized area of expertise with greater functional specialization. Concomitantly, firms of professionals have succumbed to many of the techniques of management and control applied elsewhere in the public and private sectors in the pursuit of efficiency and a competitive edge.

Yet there is also continuity. Old and new forms of organization and ideology coexist. Rival interpretations of what it means to be a professional persist. Change seems to be halting or incomplete rather than transformational. Firms switch between different modes of managing, thereby 'sedimenting' structural forms and beliefs (Cooper *et al.*, 1996). How then do we understand what is happening to the professional partnership?

This chapter aims to contribute to our understanding of change and continuity in partnerships of professionals by drawing on evidence from a large sample of UK law firms. We explore the patterns of change across several dimensions of firm behaviour and policies. We also explore the differences between firms, examining the extent to which these can be explained by organizational performance or by perceptions of change affecting the profession, because these have been identified as important contributory factors (Greenwood and Lachman, 1996). By doing this, we aim to unravel some of the dynamics that are driving change and continuity in professional firms.

The chapter extends our knowledge of professional organizations in two ways. First, much of the existing empirical work has been focused on North America where certain special conditions, such as numbers of lawyers in the population and frequency of litigation, have been used to explain the rate and nature of change in the professional partnership (Galanter and Palay, 1991). This raises questions of generalizability to other countries. We address these by focusing on change in a different jurisdiction, albeit one with a similar, Anglo-Saxon professional heritage (Johnson, 1972).

Second, accounts providing general descriptions of the nature of change in law have been developed mainly from case based research. Yet, even within tightly knit elite groups such as the professions, exceptions to institutionalized norms of organization can be found (Starbuck, 1993). For instance, studies of smaller law firms have shown considerable differences in ideology and organization compared to larger ones (e.g., Serron, 1992). We address this problem by examining variations in continuity and change in a large sample of firms.

The chapter is set out as follows. The next section outlines the literature on change in the professional firm and the research objectives following from this. After that we present the findings from survey work on law firms in the UK. The final section discusses the implications for the debate on change and continuity in professional organizations and concludes by summarizing the key findings and their implications.

Organizational innovation in professional firms

Studies of change in professional firms have been concerned with the interaction of organization structure and systems with values and images of what it means to be a professional. It has been argued that this is a complex and reciprocal process whereby changes in ideas reflect or prompt objective changes in structure as well as influencing the way structures are interpreted (Cooper *et al.*, 1996). Change has been driven by a combination of external forces operating at several levels. These include: the spread of knowledge and demystification of professional expertise; shifts in the nature and volume of client demand for professional services; technical innovations such as expert systems that can act as a substitute for professionals' advice and adjustments to regulatory systems instigated by states or super-national authorities (Freidson, 1986; Nelson and Trubek, 1992). Other influences on change in the professions have included the rivalry between occupational groups competing for access to attractive jurisdictions and competition within occupations for pre-eminence in status and resource terms (Abbott, 1988).

In response, organizations of professionals are said to have become more 'business-like'. This phrase denotes how they have reformed structures, systems, policies and practices to pursue efficiency and a more concerted, commercially oriented approach to the capture and transaction of client work (Galanter and Palay, 1991; Greenwood and Lachman, 1996). Earlier studies show that the professional firm has constantly been evolving (Smigel, 1964; Hall, 1968), but change has apparently accelerated in recent years.

While the data and focus of different accounts may vary somewhat, there is a clear overlap between them, particularly in terms of the direction and consequences they observe. The characteristic of the traditional professional partnership model of organization was its loose control over the activities of the senior professionals. This reflected a professional ideology in which partners, as co-owners of the firm, collaborated with fellow professionals in the production of the firm's services, but worked relatively autonomously. Co-ordination and control of professional work was achieved by the standardization of inputs rather than processes, with extended training creating the appropriate skills and attitudes (Mintzberg, 1983b). Central control over the activities of senior professionals with respect to pricing of work and collection of debts, task administration and professional work standards was minimal. Relatively little central coordination of strategic direction was imposed, this being the aggregate of partners' individual interests, but the partnership facilitated internal effectiveness by being highly responsive to client demands (Greenwood, Hinings and Brown, 1990).

Cooper *et al.* (1996) contrast a newer archetype, the Managed Professional Business (MPB), with this traditional form of organization. Although their analysis relates primarily to the running of multi-office firms, it also has relevance for the single-office organization because it denotes how the distribution of power is expressed through the relationship between individual partners and those with management responsibility for the whole firm. Contrary to the decentralizing tendencies of the post-bureaucratic firm (Quinn, 1993; Heckscher and Donnellon, 1994) the reformed professional partnership is a more centralized and consciously coordinated organization. The differences between the traditional, P^2 form and the MPB are summarized in Table 7.1 of this book (p. 134).

Consistent with these changes in organization are certain adjustments to the human resource flows through the firm. In the traditional model, operating on strong internal labour market principles, the up-or-out promotion system was the norm in large firms (Galanter and Palay, 1991; Gilson and Mnookin, 1985; Landers *et al.*, 1996; Malos and Campion, 1995; Siow, 1994) and profit sharing for partners was based on the seniority principle (Gilson and Mnookin, 1989). The newer model operates on different criteria. Promotion systems are adjusted to allow more frequent hiring from the external market of rainmakers and those with new or scarce skills. More exceptions to the up-or-out rule emerge, as new classes of quasi-professional are employed (Galanter and Palay, 1991; Morris and Pinnington, 1998b). Profit sharing is based more on productivity or individual contribution.

However, general models may disguise the variety of influences acting at the level of the firm. Although the changes outlined at the beginning of this section affect the whole profession, organizational level factors may affect how these are played out across firms. Change is frequently driven by external pressures building up in the environment (Gersick, 1991) but where performance has not suffered, the pressures may be less pronounced than where profits have stagnated. The impetus for change may also be less where external forces, such as demands by clients for better or new services or challenges by competing groups for jurisdictional space, are not perceived to be pressing (Abbott, 1988).

Change may be influenced, as well, by the extent to which partners value consensus in decision-making. Those at the centre, responsible for managing the firm, are most likely to want to adapt to forms of managing which streamline decision-making. They may be unable to secure the agreement of colleagues who see change as a threat to their own power or as incompatible with perceptions of their role and rights as a senior professional and owner of the firm (Hinings *et al.*, 1991; Raelin, 1989; Pierce, Rubenfeld and Morgan, 1991). Change may also be restricted to certain areas while continuity persists in others. This may be because political compromise between different interest groups limits the scope of change or certain types of change are more acceptable than others. For example, partners may welcome changes that are perceived to reduce their administrative responsibilities allowing them to concentrate on professional practice (Maister, 1993; Morris and Pinnington, 1998b; Raelin, 1989). They are more likely to oppose changes that impinge on client relationships or regulate task execution as these are central to power and professional identity (Nelson, 1988; Freidson, 1986).

The purpose of this chapter is therefore to examine some of these influences on the nature of change in professional organizations. The intention is to test how smooth the contours of change and continuity are across a sample of firms operating in the same sector. Smooth contours would imply that external factors are having a powerful effect on firms regardless of their internal arrangements. Differences in the dimensions and patterns of change would imply contingencies are experienced or interpreted differently. In this way, the chapter aims to contribute to general models of change in professional organizations that have been built on a set of very generalized environmental influences and have, thus far, been elaborated by fine grained and intensive case study work in a small number of firms.

Research method and findings

A postal questionnaire survey was circulated to the 756 partnership firms of solicitors in England and Wales with 5 or more partners. It was issued in November 1997 and a reminder letter sent out in January 1998. By February 1998, 184 usable returns were received, representing 24 per cent of the total population of firms in this size category according to Chambers Directory. Sole practitioners and small partnerships (4 or fewer equity partners) were excluded.

The questionnaire was designed for completion by the managing partner or equivalent role. It inquired about respondents' attitudes towards the internal and external environments of the partnership firm and about the organization's management structure, policy and practice. Questions were asked about how the firm's policies and practices had changed in the last three years in order to test whether they had become more managerial, that is more centralized and coordinated in the way the firm managed its internal activities and client relationships. In addition, a set of questions were posed on the performance of the firm, control systems, partners' responsibilities and involvement in the running of the firm and the selection and promotion of other lawyers. These were designed to indicate whether the MPB proposition was confirmed. The questionnaire included continuous and categorical items, gathering demographic data on the firm. In the main section, the majority of response items were ordinal data using a 4- or 5-point scale (see Table 10.1).

Table 10.1 Frequencies for the variables

Topic	Name	Variable	Mean
			Indicating 1 = A great deal; 4 = Not at all
1	Extent of diversification into new practice areas	Diversify	2.4
2	Relative importance of competitive strategies:		*Indicating 1 = Very important; 5 = Very unimportant*
	Cost-effective service	Cost-strat	2.2
	Innovative service	Innovative-strat	2.2
	Distinctive, differentiated service	Differentiated-strat	2.2
	Reputation with clients	Reputation-strat	1.4
	Specialized set of services	Niche-strat	2.2
3	Extent of change over last three years:		*Indicating 1 = A great deal; 4 = Not at all*
	Quality control policies	Quality–policies	1.7
	More focused on meeting client needs	**Client-need**	1.7
	Financial controls to monitor performance	Financial-controls	1.7
	Professional marketing methods	**Marketing-methods**	1.9
	More coordinated approach to winning clients	**New-client-business**	2.1
	Decrease scope for individual partners determining with which clients to work.	**Less-partner-autonomy**	2.9
	Linked decisions about hiring and promoting more closely the needs of the business	Recruit-for-business	1.9
4	Policies to increase productivity introduced over the last three years:		*Indicating 1 = A great deal; 4 = Not at all*
	Partners	**Partner-prod-policy**	2.2
	Other fee earners	**Fee-earner-prod-policy**	2.0
	Support staff	Support-staff-prod-policy	2.2

Table 10.1 (continued)

Topic	Name	Variable	Mean
5	Extent that partners are assessed on:		*Indicating 1 = A great deal; 4 = Not at all*
	How they perform (behaviour)	**Partner-assessment: behaviour**	2.0
	Financial controls against budgets or targets	**Partner-assessment: financial**	2.0
	Strategic goals e.g. key client areas of growth	**Partner-assessment: strategic goals**	2.2
6	Importance of the partnership in:		*Indicating 1 = Very important; 5 = Very unimportant*
	Determining overall strategic direction	Collegial-strategy	1.6
	Promotion to partner	Collegial-promotion	1.4
	Significant reorganizations or internal changes	Collegial-reorganization	1.8
	Merger with other firms	Collegial-merger	1.2
	Lateral hiring at senior positions	Collegial-recruitment	2.0
	Introduction of new performance measures	Collegial-performance-measures	2.0
7	Consensus management approach to partners		*Indicating 1 = Very important; 5 = Very unimportant*
		Partner-consensus	1.6

Note: The variables shown in bold below are used in Table 10.2

Description of sample

The average number of equity partners was 14 and the mean number of assistant solicitors (non-partner lawyers) was 21. The size range was from 5 equity partners to 187 and from 4 assistants to 527. This range covers the top corporate firms practising in the City of London to regional firms operating in markets for private and small business legal services.

During the period 1994 to 1997, firms increased in average size across all categories (equity partner, salaried partner, assistants, other fee earners and support staff) indicating growth of the firm. The largest increase in staff was in the category of support staff where the average rose from 50 in 1994 to 62 in 1997. In the same period, the average number of equity partners rose from 12 to 14. The leverage ratio of equity partner to assistant solicitors stood at 1:1.5 having been 1:1.39 at the end of 1994; if all fee earners were included, the leverage ratio rose from 2.88 in 1994 to 3.32 in 1997.

The sample of returns includes 96 firms (52 per cent) that had increased their fee income since 1994 and 72 (39 per cent) that had experienced decline. The remainder (9 per cent) made no response. Overall, fee income improved in nominal and real terms during the period 1994 to 1997. This coincided with a cyclical upturn in the economy after the deep recession of the early 1990s. We also asked firms to rate their performance relative to their competitors on a number of dimensions. These dimensions included quality, innovation, financial growth and profitability, responsiveness to clients and productivity. The reason for doing this is that detailed profit performance data are difficult to collect because partnerships are not under statutory obligation to publish their accounts and are generally unwilling to release financial information.

Analysis

To explore the direction of change, and particularly whether the MPB form had become more common, respondents were asked about the changes in the way the firm had been managed in the last three years. These changes included marketing methods and responsibilities for business generation, financial controls and quality systems. The means for these and the other variables discussed below are shown in Table 10.1. The biggest change was more focus on meeting the needs of clients, with 94 per cent rating it 1 or 2 on the scale (1 = a great deal). This was followed, in order of degree of importance attached, by introduction of more quality control policies and financial controls to monitor performance. The least change was in the autonomy of individual partners to select with which clients to work. This was shown in the response to the item asking how far the firm had 'decreased scope for individual partners to determine with which clients to work'. The mean score here was 2.9 on the 4-point scale with 14 per cent of firms indicating they had reduced partner autonomy a great deal and 20 per cent to some extent.

Respondents were also asked whether and to what extent they had introduced policies over the last three years to increase productivity for different groups of staff. Most emphasis was placed on non-partner fee earners (82 per cent rated 1 or 2), followed by partners (72 per cent rated 1 or 2), and lastly, support staff (67 per cent rated 1 or 2). A further question on partner evaluation revealed that this is based most often on 'financial controls against budgets or targets', second, on how they perform (behaviour) and, third, on strategic goals such as key areas of client growth.

In the full sample of firms, 72 per cent have introduced policies to increase partners' productivity in the last three years. Introduction of these policies is significantly associated with a reduction in the individual partner's autonomy over client selection (r = 0.410, p = 0.000) and with the assessment of partners using financial controls against targets (r = 0.401, p = 0.000). Therefore, the overall direction of change is to tighten controls over partner performance and client management.

Changes in the management of the professional firm are said to be associated with reforms to the selection and reward of partners. In the sample, 45 per cent said they used a traditional, lockstep method of profit sharing but only 12 per cent retained an up-or-out system of promotion to partner. Asked about criteria for promotion to partner, 92 per cent said that getting new business was important or very important. The relationship between the importance of this promotion criterion and changes in the way the firm was managed was statistically significant. Getting new business cross-tabulated with the following items: became more focused on meeting the needs of clients (Pearson χ^2 46.39, p = 0.0000); introduced more financial controls (Pearson χ^2 37.42, p = 0.0001); matched hiring and promotions more closely to the needs of the business (Pearson χ^2 45.98, p = 0.0000) and the lateral hiring of partners (Pearson χ^2 46.39, p = 0.0000). Thus, changes in management are associated with changes to the role and the selection of partners.

However, growth of the MPB form had not completely displaced traditional methods of managing. Asked to rate the importance of partner consensus in the management of the firm, nearly half of the respondents (44 per cent) indicated it was very important to have a high degree of consensus among partners in the management of the firm and 47 per cent rated it as important. A further question asked about partner involvement in a range of decisions (from 1 = very important to 5 = very unimportant). Partnership involvement was deemed most important in merger decisions (mean = 1.2), followed by promotion to partner (mean = 1.4), and then strategy (mean = 1.6). It was rated least important for the introduction of new performance measures and recruitment at senior positions.

To test the relationship between these dimensions of change and organizational and environmental factors, a statistical analysis of the variables was conducted for the overall sample. To reduce the complexity of the data, we selected the 9 variables where there were one or more associations significant below the 0.1 per cent level and identified with coefficient values greater than 0.5. In addition, to avoid the problem of capturing similar patterns of response among the items in any one question, only variables that were associated significantly below the 0.1 per cent level (coefficient values greater than 0.5) with at least 1 variable outside of their item group were chosen.

Pearson correlations were conducted, using a two-tailed test of significance. The results are shown in Table 10.2. The table shows there are high correlations between the different components of change that focused around how the firm carried out its marketing activities. These included becoming more focused on meeting client needs, adopting more professional marketing methods and using a more coordinated approach to winning new client business. It also shows significant but slightly less strong correlations between these change variables and the introduction of productivity policies for partners and fee earners. The introduction of new productivity policies for partners was highly associated with fee earner productivity policies and with the reduction of partner autonomy over client selection. This implies that where firms have tightened up on the performance of partners, they have also changed their client responsibilities.

Furthermore, Table 10.2 shows that partner assessment is now multi-dimensional; in other words, where partners are assessed on financial outcomes, they are also likely to be assessed on strategic goals and on behaviours.

Next, the firms were subdivided into six separate sub-samples according to relative profit-per-partner performance, perceived hostility of the external environment and competitive pressure from other professions. The perceived hostility of the external environment was assessed, first, in terms of perceptions of more demanding standards of performance from clients and, second, severity of competition from other groups seeking to enter the lawyers' jurisdiction. For each of these variables, profit-per-partner, client pressure and competitive pressure from other groups, the sample was divided at the mean response into separate groups. Ninety-six firms (52 per cent) that rated their profit-per-partner performance better formed 1 sub-sample and the 72 firms (39 per cent) that rated it the same or worse than 3 years ago were another. The remaining 9 per cent who did not respond were treated as missing data. We formed a sub-sample from the 36 per cent of firms that rated themselves above the mean in seeing the profession as subject to growing client pressures to perform more efficiently and another sub-sample from the remainder. Finally, the 80 firms (44 per cent) that rated the profession as facing growing competitive pressure from other occupations higher than the mean (for the full sample) formed a sub-sample and the 100 that perceived it to be equal to or less than the mean (54 per cent) formed the other sub-sample. These 6 sub-samples are summarized in Table 10.3.

Analysis of the sub-samples revealed some subtle differences. The group of firms with higher than average profits were likely to have introduced policies to increase partners' productivity in conjunction with reducing partners' autonomy to select their clients ($r = 0.416$, $p = 0.000$). A similar association ($r = 0.505$, $p = 0.000$) was also found in the sub-sample of firms that rated competitive pressure from other occupations relatively high. In addition, for this sub-sample, the introduction of productivity policies was correlated with more coordinated methods of competing in the client market ($r = 0.543$, $p = 0.000$) and being more focused on meeting the needs of clients ($r = 0.505$, $p = 0.000$). Thus, perceptions of a hostile environment appear to be more closely linked than high profit performance to a greater focus on the marketplace.

Table 10.2 Correlations for the selected nine variables associated with the MPB form

Pearson correlation coefficients	Cli	Mar	New	Les	Par	Fee	P:b	P:f	P:s
Client-need	1.00								
Marketing-methods	0.412****	1.00							
New-client-business	0.515****	0.677****	1.00						
Less-partner-autonomy	0.353****	0.316****	0.413****	1.00					
Partner-prod-policy	0.330****	0.371****	0.390****	0.410****	1.00				
Fee-earner-prod-policy	0.281****	0.354****	0.281****	0.332****	0.642****	1.00			
Partner-assessment: behaviour	0.215***	0.247***	0.326****	0.271***	0.344****	0.207***	1.00		
Partner-assessment: financial	0.087	0.243***	0.207***	0.131	0.401****	0.300****	0.548****	1.00	
Partner-assessment: strategic-goals	0.311****	0.293****	0.399****	0.254***	0.331****	0.270***	0.694****	0.594****	1.00

Note: (Coefficient / (Cases) / 2-tailed significance); *** p<.01; **** p<.001

Table 10.3 Sub-samples

High profit per partner (PPP)	Low profit per partner (PPP)
High client pressure	Little client pressure
High competitive pressure (from other professions)	Little competitive pressure (from other professions)

Those firms rating the pressure for change from clients as high had likewise become more coordinated in their marketing to clients ($r = 0.504$, $p = 0.000$). In this sub-sample, greater coordination in the marketplace and the introduction of more professional marketing methods were associated with the introduction of policies to raise the productivity of more junior fee earners rather than partners ($r = 0.574$, $p = 0.000$). However, no significant correlation was found with the reduction of partners' autonomy in selecting clients.

In the three other sub-samples – low profit-per-partner, little client pressure and little competitive pressure – the reduction in partner autonomy over client selection was not so strongly associated with policies to raise productivity. However, in the sub-sample of worse performing firms, there was evidence of moves towards more centralized management: policies to increase partners' productivity were associated with partners being assessed a great deal on financial controls ($r = 0.533$, $p = 0.000$) and on strategic goals such as key client areas of growth ($r = 0.581$, $p = 0.000$). A more coordinated approach to competing in the client market was also correlated with the use of assessment of partners on strategic goals ($r = 0.532$, $p = 0.000$). This suggests that, in the worse performing firms, tighter performance management has been introduced to link individual contributions to organizational goals.

These results show that change in management is not a contingent response to internal or external pressures. Analysis of the full sample and the sub-samples showed that there are slightly different emphases in the content of changes according to how well the firm has performed or perceptions of the external environment, but there were no unique patterns associated with either of these factors.

Discussion

The findings showed that change focused around a grouping of managerial practices and policies concerning the overall direction of the firm. In terms of the P^2 model, they relate to the strategic control and operating dimensions (Greenwood *et al.*, 1990) where the results showed the extension of central direction by the greater use of coordinated marketing, explicit quality control standards and productivity plans. However, in other respects the strategic dimension has remained relatively decentralized at the same time as control over operating standards has tightened. Further, emphasis continues to be placed on consensus in decision-making and partnership consultation is still rated important or very important on a range of governance issues, including the overall direction of the firm. This selective pattern of change was reinforced by the structural continuity in these firms. Even though a relatively high priority for change was placed on being more client focused, the persistence of organizational units based around professional specialization and relative rarity of client-based structures across the firm also indicates continuity.

The other dimension of change related to the role of professionals. Included in this are policies on hiring, promotion and evaluation that are central to the balance between professional authority and organizational strategy (Tolbert and Stern, 1991). Once more, the results revealed elements of change alongside continuity. Reforms to the internal labour market involving lateral hiring (recruitment from the external labour market) indicate that environmental pressure has reduced predictability in firm-level human resource flows requiring greater organizational adaptability (Malos and Campion, 1995). Similarly, the selection and evaluation of partners appears to be more closely linked to organizational than professional concerns. For instance, business potential is the most important criterion for promotion and firms indicated that they had tried to link promotions more closely to the needs of the business. Further, up-or-out is not the norm in promoting to partner and permanent career positions below partner are common.

Continuity persists as well. Even if the substantive criteria for promotion are linked more to firm factors, the procedure still emphasizes the partnership tradition of collegiality. Additionally, lockstep or parity profit sharing is still the reward mechanism of the majority of firms and neither partners' nor other professionals' earnings are tightly geared to performance. Overall, reward systems can hardly be said to be linked to firms' strategies and are more consistent with the maintenance of professional tradition. The persistence of these patterns of continuity and change, illustrated in Figure 10.1, is consistent with the argument that change has been sedimented rather than transformational in professional firms (Cooper *et al.*, 1996). Elements of older forms persist alongside newer ones.

To explain these patterns we can focus on the dynamics of the partnership form of organization. Like other firms, partnerships provide certain benefits in collaboration over market relations between independent professionals. Agency theorists concentrate on the incentive structures that firms can use (Eisenhardt, 1989a). Others have focused on the superior opportunities to cross-sell services and to learn from colleagues in hierarchical relationships over market based ones (Kogut and Zander, 1991; Grant, 1996) but partnerships are fragile organizations to the extent that the assets are relatively easily divisible. In the event of disagreement, individual partners may split away and, on the basis of their own reputation, take clients with them.

Partnership inevitably involves striking a balance between individual preferences and collective interests (Gilson and Mnookin, 1985; Morris, 1992b). Points of tension may surface around client selection, the balance of resources in the firm between different areas of specialization, the degree to which clients and client information is shared, the appropriation and distribution of earnings and

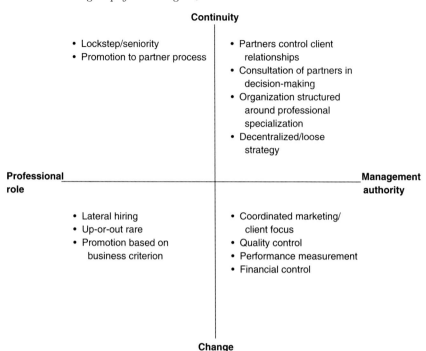

Figure 10.1 Dimensions of change and continuity in UK law firms

the relationship between effort, results and rewards. Agency and transaction cost analyses of professional firms address these conflicts between individual and firm by way of monitoring and incentive devices. Yet a partnership is unlikely to thrive for long where individuals share so little residual trust that they have to rely on close control of their colleagues' activities to ensure the firm works efficiently (Ghoshal and Moran, 1996; Donaldson, 1995). Co-operation between partners requires more than monetary incentives or the threat of punishment to work properly (Gilson and Mnookin, 1985).

Typically, therefore, partnerships are relatively loosely coordinated at the centre and reliant on consultative mechanisms to ensure partner commitment to decisions. Such commitment can be difficult to engender when partners are disinterested in active involvement in management (Hinings *et al.*, 1991), making consultation a slow and frustrating business. Nonetheless, it is important because of the potentially disruptive effects of disagreement among powerful individuals. Loose coordination may create extra decision-making costs but it is the price paid for the benefits of combination between co-owners with relatively equal power. The looseness also permits great responsiveness to client demands in different areas of specialization, as we have argued above. Continuity has persisted in the emphasis on participation in decisions and consensus building because these are the ways by which commitment to collective interests is reinforced in potentially fragile forms of organization.

At the same time, it is notable that change in the management of these firms has involved more extensive monitoring. Assessment of fee-earners and support staff is now almost universal and half of the firms formally evaluate their partners. Further, partner assessment frequently includes behaviour and contribution to broad goals rather than simply the outcomes of activities. The closer attention to promotion criteria, focusing on business contribution, is also consistent with a desire to limit the risk of making an 'underperformer' a partner. Therefore, change has been focused around ways of limiting the risks of free-riding, the downside of combining in a partnership.

Conclusions

We conclude from this research there has been a general shift towards the MPB form of the professional firm. However, elements of continuity also persist and our findings are broadly supportive of the notion of change in professional firms being a partial and recursive process rather than a transformational one. Change efforts appear to have coalesced around the operating control dimension of the firm, where coordinated marketing and quality control have been introduced and the evaluation of professionals has been extended. Continuity with the P^2 form was particularly evident in the strategic dimension where partners continued to control choices about client selection and business opportunities. Continuity in the interpretative scheme of the P^2 form was shown in the governance process where there was a preference for consultation with partners and a consensus based approach to decision-making.

Change may well be in the direction of more business-like modes of organization and control, as characterized by the MPB form, but the trade-offs or compromises that appear to occur indicate that professional partnerships retain a distinctive way of managing. Indeed, we have argued that the dynamics of partnership require a balance between the pursuit of efficiency and that of consensus and this is likely to limit the extent of change.

Existing explanations of change in professional organizations have been based on a range of broad and influential factors affecting the professions as a whole. These include changes in regulatory regimes, reduced information asymmetry between client and expert and jurisdictional competition. We assessed whether different patterns of change would result from the different experiences of firms in confronting these broad factors. We expected firms that perceived the environment to be benign relative to others would not have pursued change so much as others. We also expected firms that had performed relatively well or perceived themselves to be strong compared to competitors would have less incentive to change and more to persist with existing arrangements.

While we found variations in patterns of change related to these factors, these were a question of degree rather than qualitatively different. Better performing firms were focused on the measurement of partner performance but relatively less on central control of the client relationship than worse performers. Better performers were also more likely to emphasize consultation and consensus in decision-making, suggesting that the P^2 model is more strongly modified as a defensive response to a decline in profits. Perceptions of changes in the environment also prompted different emphases around the common themes outlined above but not different models of management. The underlying thrust was towards greater central control over the client relationship and tighter performance standards through the measurement of individual partners' activities. This leads us to conclude that the shift to MPB is not strongly contingent upon experiences or perceptions of the environment at the level of the firm. Nor is it a phenomenon that is unique to North America. For, among larger law firms in the UK the shift to a more consciously managerial style of operating in recent years closely parallels what has been observed elsewhere.

11 The restructured professional organization

Corporates, cobwebs and cowboys

David M. Brock, Michael J. Powell and C. R. Hinings

Today's accountants, lawyers and doctors work in different organizations than their professional colleagues did a generation ago. Those who still work in accounting, law and medical practices are more likely to be on contracts rather than in partnerships, receive performance-related pay rather than salary, work in specialist teams rather than generalist practices, and in larger, more international, diversified organizations. In addition, an ever increasing proportion of lawyers work for consulting firms or the legal departments of corporations, doctors are contracted to medical centres, health maintenance organizations or insurers, and accountants are more likely to be engaged in strategic planning or information system design than auditing accounts.

Three questions about the changing professional organization

This volume seeks to shed light on three interrelated questions on the changing professional organization:

- What have been the causes of change?
- How has change occurred?
- What have been the structural consequences of these changes?

The following sections revisit these three questions and consolidate what the preceding ten chapters have contributed to our understanding of the changing character of professional organizations. We conclude by addressing the question of whether the changes observed constitute new models of the professional organization.

Causes of change

The Aharoni and Rose and Hinings chapters (2 and 3) outline the forces that have driven professional service firms simultaneously to traverse national borders, expand in size, and diversify in scope. While globalization is not a new phenomenon, and there is controversy about its extent (see Parker, 1996), it is clear that organizations and their various management functions – such as production, accounting and marketing – have recently become increasingly similar from country to country (Latouche, 1996). Both Aharoni (Chapter 2) and Rose and Hinings (Chapter 3) use a contingency model to demonstrate how large professional service firms have modified their structures in response to global environmental changes.

Aharoni shows how factors like the degree of standardization of work, recognition of the impact of globalization, and need for standardized certification resulted in the different levels of globalization among accounting and law firms. In the next chapter, Rose and Hinings point out that large accounting firms have expanded into different geographical areas and industries, and developed new services and products in pursuit of their multinational clients. The resulting structure of these Global Business Advisory Firms resembles Nohria and Ghoshal's (1997) differentiated network. The loosely coupled network of the global professional service firm is integrated with new organizational structures such as an international headquarters, client management roles, and international business units and divisions.

Aharoni also points to the interest on the part of accounting firms in exploring alternative governance models, in particular the corporate limited liability model. The partnership model, in which individual partners are 'fully and severally liable' for each others' mistakes, is a serious problem in the litigious contemporary period where accounting firms are frequently sued for alleged audit failures (see Hinings, Greenwood and Cooper in Chapter 7). The corporate limited liability governance model would not only reduce the risks faced by partners in professional partnerships but also facilitate the process of raising finance in an environment where the demands of technological integration and global expansion require large amounts of capital. The adoption of a corporate governance system to replace that of the partnership would signal an important structural change in the previously dominant P^2 archetype.

In a later chapter, Kitchener examines the impact of fundamental changes in government policy on the organizational structures and interpretive schemes of public hospitals in the British National Health Service. The British health reforms sought to create an internal market in the public health system in which formerly cooperative hospitals competed with one another for patients and funding (Ferlie *et al.*, 1996). A new competitive commercial model was imposed on a health system where public service values had long held sway, along with a corporate governance model and new management structures. Viewing these changes as an attempt to undermine the prevailing public hospital variation of the professional bureaucracy, Kitchener investigates whether a new 'quasi-market' hospital archetype has succeeded in replacing it.

Chapter 4 by Caronna and Scott illustrates the impact of changes in the institutional environment of the US health care field. Through the lens of Kaiser Permanente, a significant pioneer in the development of managed care, Caronna and Scott show how the changing structure of an organizational field shapes the organizations within it. From the decades of professional control in the immediate post-war period to the dominance of the market in the 1990s, they demonstrate how Kaiser Permanente has had to alter and adapt to fit this changing institutional environment, even to the extent of modifying some key elements of the Kaiser philosophy.

The contributed chapters of this book, then, have indicated the importance of environmental factors such as globalization, client demands, the institutional arrangements of the organizational field, and changing government policy in driving organizational change. These are predominantly institutional and structural changes that have undermined the legitimacy and perceived congruence of the prevailing professional bureaucracy/P^2 archetype and encouraged change. What is less closely explored is the role of the agents of change, the individuals and firms that stand to benefit from challenging the old dominant archetype and replacing it with a new one. The chapters mentioned in the following section, however, do address the question of how such archetypal and organizational change occurs.

The process of change

Hinings *et al.* in Chapter 7 argue that an understanding of organizational change requires an awareness of both precipitating and enabling factors. The changes in environmental conditions, such as the institutional environments of health care observed by Caronna and Scott (in the US) and by Kitchener (UK), constitute precipitating factors for change or the resistance to change.

These environmental factors are necessary but not sufficient for organizational change to occur. Hinings *et al.* argue that changes in interests (e.g., shifting resources) and underlying values (e.g., collegiality or managerialism) among various stakeholders in the professions can precipitate organizational change. However, the potential for change can only be realized if groups in favour of change have the power (sufficiently concentrated) and the capability (e.g., leadership and technical skills) for the change to occur. The necessity and value of auditing is now questioned far more seriously than it was a generation ago. However, the auditors and traditional accountants in the large firms may still seek to defend auditing's pride of place in the organization because it reinforces their interests and their beliefs about the core business of an accounting firm. On the other hand, resource uncertainty due to the reduction of audit revenues provided an opportunity for rival groups within the accounting firms to develop alternative revenue flows from new products and services such as business consulting and information technology.

In Chapter 7 Hinings *et al.* apply their understanding of the dynamics of change to the emergence of a new professional archetype, the Managed Professional Business. In pointing to the importance of interests and organizational politics in the change process, Hinings *et al.* not only bring power relations into the picture but also allow for the active role of agents of change. The shift in archetype and consequent organizational change will occur only if individuals and organizations take actions to bring it about. Alternatively, the status quo will be retained as a consequence of actions taken to defend it and resist change as in the example of the public hospitals in Kitchener's study.

Power relations and interaction processes are also important in the redefinition of professional boundaries. Chapter 6 by Denis *et al.* demonstrates the continued importance of the powerful hospital physicians in the emergence of new structures such as multidisciplinary teams and integrated services. The ability of managers to impose new boundaries, or new definitions of services, on health care organizations is limited by the diluted control of the managers over the health professionals and by the continued power enjoyed by the doctors. Any new structures must be negotiated and reflect a degree of congruence with the health professional's worldview. The processes for boundary redefinition will vary according to the organizational level involved – whether intra- or inter-organizational or system-wide – but at all levels the enabling factors identified by Hinings *et al.* must be present. Otherwise, change initiatives will be derailed and fail to lead to institutionalized structures.

Gray's chapter is largely devoted to illustrating this reflexivity, the 'duality of structure and agency', in changing professional organizations and their fields. Flood's chapter also makes the point that large professional firms are products of their historical and cultural roots; they act out scripts that have been repeated time after time. Gray emphasizes that the manner in which influential partners – the power perspective – interpret the script either limits or liberates the firm. Structure does not emerge independently of either the firm's historical background or the interests and philosophies of those who have power. In Gray's chapter the powerful are the influential founding partners. Leadership and values play a critical part in shaping the direction taken by both the new and the old law firms.

The chapter by Flood shows very different sets of organizational beliefs and expectations operating in two large law firms – separated only by the Atlantic Ocean and a common language! The British firm shows far closer adherence to the traditional P^2 archetype than does the US case which, although studied a decade earlier, exhibits more corporate, managerialist tendencies. Analysis of the different legal structures in these two contexts reveals far more rigidity in the British system – e.g., the clear distinction between barristers and solicitors. This institutional rigidity and traditionalism has undoubtedly contributed to the slowness of archetypal and organizational change in the UK

Is the change process in professional organizations, then, a transformative or incremental process? Notwithstanding the radical restructuring intentions of some governmental authorities, such as in the UK National Health Service, and the consequent reorganization and reorientation of health care providers, the changes that emerged were more incremental and cumulative than transformative. Kitchener's study of British hospitals supports the general conclusions of Cooper *et al.* (1996, p. 624) that there frequently is a 'persistence of values, ideas and practices, even when the formal structures and processes seem to change, and even when there may be incoherence'. So newer aspects of professional organization – like new management systems – are superimposed on traditional professional values in a sedimented fashion. What emerges from this process may be a hybrid, or what Scott (1965) termed a 'conjoint' form, where professional and managerial values coexist.

Continuity and change in professional organizations

In previous writings the Alberta School have suggested the emergence of a new archetype for professional firms, the *Managed Professional Business* (Cooper *et al.* 1996). In Chapter 7, Hinings *et al.* provide further evidence for this emergent archetype and detail its characteristics, demonstrating how these differ from the old P² archetype.[1] While retaining certain traditional professional values and practices, the MPB signals a significant refocusing of the professional organization towards the business and management values of efficiency, cost-effectiveness, central strategic control, and internally differentiated structures. Other chapters, by Rose and Hinings, Flood, and Morris and Pinnington, also provide support for the emergence of the MPB. Rose and Hinings suggest that the largest accounting firms, which they call Global Business Advisory Firms, have already progressed a considerable distance towards the MPB. Support for the MPB is somewhat more muted in the cases of Flood and Morris and Pinnington, reflecting the more traditional and conservative UK legal profession. However, there is sufficient evidence to indicate that there is a new archetype of the professional organization emerging that incorporates explicitly the disciplines and values of the business corporation whether or not there has been formal legal adoption of the corporate business form.

Very similar to the MPB is what Kitchener calls the *quasi-market form* which reflects the position of professional organizations – such as publicly funded hospitals, universities and research institutes – that have had to move from their traditional public sector approach to a more competitive market orientation. Structural characteristics of this form in the health care area include clinical directorates, internal business units (whether profit or cost centres) and hybrid professional-manager roles. The quasi-market form shares with the MPB a deliberate and explicit intent to incorporate contemporary business and management values and approaches. It adopts the structures and systems of the modern business and applies them to these publicly funded entities, often restructured into a corporate governance form. The quasi-market model of Kitchener's chapter, then, is the MPB of Hinings *et al.* in the former professional bureaucracies of the state.

Gray's chapter reminds us of some of the other emerging forms of professional organization, such as the specialist firm working in a niche market and the star firm composed of high-flying, expensive and creative professionals. The *specialist form* is pervasive among small professional partnerships such as tax accountants, psychiatrists and mental health professionals, specialized surgeons, physicians, and lawyers. The *star form*, exemplified by Starbuck's (1992, 1993) study of the very successful New York law firm, Wachtell Lipton, essentially combines technical excellence in its work, a high degree of specialization and considerable autonomy for its high performing professional staff. It attracts those clients who want, and are willing to pay for, the highest quality professional service. The world-renowned Mayo Clinic is an example of such a 'star' organization in the health care world. The star form combines the traditional professional values of excellence, creativity, and individual autonomy with rewards based on performance and a culture not too dissimilar from the high-energy software, advertising, and investment banking worlds (see Eccles and Crane, 1988).

Finally, we see another emergent form – the *multidisciplinary form* (MDF) or the professional conglomerate – typified by the huge multinational GBAFs (Chapter 3) noted above and giant health care systems such as Kaiser Permanente (Chapter 4). This form also fits the MPB archetype, but is typically international in scope; and it also combines not just different disciplines within the one profession, but professionals from a variety of professions, working in autonomous, differentiated business units. It is not just multidisciplinary but multi-professional. We discuss this and the other forms in more detail in the next section of this chapter.

While the chapters of this book point to diverse new forms of professional organization, and perhaps to a new emergent archetype, it is also clear that significant elements of the traditional professional organizational form remain. Morris and Pinnington's study of a large sample of British law firms found evidence of both change towards more corporate structures as well as continuity of significant aspects of the traditional professional partnership, particularly in the maintenance of consensus-style governance structures. Moreover, they found that it was the firms that were performing less well that were more likely to demonstrate more corporate, managerialist tendencies, perhaps indicating their resource dependence needs. Better performing firms were more likely to emphasize a blend of the traditional and new managerial structures and processes: senior management teams with partnership meetings, performance appraisal with lockstep remuneration systems, public relations and marketing functions along with individual control of clients. In these firms, professional autonomy and discretion remained unchallenged with management leaving client relationships to the professionals.

Morris and Pinnington's finding of significant continuity alongside evident change is supported by Kitchener's study of the adoption of the quasi-market archetype by UK hospitals. Similarly, Kitchener finds substantial continuity in the interpretive schemes and in the evaluative systems. Like Morris and Pinnington, Kitchener argues for an emergent hybrid form that combines the old and the new in a process similar to that of sedimentation (Cooper *et al.*, 1996).

Figure 11.1 summarizes the changes and continuities observed by the contributed chapters. The drivers of change can be viewed as precipitating factors in the Hinings *et al.* analysis of the process of change. Their impact on the change process is mediated by the interests and power of various stakeholders, issues of resource dependency, and the reflexive interaction between changing structures and institutions and individual agency. The outcomes of the change processes that have been identified are listed in column three with respect to both the new structures and the continuities with the previously dominant model. These

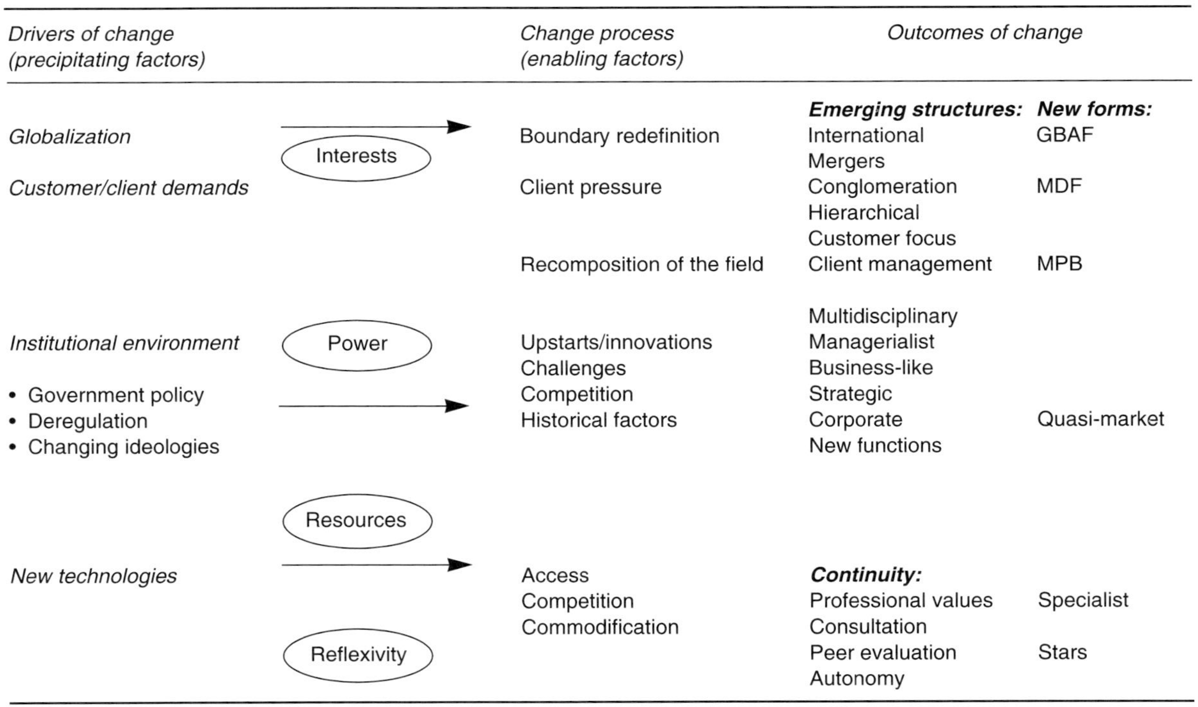

Drivers of change (precipitating factors)	Change process (enabling factors)	Outcomes of change	New forms:
		Emerging structures:	
Globalization	Boundary redefinition	International Mergers	GBAF
Customer/client demands	Client pressure	Conglomeration Hierarchical Customer focus	MDF
		Client management	MPB
	Recomposition of the field		
(Interests)		Multidisciplinary Managerialist Business-like	
(Power)	Upstarts/innovations Challenges Competition	Strategic Corporate New functions	
Institutional environment • Government policy • Deregulation • Changing ideologies	Historical factors		Quasi-market
(Resources)			
New technologies	Access Competition Commodification	**Continuity:** Professional values Consultation	Specialist
(Reflexivity)		Peer evaluation Autonomy	Stars

Figure 11.1 The changing professional organization

outcomes have given rise to several new organizational forms, from Global Business Advisory Firms to hybrid quasi-market forms to the free-ranging star model. These new forms all combine aspects of the old and the new but differ in significant respects from earlier models of the professional organization.

An emergent archetype?

As foreshadowed in Chapter 1 of this book, our intention was to discover whether a new dominant organizational archetype has emerged to take over from the earlier archetype identified by Mintzberg (1979) and Greenwood *et al.* (1990). We raised the question of whether the professional organization will retain its distinctive characteristics as we enter a new millennium or be absorbed by other dominant organizational archetypes such as the corporate business model. We argued that the extant archetype may undergo a process of delegitimation and de-institutionalization as a consequence of the many forces for change identified in the chapters in this book. We also pointed to the active search for new resources on the part of individuals and professional organizations seeking to reduce their dependence on diminishing resource flows and to develop new growth markets or services. The combination of the delegitimation of the existing dominant archetype and the need for new resources could well lead to the emergence of a new, or substantially different, archetype of the professional organization.

New environmental conditions and new resource strategies generally require changed structures (Chandler, 1977). As indicated in the previous section, the contributed chapters in this book point to the emergence of several new organizational forms such as the Global Business Advisory Firm and the Managed Professional Business. There is also the suggestion, most clearly in Hinings *et al.*'s chapter, of the emergence of a new potentially dominant archetype. The issue remains as to whether the changes in organizational forms identified in this book contribute to a single new archetype of the professional organization, to archetypal incoherence or, perhaps, to a number of competing archetypes reflecting a variety of organizational forms.

There are recurring themes and structures in these new organizational forms such as *managerialism, business-like, corporate governance, larger size,* and *greater complexity and internal differentiation.* The question is whether these common themes and similar structures constitute a new emerging archetype of the professional organization.

However, there is another common theme, explicit in the 'Continuity and change' title of Morris and Pinnington's chapter and supported by Kitchener and Hinings *et al.*: below the surface of change one still finds evidence of traditional professional values and structures like collegiality, consensual decision-making, and professional autonomy. Indeed, in Chapter 9, Kitchener describes a hybrid interpretive scheme resulting from the attempt to introduce quasi-market structures to the National Health Service in the UK. The same idea is also present in the concept of '*sedimentation*' used by Cooper *et al.* (1996) to explain the process of archetypal change associated with the emergence of the MPB form.

In the wider organizational literature we see contemporary researchers pointing to the emergence of similar complex, hybrid, old/new structures (e.g. Powell, 1990). Such hybrid structures are especially likely to emerge when traditional organizational forms are confronted with new, global, information-age structural challenges. For example, in explaining how multinational corporations resolve the structural dilemma of operating effectively across borders in the knowledge age, Nohria and Ghoshal (1997) point to the emergence of the '*differentiated network*.' This structure consists of diverse sub-units, each with its own internal structures and with different relationships with headquarters and other affiliates, sharing information and resources where appropriate but retaining quite distinctive local organizational structures.

Elsewhere, explaining why the introduction of new information technology frequently does not have the anticipated effect of eliminating bureaucracy, Schwarz and Brock (1998) suggest that hybrid structures may be quite common. They term the organization characterized by coexisting traditional, hierarchical organizational and contemporary network structures as the '*coexistent organization*.' Again, this hybrid form fits the concept of sedimentation, as the original structural artifacts persist while new organizational arrangements are apparent at the surface.

If there is a new emergent archetype of the professional organization, we would expect it to reflect a similar sedimented structure – displaying aspects of both change and continuity. However, the new archetype would need to be substantially different from the old in order to constitute a new archetype, as is argued by Hinings *et al.* in Chapter 7 where they suggest the MPB constitutes a new archetype for the large accounting firm. As we have already indicated, we see key aspects of the MPB in the other emergent organizational forms identified in this book. These common features may be viewed as key themes of the new emergent, potentially dominant, archetype.

Key themes of the new archetype

*   *Managerialism and becoming more 'business-like'*. Many of the chapters agree with Cooper *et al.* (1996) in describing contemporary professional organizations as more business-like. The language of business: customers, market share, efficiency and – importantly – profit, is increasingly the norm. Furthermore, there is widespread adoption of new management structures, functions and methods such as performance appraisal systems, strategic business units, marketing and business development, cross-selling, chief executive positions and senior management team structures and so forth.
*   *Less reliance on informal networks*. It is a well-established proposition that informal networks can be more effective than formal relationships in facilitating cooperation between potentially rival organizations (Chisolm, 1989). Kitchener relates a medical professional remembering the 'good old days' when expensive machinery would be informally loaned, and other personal favours done by supposedly competing professionals. However, in the new

world of the marketplace with more formalized performance controls, there is more reliance on formal networks and an eschewing of informal links. In keeping with the more business-like theme, relationships are more likely to be contractual. Surgeons frequently contract to share office space and facilities with other professionals, join specialist referral networks, and secure multi-year contracts with technical laboratories. Family physicians and independent specialists establish formal networks of practitioners such as Independent Practitioner Associations in the United States and New Zealand to ensure continued resource flows. Small law firms around the world may be linked to form 'virtual multinational' law firms. Some GBAFs use a franchise system, whereby local accounting offices get to use the Big Five brand name in exchange for a fee.

- *A tendency towards individualized rewards.* While many traditional partnership agreements are still in force, specifying equal sharing of profits, more and more 'eat-what-you-kill' (or piecework) remuneration systems are being put in place throughout the professions (Galanter and Palay, 1991). Flood's chapter shows the link between productivity and influence and power in his US case study. Traditional professional bureaucracies, such as hospitals, introduce performance-based pay in order to 'incentivize' the health professionals.

- *A tendency away from partnership.* The trend towards corporatization of health care is well documented (see Starr, 1982; Light, 1986). In Chapter 2, Aharoni indicates that large accounting firms are seriously considering adopting a corporate, limited liability status. Even in large professional partnerships, increased size and consequent dilution in partnership shares, and the introduction of different levels of partnership, effectively means that the vast majority of 'partners' (all but the few most senior) are little different from middle managers in terms of their control and remuneration.

- *A tendency towards globalization.* As discussed in Chapter 1, professional organizations both contribute to and are affected by the general trends towards globalization. New communication and travel technologies present opportunities for professional organizations to pursue resource acquisition internationally. Aharoni asserts that this propensity is a function of various characteristics of particular professions (such as certification and standardization) which explain why the accounting profession has been more globally oriented than law. It is not just accounting and law firms that seek resources in international markets; increasingly, health and educational organizations are attempting to supplement their uncertain domestic revenue streams with new international business. And, of course, the diffusion of Internet technology has enormous implications for all professions.

- *From generalist to specialist to multidisciplinary practice.* While the trend from generalist to specialist practices has been apparent for some time, the corollary is more specialized professional organizations appealing to particular markets or providing particular services. However, we see a further trend from specialist to multidisciplinary practice. Rose and Hinings in

Chapter 3 describe the tendency for professional firms to follow their expanding global clients so that they can deal with one GBAF wherever they are in the world. By the same logic, the GBAF has to offer the full range of professional services that the client might require. We thus observe the strategic shift towards implementing the 'one-stop shop' for professional and business advisory services. In health care the most rapidly growing group of physicians is the multidisciplinary, spatially separated network of specialists (Shortell *et al.*, 1996). These 'virtual' arrangements have the advantages of loose coupling, flexibility, local initiative, and incentives while retaining practice autonomy (see Robinson, 1997).

These common themes suggest that there is an emergent archetype of the changing professional organization that is different in significant respects from the old professional bureaucracy and P^2 forms. However, Hinings and Greenwood (1988a) remind us that change processes are rarely linear and successful. While there may be a potentially dominant archetype waiting in the wings, the plurality of organizational forms identified by the contributors to this volume would suggest that it is far from achieving dominance. Indeed, we suggest that competing archetypes as the professional organization undergoes transition.

Towards a typology of professional organizations

Given that we are faced with a plurality of professional organizational forms as we approach the new millennium, it may be helpful to array them in a typology that demonstrates their differing governance structures and strategic responses to the changed environment. Such a typology is presented in Figure 11.2.

Strategy is conceptualized here as the breadth of service focus of the organization, whether generalist, specialist or multidisciplinary. *Governance structure* is the type of ownership and control, from sole traders and small partnerships to larger, more complex corporate forms, franchises and other networks. A related

Governance structure	Generalist	Specialist	Multidisciplinary
Global network / Franchise / Corporate	c	f	i
Local network / Group practice	b	e	h
Partnership / Solo practice	a	d	g

Strategy

Figure 11.2 A typology of professional organizations

structural dimension is size, which we assume will be largely coterminous with the vertical governance dimension.

The nine small letters in Figure 11.2 represent a possible combination of these strategy–structure dimensions. We propose the following explanations to the nine possible combinations of the typology beginning with the left column:

a: Generalist sole operator or small partnership, like the traditional family doctor or neighbourhood law practice.

b: Medium-sized partnership or network of generalists, like small-town law firms or local accountants franchised to a larger entity; multi-site practices.

c: Large networks of generalists or franchised generalist clinics or offices.

d: Specialist sole operator or small partnership, such as a tax accountant or psychiatrist in a one or two person practice.

e: Medium-sized partnership of specialists, often boutique operations, like many surgical practices or specialty law firms.

f: Large corporate or franchised specialists, like tax preparation services or over-the-counter medical and pharmaceutical services.

g: Small partnerships of diverse specialists (unusual).

h: Medium-sized multidisciplinary practices, such as local or regional networks of specialist medical practices or medium sized accounting or consulting firms.

i: Large, often global, professional service organizations with autonomous specialized business units, like the largest medical centres, accounting and law networks.

Organizational clusters

We suggest that the different professional organizational types in this typology reflect clusters of similar organizations. First, the traditional professional bureaucracy and P^2 (types a and b in the typology) are clearly still with us. They are clustered around the bottom left-hand corner of the matrix. While new technology and population growth provide the opportunity for new small professional practices to be born, these same forces cause successful practices to grow – thus moving upwards in the matrix.

The second clustering is a function of new technology, environmental complexity, and the information age. These create opportunities for more specialization in the professions. Specialists can work in small or medium-sized practices. However, the trend appears to be for medium-sized practices to move to the right in the typology in an attempt to secure flows of clients by affiliating with different specialty practices to form multidisciplinary practices (types h or i) rather than networks of same-type specialists (type f).

Several of the contributed chapters in this volume suggest a vector of change from the bottom left-hand corner of the typology towards the upper right-hand cell. Here are found the GBAFs, Kaiser Permanentes and Baker & McKenzies (a large, franchised international law firm). All grow through mergers, franchising, and sheer market power, attracting smaller firms from elsewhere in the professional organization typology that have problems ensuring a steady resource flow or that seek to increase their opportunities for resource acquisition.

Having presented a typology of professional organizations and identified three important clusters of organizational types, we return to our earlier focus on archetypal change. Is one of these clusters the emerging, potentially dominant, archetype identified earlier in the chapter? Or are there multiple, competing archetypes which together contribute to archetype incoherence?

Competing archetypes

An archetype is an ideal type and, thus in theory, one would expect to find only one archetype in an organizational field. However, having established that archetypes do change, it is unlikely that these changes will take place instantaneously. Rather, it is more likely that there will be a period of archetype incoherence when several competing archetypes coexist. There is some research evidence for more than one archetype coexisting at a point in time. Hinings and Greenwood (1988a) showed how different British local government archetypes coexisted during a decade of change and transition. Kikulis *et al.* (1992) went a step further and found three competing sports governance archetypes coexisting in the sports industry for a time.

In the previous section we identified several clusters of organizational types which may point to as many as three competing archetypes of professional organizations coexisting today. The traditional archetype – in the P^2 typology – may well be on the decline. However it shows much resilience amid the trend to larger professional forms. While solo practice and very small firms are decreasing in prominence, it is clear they will continue to exist in the foreseeable future. At this juncture we can only suggest that further research is indicated to study the persistence of and changes in these ubiquitous small organizations.

At the other end of the diagonal running across the typology we find the large, business-like, diversified, networks of professional service firms, frequently with global reach. For brevity we use the acronym GPN or Global Professional Networks to identify this emerging archetype. The pervasive trends of deregulation, globalization, new technology, increased competition, and client demands all feed into the growth of GPNs. A superficial view of the structures of GPNs hardly differentiates them from other large industrial and commercial enterprises and multinationals. However, the other theme highlighted in this book – that of continuity and sedimentation – is critical here. It implies that many of the internal processes of contemporary GPNs still rest on traditional professional values of collegiality, consensus, quality of service, and technical autonomy in serving clients. In this sense, it reflects the emergence of a conjoint, or hybrid archetype, as noted earlier, combining new business values and structures with central elements of the old professional interpretive scheme.

A third possible archetype that the typology suggests is that of a medium-sized, highly specialized professional firm that persists in that form (i.e., resists merger or significant growth) by a fixation on the highest professional quality standards and a commitment to individual excellence. Evidence of this archetype is presented by Starbuck's (1992, 1993) Wachtell Lipton case and by Gray's (Chapter 5) 'star' form. Like the GPN, the star archetype is a hybrid with the critical professional and partnership dimensions of the P^2 still very much in evidence. And managerial systems and controls are not prevalent. The star firm or organization is so successful that it can afford some organizational slack. However, in recognition of the critical roles of extremely talented and innovative individuals, reward systems are unlikely to be equal or lockstep. In addition to performance-related remuneration systems, individuals in star organizations are all expected to bring in new business and revenues through aggressive pursuit of big deals and wealthy clients. The relative absence of hierarchy and bureaucratic controls, and the focus on the successful individual professional rather than the organization or team, distinguishes the star archetype from the GPN. It has more in common with smaller and highly successful advertising agencies or investment banking dealmaking units than the large GBAFs that populate the right-hand apex of the typology of professional organizations. In the medium term, we suspect that the star may be a viable competing professional organization archetype. Perhaps it is likely to be more pervasive in law and medicine where localism and national borders inhibit global growth.

The three competing archetypes are presented in Figure 11.3. They overlap with each other, which is yet another indication that this is a period of archetype incoherence or instability. We anticipate, following Greenwood *et al.* (1993), that there will be pressure towards archetypal coherence and convergence. Certainly, the GPN archetype bears considerable similarity with the MPB developed by Hinings *et al.* in Chapter 7. We have noted the common elements of these hybrid organizational forms, all of which fit well with the MPB or GPN archetypes that promise to be the dominant archetypal forms in the new millennium.

The professional organization is undergoing substantial change. This process is likely to continue in the future. However, even should one archetype achieve dominance, the evidence presented in this volume suggests that it will retain a strong and distinctive professional character. There is little evidence to suggest

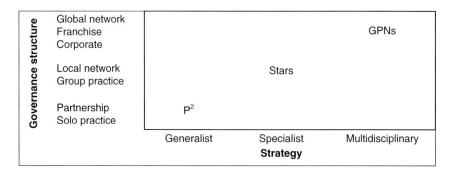

Figure 11.3 Location of clusters and archetypes

that professional organizations will completely lose their distinctiveness and simply be subsumed under a monolithic corporate business archetype. Further research is needed to delineate the changing dimensions of professional organizations as they transform themselves to meet the demands of new institutional environments and uncertain resource flows.

Notes

1   A comprehensive summary of the MPB's features is in Table 7.1 (p. 134) of this book.

References

Abbott, A. (1988). *The System of Professions: An Essay on the Division of Expert Labor*. Chicago: University of Chicago Press.

Abel, R. (1989). *American Lawyers*. New York: Oxford University Press.

Accountancy. (1997). Big Six Legal Link-ups Take a Global Hold. International edition, 120(1250), October, 10.

Acher, G. (1998). 'The Challenge of Change'. *Accountancy*, 121(1253), January, 34–35.

Ackroyd, S. (1996). 'Organization Contra Organizations: Professions and Organizational Change in the United Kingdom'. *Organization Studies*, 17(4), 599–621.

Ackroyd, S., Hughes, J. and Soothill, K. (1989). 'Public Sector Services and Their Management'. *Journal of Management Studies*, 26(6), 603–620.

Adams, S. B. (1997). *Mr. Kaiser Goes to Washington: The Rise of a Government Entrepreneur*. Chapel Hill, NC: University of North Carolina Press.

Addams, H. L., Davis B., Mano, R. M., and Nycum, V. (1997). 'Why Are Partners and Managers Leaving the Big Six?', *Journal of Applied Business Research*, 13(4), 75–82.

Aharoni, Y. (1993a). *Coalitions and Competition: The Globalization of Professional Business Services*. London: Routledge.

Aharoni, Y. (1993b). 'Globalization of Professional Business Services'. In Yair Aharoni (ed.). *Coalitions and Competition: The Globalization of Professional Business Services* (pp. 1–9). London: Routledge.

Aharoni, Y. (1993c). 'Ownership, Networks and Coalitions'. In Yair Aharoni (ed.). *Coalitions and Competition: The Globalization of Professional Business Services* (pp. 121–142). London: Routledge.

Aharoni, Y. (1995). 'A Note on the Horizontal Movement of Knowledge within Organizations'. Paper presented at the Conference on Change in Knowledge Based Organizations, University of Alberta, Edmonton, Alberta, Canada. May.

Aharoni, Y. (1996). 'The Organization of Global Service MNES'. *International Studies of Management and Organization*, 26(2), 6–23.

Alcock, M. (1998). 'Marking Time'. *Legal Business*, July–August, 42–45.

Alford, R. (1975). *Health Care Politics; Ideological and Interest Group Barriers to Reform*. Chicago: University of Chicago Press.

Allen & Overy. (n.d). Allen & Overy. London.

American Medical Association. (1970). *Informational Papers: Health Care Delivery Systems, Health Care Financing, Manpower and Facilities, Quality of Care and Evaluation*. Chicago: AMA.

American Medical Association. (1997). *AMA Membership 1847–1996*. Internal reports. Chicago: Division of Library and Information Services, AMA.

Anders, G. (1994). 'Aches and Pains: In the Age of the HMO, Pioneer of the Species Has Hit a Rough Patch; Kaiser Permanente can't cut prices as much as rivals that lack its fixed costs teaching doctors to be nice'. *Wall Street Journal*, 1 December, A1.

Anderson, T. and Zeghal, D. (1994). 'The Pricing of Audit Services: Further Evidence from the Canadian Market'. *Accounting and Business Research*, 24(Summer), 195–207.

Anonymous. (1996). 'Sweeping Changes in Practice Accelerate Growth'. *Practical Accountant*, 4, 29 April, 18–19.

Anonymous. (1997). 'Accountants Lose Dutch Bar Case'. *International Financial Law Review*, 16(3), 4 March.

Appadurai, A. (1996). *Modernity at Large: Cultural Dimensions of Globalization*. Minneapolis: University of Minnesota Press.

Appleby, J. (1997). 'Operating on Kaiser'. *The Sunday Times*, 3 August, D1, D6.

Asian Business Review. (1995). Lawyers in a Successful Multinational Partnership, October, 54.

Australian Bureau of Statistics. (1997). *Legal and Accounting Services*. Catalogue 8678.0, Canberra: AGPS.

Baker, W. (1990). 'Market Networks and Corporate Behavior'. *American Journal of Sociology*, 96, 589–625.

Baldwin, R. (1998). 'Regulating the Legal Profession'. In *Proceedings of the RPPU Research Conference 1998*. London: Law Society.

Banks, H. (1997). 'Global Lawyers'. *Forbes*, 160(10), November, 340–344.

Barley, S. R. (1986). 'Technology as an Occasion for Structuring: Evidence from Observations of CT Scanners and the Social Order of Radiology Departments'. *Administrative Science Quarterly*, 31(1), 78–108.

Barnard, C. (1948). *Organization and Management*. Cambridge, MA: Harvard University Press.

Baron, J. N., Dobbin, F. R. and Jennings, P. D. (1986). 'War and Peace: The Evolution of Modern Personnel Administration in U.S. Industry'. *American Journal of Sociology*, 92, 350–383.

Baroody, W. J. (1981). 'Foreword'. In Mancur Olson (ed.), *A New Approach to the Economics of Health Care* (pp. xv–xvi). Washington, DC: American Enterprise Institute.

Bartlett, C. and Ghoshal, S. (1989). *Managing Across Borders: The Transnational Solution*. Boston: Harvard Business School Press.

Beck, U. (1992). *Risk Society: Towards a New Modernity*. London: Sage.

Bégin, C. and Labelle, B. (1989). 'Les centres de santé: Réalités et opportunités face au défi de l'intégration'. *Rapport de l'étude sur les centres de santé au Québec Bilan d'une expérience*, Faculté des sciences de l'administration, Université Laval, Décembre,

Benson, K. J. (1975). 'The Interorganizational Network as a Political Economy'. *Administrative Science Quarterly*, 20, 229–249.

Benson, K. J. (1977). 'Organizations: A Dialectical View'. *Administrative Science Quarterly*, 22, 1–21.

Bergthold, L. (1990). *Purchasing Power in Health: Business, the State, and Health Care Politics*. New Brunswick: Rutgers University Press.

Berwick, D. M., Godfrey, A. B. and Roessner, J. (1990). *Curing Health Care*. San Francisco: Jossey-Bass.

Blackler, F. (1995). 'Knowledge, Knowledge Work and Organizations: An Overview and Interpretation'. *Organization Studies*, 16(6), 1021–1046.

Blau, J. (1984). *Architects and Firms*. Cambridge, MA: MIT Press.

Bledstein, B. J. (1978). *The Culture of Professionalism*. New York: W.W. Norton and Co.

Boddewyn, J. J., Halbrich, M. B. and Perry, A. C. (1986). 'Service Multinationals:

Conceptualization, Measurement and Theory'. *Journal of International Business Studies*, 17, 41–57.

Boerstler, H., Foster, R. W., O'Connor, E. J. and O'Brien, J. L. (1996). 'Implementation of Total Quality Management: Conventional Wisdom vs. Reality'. *Hospital and Health Services Administration*, 41(2), 143–159.

Bohman, J. (1996). *Public Deliberation*. Cambridge: MIT Press.

Bolman, L. and Deal, T. (1997). *Reframing Organizations: Artistry, Choice, and Leadership*. San Francisco: Jossey Bass.

Boston, J., Martin, J., Pallot, J. and Walsh, P. (1991). *Reshaping the State: New Zealand's Bureaucratic Revolution*. Auckland: Oxford University Press.

Bourdieu, P. (1990). *The Logic of Practice*. Cambridge: Polity Press.

Bourdieu, P. and Wacquant, L. (1992). *An Invitation to Reflexive Sociology*. Chicago: University of Chicago Press.

Bourn, J. (1986). 'How Businesses Find Lawyers: A Study of Organizational Information Gathering'. Ph.D. dissertation, Northwestern University.

Brill, S. (1985). 'Headnotes: War of the Tombstones'. *American Lawyer*, March, 1.

Briston, R. J. (1979). 'The U.K. Accountancy Profession: The Move Towards Monopoly Power'. *The Accountants Magazine*, 83(November), 458–460.

Brown, J. L., Cooper, D. J., Greenwood, R. and Hinings, C. R. (1996). 'Strategic Alliance within a Big Six Accounting Firm: A Case Study'. *International Studies of Management and Organization*, 26(2), Summer, 59–79.

Bruce, R. (1996). 'Whiter than White?' *Accountancy*, 117(1233), May, 56–57.

Brunsson, N. and Olsen, J. (1993). *The Reforming Organization*. Cambridge: Cambridge University Press.

Bucher, R. and Stelling, J. (1969). 'Characteristics of Professional Organizations'. *Journal of Health and Sociological Behavior*, 10(1), 3–15.

Buckley, P. and Casson, M. (1998). 'Models of the Multinational Enterprise'. *Journal of International Business Studies*, 29, 21–44.

Business Week. (1988). 'An Identity Crisis at Arthur Andersen'. October, 24, 34.

Cairns, D., Lafferty, M. and Mantle, P. (1984). *IAB Survey of Accounts and Accountants 1983–84*. London: Lafferty Publications.

Campion, F. D. (1984). *The AMA and U.S. Health Policy Since 1940*. Chicago: Chicago Review Press.

Cannon, P. (1997). 'International Practice: The Big Six Move In'. *International Financial Law Review*, 16(11) November, 25–28.

Caplan, L. (1993). *Skadden: Power, Money, and the Rise of a Legal Empire*. New York: Farrar Strauss Giroux.

Carman, J. M., Shortell, S. M., Foster, R. W., Hughes, E. F., Boerstler, H., O'Brien, J. L. and O'Connor, E. J. (1996). 'Keys for Successful Implementation of Total Quality Management in Hospitals'. *Health Care Management Review*, 21(1), 48–60.

Castells, M. (1996). *The Rise of Network Society*. Vol. 1 of 3 volumes. Oxford: Blackwell.

Caves, R. E. (1996). *Multinational Enterprise and Economic Analysis*. Second edition. Cambridge, UK: Cambridge University Press.

Champagne, F., Denis, J.-L. and Bilodeau, H. (1998). 'Les intérêts médicaux et hospitaliers: La reconciliation sera-t-elle possible?'. *Ruptures*, 5(1), 53–61.

Champagne, F., Denis, J.-L., Pineault, R. and Contandriopoulos, A.-P. (1995). *Évaluation du projet pilote ACCÈS*. Groupe de recherche interdisciplinaire en santé, August.

Chan, P., Ezzamel, M. and Gwilliam, D. (1993). 'Determinants of Audit Fees for Quoted U.K. Companies'. *Journal of Business Finance and Accounting*, 20(November), 765–786.

Chandler, A. D., Jr (1977). *The Visible Hand: The Managerial Revolution in American Business.* Cambridge, MA: Harvard University Press.

Chesanow, N. (1997). 'Making Doctors' Lives Easier – and Patients Happier'. *Medical Economics*, 74(16), 118–131.

Child, J., and Smith, C. (1987). 'The Context and Process of Organizational Transformation: Cadbury Ltd in its Sector'. *Journal of Management Studies*, 24, 565–594.

Chisolm, D. (1989). *Coordination without Hierarchy: Informal Structures in Multiorganizational Systems.* Berkeley, CA: University of California Press.

Christianson, J. B., Sanchez, S. M., Wholey, D. R. and Shadle, M. (1991). 'The HMO Industry: Evolution in Population Demographics and Market Structures'. *Medical Care Review*, 48, 3–46.

City of London Law Society. (1989). *The Work and Organization of the Legal Profession: A Response to the Government's Green Paper.* London: CLLS.

Clarke, J. and Newman, J. (1997). *The Managerialist State.* London: Sage.

Clegg, S. R. (1989). *Frameworks of Power.* London: Sage.

Cohen, M. D. and March, J. G. (1986). *Leadership and Ambiguity.* Boston: Harvard Business School Press.

Cohen, M. D., March, J. G. and Olsen, J. P. (1972). 'A Garbage Can Model of Organizational Choice'. *Administrative Science Quarterly*, 17, 1–25.

Cohen, W. M. and Levinthal, D. A. (1990). 'Absorptive Capacity: A New Perspective on Learning and Innovation'. *Administrative Science Quarterly*, 35, 128–152.

Cooper, D., Greenwood, R., Hinings, B. and Brown, J. (1998). 'Globalization and Nationalism in A Multinational Accounting Firm: The Case of Opening New Markets in Eastern Europe'. *Accounting, Organizations and Society*, 23, 531–548.

Cooper, D. J., Hinings, C. R., Greenwood, R. and Brown, J. L. (1996). 'Sedimentation and Transformation in Organizational Change: The Case of Canadian Law Firms'. *Organization Studies*, 17(4), 623–647.

Crozier, M. (1964). *The Bureaucratic Phenomenon.* Chicago: University of Chicago Press.

Crozier, M. and Friedberg, E. (1978). *L'acteur et le système.* Paris: Seuil.

Cutting, C. C. (1986). 'History of the Kaiser Permanente Medical Care Program: An Oral History Conducted in 1985 by Malca Chall'. Berkeley, CA: Regional Oral History Office, The Bancroft Library, University of California.

Cypert, S. A. (1991). *Following the Money: The Inside Story of Accounting's First Mega-Merger.* New York: AMACOM.

D'Amour, D. (1997). Structuration de la collaboration interprofessionnelle dans les services de santé de première ligne au Québec. Doctoral thesis, University of Montreal.

Daniels, P. W., Thrift, N. J. and Leyshon, A. (1989). 'Internationalization of Professional Provider Services: Accountancy Conglomerates'. In Peter Enderwick (ed.), *Multinational Service Firms* (pp. 79–105). London: Routledge.

Daoust, M. (1998). Analyse d'une démarche de concertation réseau pour assurer une continuité des services. Master's paper, University of Montreal.

Davidson, N. (1987). *A Question of Care: The Changing Face of the National Health Service.* London: Michael Joseph.

Demers, L. and Bégin, C. (1990). 'Pouvoirs et contre-pouvoirs dans le secteur de la santé Deux cas de fusion'. *Recherches sociographiques*, 31(3), 381–404.

Denis, J.-L. (1988). Un modèle politique d'analyse du changement dans les organisations: Le cas de l'implantation de la vacation dans les centres d'hébergement. Ph.D. thesis, Université de Montréal.

Denis, J.-L. (1997). 'Trois idées et trois terrains pour penser la décentralisation'. Paper presented at the Colloquium La santé de demain vers un système de soins sans murs, Lyon, December.

Denis, J.-L. and Valette, A. (1997). 'La régulation au concret: L'expérience des DRASS'. *Politiques et Management Public*, 15(4), 1–25.

Denis, J.-L. and Valette, A. (1998). 'Décentraliser pour transformer la régulation La création des agences régionales d'hospitalisation'. Paper presented at the Seminar of the Institut National de la Santé et de la Recherche Médicale, Paris.

Denis, J.-L., Lamothe, L. and Langley, A. (1998). 'The Dynamics of Teaching Hospital Mergers'. Paper presented at the Academy of Management Meeting, San Diego.

Denis, J.-L., Langley, A. and Cazale, L. (1996). 'Leadership and Strategic Change under Ambiguity'. *Organization Studies*, 17(4), 673–699.

Denis, J.-L., Langley, A. and Contandriopoulos, A.-P. (1998). 'From Institutional Discourse to Organizational Action: The Dynamics of Legitimation'. Paper presented at the Academy of Management Meeting, San Diego.

Denis, J.-L., Fleury, M. J., Champagne, F., Contandriopoulos, A.-P., Pineault, R., Sicotte, C. and Langley, A. (1996). 'La planification et le changement Analyse de l'expérience des PROS dans le système de santé du Québec'. *La planification régionale des services sociaux et de santé* (eds M. Tremblay, H. Nguyen and J. Turgeon), Québec Publications du Québec, 41–50.

Dennett, L. (1989). *Slaughter and May: A Century in the City*. Cambridge: Granta Editions.

Dent, M. (1996). 'The New National Health Service: A Case of Postmodernism?'. *Organization Studies*, 16(5), 875–899.

Department of Health and Social Security. (1983). *A Report on the Collection and Use of Financial Information in the NHS*. Sixth report of the Steering Group on Health Services Information. London: HMSO.

Department of Health. (1989). *Working for Patients*. Cm 555. London: HMSO.

Derber, C. (1982). *Professionals as Workers: Mental Labor in Advanced Capitalism*. Boston: G.K. Hall & Co.

Dezalay, Y. (1997). 'Accountants as "New Guard Dogs" of Capitalism: Stereotype or Research Agenda?'. *Accounting, Organizations and Society*, 22(8), November, 825–829.

Dillon, K. (1992). 'Profile: Top Billing'. *Legal Business*, April, 22–25.

DiMaggio, P. J. (1988). 'Interest and Agency in Institutional Theory'. In Lynne G. Zucker (ed.), *Institutional Patterns and Organizations: Culture and Environment*, (pp. 3–21). Cambridge, MA: Ballinger.

DiMaggio, P. J. (1991). 'Constructing an Organizational Field as a Professional Project: U.S. Art Museums, 1920–1940'. In W.W. Powell and P.J. DiMaggio, (eds), *The New Institutionalism in Organizational Analysis*, (pp. 267–292). Chicago: University of Chicago Press.

DiMaggio, P. J. and Powell, W. W. (1983). 'The Iron Cage Revisited: Institutional Isomorphism and Collective Rationality in Organizational Fields'. *American Sociological Review*, 48(2), 147–160.

Donaldson, L. (1985). *In Defence of Contingency Theory: A Reply to the Critics*. New York: Cambridge University Press.

Donaldson, L. (1995). *American Anti-Management Theories of Organization: A Critique of Paradigm Proliferation*. Cambridge: Cambridge University Press.

Donaldson, L. (1996). *For Positivist Organization Theory. Providing the Hard Core*. Thousand Oaks, CA: Sage.

Drucker, P.F. (1988). 'The Coming of the New Organization'. *Harvard Business Review*, January–February, 45–53.

Dunning, J. (1998). 'Location, and the Multinational Enterprise: A Neglected Factor'. *Journal of International Business Studies*, 29(1), 45–67.

Eccles, R. G. and Crane, D. B. (1988). *Doing Deals: Investment Banks at Work*. Cambridge, MA: Harvard Business School.

Economist, The. (1988). 'Accountant, Consult Thyself'. 10 September, 89–90.

Economist, The. (1992). All Change. 17 October, 19–21.

Edmonton Capital Health Authority. (1994). 'A New Direction for Health'. Business Plan presented to Alberta Health, 15 September.

Eisenhardt, K. M. (1989a). 'Agency Theory: An Assessment and Review'. *Academy of Management Review*, 14, 57–74.

Eisenhardt, K. M. (1989b). 'Building Theories from Case Study Research'. *Academy of Management Review*, 14, 532–550.

Eisler, K. (1991). *Shark Tank: Greed, Politics and the Collapse of Finley Kumble, One of America's Largest Law Firms*. New York: Plume.

Enthoven, A. (1985). *Reflections on the Management of the National Health Service*. Occasional paper No. 5. London: Nuffield Provincial Hospital Trust.

Enthoven, A. C. and Kronick, R. (1989). 'A Consumer Choice Health Plan for the 1990s'. *New England Journal of Medicine*, 320(1), 29–37, 320(2), 94–101.

European Accounting Focus. (1994). 'Developing the Right Network'. September, 13–15.

Evans, P. (1992). 'Management Development as Glue Technology'. *Human Resource Planning*, 15(1), 85–106.

Evans, P. (1993). 'Dosing the Glue: Applying Human Resource Technology to Build the Global Organization'. *Research in Personnel and Human Resource Management*, 3, 21–54. JAI Press Inc.

Fairtlough, G. (1994). *Creative Compartments: A Design for Future Organisation*. London: Adamantine Press.

Federal Bar Council (1984). 'The Changing Nature of the Practice of Law'. In *Bench and Bar Conference Proceedings*. Dorado, Puerto Rico.

Feldstein, P. J. (1986). 'The Emergence of Market Competition in the U.S. Health Care System: Its Causes, Likely Structure, and Implications'. *Health Policy*, 6, 1–20.

Ferlie, E., Ashburner, L., Fitzgerald, L. and Pettigrew, A. (1996). *The New Public Management in Action*. Oxford: Oxford University Press.

Ferner, A., Edwards, P. and Sisson, K. (1995). 'Coming Unstuck? In Search of the "Corporate Glue" in an International Professional Service Firm'. *Human Resource Management*, 34(3), Fall, 343–361.

Firth, M. (1985). 'An Analysis of Audit Fees and Their Determinants'. *Auditing: A Journal of Practice and Theory*, 4, Spring, 23–37.

Fischer, M. J. (1996). 'Realizing the Benefits of New Technologies as a Source of Audit Evidence: An Interpretive Field Study'. *Accounting, Organizations & Society*, 21(2), 3, 219–242.

Fitzpatrick, J. (1989). 'Legal Future Shock: The Role of Large Law Firms by the End of the Century'. *Indiana Law Journal*, 64, 461–471.

Flam, H. (1993). 'Fear, Loyalty and Greedy Organizations'. In S. Fineman (ed.) *Emotion in Organizations*, pp. 58–75. London: Sage.

Flanagan, C. (1998). 'The Second Coming'. *Legal Business*, June, 58–65.

Flood, J. (1987). Anatomy of Lawyering: An Ethnography of a Corporate Law Firm. Ph.D. dissertation, Northwestern University.

Flood, J. (1989). 'Megalaw in the U.K.: Professionalism or Corporatism? A Preliminary Report'. *Indiana Law Journal*, 64, 569–592.

Flood, J. (1994). 'Shark Tanks, Sweatshops, and the Lawyer as Hero? Fact as Fiction'. *Journal of Law and Society*, 21, 396–405.

Flood, J. (1996). 'Megalawyering in the Global Order: The Cultural, Social and Economic Transformation of Global Legal Practice'. *International Journal of the Legal Profession*, 3, 169–214.

Flood, J. (1998). 'Fatal Attraction: A Tale of a Failed MDP'. Paper presented at Research and Policy Planning Unit, Law Society, London.

Flood, J., Boon, A., Whyte, A., Skordaki, E., Abbey, R. and Ash, A. (1996). *Reconfiguring the Market for Advocacy Services: A Case Study of London and Four Fields of Practice*. Report for the Lord Chancellor's Advisory Committee on Legal Education and Conduct.

Ford, J. D. and Baucus, D. A. (1987). 'Organizational Adaptation to Performance Downturns: An Interpretation-based Perspective'. *Academy of Management Review*, 12(2), 366–380.

Forsgren, M. (1990). 'Managing the International Multi-centre Firm'. *European Management Journal*, 8(2), 261–267.

Fortune (1998). *Consultants Have a Big People Problem*. 13 April, 163–166.

Foster, M. S. (1989). *Henry J. Kaiser: Builder in the Modern American West*. Austin, TX: University of Texas Press.

Foucault, M. (1977) *Discipline and Punish: The Birth of the Prison*. Translated by A. S. Smith, New York: Pantheon.

Francis, J. R. (1984). 'The Effect of Audit Firm Size on Audit Prices: A Study of the Australian Market'. *Journal of Accounting and Economics*, 6, August, 133–151.

Francis, J. R. and Stokes, D. J. (1986). 'Audit Prices, Product Differentiation and Scale Economies: Further Evidence from the Australian Market'. *Journal of Accounting Research*, 24, Autumn, 383–393.

Freidson, E. (1970). *Profession of Medicine: A Study in the Sociology of Applied Knowledge*. New York: Dodd, Mead.

Freidson, E. (1986). *Professional Powers: A Study of the Institutionalization of Formal Knowledge*. Chicago: University of Chicago Press.

Freidson, E. (1994). *Professionalism Reborn: Theory, Prophecy and Policy*. Cambridge: Polity.

Friedberg, E. (1993). *Le pouvoir et la règle*. Paris: Seuil.

Friedman, M. (1962). *Capitalism and Freedom*. Chicago: University of Chicago Press.

Galanter, M. and Palay, T. (1991). *Tournament of Lawyers: The Transformation of the Big Law Firm*. Chicago: University of Chicago Press.

Garcia, M. R., (1997). 'Knowledge Central'. *Information Week*, September, 649, 252–256.

Garfinkel, H. (1967). *Studies in Ethnomethodology*. Englewood Cliffs, NJ: Prentice-Hall.

Gaston, S. J. (1992). 'Matters of Interest'. *CA Magazine*, May, 19–31.

Gazette (1997). 'Alarm Raised Over "Big Six" Threat'. *Gazette*, 14 August.

Gersick, C. J. G. (1991). 'Revolutionary Change Theories: A Multilevel Exploration of the Punctuated Equilibrium Paradigm'. *Academy of Management Review*, 16(1), 10–36.

Ghoshal, S., and Bartlett, C. (1990). 'The Multinational Corporation as an Interorganizational Network'. *Academy of Management Review*, 40(1), January, 96–110.

Ghoshal, S. and Moran, P. (1996). 'Bad for Practice: A Critique of Transaction Cost Theory'. *Academy of Management Review*, 21(1), 13–47.

Giacomini, M., Hurley, J., Lomas, J., Bhatia, V. and Goldsmith, L. (1996). *The Many Meanings of Money. A Health Policy Analysis Framework for Understanding Financial Incentives*. Centre for Health Economics and Policy Analysis, McMaster University.

Giddens, A. (1976). *New Rules of Sociological Method*. London: Hutchinson.

Giddens, A. (1979). *Central Problems in Social Theory: Action, Structure and Contradiction in Social Analysis*. Berkeley, CA: University of California Press.

Giddens, A. (1984). *The Constitution of Society*. Cambridge: Cambridge University Press.

Gilson, R. and Mnookin, R. (1985). 'Sharing Among the Human Capitalists: An Economic Inquiry into the Corporate Law Firm and How Partners Split Profits'. *Stanford Law Review*, 37, 313–392.

Gilson, R. and Mnookin, R. (1989). 'Coming of Age in a Corporate Law Firm: The Economics of Associate Career Patterns'. *Stanford Law Review*, 41, 567–595.

Girin, J. (1995). Les agencements organisationnels. *Les savoirs en action* (ed. F. Charue-Duboc), Paris: L'Harmattan.

Goldacre, M. J., Lambert, T. W. and Parkhouse, J. (1998). 'Views of Doctors in the United Kingdom about Their Own Professional Position about the National Health Service Reforms'. *Journal of Public Health Medicine*, 20(1), 86–92.

Graham, E. M. (1978). 'Transatlantic Investment by Multinational Firms: A Rivalistic Phenomenon'. *Journal of Post-Keynsian Economics*, 1(1), Fall, 82–99.

Granovetter, M. (1985). 'Economic Action and Social Structure: The Problem of Embeddedness'. *American Journal of Sociology*, 91, 481–510.

Grant, R. (1996). 'Towards a Knowledge-based Theory of the Firm'. *Strategic Management Journal*, 17(Special issue), 109–122.

Gray, J. T. (1999). The Organising Modes of Law Firms. Unpublished doctoral dissertation. Sydney: UWS.

Gray, J. T., King, P. and Woellner, R. (1998). 'Strategic Change in Successful Law Firms'. *NSW Law Society Journal*, April edition, Sydney: Law Society of NSW.

Greenwood, R., Cooper, D. J., Hinings, C. R. and Brown, J. L. (1993). 'Biggest is Best? Strategic Assumptions and Actions in the Canadian Audit Industry'. *Canadian Journal of Administrative Sciences*, 10(4), 308–321.

Greenwood, R. and Hinings, C. R. (1988). 'Organizational Design Types, Tracks and the Dynamics of Strategic Change'. *Organization Studies*, 9(3), 293–316.

Greenwood, R. and Hinings, C. R. (1993). 'Understanding Strategic Change: The Contribution of Archetypes'. *Academy of Management Journal*, 36, 1052–1081.

Greenwood, R. and Hinings, C. R. (1996). 'Understanding Radical Organizational Change: Bringing Together the Old and New Institutionalism'. *Academy of Management Review*, 21, 1022–1054.

Greenwood, R., Hinings, C. R. and Brown, J. (1990). '"P²-form" Strategic Management: Corporate Practices in Professional Partnerships'. *Academy of Management Journal*, 33(4), 725–755.

Greenwood, R., Hinings, C. R., Brown, J. and Cooper, D. (1997). 'Promoting the Professions'. *Business Quarterly*, 61: 64–70.

Greenwood, R., Hinings, B., and Cooper, D. (1999). 'An Institutional Theory of Change: Contextual and Interpretive Dynamics in the Accounting Industry'. In W. Powell and D. Jones (eds). *Bending the Bars of the Iron Cage: Institutional Dynamics and Processes*.

Greenwood, R. and Lachman, R. (1996). 'Change as an Underlying Theme in Professional Service Organizations: An Introduction'. *Organization Studies*, 17(4), 563–572.

Greenwood, R., Rose, T., Hinings, B., Cooper, D. and Brown, J. (1998b). 'The Global Management of Professional Services: The Example of Accounting'. In S. Clegg, E. Ibarra, and L. Bueno (eds). *Theories of Management Process: Making Sense Through Difference*.

Greenwood, R., Suddaby, R. and Hinings, B. (1998a). 'The Role of Professional Associations in the Transformation of Institutionalized Fields'. Paper presented at the SCORE Conference, Standford University, September.

Hagedoorn, J. (1996). 'The Economics of Cooperation Among High-Tech Firms: Trends and Patterns in Strategic Partnering Since the Early Seventies'. In Georg Koopmans and Hans-Eckart Scharrer (eds). *The Economics of High-Technology: Competition and Cooperation in Global Markets* (pp. 173–198). Hamburg: HWWA.

Hall, R. (1968). 'Professionalization and Bureaucratization'. *American Sociological Review*, 33, 92–104.

Han, S. (1994). 'Mimetic Isomorphism and its Effect on the Audit Services Market'. *Social Forces*, 73, 637–664.

Hanlon, G. (1994). *The Commercialization of Accountancy: Flexible Accumulation and the Transformation of the Service Class*, (p. 842). London: Macmillan.

Hanlon, G. (1997). 'Commercializing the Service Class and Economic Restructuring: A Response to My Critics'. *Accounting, Organizations and Society*, 22(8), November, 843–855.

Hanson, J. D. (1989). 'Internationalization of the Accounting Firm'. In A. Hopwood (ed.). *International Pressures for Accounting Change*. Englewood Cliffs, NJ: Prentice-Hall.

Harrison, S. and Pollitt, C. (1994). *Controlling Health Professionals: The Future of Work and Organization in the NHS*. Buckingham: Open University Press.

Haug, M. R. (1973). 'De-professionalization: An Alternative Hypothesis for the Future'. *Sociological Review Monograph*, 20, 195–211.

Haugh, R. (1998). 'Who's Afraid of Capitation Now'. *Hospitals and Health Networks*, 72(11), 5 June, 30–37.

Hayes, M. V. and Dunn, J. R. (1998). *Population Health in Canada: A Systematic Review*. CPRN Study No. H01, Canadian Policy Research Networks Inc.

Health Canada. (1993). *Quest for Quality in Canadian Health Care Continuous Quality Improvement*. Minister of Supply and Services, Canada.

Hecksher, C. and Donnellon, A. (1994). *The Post-bureaucratic Organization: New Perspectives on Organizational Change*. London: Sage.

Hedlund, G. (1986). 'The Hypermodern MNC'. *Human Resource Management*, 25, 9–36.

Hedlund, G. (1994). 'A Model of Knowledge Management and the N-form Corporation'. *Strategic Management Journal*, 15, 73–90.

Heinz, J. and Laumann, E. (1982). *Chicago Lawyers: The Social Structure of the Bar*. Chicago: American Bar Foundation. New York: Basic Books.

Hendricks, R. (1991). 'Medical Practice Embattled: Kaiser Permanente, the American Medical Association, and Henry J. Kaiser on the West Coast, 1945–1955'. *Pacific Historical Review*, 60, 439–473.

Hendricks, R. (1993). *A Model For National Health Care: The History of Kaiser Permanente*. New Jersey: Rutgers University Press.

Hickson, D. J., Hinings, C. R., Schneck, R., Lee, C. A. and Pennings, J. (1971). 'A Strategic Contingencies Theory of Power'. *Administrative Science Quarterly*, 16, 216–229.

Hinings, C. R. and Greenwood, R. (1988a). *The Dynamics of Strategic Change*. Oxford: Basil Blackwell.

Hinings, C. R. and Greenwood, R. (1988b). 'The Normative Prescription of Organizations'. In L. Zucker (ed.), *Institutional Patterns and Organizations: Culture and Environment*, (pp. 53–70). Cambridge, MA: Ballinger.

Hinings, C. R., Brown, J. and Greenwood, R. (1991). 'Change in an Autonomous Professional Organization'. *Journal of Management Studies*, 28(4), 375–393.

Hirsch, S. (1989). 'Services and Service Intensity in International Trade'. *Weltwirtschaftliches Archiv*, 125, 45–60.

Hofstede, G. (1980). *Culture's Consequences: International Differences in Work-related Values*. Beverly Hills, CA: Sage.

Hoggett, P. (1996). 'New Modes of Control in the Public Service'. *Public Administration*, 74, 9–32.

Hood, C. (1991). 'A Public Management for all Seasons?'. *Public Administration*, 69(Spring), 3–19.

Hoult, P. (1998). 'Matchmaker on a Mission'. *The Lawyer*, 11, August, 15.

Howard, J. H. (1991). 'Leadership, Management and Change in the Professional Service Firm'. *Business Quarterly*, Spring, 111–118.

Hymer, S. (1976). *The International Operations of National Firms*. Cambridge, MA: MIT Press.

Illich, I. (1975). *Medical Nemesis: The Expropriation of Our Health*. New York: Pantheon.

Illich, I., Zola, I. K., McKnight, J., Caplan, J. and Shaiken, H. (1977). *Disabling Professions*. Salem, NH: Marion Boyars.

International Federation of Accountants (1995). *Auditors' Legal Liability in the Global Market Place: A Case for Limitation*. New York: International Federation of Accountants.

Jérôme-Forget, M., White, J. and Weiner, J. M. (1995). *Health Reform through Internal Markets*. Montreal Institute for Research on Public Policy.

Johnson, S. K. (1974). 'Health Maintenance: It works'. *New York Times Magazine*, 28 April, 34.

Johnson, T. (1972). *Professions and Power*. London: Macmillan.

Johnson, T. (1993). 'Expertise and the State'. In M. Gane and T. Johnson (eds). *Foucault's New Domains* (pp. 139–152). London: Routledge.

Jones, C., Hesterly, W. and Borgatti, S. (1997). 'A General Theory of Network Governance: Exchange Conditions and Social Mechanisms'. *Academy of Management Review*, 22(4), 911–945.

Jones, E. (1981). *Accountancy and the British Economy 1840–1980: The Evolution of Ernst & Whinney*. London: Batsford Books.

Jones, M. (1998). 'The IASC: Twenty-five Years Old This Year'. *Management Accounting*, 76(5), 30–32.

Journal of Accountancy. (1998). *Bigger Pieces of the Audit Pie*. 185(1), January, 20.

Kaiser Permanente Medical Care Program (1987, 1994a). *Annual Report*. Oakland, CA: Kaiser Permanente.

Kaiser Permanente Medical Care Program. (1994b). *How We Measure Up: A Report on Our Performance*. Oakland, CA: Kaiser Foundation Health Plan.

Karpin, D. (Chairman) (1995). *Enterprising Nation: Australia's Inquiry into Leadership and Management Skills for the 21st Century*. Canberra: DEETYA.

Keat, R. (1991). Consumer Sovereignty and the Integrity of Professional Practices. In R. Keat and N. Abercrombie (eds), *The Enterprise Culture*. London: Routledge.

Kerry J. and Brown, H. (1993). *The BCCI Affair: A Report to the Committee of Foreign Relations* (p. 842). Washington: U.S. Government Printing Office.

Kertesz, L. (1997). 'Which Is the Real Kaiser?'. *Modern Healthcare*, 25 August, 27, 61–62, 64, 66, 68, 70.

Kikulis, L., Slack, T. and Hinings, C. R. (1992). 'Institutionally Specific Design Archetypes: A Framework for Understanding Change in National Sport Organizations'. *International Review for the Sociology of Sport*, 27, 343–370.

Kilimnik, K. S. (1994). 'Lawyers Abroad: New Rules for Practice in a Global Economy'. *Dickinson Journal of International Law*, 12(Winter), 269–325.

King's Fund Institute. (1988). *Health Finance: Assessing the Options*. London: King's Fund Institute.

Kitchener, M. (1994). 'Investigating Marketing Change: A Comparative-intensive Approach'. In V. Wass and P. Wells (eds). *Principles and Practice in Business and Management Research* (pp. 207–234). Aldershot: Dartmouth.

Kitchener, M. (1998). 'Institutional Change in U.K. Hospitals'. *Public Administration*, 76(1), 73–95.

Kitchener, M. and Whipp, R. (1997). 'Tracks of Change in Hospitals: A Study of Quasi-market Transformation'. *International Journal of Public Sector Management*, 10(1), 2, 47–62.

Kleinfield, N. R. (1983). 'The King of the HMO Mountain'. *New York Times*, 31 July, 132, 3, 1, 23.

Knickerbocker, F. T. (1973). *Oligopolistic Reaction and Multinational Enterprise*. Boston: Harvard Business School Press.

Kobrin, S. J. (1991). 'An Empirical Analysis of the Determinants of Global Integration'. *Strategic Management Journal*, 12, 17–31.

Kogut, B. (1985). 'Designing Global Strategies: Profiting from Operational Flexibility'. *Sloan Management Review*, 26(4), 27–38.

Kogut, B. and Zander, U. (1991). 'Knowledge of the Firm, Combinative Capabilities and the Replication of Technology'. *Organization Science*, 3, 383–397.

Kondra, A. Z. and Hinings, C. R. (1998). 'Organizational Diversity & Change in Institutional Theory'. *Organization Studies*, 19, 743–767.

Kramon, G. (1989). 'Why Kaiser is Still the King'. *New York Times*, 2 July, 138, 3, 1, 9.

Krause, E. (1997). *Death of the Guilds: Professions, States and the Advance of Capitalism, 1930 to the Present*. New Haven, CT: Yale University Press.

Kroll, K. M. (1997). 'Closing the GAAP?'. (Differences in National Accounting Standards). *Industry Week*, 246, 61–62 plus il. tab.

Lamothe, L. (1996). 'La structure professionnelle clinique de facto d'un hôpital de soins ultraspécialisés'. Ph.D. Thesis, Faculty of Management, McGill University, July.

Landers, R., Rebitzer J. and Taylor, L. (1996). 'Rat Race Redux: Adverse Selection in the Determination of Work Hours in Law Firms'. *American Economic Review*, 86, 329–348.

Lane, P. J. and Lubatkin, M. (1998). 'Relative Absorptive Capacity and Inter-organizational Learning'. *Strategic Management Journal*, 19, 461–477.

Langhorn, K. and Hinings, C. R. (1987). 'Integrated Planning and Organizational Conflict'. *Canadian Public Administration*, 30, 558–565.

Larson, M. S. (1977). *The Rise of Professionalism: A Sociological Analysis*. Berkeley: University of California Press.

Latouche, S. (1996). *The Westernization of the World: The Significance, Scope and Limits of the Drive towards Global Uniformity*. Cambridge: Polity Press.

Lawless, J. (1992). U.K. Law Opens Euro Door (British Lawyers Form Alliances with Foreign Counterparts). *International Management* (Europe edition), 47, 40–41.

Lawrence, P. and Lorsch, J. (1967). *Organization and Environment*. Cambridge, MA: Harvard University Press.

Lawrence, T. (1993). 'Institutional Entrepreneurs in Emerging Industries'. Ph.D. thesis, University of Alberta.

The Lawyer (1998a). 'Law Society Votes on MDP Models'. *The Lawyer*, 27, January, 1.

The Lawyer (1998b). 'ABA Task Force to Probe Threat Posed by MDPs'. *The Lawyer*, 11, August, 1.

Leatt, P., Lemieux-Charles, L. and Aird, C. (1994). *Program Management and Beyond Management Innovation in Ontario Hospitals*. Ottawa Canadian College of Health Service Executives.

Leblebici, H., Salancik, G. R., Copay, A. and King, T. (1991). 'Institutional Change and the Transformation of Interorganizational Fields: An Organizational History of the U.S. Radio Broadcasting Industry'. *Administrative Science Quarterly*, 36, 333–363.

Lee, D. S. (1994). 'Further Evidence on Auditor Concentration: The Case of a Growing Market'. *International Journal of Accounting*, 29, 234–250.

Lee, D. S. (1996). 'Auditor Market Share, Product Differentiation and Audit Fees'. *Accounting and Business Research*, 26(4), 315–324.

Lee, P. (1997). 'International Financial Law Review 50: Setting the Law Firm Standard'. *International Financial Law Review*, November, 16–24.

LeGrand, J. and Bartlett, W. (1993). *Quasi-Markets and Social Policy*. Basingstoke: Macmillan.

Leifer, E. (1985). 'Markets as Mechanisms: Using a Role Structure'. *Social Forces*, 64, 442–472.

Leonard-Barton, D. (1996). *Wellsprings of Knowledge Building and Sustaining the Sources of Innovation*. Boston: Harvard Business School Press.

Levine, S. (1996). Phone interview conducted by Carol Caronna.

Light, D.W. (1986). 'Corporate Medicine for Profit'. *Scientific American*, 255, 38–54.

Lindsay, R. (1998a). 'PW Set to Swoop on Wilde Sapte'. *The Lawyer*, 9(June), 1.

Lindsay, R. (1998b). 'The Perfect Match That Never Was'. *The Lawyer*, 9(June), 2.

Little, M. and Fearnside, M. (1997). 'On Trust'. *The Online Journal of Ethics*, 2, http://www.depaul.edu/ethics/ontrust.html.

Lomas, J. and Contandriopoulos, A.-P.(1994). 'Regulating Limits to Medicine towards Harmony in Public and Self-Regulation'. In R. G. Evans, M. L. Barer and T. R. Marmor (eds). *Why are Some People Healthy and Others Not? The Determinants of Health of Populations* (pp. 253–283). Hawthorne, NY: Aldine de Gruyter.

London Economics Ltd (1994). *The Competitive Advantage of Law and Accountancy in the City of London*. London: Corporation of London.

Lord Chancellor's Department (1998). *Rights of Audience and Rights to Conduct Litigation in England and Wales: The Way Ahead*. London: HMSO.

Løwendahl, B. R. (1992). Global Strategies for Professional Business Service Firms. Unpublished Ph.D. dissertation. Philadelphia: The Wharton School, University of Pennsylvania.

Løwendahl, B. R. (1997). *Strategic Management of Professional Service Firms*. Denmark: Handelshojskolens Forlag.

Løwendahl, B. R. and Revang, Ø. (1998). 'Challenges to Existing Strategy Theory in a Post-industrial Society'. *Strategic Management Journal*, 19(8), 755–774.

Lozeau, D. (1997). 'L'effondrement tranquille de la gestion de la qualité: Résultats d'une étude réalisée dans douze hôpitaux publics du Québec'. *Ruptures*, 3(2), 187–208.

Luft, H. S. (1987). *Health Maintenance Organizations: Dimensions of Performance*. New Brunswick: Transaction Books.

Luhmann, N. (1979). *Trust and Power*. Chichester: John Wiley.

Maister, D. H. (1982). 'Balancing the Professional Service Firm'. *Sloan Management Review*, Fall, 15–30.

Maister, D. H. (1989). *Professional Service Firm Management*. Boston: Maister Associates.

Maister, D. H. (1993). *Managing the Professional Service Firm*. Boston, MA: HBS.

Maister, D. H. (1997). *True Professionalism*. New York: Free Press.

Malos, S. B. and Campion, M. A. (1995). 'An Options-based Model of Career Mobility in Professional Service Firms'. *Academy of Management Review*, 20, 611–645.

Margerion, T. (1980). *The Making of a Profession*. London: The Institute of Chartered Accountants in England and Wales.

Markham, B. and Lomas, J. (1995). 'Review of the Multi-hospital Arrangement Literature:

Benefits, Disadvantages and Lessons for Implementation'. *Healthcare Management Forum*, 8(3), 24–35.

Marmor, T. R. (1970). *The Politics of Medicare*. Chicago: Aldine.

Martinez, J. and Jarillo, J. (1989). 'The Evolution of Research on Coordination Mechanisms in Multinational Corporations'. *Journal of International Business Studies*, 20(3), 489–514.

McKee, D. and Garner, D. (1996). *Accounting: Services Growth and Change in the Pacific Basin*. Westport, CT: Quorum.

McKinlay, J. B. and Arches, J. (1985). 'Toward the Proletarianization of Physicians'. *International Journal of Health Services*, 15(2), 161–195.

McNulty, T., Whittington, R., Whipp, R. and Kitchener, M. (1994). 'Putting Marketing into NHS Hospitals: Issues about Implementation'. *Journal of Public Money and Management*, 14(3), 51–59.

Metcalfe, L. and Richards, S. (1990). *Improving Public Management*. London: Sage.

Meyer, J. and Rowan, B. (1977). 'Institutionalized Organizations: Formal Structure as Myth and Ceremony'. *American Journal of Sociology*, 83(2), 340–363.

Miller, D. (1990). *The Icarus Paradox*. New York: Harper.

Miller, D. and Friesen, P.H. (1984). *Organizations: A Quantum View*. Englewood Cliffs, NJ: Prentice-Hall.

Mills, P., Hall, J., Leidecker, J. and Margulies, N. (1983). 'Flexiform: A Model for Professional Service Organizations'. *Academy of Management Review*, 8(1), 118–131.

Mintzberg, H. (1979). *The Structuring of Organizations: A Synthesis of the Research*. Englewood Cliffs, NJ: Prentice-Hall.

Mintzberg, H. (1983a). *Power in and Around Organizations*. Englewood Cliffs, NJ: Prentice-Hall.

Mintzberg, H. (1983b, 1993). *Structure in Fives: Designing Effective Organizations*. Englewood Cliffs, NJ: Prentice-Hall.

Montagna, P. (1968). 'Professionalization and Bureaucratization in Large Professional Organizations'. *American Journal of Sociology*, 74, July, 138–145.

Montgomery, K. and Oliver, A. (1996). 'Responses by Professional Organizations to Multiple and Ambiguous Institutional Environments: The Case of AIDS'. *Organization Studies*, 17(4), 649–671.

Morris, T. (1992a). 'New Forms of Partnership'. Paper presented to the Conference on Knowledge Workers in Contemporary Organizations, Lancaster, England.

Morris, T. (1992b). 'The End of Partnership?' Proceedings of Conference on Knowledge Based Organizations, Lancaster University, UK.

Morris, T. and Pinnington, A. (1998a). *Change, Management and Performance in Law Firms*. London: London Business School.

Morris, T. and Pinnington, A. (1998b). 'Promotion to Partner in Professional Service Firms'. *Human Relations*, 51, 3–24.

Morrison, E. M. and Luft, H. S. (1990). 'Health Maintenance Organization Environments in the 1980s and Beyond'. *Health Care Financing Review*, 15, 62–73.

National Forum on Health (1997). *Canada Health Action Building on the Legacy*. Ottawa Department of Public Works and Government Services.

Nault, B. R. (1997). 'Mitigating Underinvestment through an IT-Enabled Organization Form'. *Organization Science*, 8(3), 223–234.

Nelson, R. (1988). *Partners with Power: The Social Transformation of the Large Law Firm*. Berkeley: University of California Press.

Nelson, R. and Trubek, D. (1992). 'Introduction: New Problems and New Paradigms in Studies of the Legal Profession'. In Nelson, R., Trubek, D. and Solomon, R. (eds).

Lawyers' Ideals/Lawyers' Practices: Transformations in the American Legal Profession (pp. 1–29). Ithaca, NY: Cornell University Press.

New York Times. (1998) 'Paris Lawyers Are Seeking Barricades Against Big 6'. 8 June, 2.

Nohria, N. and Ghoshal, S. (1997). *The Differentiated Network: Organizing Multinational Corporations for Value Creation.* San Francisco, CA: Jossey-Bass Publishers.

Nystrom, P. (1986). 'Comparing Beliefs of Line and Technostructure Managers'. *Academy of Management Journal*, 29, 812–819.

Oakes, L. S., Townley, B. and Cooper, D. J. (1998). 'Business Planning as Pedagogy: Language and Control in a Changing Institutional Field'. *Administrative Science Quarterly*, 43(2), 257–292.

Oliver, C. (1991). 'Strategic Responses to Institutional Processes'. *Academy of Management Review*, 16, 145–179.

Oliver, C. (1992). 'The Antecedents of Deinstitutionalization'. *Organization Studies*, 13(4), 565–588.

Orru, M., Biggart, N. W. and Hamilton, G. G. (1991). 'Organizational Isomorphism in East Asia'. In Walter W. Powell and Paul J. DiMaggio (eds), *The New Institutionalism in Organizational Analysis* (pp. 361–389). Chicago: University of Chicago Press.

Orru, M., Biggart, N. W. and Hamilton, G. G. (1997). *The Economic Organization of East Asian Capitalism.* Thousand Oaks, CA: Sage.

Ouchi, W. G. (1980). 'Markets, Bureaucracies and Clans'. *Administrative Science Quarterly*, 25(1), 129–141.

Palmer, R. E. (1989). 'Accounting as a "Mature Industry"'. *Journal of Accountancy*, May, 84–88.

Palmrose, Z. V. (1986). 'Audit Fees and Auditor Size'. *Journal of Accounting Research*, 24(Spring), 97–110.

Parker, B. (1996). 'Evolution and Revolution: From International Business to Globalization'. In S. R. Clegg, C. Hardy and W. R. Nord (eds), *Handbook of Organizational Studies.* London: Sage.

Peel, M. J. (1997). U.K. Auditor Concentration: A Descriptive Note. *Accounting & Business Research*, 27(4), 311–322.

Peters, T. (1992). *Liberation Management.* London: Macmillan.

Pettigrew, A. (1973). *The Politics of Organizational Decision Making.* London: Tavistock.

Pettigrew, A. (1985). *The Awakening Giant: Continuity and Change in Imperial Chemical Industries.* Oxford: Basil Blackwell.

Pettigrew, A., Ferlie. E. and McKee, L. (1992). *Shaping Strategic Change.* London: Sage.

Pfeffer, J. (1981). *Power in Organization.* Boston: Pitman.

Pfeffer, J. and Salancik, G. R. (1978). *The External Control of Organizations.* New York: Harper & Row.

Phelps-Brown, H. (1983). *The Origins of Trade Union Power.* Oxford: Clarendon.

Pierce, J. L., Rubenfeld, S. and Morgan, S. (1991). 'Employee Ownership: A Conceptual Model of Process and Effects'. *Academy of Management Review*, 16, 121–144.

Podolny, J. (1993). 'A Status-based Model of Market Competition'. *American Journal of Sociology*, 98, 829–872.

Pollitt, C. (1993a). *Managerialism and the Public Services: The Anglo-American Experience.* London: Macmillan.

Pollitt, C. (1993b). 'The Struggle for Quality: The Case of the National Health Service'. *Policy and Politics*, 21(3), 161–170.

Pollitt, C. (1995). 'Justification by Works or by Faith? Evaluating the New Public Management'. *Evaluation: The International Journal of Theory Research and Practice*, 1(2), 133–154.

Pollitt, C., Harrison, S., Hunter, D. J. and Marnoch, G. (1991). 'General Management in the NHS: The Initial Impact 1983–88'. *Public Administration*, 69, 61–83.

Pong, C. M. and Whittington, G. (1994). 'The Determinants of Audit Fees: Some Empirical Models'. *Journal of Business Finance & Accounting*, 21, December, 1071–1095.

Porter, M. (1985). *Competitive Advantage: Creating and Sustaining Superior Performance*. New York: Free Press.

Post, H. A. (1995). Internationalization of Professional Services: A Study of Large Dutch Accounting and Software Firms. Paper presented at European International Business Association Conference, Urbino, Italy.

Post, H. A. (1996). 'Internationalization and Professionalization in Accounting Services: The Cases of BDO Binder and BDO CampsObers'. *International Studies of Management & Organization*, 26(2), 80–103.

Powell, M. J. (1985). 'Developments in the Regulation of Lawyers: Competing Segments and Market, Client and Government Controls'. *Social Forces*, 64, 281–305.

Powell, M. J. (1993). 'Professional Innovation: Corporate Lawyers and Private Lawmaking'. *Law & Social Inquiry*, 18, 423–452.

Powell, W. W. (1990). 'Neither Market Nor Hierarchy: Network Forms of Organization'. In B. M. Staw and L. L. Cummings, (eds). *Research in Organizational Behavior*. Vol. 12. Greenwich, CT: JAI Press.

Powell, W. W. (1991). 'Expanding the Scope of Institutional Analysis'. In W. W. Powell and P. J. DiMaggio, (eds). *The New Institutionalism in Organizational Analysis* (pp. 183–203). Chicago: University of Chicago Press.

Powell, W. W. and DiMaggio, P. J. (eds) (1991). *The New Institutionalism in Organizational Analysis*. Chicago: University of Chicago Press.

Pralahad, C. K. and Doz, Y. L. (1989). *The Multinational Mission: Balancing Local Demands and Global Vision*. New York: Free Press.

Pugh, D., Hickson, D., Hinings, C. and Turner, C. (1968). 'Dimensions of Organizational Structure'. *Administrative Science Quarterly*, 13, 65–105.

Quinn, J. B. (1993). *Intelligent Enterprise: A New Paradigm for a New Era*. New York: The Free Press.

Quinn, J. B., Anderson, P. and Finkelstein, S. (1996). 'Leveraging Intellect'. *The Academy of Management Executive*, 10(3), 7–27.

Rachlis, M. and Kushner, C. (1994). *Strong Medicine*. Toronto, ON: HarperCollins.

Raelin, J. (1989). *Clash of Cultures*. Boston: Harvard Business School Press.

Raelin, J. (1991). *The Clash of Cultures. Managers Managing Professionals*. Boston: Harvard Business School Press.

Ranade, W. (1995). 'The Theory and Practice of Managed Competition in the National Health Service'. *Public Administration*, 73, 241–262.

Ranson, S., Hinings, B. and Greenwood, R. (1980). 'The Structuring of Organizational Structures'. *Administrative Science Quarterly*, 25, 1–17.

Rea, C. (1995). Clinical Directorates. *British Journal of Hospital Medicine*, 53(5), 231–232.

Reed, M. (1996) 'Expert Power and Control in Late Modernity: An Empirical Review and Theoretical Synthesis'. *Organization Studies*, 17(4), 573–597.

Report on Business Magazine, (1998). 'They Like to Watch'. May, 82–86.

Reynolds, B. (1993). *Excellence in Accountancy*. London: Macmillan.

Rhode, D. (1981). 'Policing the Professional Monopoly: A Constitutional and Empirical Analysis of Unauthorized Practice Prohibitions'. *Stanford Law Review*, 34, 1–112.

Richards, A. B. (1981). *Touche Ross and Co. 1899–1981*. London: Touche Ross and Co.

Roberts, J. (1998). *Multinational Business Service Firms: The Development of Multinational Organisational Structures in the U.K. Business Services Sector*. Aldershot: Ashgate.

Robinson, J. C. (1997). 'Physician–Hospital Integration and the Economic Theory of the Firm'. *Medical Care Research and Review*, 54(1), 3–24.

Rochon, J., Gélineau, G. Barkun, H., Bernatchez-Simard, J., Bertrand, R., Duplantie, J.-P. and Rodrigue, N. (1988). *Rapport de la Commission d'enquête sur les services de santé et les services sociaux*. Gouvernement du Québec.

Romanelli, E. and Tushman, M. L. (1993). 'Organizational Transformation as Punctuated Equilibrium: An Empirical Test'. *Academy of Management Journal*, 36(5), 1141–1156.

Rose, T. (1998). Coordination and Integration Processes in Global Business Advisory Firms: The Role of Global Clients. Unpublished doctoral dissertation, University of Alberta, Edmonton.

Sackett, D. L., Richardson, W. S., Rosenberg, W. and Haynes, R. B. (1997). *Evidence-based Medicine*. New York: Churchill-Livingstone.

Saltman, R. B. and von Otter, C. (1987). 'Revitalizing Public Health Services: A Proposal for Public Competition in Sweden'. *Health Policy*, 7, 21–40.

Sander, R. and Williams, D. (1989). 'Why Are There So Many Lawyers? Perspectives on a Turbulent Market'. *Law & Social Inquiry*, 14, 431–479.

Sassen, S. (1991). *The Global City: New York, London, Tokyo*. Princeton: Princeton University Press.

Schein, E. H. (1985). *Organizational Culture and Leadership*. San Francisco: Jossey-Bass.

Schultz, M. (1995). *On Studying Organizational Cultures: Diagnosis and Understanding*. Berlin: de Gruyter.

Schulz, R. and Detmer, D. (1977). 'How to Get Doctors Involved in Governance and Management'. *Hospital Medical Staff: Selected Readings 1972–1976*. Chicago: American Hospital Association.

Schumpeter, J. A. (1934). *The Theory of Economic Development: An Inquiry into Profits, Capital, Credit, Interest, and the Business Cycle*. Cambridge, MA: Harvard University Press.

Schwarz, G. M. and Brock, D. M. (1998). 'Waving Hello or Waving Good-bye? Organizational Change in the Information Age'. *The International Journal of Organization Analysis*, 6(1), 65–90.

Scott, P. (1998). 'Take the Lead or Take the Consequences'. *The Lawyer*, 13 (January), 10.

Scott, W. R. (1965). 'Reactions to Supervision in a Heteronomous Professional Organization'. *Administrative Science Quarterly*, 10, 65–81.

Scott, W. R. (1987). *Organizations: Rational, Natural and Open Systems*. Second edition. Englewood Cliffs, NJ: Prentice Hall.

Scott, W. R. (1995). *Institutions and Organizations*. Thousand Oaks, CA: Sage.

Scott, W. R., Mendel, P. and Pollack, S. (forthcoming). 'Environments and Fields: Studying the Evolution of a Field of Medical Care Organizations'. To appear in Walter W. Powell (ed.). *Remaking the Iron Cage: Institutional Dynamics and Processes*.

Scott, W. R., Ruef, M., Mendel, P. and Caronna, C. A. (2000). *Institutional Change and Organizations: Transformation of a Healthcare Field*. Chicago: University of Chicago Press.

Serron, C. (1992). 'Managing Entrepreneurial Legal Services: The Transformation of Small-Firm Practice'. In Nelson, R., Trubek, D. and Solomon, R. (eds) *Lawyers Ideals/Lawyers Practices*, pp. 63–92.

Shortell, S. M. (1997). 'Commentary'. *Medical Care Research and Review*, 54(1), 25–31.

Shortell, S. M., Gillies, R. R., Anderson, D. A., Erickson, K. M. and Mitchell, J. B. (1996). *Remaking Health Care in America*. San Francisco, CA: Jossey-Bass.

Simon, D. T. (1997). 'Additional Evidence on the Large Audit-Firm Fee Premium as an Indication of Auditor Quality'. *Journal of Applied Business Research*, 13, 21–29.

Simpson, B. and Powell, M. J. (1999). 'Designing Research Organizations for Science Innovation'. *Long Range Planning*, forthcoming.

Siow, A. (1994). 'Hierarchical Careers'. *Industrial Relations*, 33, 83–105.

Slack, T. and Hinings, B. (1994). 'Institutional Pressures and Isomorphic Change: An Empirical Test'. *Organization Studies*, 15(6), 803 827.

Slinn, J. (1984). *A History of Freshfields*. London: Freshfields.

Smigel, E. (1964). *Wall Street Lawyer: Professional Organization Man?* New York: The Free Press.

Smillie, J. G. (1991). *Can Physicians Manage the Quality and Costs of Care?: The Story of the Permanente Medical Group*. New York: Mc-Graw Hill.

Smoller, M. (1996). Interview conducted by Carol Caronna.

Somers, A. R. (1971a). *Health Care in Transition: Directions for the Future*. Chicago: Hospital Research and Education Trust.

Somers, A. R. (ed.). (1971b). *The Kaiser-Permanente Medical Care Program: One Valid Solution to the Problem of Health Care Delivery in the United States*. New York: The Commonwealth Fund.

Sommerlad, H. (1995). 'Managerialism and the Legal Profession: A New Professional Paradigm'. *International Journal of the Legal Profession*, 2, 159–185.

Spangler, E. (1986). *Lawyers for Hire: Salaried Professionals at Work*. New Haven: Yale University Press.

Spar, D. L. (1997). 'Lawyers Abroad: The Internationalization of Legal Practice'. *California Management Review*, 39, 8–28.

St George, A. (1995). *A History of Norton Rose*. Cambridge: Granta Editions.

Starbuck, W. H. (1992). 'Learning by Knowledge-intensive Firms'. *Journal of Management Studies*, 29(6), 713–740.

Starbuck, W. H. (1993). 'Keeping a Butterfly and an Elephant in a House of Cards: The Elements of Exceptional Success'. *Journal of Management Studies*, 30, 885–921.

Starbuck, W. H., Greve, A. and Hedberg, B. (1978). 'Responding to Crises'. *Journal of Business Administration*, 9, 111–137.

Starr, P. (1982). *The Social Transformation of American Medicine*. New York: Basic Books.

Statement of Position. (1992). 'A Statement of Position by the Six Largest Public Accounting Firms on the Liability Crisis Facing the Accounting Profession' New York: Submission to SEC.

Stevens, M. (1981). *The Big Eight*. New York: Macmillan Book Publishing Co.

Stevens, M. (1987). *Power of Attorney: The Rise of the Giant Law Firms*. New York: McGraw-Hill.

Stevens, M. (1991). *The Big Six*. New York: Simon & Schuster.

Stewart, T. A. (1997). *Intellectual Capital*. London: Nicholas Bradley.

Stopford, J. and Wells, L. (1972). *Managing the Multinational Enterprise*. New York: Basic Books.

Strauss, A., Schatzman, L., Bucher, R., Ehrlich, D. and Sabshin, M. (1964). *Psychiatric Ideologies and Institutions*. New York: Free Press.

Strauss, A., Schatzman, L., Ehrlich, D., Bucher, R. and Sabshin, M. (1963). 'The Hospital and its Negotiated Order'. In E. Friedson (ed.), *The Hospital in Modern Society* (pp. 147–169). London: Collier-Macmillan.

Suchman, M. C. (1995). 'Localism and Globalism in Institutional Analysis: The Emergence of Contractual Norms in Venture Finance'. In W. Richard Scott and

Soren Christensen (eds), *The Institutional Construction of Organizations: International and Longitudinal Studies* (pp. 39–63). Thousand Oaks, CA: Sage.

Suchman, M. and Edelman, L. (1996). 'Legal Rational Myths: The New Institutionalism and the Law and Society Tradition'. *Law & Social Inquiry*, 21, 903–941.

Swaine, R. (1946). *The Cravath Firm and its Predecessors, 1819–1947.* (2 vols) New York: Ad Press.

Swann, G. (1998). 'The Name is Bond. Project Bond'. *Legal Business*, June, 54–57.

Taylor, S., Beechler, S. and Napier, N. (1996). 'Toward an Integrative Model of Strategic Human Resource Management'. *Academy of Management Review*, 21(4), 959–985.

Thompson, J. (1967). *Organization in Action: Social Science Bases of Administrative Theory.* New York: McGraw-Hill.

Thorne, Ernst & Whinney. (1986). *Merger Report.* Toronto, ON.

Tichy, N. and Ulrich, D. (1984). 'Revitalizing Organizations: The Leadership Role'. In J. R. Kimberly and R. E. Quinn (eds), *Managing Organizational Transitions.* Homewood, IL: Irwin.

Tolbert, P. S. (1988). 'Institutional Sources of Organizational Culture in Major Law Firms'. In Lynne G. Zucker (ed.), *Institutional Patterns and Organizations: Culture and Environment* (pp. 101–113). Cambridge, MA: Ballinger.

Tolbert, P. and Stern, R. (1991). 'Organizations of Professionals: Governance Structures in Large Law Firms'. In Tolbert, P. and S. Barley (eds). *Research in the Sociology of Organizations: Vol. 8 Organizations and Professions* (pp. 97–118). London: JAI Press.

Tolbert, P. S. and Zucker, L. G. (1983). 'Institutional Sources of Change in the Formal Structure of Organizations: The Diffusion of Civil Service Reform, 1880–1935'. *Administrative Science Quarterly*, 30, 22–39.

Trapp, R. (1994). 'Fears Grow Among Auditors as the Liability Claims Soar'. *Independent on Sunday*, 6 March.

Traska, M. R. (1988, June 5). 'Vohs: Kaiser Has Withstood the Test of Time'. *Hospitals*, 62, 108–109.

Trice, E. and Beyer, J. (1994). *The Culture of Work Organisations.* Englewood Cliffs, NJ: Prentice-Hall.

Tushman, M. and Romanelli, E. (1985). 'Organizational Evolution: A Metamorphosis Model of Convergence and Reorientation'. In L. L. Cummings and B. Staw (eds). *Research in Organizational Behavior.* Greenwich, CT: JAI Press.

Tyler, R. (1998). 'Feature: France – War of the Words'. *The Lawyer*, 4 August, 15–16.

UNCTAD (1995). *World Investment Report 1995: Transnational Corporations and Competitiveness.* New York and Geneva: UN.

UNCTAD (1997). *World Investment Report 1997: Transnational Corporations, Market Structure and Competition Policy.* New York and Geneva: UN.

UNCTC (1990). *Transnational Corporations, Services and the Uruguay Round.* New York: United Nations.

United Nations (1993). *The Transnationalization of Service Industries.* Transnational Corporations and Management Division, Department of Economic and Social Development. ST/CTC/SER.A/23.

Vaughan, D. (1992). 'Theory Elaboration: The Heuristics of Case Analysis'. In Charles C. Ragin and Howard S. Becker (eds), *What is a Case?: Exploring the Foundations of Social Inquiry* (pp. 173–202). New York: Cambridge University Press.

Vernon, R. (1966). 'International Investment and International Trade in the Product Life Cycle'. *Quarterly Journal of Economics*, 190–207.

Vijayan, J. and Hoffman, T. (1997). 'IT Services Boom Sets Megamerger in Motion'. *Computerworld*, 31(38), September, 4.

Walsh, K., Hinings, C. R., Ranson, S. and Greenwood, R. (1981). 'Power and Advantage in Organizations'. *Organization Studies*, 2, 131–152.

Wasserman, E. (1996). 'Kaiser Discussing Hospital Alliances'. *San Jose Mercury News*, 27 January, 1B, 2B.

Weick, K. E. (1976). 'Educational Organizations as Loosely Coupled Systems'. *Administrative Science Quarterly*, 21, 1–19.

Weiner, B. J., Shortell, S. M. and Alexander, J. A. (1997). 'Promoting Clinical Involvement in Hospital Quality Improvement Efforts: The Effects of Top Management, Board and Physician Leadership'. *Health Services Research*, 32(4), 491–510.

White, H. (1981). 'Where Do Markets Come From?'. *American Sociological Review*, 87, 517–547.

Whitford, D. (1997). 'Arthur, Arthur [.]'. *Fortune*, 10 November, 169–178.

Williams, G. (1971). *Kaiser-Permanente Health Plan: Why It Works*. Oakland, CA: Henry J. Kaiser Foundation.

Willmott, H. and Sikka, P. (1997). 'On the Commercialization of Accountancy Thesis: A Review Essay'. *Accounting, Organizations and Society*, 22(8), November, 831–842.

Winsbury, R. (1977). *Thomson McLintock and Co.: The First Hundred Years*. London: Seeley, Service.

Winslow, R. (1994). 'Technology and Health: Kaiser Permanente Will Allow Members to Get Care from Non-plan Physicians'. *Wall Street Journal*, 28 January, B2.

Woodward, J. (1965). *Industrial Organization: Theory and Practice*. London: Oxford University Press.

Wooton, C. W., Tonge, S. D. and Wolk, C. M. (1990). 'From the 'Big Eight' to the 'Big Six' Accounting Firms'. *Ohio CPA Journal*, Spring, 19–23.

Zeff, S. A. (1998). 'Whither the Independent Audit?'. *Chartered Accountant Journal of New Zealand*, 77, 41–6.

Zeithaml, V. A., Parasuraman, A. and Berry, L. (1990). *Delivering Quality Service: Balancing Customer Perceptions and Expectations*. New York: Free Press.

Zucker, L. G. (1987). 'Normal Change or Risky Business: Institutional Effects on the Hazard of Change in Hospital Organizations, 1959–1979'. *Journal of Management Studies*, 24(6), 671–700

Author index

note: for '*et al.*' references in the text of the book, often only the first author is referenced in this index

Abbey, R. 155, 173
Abbott, A. 72, 110, 155, 188, 201, 202
Abel, R. 105, 157
Acher, G. 33
Ackroyd, S. 107, 112, 185, 188
Adams, S. 75
Addams, H. L. 32
Aharoni, Y. 12, 15–16, 20, 24, 29–30, 41, 44, 53–4, 136, 215–16, 224
Aird, C. 116
Alcock, M. 181
Alford, R. 147
Anders, G. 79–80
Anderson, D. A. 9, 105
Anderson, P. 115, 117
Anderson, T. 26
Appadurai, A. 12
Appleby, J. 79–80
Arches, J. 8
Ashburner, L. 121, 183, 216
Ash, A. 155, 173

Baker, W. 158
Baldwin, R. 155
Banks, H. 39
Barkun, H. 126
Barley, S. R. 110
Barnard, C. 88
Baron, J. N. 81
Baroody, W. J. 78
Bartlett, C. 24, 43–4, 49, 52
Bartlett, W. 183, 190
Baucus, D. A. 151
Beck, U. 156
Beechler, S. 54

Bégin, C. 106, 119, 122
Benson, K. J. 118, 144, 172
Bergthold, L. 78
Bernatchez-Simard, J. 126
Berry, L. 54
Bertrand, R. 90, 92–7, 99, 100-1, 104, 126
Berwick, D. M. 107, 115, 117
Beyer, J. 94
Bhatia, V. 128
Biggart, N. W. 81
Bilodeau, H. 109
Blackler, F. 115, 129
Blau, J. 4, 148
Bledstein, B. J. 2
Boddewyn, J. J. 27
Boerstler, H. 116–17
Bohman, J. 128
Bolman, L. 88
Boon, A. 155, 173, 182
Borgatti, S. 65
Boston, J. 14
Bourdieu, P. 157
Bourn, J. 157, 163
Brill, S. 177
Briston, R. J. 25
Brock, D. M. 1, 182, 215, 223
Brown, H. 33
Brown, J. 2, 7, 8, 30, 31, 41, 44, 51, 67–9, 89, 97, 99, 102–3, 108, 131–2, 135, 145, 148, 155, 185, 198, 200, 202–3
Bruce, R. 32
Brunsson, N. 188
Bucher, R. 5, 106, 110
Buckley, P. 42, 66

Cairns, D. 29
Campion, F. D. 76
Campion, M. A. 202, 211

Cannon, P. 39, 182
Caplan, J. 14
Caplan, L. 157
Carman, J. M. 116–17
Caronna, C. A. 12, 16–17, 68, 76, 78, 106, 216–17
Casson, M. 42, 66
Castells, M. 87–8, 101
Caves, R. E. 27
Cazale, L. 111, 195
Champagne, F. 109, 125
Chan, P. 26
Chandler, A. D. Jr 8, 222
Chesanow, N. 117
Child, J. 150
Chisolm, D. 223
Christianson, J. B. 79
Clarke, J. 183
Clegg, S. R. 89, 96, 100, 143
Cohen, M. D. 5, 112
Cohen, W. M. 38
Contandriopoulos, A-P. 106, 115, 125
Cooper, D. 2, 8, 14, 18, 28, 41–4, 51, 53, 67–9, 89, 97, 99, 102–3, 108, 129, 130–1, 135, 140, 145–6, 155, 180, 185–6, 196, 198, 200–2, 211, 218–19, 220, 222–3
Copay, A. 84
Crane, D. B. 220
Crozier, M. 110–11
Cutting, C. C. 71, 77
Cypert, S. A. 24, 53

Daniels, P. W. 29
Daoust, M. 121–2
Davidson, N. 189–90
Deal, T. 88
Demers, L. 119
Denis, J-L. 17, 19, 105–6, 109, 111, 117, 119, 124–5, 128, 195, 218
Dennett, L. 155, 172
Dent, M. 190
Derber, C. 8
Detmer, D. 191, 197
Dezalay, Y. 32
Dillon, K. 154
DiMaggio, P. 3, 69, 81, 85–6, 138, 155, 185, 196
Dobbin, F. R. 81
Donaldson, L. 46, 212
Donnellon, A. 202
Doz, Y. L. 24
Drucker, P. F. 1
Dunn, J. R. 105

Dunning, J. 43
Duplantie, J.-P. 126

Eccles, R. G. 220
Edelman, L. 178
Edwards, P. 32, 54
Ehrlich, D. 106, 110
Eisenhardt, K. 68, 129, 211
Eisler, K. 157
Enthoven, A. 107, 189
Erickson, K. M. 105
Evans, P. 54

Fairtlough, G. 100
Feldstein, P. J. 78
Ferlie, E. 121, 183, 216
Ferner, A. 32, 34, 54
Firth, M. 26
Finkelstein, S. 115, 117
Fischer, M. J. 25
Fitzgerald, L. 121, 183, 216
Fitzpatrick, J. 177
Flam, H. 172
Flanagan, C. 179
Fleury, M. J. 106, 125
Francis, J. R. 26
Friesen, P. H. 96–7, 185, 187, 196
Flood, J. 13, 15, 18, 91, 103, 154–5, 158, 160, 172–3, 179–82, 218–19, 224
Ford, J. D. 151, 181
Forsgren, M. 24
Foster, M. S. 71, 73–5
Foster, R. W. 116–17
Foucault, M. 91
Freidson, E. 2, 5–6, 19, 72, 188, 201, 203
Friedberg, E. 110, 126, 129
Friedman, M. 14

Galanter, M. 131, 154–5, 159, 200–2
Garcia, M. R. 33
Garfinkel, H. 88
Garner, D. 41
Gaston, S. J. 138
Gélineau, G. 126
Gersick, C. J. G. 202
Ghoshal, S. 24, 39, 43–4, 46, 49, 52, 62, 136, 212, 216, 223
Giacomini, M. 128
Giddens, A. 13, 85, 89
Gillies, R. R. 105
Gilson, R. 167, 172, 202, 211–12
Girin, J. 111
Godfrey, A. B. 107, 115
Goldacre, M. J. 196

Goldsmith, L. 128
Granovetter, M. 91, 103, 158
Grant, R. 30, 140, 211
Gray, J. T. 17, 87, 95, 97, 99, 102, 182, 218–19, 228
Greenwood, R. 2–4, 7, 8, 13, 14–15, 18–19, 29, 33–4, 41–2, 44, 51, 53–5, 63–4, 67–70, 81, 85, 89–90, 94–9, 102–3, 108, 131–2, 135, 140, 143, 145–6, 148, 155, 183–6, 195–8, 200–3, 210, 216–20, 222–3, 225, 227–9
Greve, A. 148

Hagedoorn, J. 23
Halbrich, M. 27
Hall, J. 37
Hall, R. 5, 201
Hamilton, G. G. 81
Han, S. 178, 181
Hanlon, G. 21, 31, 32–3
Hanson, J. D. 26
Harrison, S. 186–8, 195
Haug, M. R. 8, 197
Haugh, R. 105
Hayes, M. V. 105
Haynes, R. B. 116
Hedberg, B.148
Hedlund, G. 24, 43, 46
Heinz, J. 157, 168, 181
Hendricks, R. 70, 73–5
Hesterly, W. 65
Hickson, D. J. 67, 148
Hinings, C. R. 1–4, 7–8, 12–6, 18–19, 28, 32, 40–2, 44, 51, 63, 67–70, 81, 85, 89, 90, 94–9, 102–3, 108, 131–2, 135, 140, 142–6, 148, 150, 155, 182, 184–6, 195–8, 200, 202–3, 212, 215–16, 217–20, 222–5, 227–9
Hirsch, S. 37
Hoffman, T. 27, 40
Hofstede, G. 27, 46
Hoggett, P. 183
Hood, C. 14, 183
Hoult, P. 182
Howard, J. H. 150
Hughes, E. F. 116
Hughes, J. 107, 112, 185
Hunter, D. J. 186
Hurley, J. 128
Hymer, S. 27

Illich, I. 14

Jarillo, J. 43

Jennings, P. D. 81
Jérôme-Forget, M. 107
Johnson, S. K. 73, 76
Johnson, T. 29, 155, 172, 201
Jones, C. 65–6
Jones, E. 20–1
Jones, M. 35

Karpin, D. 88
Keat, R. 192
Kerry, J. 33
Kertesz, L. 70–1, 79–80
Kikulis, L. 227
Kilimnik, K. S. 36
King, P. 87, 95, 97, 99, 102
King, T. 84
Kitchener, M. 18–19, 106, 183–4, 186–9, 196, 216–20, 222–3
Kleinfield, N. R. 78
Kobrin, S. J. 31
Kogut, B. 43, 211
Kondra, A. Z. 140
Kramon, G. 79
Krause, E. 76
Kroll, K. M. 35, 40
Kronick, R. 107
Kushner, C. 108

Labelle, B. 106, 122
Lachman, R. 183, 200–1
Lafferty, M. 29
Lambert, T. W. 196
Lamothe, L. 17, 105–6, 108–10, 115–16, 125
Landers, R. 202
Lane, P. J. 38
Langhorn, K. 144
Langley, A. 17, 105–6, 111, 125, 195
Larson, M. S. 188
Latouche, S. 12, 216
Laumann, E. 157, 168, 181
Lawless, J. 35
Lawrence, P. 43–4, 53, 143
Lawrence, T. 136, 139
Leatt, P. 116
Leblebici, H. 84
Lee, C. A. 148
Lee, D. S. 26
Lee, P. 180
LeGrand, J. 183, 190
Leifer, E. 158
Lemieux-Charles, L. 116
Leonard-Barton, D. 115
Levine, S. 78, 158

Levinthal, D. A. 38
Light, D.W. 8, 224
Lindsay, R. 180
Little, M. 157, 210
Lomas, J. 115, 118–19, 128
Lorsch, J. 43–4, 53, 143
Løwendahl, B. R. 130
Lozeau, D. 106, 115–16
Lubatkin, M. 38
Luft, H. S. 78, 80, 86

McNulty, T. 186
Maister, D. H. 26, 34, 38, 133, 203
Malos, S. B. 202, 211
Mantle, P. 29
March, J. G. 5, 112, 169
Margerion, T. 21
Markham, B. 118–19
Marmor, T. R. 72, 75
Marnoch, G. 186
Martin, J. 178, 183
Martinez, J. 43
McKee, D. 41
McKinlay, J. B. 8
McNulty, T. 186
Mendel, P. 68, 72, 76, 78
Metcalfe, L. 195
Meyer, J. 69, 117, 185
Miller, D. 96–7, 148, 185, 187, 196
Mills, P. 37
Mintzberg, H. 2, 6–7, 29, 97, 105–6,
    108–9, 112, 183–4, 187–8, 191, 195,
    198, 202, 222
Mitchell, J. B. 105
Mnookin, R. 167, 172, 202, 211–12
Montagna, P. 2, 5, 30
Montgomery, K. 130, 190, 198
Moran, P. 212
Morgan, S. 203
Morris, T. 18–19, 102–3, 142, 167, 172,
    200, 202–3, 211, 219–20, 222
Morrison, E. M. 78, 86

Napier, N. 54
Nault, B. R. 38
Nelson, R. 2, 4, 8, 131, 154, 156, 161,
    201, 203
Newman, J. 183
Nohria, N. 39, 43–4, 46, 52, 62, 136, 216,
    223
Nystrom, P. 143

Oakes, L. S. 129
Oliver, A. 130, 190, 198

Oliver, C. 13, 69–70, 84–5, 185, 195,
    197–8
Olsen, J. 5, 188
Orru, M. 81
Ouchi, W. G. 6, 129

Palay, T. 154–5, 159, 200–2
Palmer, R. E. 135
Palmrose, Z. V. 26
Parasuraman, A. 54
Parker, B. 215
Parkhouse, J. 196
Peel, M. J. 25
Pennings, J. 148
Perry, A. 27
Peters, T. 1
Pettigrew, A. 121, 143–4, 150, 183,
    216
Pfeffer, J. 15, 118, 148
Phelps-Brown, H. 188
Pierce, J. L. 203
Pineault, R. 125
Pinnington, A. 18–19, 102–3, 167, 172,
    200, 202–3, 219–20, 222
Podolny, J. 158
Pollack, S. 72
Pollitt, C. 115, 183, 186–9, 191, 195
Pong, C. M. 26
Porter, M. 87
Post, H. 34, 41, 54
Powell, M. J. 1–2, 12, 15, 162, 182,
    196, 215
Powell, W. W. 3, 15, 69, 85–6, 97–8,
    139, 155, 185, 223
Pralahad, C. K. 24
Pugh, D. 67

Quinn, J. 1, 115, 117, 202

Rachlis, M. 108
Raelin, J. 30, 203
Ranade, W. 190
Ranson, S. 89–90, 94–7, 143, 185,
    195
Rea, C. 190
Rebitzer, J. 202
Reed, M. 197
Revang, Ø. 130
Reynolds, B. 31
Rhode, D. 155
Richards, A. B. 20–1
Richards, S. 195
Richardson, W. S. 116
Roberts, J. 31, 35

Robinson, J. C. 120–1, 225
Rochon, J. 105, 107, 126
Rodrigue, N. 126
Roessner, J. 107, 115
Romanelli, E. 148, 150, 196
Rose, T. 12, 16, 40–2, 44–5, 47, 53, 67, 215–16, 219, 224
Rosenberg, W. 116
Rowan, B. 69, 117, 185
Rubenfeld, S. 203
Ruef, M. 68, 76, 78, 86

Sabshin, M. 106, 110
Sackett, D. L. 116
Salancik, G. R. 15, 84, 118
Saltman, R. B. 107
Sanchez, S. M. 79
Sander, R. 157
Sassen, S. 172
Schatzman, L. 106, 110
Schein, E. H. 100, 150
Schneck, R. 148
Schultz, M. 178
Schulz, R. 191, 197
Schumpeter, J. A. 87
Schwarz, G. M. 223
Scott, P. 180
Scott, W. R. 5, 7, 12, 15–17, 63, 68–9, 72, 76, 78, 81, 84, 86, 106, 132, 216–17, 219
Serron, C. 201
Shadle, M. 79
Shortell, S. M. 2, 9, 105, 116, 121, 124, 225
Sikka, P. 32
Simon, D. T. 26
Simpson, B. 2
Siow, A. 202
Sisson, K. 32, 54
Skordaki, E. 155, 173, 182
Slack, T. 198, 227
Slinn, J. 155, 157, 172
Smigel, E. 201
Smillie, J. G. 70–1, 73–7
Smith, C. 150
Smoller, M. 79
Somers, A. R. 71, 76–7
Sommerlad, H. 179
Soothil, K. 107, 112
Spangler, E. 8, 181
Spar, D. L. 26, 28, 36, 39
St George, A. 155
Starbuck, W. H. 17, 55, 99, 148, 201, 219, 228

Starr, P. 8, 68, 70, 72, 75–6, 78, 224
Stelling, J. 5, 110
Stern, R. 211
Stevens, M. 20–1, 39, 53, 131, 160
Stewart, T. A. 23
Stokes, D. J. 26
Stopford, J. 42–3
Strauss, A. 106, 110
Suchman, M. 81, 178
Suddaby, R. 63
Swaine, R. 154
Swann, G. 179

Taylor, L. 202
Taylor, S. 54
Thompson, J. 43–4, 53, 111
Thrift, N. J. 29
Tichy, N. 150
Tolbert, P. S. 69, 81, 211
Tonge, S. D. 135
Townley, B. 129
Trapp, R. 33
Traska, M. R. 78
Trice, E. 94
Trubek, D. 201
Turner, C. 67, 89–97, 99, 101–2
Tushman, M. L. 148, 150, 196
Tyler, R. 182

Ulrich, D. 150

Valette, A. 17, 105–6, 124, 128
Vaughan, D. 68
Vernon, R. 42
Vijayan, J. 27, 40

Walsh, K. 143–4
Walsh, P. 14
Wasserman, E. 79
Weick, K. E. 188
Weiner, B. J. 116–17
Weiner, J. M. 107,
Wells, L. 42–3
Whipp, R. 184, 186, 188
White, H. 157, 158
White, J. 107
Whitford, D. 53, 61
Whittington, G. 26
Whittington, R. 186
Wholey, D. R. 79
Whyte, A. 155, 173
Williams, D. 157
Williams, G. 71, 76
Winsbury, R. 21

Winslow, R. 79
Woellner, R. 87, 95, 97, 99, 102
Wolk, C. M. 135
Woodward, J. 67
Wooton, C. W. 135

Zander, U. 211
Zeff, S. A. 30
Zeghal, D. 26
Zeithaml, V. A. 54
Zucker, L. G. 81, 184

Subject index

accountability 51, 95, 107, 117, 125, 133–4, 196

accountant 47, 138, 142, 226

accounting 1, 2, 5, 9, 10, 12, 14–16, 20–40, 41–67, 69, 94, 131–53, 156, 177, 179–81, 187, 215–17, 219, 223–4, 226

advertising 9, 21, 24–5, 47, 72–3, 135, 158, 220, 228

advocates 158, 173–4, 176, 180

agency 12, 15, 73, 89, 96, 165, 211–12, 220

Allen & Overy 173

alliance 23, 29, 38, 80, 177, 180; alliance capitalism, 23

American Bar Association (ABA) 163–5, 182

American Medical Association (AMA) 72, 74, 76, 78, 82

Andersen, Arthur Andersen, Andersen Consulting, Andersen International, Andersen Worldwide 21, 24, 27–9, 33, 39–40, 79, 91, 145, 148, 180

archetype, archetypal 3–5, 7, 8, 12–16, 18–19, 51, 96–9, 102–3, 107–8, 113, 120–1, 124, 132–3, 141–3, 147, 149–52, 155, 167, 180, 184–91, 195–6, 202, 216–20, 222–3, 225, 227–9

Asian Business Review 35

audit, auditing 3, 10, 14–15, 20–1, 25–6, 30, 31–4, 36–8, 40, 44–50, 53, 55, 57–8, 61, 67, 87, 135–9, 142, 145, 147–8, 181–2, 191, 195, 215–17

Australia 16–17, 26, 35, 87, 90–2, 99, 101; Australian Bureau of Statistics, 87

autonomy 5, 29, 35, 51, 58, 62, 74–5, 94–5, 107, 113, 118, 121, 123–4, 126, 128–9, 131, 146, 188–9, 192–4, 197–8, 206–8, 210, 219–20, 225, 227

Baker & McKenzie 27, 39, 226

barrister 103, 155, 158, 173–6, 181, 218

BDO 140

Big Eight 20, 28, 36

Big Five 1, 15–16, 20–1, 24, 29, 34, 37, 40–1, 55, 61–4, 180, 224

Big Six 20–1, 25–8, 32, 37, 40, 92–3, 181

boundary, crossing 64, 106, 108, 111–13, 116, 119, 123–4

Britain 49, 69, 137–8, 178

bureaucracy 2, 5–7, 18–19, 79, 93, 108, 114, 125, 142, 152, 183–4, 195–6, 198, 216–17, 223, 225–6

business development 10, 32, 80, 223

business-like 200–1, 213, 222–4, 227

business service 2, 11, 15–16, 25, 27, 35, 38–9, 45–6, 53, 87–8, 102, 132, 135–6, 139

business unit 42, 55, 58, 60, 62, 145, 216, 219–20, 223, 226

Business Week 25, 136, 139

Canada 16–17, 26, 60, 67, 69, 107, 111–12, 119, 124–5, 127, 130, 136–8, 149–50

capitation 71, 128

centralization 30, 51, 77, 81–2, 134, 142 (*see also* decentralization)

change tracks 3, 185, 189

China 15, 25, 31, 40, 53, 145

circuits of power 96, 98, 100

City of London Law Society 172 (*see also* Law Society)

clan 6–7, 32, 129

client 5, 11, 14, 16, 21, 27, 32–4, 37, 40–66, 90, 92–3, 99–100, 109, 125, 128, 135–6, 141–2, 150, 154–71, 173–7, 180–2, 201–5, 207–8, 210–14, 216–17, 220, 225, 227; command of

178, control of 100, 154, 159–71,
    173–9, 204, 208, 220; management 16,
    87, 141–2, 207, 216; structures 16,
    47–9, 55, 57–9, 62–3
clinical 106, 111, 113, 116–17, 119–20,
    127–9, 184, 188–96, 198, 219
coalition 95, 98, 101, 103, 148
coexistent organization 223
collaborate, collaboration 79, 105–13,
    116–18, 120, 121–3, 125, 127–30, 197,
    211
collegial, collegiality 7, 32, 64, 91, 93, 95,
    100, 131, 145, 155, 172, 187, 211,
    217, 222, 227
commodification 11, 92, 135
competition 1, 5, 9, 11, 14–15, 17, 20, 32,
    38–9, 43, 48, 71, 78–84, 87, 91, 95,
    102, 107, 114, 118, 124, 129, 135–6,
    140–1, 146, 156, 158, 172, 177,
    180–1, 190–2, 196, 200–1, 208, 213,
    227
consultancy, consultant, consulting 9–10,
    15–16, 20–1, 24–6, 32, 37–40, 42,
    46–50, 53, 55–6, 59, 60–3, 77, 93,
    136, 139, 141–2, 145–8, 152, 163–4,
    191–4, 215, 217, 226
contingency theory 21–2, 34–5, 46
convergence 18, 102, 156, 228
coordination 5, 14, 28–32, 41, 43, 45,
    53–5, 63, 83, 101, 105–10, 112–13,
    116–17, 120–5, 133
corporate 2–3, 5, 8–10, 14, 25, 30, 32,
    35–6, 42, 53, 66, 69, 72–75, 78, 81,
    86–90, 92–3, 99, 131, 136, 139,
    141, 143, 146–7, 154–7, 159, 161,
    163, 165–73, 179–80, 182, 191–2,
    196–7, 206, 216, 218–20, 222, 224–6,
    229
Cravath 154–5
customer 13, 21, 24, 32, 47, 67, 80, 87,
    91, 95, 102–3, 192

decentralization 140
de-institutionalization 13, 138, 196, 222
    (*see also* reinstitutionalization)
delegitimation 4, 13–15, 222 (*see also*
    legitimacy)
Deloitte, Deloitte and Haskins Sells,
    Deloitte Touche, Deloitte Touche
    Tohmatsu 20, 28, 31, 39, 47
Department of Health, Department of
    Health and Social Security (DoH) 184,
    187, 190–1, 196
dependence 37, 70, 95–8, 101, 103, 137,

220, 222 (*see also* independence,
    resource dependency theory)
deprofessionalization 8, 12
deregulation 9, 11–12, 14, 77, 179, 221,
    227
deviant 13, 17, 75, 82, 84–5
differentiated network 52, 62, 66, 216,
    223
differentiation 7, 26, 32, 42–4, 46, 52–3,
    62–3, 97, 142–4 (*see also* internal
    differentiation)
diffusion 84–5, 102–3, 224
diversification 37–8, 50, 138, 143, 204
drivers of change 9, 12–13, 113, 115, 220

'eat-what-you-kill' 4, 145, 224,
Edmonton Capital Health Authority
    123–4
environment 2, 9, 12–14, 16–18, 32, 34,
    37, 42–4, 46, 52–3, 69–70, 72, 84–5,
    91, 93, 97–8, 101, 117, 119, 133, 135,
    138, 142, 155, 178, 187, 194, 202,
    208, 210, 213–14, 216–17, 225
Ernst and Whinney, Ernst and Young,
    Arthur Young, Thorne Ernst and
    Whinney (TEW) 27–8, 39–40, 136
exceptionalism 6, 12

Federal Bar Council 156, 160
federated structure 29, 51
fiduciary role 21
foreign direct investment 22, 24, 27
Fortune 9, 50, 136, 139
franchise, franchising 22, 29, 172, 224–6,
    228

generalist 215, 224–6
Global Business Advisory Firm (GBAF)
    16, 40–3, 46–7, 49–52, 54–5, 58–60,
    216, 221–2, 225
Global Professional Network (GPN) 227–8
globalization 3, 9, 12, 16, 19, 21–8, 35–6,
    39, 87–8, 91, 100, 135–6, 177,
    215–17, 224, 227
governance 2, 8, 10, 24, 30–1, 44–5, 65,
    68–72, 74–8, 80–7, 93, 111, 114,
    123–4, 129, 133, 141–3, 210, 213,
    216, 219–20, 222, 225–7; field 72, 78,
    81, 85
government 1–2, 9, 14–15, 23, 69, 72,
    75–8, 80–83, 86, 107, 130, 137–8,
    157, 172–3, 179, 183, 187–90, 195–8,
    216–17, 221, 227
Grant Thornton 30, 140

group practice 68, 70–1, 76–8, 82

Health Canada 107
health care 3, 5, 10–11, 13, 16–17, 58,
 68–86, 105–30, 183–99, 216–20,
 224–5
Health Maintenance Organization
 (HMO) 76, 78–80
Health Plan 71, 73–5, 79–80, 83 (*see also*
 Kaiser Permanente)
hospital 1, 5, 9–10, 17, 68, 70, 72, 74,
 76–9, 84, 106, 108–9, 111, 114,
 118–19, 128, 130, 184, 186–98, 216,
 218
human assets, human resource (HR) 26,
 61, 145–6

ideology 29, 65, 107–9, 120, 122, 187,
 189, 192, 200–1
independence 6–7, 15, 28–30, 32–5, 39,
 60, 71, 84, 93, 95, 107, 110, 115, 150,
 184, 190, 211
inertia 151, 185, 188, 192
informal 80, 95, 110–12, 116–17, 120,
 127, 223–4
information system, 23, 136, 184, 187,
 190
information technology (IT) 15, 23, 38,
 40, 45, 47–8, 53, 63, 87, 90–2, 95,
 114, 136, 140, 142, 217, 223
innovation 24, 87, 91, 131, 206
institutional 12, 14, 35, 68–70, 81, 84–6,
 94, 98, 103, 106–7, 117–18, 121, 135,
 137–40, 144, 151–2, 155, 177–8, 180,
 183, 190, 196, 198, 216–17, 229
integration 5, 17, 23, 29–32, 34, 36,
 42–6, 51, 53–4, 59, 61–6, 80, 101,
 105–9, 112–14, 116, 118–27, 142, 193,
 216
intellectual capital 23, 43, 115
internal differentiation 5, 53, 59, 133,
 142–4, 222
international 1, 3, 9, 11, 16, 22, 24, 26,
 29–31, 33–5, 39, 41–3, 45–6, 48, 51,
 55–7, 59, 62–7, 90, 93, 136–7, 141,
 146, 150–2, 177, 180, 215–16, 220,
 224, 226
International Federation of Accountants
 33
interpretive scheme 3–4, 10, 13–14,
 17–19, 94, 96–8, 107, 132–3, 141–2,
 146–53, 185, 188–9, 191–2, 195–8,
 216, 220, 222, 227
isomorphic, isomorphism 13, 185, 190

Journal of Accountancy 40

Kaiser Permanente, Medical Care
 Program (KP) 68, 70–85
knowledge 3, 6, 14, 23, 27, 30, 33–4,
 37–40, 42, 44–9, 54–6, 58–9, 61, 62,
 64–6, 82, 98, 109, 114, 116, 122,
 124–5, 127, 129, 133–4, 149–51, 158,
 162–3, 200–1, 223
KPMG 28–9, 33, 47, 53, 59, 136,
 140–1

law firm 1–4, 8–13, 15–19, 21, 24–7, 35,
 39, 63, 69, 87–104, 132, 136, 154–82,
 185, 196, 200–14, 216, 218–20, 224,
 226
Law Society 24, 172
lawyer 35, 91, 94–5, 154–5, 159–71, 181
lead partner 49, 50, 57–8
leadership 39, 61, 111, 149–51, 217
legal department 157, 215
legitimacy, legitimate 4, 15, 68–9, 84–5,
 96–9, 101–3, 108, 119, 124, 132, 135,
 137, 139, 143, 152, 170, 178–9,
 184–5, 191–2, 194, 196–7, 217
leverage 15, 52, 56, 59, 92, 124, 206
liability 33–6, 55, 91, 99, 137, 155, 178,
 216, 224; limited, 33–6, 91, 178, 216,
 224
litigation 21, 33, 39, 44, 101, 104, 136–7,
 156, 158–9, 165–7, 173–6, 182, 200
lockstep 4, 93, 167, 172, 178–80, 207,
 211, 228
London Economics Ltd. 27
Lord Chancellor's Department 181–2

Managed Professional Business (MPB) 8,
 19, 51, 97, 99–100, 102, 131–2, 134,
 140–6, 149–51, 153, 180, 202–3,
 206–7, 209, 213–14, 219–23, 228–9
managerialism 8, 14, 93, 103, 217, 222
managerialist 93, 95, 99, 102, 218, 220
marketing 1, 9, 10, 30, 37, 55, 83, 91–3,
 134, 141–2, 145–6, 150, 160, 162,
 191, 204, 206, 208, 210, 213, 216,
 220, 223
medical 1–3, 8, 68, 70–8, 80, 82, 83–4,
 108–9, 111, 115–16, 119, 157, 184,
 186–95, 197, 215, 223, 226
mergers 3, 9, 10, 17, 20, 24–5, 30, 32, 40,
 64, 80–1, 90, 105–6, 114, 118–19,
 120–1, 127–8, 130, 136–8, 146, 152,
 172, 226
mimetic 98, 190, 196

multidisciplinary 40, 107, 109, 116, 218, 220, 224–6; form (MDF) 220–1; practice 224, 226
multinational 3, 16, 21–2, 24–5, 27–8, 35–6, 38, 41, 43, 49, 57, 60, 88, 152, 159, 179, 216, 220, 223–4; corporation (MNC) 3, 21–2, 223; enterprise (MNE) 22, 24, 27–8, 41, 43, 64

National Forum on Health 130
National Health Service (NHS) 10, 18, 115, 183, 186–9, 195, 216, 218, 222
network 21–4, 26–31, 33–5, 39, 41, 44, 52, 55, 62–6, 78, 92, 101–2, 125, 137, 155, 216, 223, 225–6, 228; (*see also* differentiated network)
new public management (NPM) 183–4, 190, 196
New Zealand 10, 15, 26
non-conformity 69, 85, 198
norms 13, 28, 34–5, 68, 70, 72, 75, 82, 84–5, 91, 119, 129, 178, 201

'one-stop shop' 9, 15, 45, 137, 177, 225
operating unit 109, 118, 120, 126
organizational field 12–13, 16–17, 132, 138–9
organized anarchy 5

Philippines 35, 150
population-driven 107–8, 113, 120–1, 124, 127
power 6–8, 10, 14, 18–19, 21, 24, 54, 72–3, 76–8, 81, 89, 95–8, 100–1, 103, 108, 110–13, 115, 119, 121, 124, 127, 143, 148–52, 155–7, 160, 163, 167, 178, 183, 185, 188–9, 192, 195, 197–8, 202–3, 212, 217–18, 220, 224, 227; 'circuits of power' 96, 98, 100
Price Waterhouse 20–1, 24, 27–8, 31, 33, 39–40, 136
productivity 27, 141, 202, 204, 206–8, 210, 224
professional autonomy 34, 74, 81, 106, 111, 115–16, 129, 183, 187, 193, 195, 197, 220, 222
professional bureaucracy (PB) 2, 6–7, 18–19, 108, 142, 152, 183–4, 186–9, 191–2, 195–8, 216–17, 225–6,
professional dominance 2, 5, 8, 12, 14, 72, 75, 82, 84, 117
professional entrepreneurs 6
professional influence 109–10, 126
professionalism 2, 4, 7, 13, 29–30, 34, 45, 58, 93, 94–5, 103, 132, 141, 143, 146, 150, 155, 178
professionalization 1, 5, 14, 155
professional partnership (P^2) 2, 4, 7–8, 18, 26, 29, 51, 58, 69, 97, 99–100, 102, 131–4, 140–3, 145–7, 150, 152–3, 180, 200, 202, 210, 213–14, 216–20, 225–8
profit sharing 29, 56, 202, 207, 211
proletarianization 8, 12
provider capture 14
provider-driven 107–8, 120, 127

quality 6, 11, 24, 26, 34, 37, 42, 44–5, 51, 55, 57, 60–1, 79–81, 83, 93, 105, 115–17, 133–4, 136, 142, 158, 179, 184, 187, 191, 195, 197, 206, 210, 213, 220, 227–8; total quality management (TQM) 107, 114–16, 130, 136
quasi-market (QM) 183–4, 186, 189–93, 195–8, 216, 219, 220, 222

rainmaker 99, 167–9, 171
rationalization 9–10, 19, 111–12, 114, 120, 141, 192
reflexivity 13, 89, 101, 102, 218
reinstitutionalization 138 (*see also* de-institutionalization)
Report on Business Magazine 137
reputation 24, 26, 29, 37, 54, 75, 92, 155, 159, 161–2, 180, 211
resource dependency theory 15, 96, 220
rewards 54, 78, 86, 167, 178, 212, 220, 224
routinization 8, 11, 34, 36, 61
Russia 40, 46, 145

Securities and Exchange Commission (SEC) 21, 67, 138, 177
sedimentation 69, 180, 185, 198, 220, 222–3, 227
sedimented change 19
senior partner 154, 160–1, 165–6, 169
shared values 30, 40, 44, 52, 65
size 20, 24–7, 30, 36–7, 78, 91, 92, 95, 100–1, 155, 159, 172, 203, 206, 215, 222, 224, 226
Skadden Arps 15, 156
socialization 32, 38, 39, 69, 94
solicitors 103, 155, 158, 172–7, 181–2, 203, 206, 218
specialization 38, 58–61, 114–15, 133–4, 136, 140, 142, 144, 150, 200, 211–12, 219, 226

standardization 6–7, 31, 34, 36, 44, 55, 61, 112, 114, 116, 140, 202, 216, 224
star (form) 132, 148, 161, 219, 220
strategy 6–7, 17, 31, 34, 37–9, 42, 44, 46, 48, 55, 57, 59, 64, 73, 87, 90–3, 95, 97, 100–1, 119, 136–7, 140–1, 150, 177, 191, 207, 211
structure and agency 13, 89, 218
surgery, surgical 1, 10, 109, 226

tax 9, 20, 33, 37, 40, 45, 47, 53, 55, 58, 61, 136, 138–40, 142, 146, 158, 167, 219, 226
technology 22–3, 31, 33, 55–7, 61–3, 67, 88, 91, 105, 109–10, 115, 118, 124, 224, 226–7
The Lawyer 180, 182
Touche, Touche Ross 28, 32, 135, 163
tracks 185, 189 (*see also* change tracks)
transaction cost 27, 28, 158, 212
transnational 31, 43–4, 52
trust 37, 50, 65, 73, 110, 157–8, 193, 212

typology 69, 85, 225–8

UNCTAD 22
UNCTC 25
United Kingdom (UK) 16, 21, 27, 30, 39, 154, 183, 219
United Nations 27
United States (USA, US) 16, 20–3, 25–7, 30, 32–3, 35, 59, 67–8, 117, 137–8, 141, 150, 154
university 5–6
'up-or-out' 202, 207, 211

values 3–4, 6–8, 10, 13, 17–19, 38, 58, 65, 78, 93–6, 98, 100–1, 108, 132, 143–51, 155, 184–9, 194–5, 198, 200–1, 207, 216–22, 227
virtual 27, 38, 60, 121, 224, 225; corporation 27, 38

Wachtell Lipton Rosen & Katz, Wachtell Lipton 17, 219, 228
whirlpool organization 88, 90